# SocialCapital

*A Multifaceted Perspective*

# SocialCapital

## A Multifaceted Perspective

Partha Dasgupta
Ismail Serageldin

*The World Bank*
Washington, D.C.

ISBN 0-8213-4562-1

**Library of Congress Cataloging-in-Publication Data has been
applied for.**

# Contents

## Statistical Analysis

## Overview

## Figures and Tables

# Preface

**Partha Dasgupta**
*University of Cambridge*

and

**Ismail Serageldin**
*World Bank*

A number of essays in this volume were presented at a workshop organized at the World Bank in April 1997. The workshop was an outcome of a series of meetings convened over time beginning in autumn 1993 with a group drawn from various parts of the world. The group, which acted as an Advisory Council to the Vice Presidency for Environmentally Sustainable Development at the World Bank, consisted of academics and leaders of nongovernmental organizations.[1] The idea in creating the Council was to help identify and formulate those societal problems that are likely to be the most telling as we enter the new millennium, and to indicate the various directions in which progress could be made in our understanding of them.

It will come as no particular surprise to anyone that the group felt that poverty, the environment, and the ability of communities to live with one another would remain the dominant themes of societal concern over the coming decades. Members of the group observed, however, that even though these particular themes have been explored for many years, the way questions that have a bearing on them are framed has changed considerably over time. They noted that our understanding is deeper today than in the past. And they added that while this does not necessarily mean that solutions to the concomitant social problems are within easy reach, it does mean that we know better today where to look for solutions and what to avoid. If in earlier days social

---

[1]  The members were Nancy Birdsall, Kamla Chowdhry, the late Jacques-Yves Cousteau, Partha Dasgupta, Kathryn Fuller, Clifford Geertz, Saad Eddin Ibrahim, Yolanda Kakabadse, David Pearce, Robert Putnam, Edward Said, Amartya Sen, Hari Shankar Singhania, Maurice Strong, M. S. Swaminathan, Alain Touraine, and Mohammad Yunus.

scientists looked for policies to shape social outcomes for the better, their focus today is more on the character of institutions within which decisions are made by various parties in society. But if policies that read well often come to naught in dysfunctional institutions, the study of institutions on their own is not sufficient: good policies cannot be plucked out of the air. There is mutual influence here, and the task before the social scientist is to study it.

Even though economists have traditionally been much engaged in the study of markets, political scientists in the study of the State, and anthropologists and sociologists in the study of interpersonal networks, in recent years each group has begun to peer into the others' publications to see whether they can better understand the links connecting their particular objects of interest. One of the outcomes of this enterprise, since especially the publication of a classic 1987 article by the late James Coleman (reprinted here), has been the development of "social capital" as an organizing concept in the social sciences. It is difficult to think of an academic notion that has entered the common vocabulary of social discourse more quickly than the idea of social capital. Not only do academic journals devote special issues to discuss the concept, journalists make frequent references to it and politicians pay regular homage to it. The reference to "capital" suggests that all who use the term see it as an ingredient of resource allocation mechanisms. Thus, whatever else social capital may be, it is emphatically an economic good. And yet, while the term has gained wide currency, it has not found favor among economists.

Some authors have identified social capital with such features of social organizations as trust. Then there are those who think of it as an aggregate of behavioral norms. Some view it as social networks, and there are those who think of it as a combination of them all. So it would seem that social capital means different things to different people. What is not uncommon, however, is the temptation among those who are enthusiastic about the concept to use it as a peg on which to hang all those informal engagements we like, care for, and approve of. Thus, one frequently hears the view that if a society harbors widespread opportunistic behavior, such as free-riding, rent-seeking, and bribery and corruption, it is because citizens have not invested sufficiently in the accumulation of social capital. But if the concept is to serve any purpose, this particular temptation should be resisted. Indeed, the reluctance of economists to embrace the term even when engaged in similar research endeavors as those who make use of it may well be because of a certain lack of intellectual discipline in some of the more popular writings on social capital. Terminology is not the only issue—neither, in particular, is the fact that social capital refers to something intangible. A firm's goodwill is intangible too, but economists are comfortable with the notion. The problem with social capital is that the concept has not been nailed down sufficiently to be useable in quantitative research into the character of societies.

One way to try to pin it down would be to explore the issues that the concept was designed to illuminate, with an attention to both theoretical and empirical detail. The workshop at the World Bank in April 1997 was devoted to such an exploration. Inevitably, the occasion was interdisciplinary, but participants were encouraged to study the concept of social capital by peering through their own disciplinary lenses. It meant that even though the workshop had a very sharp focus, the papers presented were heterogeneous, not only in the way authors formulated their common concerns, but also in the style in which the arguments were conducted. The resulting combination of commonality and differences gave the workshop an unusual form of intellectual vitality: the contributions were all of a probing nature, none pretended to be definitive. In the event, the workshop was found by all who took part in it to be so interesting that we joined forces to edit the proceedings for publication.

The literature on social capital is highly dispersed. It soon became apparent that we could aim at a comprehensive collection of essays, one that would provide a reasoned account of our current understanding of the concept, if we were to include articles on aspects not covered at the workshop. This meant reprinting a few articles. In addition, Elinor Ostrom and Robert Solow wrote their thoughts for us even though they had been unable to attend the workshop. The present volume is the result.

The volume covers both theoretical and empirical studies and it has been divided into such sections. While most of the contributions fall exclusively into one or the other of the two categories, several contain both theory and empirics (the subject would seem to lend itself to a combined treatment). Empirical studies on social capital come in two shapes. One consists of studies of particular institutions (otherwise known as "case studies") and relies on the powerful way examples can illuminate our understanding. The other makes use of statistical information, be it spatial or temporal, to identify and to make sense of the links connecting key socioeconomic variables. But just as empirical findings discipline theorizing, theory disciplines empirical work. The mutual influence is striking in the present collection. It helps explain why the literature on social capital has been so rich and fast-moving.

Inevitably, when concepts are discussed, methodological reflections creep in. The present volume is no exception. But the contributors have kept such reflections to a minimum; not because they are unimportant or uninteresting, but because in studies that explore concepts, there is a danger of falling prey to what one could call "concept fetishism." The danger could have been especially prominent in the present context because of the widespread use of the term "social capital" in contemporary writings. In fact, however, there was never much risk of that at the

April 1997 workshop. Reflections on social capital are no mere academic matter, because the issues involved in it—the ones the contributors to this volume are addressing—are momentous: their explorations are a part of a permanent inquiry into the character of those institutions that would enable people to have a good chance of pursuing well-lived lives.

We would be remiss if we did not acknowledge the group of people who contributed their time and wisdom to the workshop and to this publication. Deserving mention and sincere thanks are the many distinguished academicians who attended the 1997 workshop: Francis Fukuyama (George Mason University), Geoffrey Heal (Columbia University), Saad Eddin Ibrahim (American University, Cairo), Robert Klitgaard (University of Natal, South Africa), Mancur Olson (University of Maryland), Martin Paldam (University of Aarhus, Denmark), and Michael Woolcock (Brown University). Most of the authors in this book and many World Bank economists, social scientists, and executive directors Michael Cernea, Gloria Jean Davis, John Dixon, Alan Gelb, Jean-Daniel Gerber, Leonard Good, Tariq Husain, John M. Page, Jr., Robert Picciotto, Jan Piercy, Joanne Salop, Andrew Steer, Vinod Thomas, and John Williamson also participated in the workshop and continue to contribute to the ongoing dialogue. Special thanks go to Paul Nielson, then Minister of Development, Denmark; Jacques Baudot, senior advisor to the Danish Foreign Ministry; and the Danish Trust Fund for providing the resources that made the workshop and this publication possible. Our sincere gratitude go to the staff of the World Bank Publisher's Office, Lisa Carlson, Sarwat Hussain, and Sheldon Lippman for organizing the minutiae that ultimately resulted in the fashioning of this provocative book.

# Introduction

# Observations on social capital

Kenneth J. Arrow
*Stanford University*

The concept of "social capital" has received considerable attention recently among sociologists, economists, and political scientists. The question before the workshop (see below) is the degree to which the concept can be made operational for the purposes of analysis and policy. What follows is a series of observations, partly but not entirely based on discussions at the World Bank's workshop, *Social Capital: Integrating the Economist's and the Sociologist's Perspectives*, held in spring 1997.

There seems to be widespread consensus on the plausibility of the hypothesis that social networks can affect economic performance. At the workshop, the most cited element was that of trust. That trust can promote economic progress has long been argued, even by economists, and given some theoretical foundation by "reputation effects" in game theory. But there is also a literature, not much cited at the workshop, that social interactions can have negative as well as positive effects. One model that has been studied recently involves cases in which choices of good and bad behavior (for example, years of education, illegitimacy, and crime) are influenced by one's neighbors in the network (which may be ordinary geographical space or something else); see Glaser, Sacerdote, and Scheinkman (1995). Good behavior spreads; so does bad.

There is considerable consensus also that much of the reward for social interactions is intrinsic—that is, the interaction is the reward—or at least that the motives for interaction are not economic. People may get jobs through networks of friendship or acquaintance, but they do not, in many cases, join the networks for that purpose.

This is not to deny that networks and other social links may also form for economic reasons. One line of reasoning is that the social networks guard against market failure that is caused by asymmetric information; they are supplementary activities that exploit monitoring devices not otherwise available.

Under some circumstances, when the rewards are large or there is outside intervention, social organizations may be created by deliberate action (for example, irrigation districts). It has been claimed that when there is genuine participation, these organizations are more efficient than when they are under top-down management. Are these a form of social "capital" with the same consequences as self-organizing "spontaneous" social networks? In any case, is it really verified that they are superior in efficiency in all cases or in a well-defined subset of them?

The most far-reaching part of the "social capital" hypothesis has been the one associated with Robert Putnam. His claim is that membership in associations strengthens political and economic efficiency even though the associations themselves play no role in either the polity or the economy. Structurally, this proposition is reminiscent of Max Weber's thesis on the importance of religion in the workings of the economy. In both cases, there is a transfer of ways of thinking from one realm to another. The Weber thesis is still in dispute, after almost a century. Specific tests fail, yet the overall impression remains that there is something to it. Is the Putnam thesis going to have the same fate?

The concept of measuring social interaction may be a snare and a delusion. Instead of thinking of more and less, it may be more fruitful to think of the existing social relations as a preexisting network into which new parts of the economy (for example, development projects) have to be fitted. We would want to fit new projects so as to exploit complementarity relations and avoid rivalries. Of course, new projects will create their own unintended social relations, possibly destroying existing ones.

More specifically, I would urge abandonment of the metaphor of capital and the term, "social capital." The term "capital" implies three aspects: (a) extension in time; (b) deliberate sacrifice in the present for future benefit; and (c) alienability. The last is not true for human capital and not even entirely true for physical investment (namely, the presence of irreversible investments). The aspect defined as (a) above may hold in part; we speak of building a reputation or a trust relation. But these are not like physical investment; a little trust has not much use. But it is especially (b) that fails. The essence of social networks is that they are built up for reasons other than their economic value to the participants (see the point made above in the third paragraph of this article, that much of the reward for social interactions is intrinsic). Indeed, that is what gives them their value in monitoring. I certainly found no consensus at the workshop for *adding* something called "social capital," to other forms of capital.

Several studies based on indexes of social *dis*organization (for example, crime or corruption) were presented to workshop participants. These are related to a number of studies that have sought to link economic development to "good government"—for example, Robert Hall and Charles Jones (1997). These verge on a field related to but perhaps somewhat distinct from social networks, that is, to macroinstitutional analysis (I take social networks to be found on a microinstitutional level, what is frequently referred to as "civil society"). A preference for these studies may be based on greater measurability. But a more mainstream view would be that the workings of large institutions, such as government, are in fact more important than social networks. Can we find some evidence on this matter?

The relations between the market and social interactions appear to be two-sided. On the one hand, modern economic theory emphasizes that even in advanced countries, the market needs supplementation (for efficiency) by nonmarket relations. This is true, first of all, within the firm, and also true in markets in which personal relations are important (for example, relations formed with higher levels of labor or suppliers). On the other hand, labor or supplier turnover in response to prices may destroy the willingness to offer trust or, more generally, to invest in the future of the relation. This leads to an important and long-standing question: does the market (or, for that matter, the large, efficient, bureaucratic state) destroy social links that have positive implications for efficiency?

## References

Glaeser, Edward L., Bruce Sacerdote, and Jose A. Scheinkman. 1995. "Crime and Social Interactions." *Quarterly Journal of Economics* 111: 507–48.

Hall, Robert E., and Charles I. Jones. 1997. "Levels of Economic Activity across Countries." *American Economic Review (Papers and Proceedings)* 87(2): 173–77.

# Notes on social capital and economic performance

**Robert M. Solow**
*Massachusetts Institute of Technology*

These comments began life as notes for a panel discussion following a talk by Francis Fukuyama at New York University's Stern School of Business in April 1997. It should be noted that they have not acquired much embellishment since then. They should be taken more as suggesting an agenda for discussion and research than as finished thoughts.

To sum up, I am going to be critical of the concept of social capital and the way it is used. That does not mean I think the underlying ideas are unimportant or irrelevant to economic performance. On the contrary, I think that those who write and talk about social capital are trying to get at something difficult, complicated, and important: the way a society's institutions and shared attitudes interact with the way its economy works. It is a dirty job, but someone has to do it; and mainstream economics has puristically shied away from the task. My problem is that I would like to see the job done well, in the hope that serious research will uncover defensible answers. So far I have seen only vague ideas and casual empiricism.

Start with the phrase itself. Why social *capital*? I think it is an attempt to gain conviction from a bad analogy. Generically "capital" stands for a stock of produced or natural factors of production that can be expected to yield productive services for some time. Originally anyone who talked about capital had in mind a stock of tangible, solid, often durable things such as buildings, machinery, and inventories. You could think meaningfully about the rate of return on capital, its earnings expressed somehow as a fraction of its value, though God knows that pinning down the numerator and the denominator numerically could employ armies of accountants (and, fortunately, professors of accounting). It is clear how a firm or a nation adds to its stock of capital in that sense: it builds factories and machines and offices faster than the existing ones wear out.

Within the past 30 years or so, it has occurred to some economists that there was a close analogy between tangible capital and what they called "human capital." A city's or a nation's labor force embodies a lot

6

of past investment in the form of education, training, and even research. It is logically a stock; there is a certain amount of it in existence at any particular time. It is added to (in terms of manual and brain power) as new or veteran workers are schooled and trained in up-to-date skills, and it is subtracted from as people retire or die, and as knowledge and skills become obsolete. In principle you might try to calculate the annual earnings of human capital—what people are paid over and above their base, uneducated earning capacity—and you can even try to express this quantity as a proportion of the original cost, or even the reproduction cost, of the cumulated education and training embodied in today's labor force. There is certainly more inference, and riskier inference, involved in measuring these quantities than in the parallel case of tangible capital. But it is the same sort of exercise. And the exercise has paid off in terms of understanding, for instance, differences in productivity between one place and another, and between one time and another.

Okay, so what about social capital? Such things as trust, the willingness and capacity to cooperate and coordinate, the habit of contributing to a common effort even if no one is watching—all these patterns of behavior, and others, have a payoff in terms of aggregate productivity. What could be more natural than to latch on to the outstanding intellectual success of the human-capital notion by adding a plausible and natural-sounding third leg to the stool? So these important, and previously unanalyzed influences on production can be lumped together as social capital, and the whole apparatus of analysis becomes available.

But does it really? Just what is social capital a stock of? Any stock of capital is a cumulation of past flows of investment, with past flows of depreciation netted out. What are those past investments in social capital? How could an accountant measure them and cumulate them in principle? I am not now worrying about where the numbers would come from, I am wondering about what instructions you would give a search party. Could one talk seriously about whether straight-line or double-declining-balance depreciation is appropriate for social capital? If I told you that the rate of return on social capital had fallen from 10 percent a year to 6 percent a year since 1975, would that convey any clear picture to you? I have never asked so many rhetorical questions in my life; but that is the quickest way to explain why I doubt that "social capital" is the right concept to use in discussing whatever it is we are discussing—the behavior patterns I mentioned earlier, for instance.

"Behavior patterns" may be the right phrase, drab as it is, though I would be glad to accept something more colorful. The simple combination of rationality and individual greed that provides the behavioral foundation for most of economics will go only so far. There are important aspects of economic life and economic performance that cannot be analyzed that way. More accurately it is part of the athleticism of economics to analyze everything this way; but the attempt often fails. This is not news. The story gets more interesting when it has to allow for the fact that a lot of economically relevant behavior is socially determined. Patterns of behavior, of acceptable and expectable behavior, start off as social norms, enforced by parental pressure or peer pressure or religious instruction, or in some other way, and are eventually internalized. There are some things you do and others you do not do.

Let me take one important example that has to do with the recent emphasis, by Fukuyama and others, on trust. I will be superficial because I do not have anything deep to say. Contracts are almost always incomplete. During the life of any contract, contingencies will arise that were not provided for when the contract was drawn up. Not every contingency can be foreseen or even imagined. Even if they could, it might be unprofitable, given what lawyers make, to spell out the obligations of the parties in all of the low-probability cases. Pretty clearly transactions costs will be lower, defensive behavior will be diminished, and economic performance will be better if the parties can legitimately expect each other to be "reasonable" or nonexploitative if one of those uncovered contingencies should pop up. How could that kind of confidence, that kind of trust, emerge?

One important possibility requires no special influence from outside the sort of situation we are analyzing. A reputation for trustworthiness in this sense can be highly valuable; it can make you a desirable partner in just such enterprises. Such a reputation can be built up by repeated exhibitions of trustworthy behavior in similar circumstances. So trust can emerge without any sort of societal superego to enforce it. This is not always the case: in some repeated games it is the ruthless guardhouse lawyer who wins. More to the point, many economically important situations are too anonymous or too idiosyncratic or too rare for reputation-building to be a useful strategy.

Well, I do think that societies and groups have ways of instilling norms of behavior and causing conformity with them to be seen as right or natural. There may be an evolutionary force at work, a tendency for the bearers of successful behavior patterns to survive deferentially. But it may be that different subcultures, with different instilled behavior patterns, can coexist, either because the competition between them is not very stiff, or because neither set of behavior traits is noticeably more functional than the other.

It seems to me that this is what we should be studying: what is the available repertoire of behavior patterns in this situation or that, and how does one of them come to be entrenched as the standard? More generally, what kinds of institutions and habits make an economy or a society better able to adapt to changing circumstances by finding and imposing appropriate norms of behavior? I do not see how dressing this set of issues in the language and apparatus of capital theory helps much one way or another.

To dispel the impression that all this is merely abstract and remote theorizing, I will finish by mentioning two topical applications.

Many observers have noticed that the employment relationship seems to be changing its character. The increase in the proportion of temporary, contingent, and part-time workers; the apparently growing ease of mobility of executives and even professors; the decay of trade unionism; and other similar trends, if they are not illusory, all confirm that observation. A recent *New Yorker* cartoon shows a personnel manager sitting behind a desk and interviewing a candidate for a suit-and-tie job. The personnel manager is saying: "We don't expect much loyalty. And we don't offer much security." That is not what personnel managers used to say. Two questions suggest themselves. Why is this happening? Are the causes narrowly economic—tougher international competition, for example, or a shift in the supply-demand balance in labor markets—or do they have something to do with broader changes in the society? And the second question is: how will this change affect the profitability of firms and the functioning of the labor market?

If human capital is getting more transferable, what might take its place as a source of loyalty and security? Steeper seniority gradients? Something quite different?

The second example is at another level. It is often opined that the rapidly growing East Asian economies—Hong Kong, Republic of Korea, Singapore, and Taiwan (China) in the first instance and now perhaps Indonesia, Malaysia, and Thailand—exemplify the value of some specifically Asian virtues of character and social organization: diligence, teamwork, compromise, and so on. Japan used to be the prize exemplar of these characteristics, apparently not anymore. The main finding of recent research—Kim and Lau (1996), and Collins and Bosworth (1996)—is that the extraordinarily fast growth of the four "Tigers" does not owe anything to any special proclivity or talent, but is imputable to very intense accumulation of physical and human capital. (This finding is sometimes disputed, but so far it has won the day.)

One inference could be *either* that there are no special behavior patterns underlying the Asian success stories, just conventional production economics, *or* that the relevant behavior patterns are precisely what account for the ability of those societies to accumulate capital and to mobilize skilled labor so fast and so effectively.

Either way, there is something to look for that is at least capable of being found.

## References

Collins, Susan M., and Barry P. Bosworth. 1996. "Economic Growth in East Asia: Accumulation versus Assimilation." *Brookings Papers on Economic Activity*, No. 2: 135–203.

Kim, Jong-il, and Lawrence J. Lau. 1996. "The Sources of Asian Pacific Economic Growth." *Canadian Journal of Economics* 29, Special Issue Part 2: 5448–54.

# Analytical Foundations

# Social capital in the creation of human capital

James S. Coleman
*University of Chicago*

*In this paper, the concept of social capital is introduced and illustrated, its forms are described, the social structural conditions under which it arises are examined, and it is used in an analysis of dropouts from high school. Use of the concept of social capital is part of a general theoretical strategy discussed in the paper: taking rational action as a starting point but rejecting the extreme individualistic premises that often accompany it. The conception of social capital as a resource for action is one way of introducing social structure into the rational action paradigm. Three forms of social capital are examined: obligations and expectations, information channels, and social norms. The role of closure in the social structure in facilitating the first and third of these forms of social capital is described. An analysis of the effect of the lack of social capital available to high school sophomores on dropping out of school before graduation is carried out. The effect of social capital within the family and in the community outside the family is examined.*

There are two broad intellectual streams in the description and explanation of social action. One, characteristic of the work of most sociologists, sees the actor as socialized and action as governed by social norms, rules, and obligations. The principal virtues of this intellectual stream lie in its ability to describe action in social context and to explain the way action is shaped, constrained, and redirected by the social context.

The other intellectual stream, characteristic of the work of most economists, sees the actor as having goals independently arrived at, as acting independently, and as wholly self-interested. Its principal virtue lies in having a principle of action, that of maximizing utility. This principle of action, together with a single empirical generalization (declining marginal utility) has generated the extensive growth of neoclassical economic theory, as well as the growth of political philosophy of several varieties: utilitarianism, contractarianism, and natural rights.[1]

In earlier works (Coleman 1986a, 1986b), I have argued for and engaged in the development of a theoretical orientation in sociology that includes components from both these intellectual streams. It accepts the principle of rational or purposive action and attempts to show how that principle, in conjunction with particular social contexts, can account not only for the actions of individuals in particular contexts but also for the development of social organization. In the present paper, I introduce a conceptual tool for use in this theoretical enterprise: social capital. As background for introducing this concept, it is useful to see some of the criticisms of and attempts to modify the two intellectual streams.

### Criticisms and revisions

Both these intellectual streams have serious defects. The sociological stream has what may be a fatal flaw as a theoretical enterprise: the actor has no "engine of action." The actor is shaped by the environment, but there are no internal springs of action that give the actor a purpose or direction. The very conception of action as wholly a product of the environment has led sociologists themselves to criticize this intellectual stream, as in Dennis Wrong's (1961) "The Oversocialized Conception of Man in Modem Sociology."

The economic stream, on the other hand, flies in the face of empirical reality: persons' actions are shaped, redirected, constrained by the social context; norms, interpersonal trust, social networks, and social organization are important in the functioning not only of the society but also of the economy.

A number of authors from both traditions have recognized these difficulties and have attempted to impart some of the insights and orientations of the one intellectual stream to the other. In economics, Yoram Ben-Porath (1930) has developed ideas concerning the functioning of what he calls the "F-connection" in exchange systems. The F-connection is families, friends, and firms, and Ben-Porath, drawing on literature in anthropology and sociology as well as economics, shows the way these forms of social organization affect economic exchange. Oliver Williamson has, in a number of publications (e.g., 1975, 1981), examined the conditions under which economic activity is organized in different institutional forms, that is, within firms or in markets.

---

[1]   For a discussion of the importance of the empirical generalization to economics, see Black, Coats, and Goodwin (1973).

There is a whole body of work in economics, the "new institutional economics," that attempts to show, within neoclassical economic theory, both the conditions under which particular economic institutions arise and the effects of these institutions (i.e., of social organization) on the functioning of the system.

There have been recent attempts by sociologists to examine the way social organization affects the functioning of economic activity. Baker (1983) has shown how, even in the highly rationalized market of the Chicago Options Exchange, relations among floor traders develop, are maintained, and affect their trades. More generally, Granovetter (1985) has engaged in a broad attack on the "undersocialized concept of man" that characterizes economists' analysis of economic activity. Granovetter first criticizes much of the new institutional economics as crudely functionalist because the existence of an economic institution is often explained merely by the functions it performs for the economic system. He argues that, even in the new institutional economics, there is a failure to recognize the importance of concrete personal relations and networks of relations— what he calls "embeddedness"—in generating trust, in establishing expectations, and in creating and enforcing norms.

Granovetter's idea of embeddedness may be seen as an attempt to introduce into the analysis of economic systems social organization and social relations not merely as a structure that springs into place to fulfill an economic function, but as a structure with history and continuity that give it an independent effect on the functioning of economic systems.

All this work, both by economists and by sociologists, has constituted a revisionist analysis of the functioning of economic systems. Broadly, it can be said to maintain the conception of rational action but to superimpose on it social and institutional organization—either endogenously generated, as in the functionalist explanations of some of the new institutional economists, or as exogenous factors, as in the more proximate–causally oriented work of some sociologists.

My aim is somewhat different. It is to import the economists' principle of rational action for use in the analysis of social systems proper, including but not limited to economic systems, and to do so without discarding social organization in the process. The concept of social capital is a tool to aid in this. In this paper, I introduce the concept in some generality, and then examine its usefulness in a particular context, that of education.

## Social capital

Elements for these two intellectual traditions cannot be brought together in a pastiche. It is necessary to begin with a conceptually coherent framework from one and introduce elements from the other without destroying that coherence.

I see two major deficiencies in earlier work that introduced "exchange theory" into sociology, despite the pathbreaking character of this work. One was the limitation to microsocial relations, which abandons the principal virtue of economic theory, its ability to make the micro-macro transition from pair relations to system. This was evident both in Homans's (1961) work and in Blau's (1964) work. The other was the attempt to introduce principles in an ad hoc fashion, such as "distributive justice" (Homans 1974, p. 241) or the "norm of reciprocity" (Gouldner 1960). The former deficiency limits the theory's usefulness, and the latter creates a pastiche.

If we begin with a theory of rational action, in which each actor has control over certain resources and interests in certain resources and events, then social capital constitutes a particular kind of resource available to an actor.

Social capital is defined by its function. It is not a single entity but a variety of different entities, with two elements in common: they all consist of some aspect of social structures, and they facilitate certain actions of actors—whether persons or corporate actors—within the structure. Like other forms of capital, social capital is productive, making possible the achievement of certain ends that in its absence would not be possible. Like physical capital and human capital, social capital is not completely fungible but may be specific to certain activities. A given form of social capital that is valuable in facilitating certain actions may be useless or even harmful for others.

Unlike other forms of capital, social capital inheres in the structure of relations between actors and among actors. It is not lodged either in the actors themselves or in physical implements of production. Because purposive organizations can be actors ("corporate actors") just as persons can, relations among corporate actors can constitute social capital for them as well (with perhaps the best-known example being the sharing of information that allows price-fixing in an industry). However, in the present paper, the examples and area of application to which I will direct attention concern social capital as a resource for persons.

Before I state more precisely what social capital consists of, it is useful to give several examples that illustrate some of its different forms.

1.  Wholesale diamond markets exhibit a property that to an outsider is remarkable. In the process of negotiating a sale, a merchant will hand over to another merchant a bag of stones for the latter to examine in private at his leisure, with no formal insurance that the latter will not substitute one or more inferior stones or a paste replica. The merchandise may be worth thousands, or hundreds of thousands, of dollars. Such free exchange of stones for inspec-

tion is important to the functioning of this market. In its absence, the market would operate in a much more cumbersome, much less efficient fashion.

Inspection shows certain attributes of the social structure. A given merchant community is ordinarily very close, both in the frequency of interaction and in ethnic and family ties. The wholesale diamond market in New York City, for example, is Jewish, with a high degree of intermarriage, living in the same community in Brooklyn, and going to the same synagogues. It is essentially a closed community.

Observation of the wholesale diamond market indicates that these close ties, through family, community, and religious affiliation, provide the insurance that is necessary to facilitate the transactions in the market. If any member of this community defected through substituting other stones or through stealing stones in his temporary possession, he would lose family, religious, and community ties. The strength of these ties makes possible transactions in which trustworthiness is taken for granted and trade can occur with ease. In the absence of these ties, elaborate and expensive bonding and insurance devices would be necessary— or else the transactions could not take place.

2. The *International Herald Tribune* of June 21–22, 1986, contained an article on page 1 about South Korean student radical activists. It describes the development of such activism: "Radical thought is passed on in clandestine 'study circles,' groups of students who may come from the same high school or hometown or church. These study circles . . . serve as the basic organizational unit for demonstrations and other protests. To avoid detection, members of different groups never meet, but communicate through an appointed representative."

This description of the basis of organization of this activism illustrates social capital of two kinds. The "same high school or hometown or church" provides social relations on which the "study circles" are later built. The study circles themselves constitute a form of social capital—a cellular form of organization that appears especially valuable for facilitating opposition in any political system intolerant of dissent. Even where political dissent is tolerated, certain activities are not, whether the activities are politically motivated terrorism or simple crime. The organization that makes possible these activities is an especially potent form of social capital.

3. A mother of six children, who recently moved with husband and children from suburban Detroit to Jerusalem, described as one

reason for doing so the greater freedom her young children had in Jerusalem. She felt safe in letting her eight year old take the six year old across town to school on the city bus and felt her children to be safe in playing without supervision in a city park, neither of which she felt able to do where she lived before.

The reason for this difference can be described as a difference in social capital available in Jerusalem and suburban Detroit. In Jerusalem, the normative structure ensures that unattended children will be "looked after" by adults in the vicinity, while no such normative structure exists in most metropolitan areas of the United States. One can say that families have available to them in Jerusalem social capital that does not exist in metropolitan areas of the United States.

4.   In the Kahn El Khalili market of Cairo, the boundaries between merchants are difficult for an outsider to discover. The owner of a shop that specializes in leather will, when queried about where one can find a certain kind of jewelry, turn out to sell that as well—or, what appears to be nearly the same thing, to have a close associate who sells it, to whom he will immediately take the customer. Or he will instantly become a money changer, although he is not a money changer, merely by turning to his colleague a few shops down. For some activities, such as bringing a customer to a friend's store, there are commissions; for others, such as money changing, merely the creation of obligations. Family relations are important in the market, as is the stability of proprietorship. The whole market is so infused with relations of the sort I have described that it can be seen as an organization, no less so than a department store. Alternatively, one can see the market as consisting of a set of individual merchants, each having an extensive body of social capital on which to draw, through the relationships of the market.

The examples above have shown the value of social capital for a number of outcomes, both economic and noneconomic. There are, however, certain properties of social capital that are important for understanding how it comes into being and how it is employed in the creation of human capital. First, a comparison with human capital, and then an examination of different forms of social capital, will be helpful for seeing these.

## Human capital and social capital

Probably the most important and most original development in the economics of education in the past 30 years has been the idea that the concept of physical capital as embodied in tools, machines, and other productive equipment can be extended to include human capital as well (see Schultz 1961; Becker 1964). Just as physical capital is created by changes in materials to form tools that facilitate production, human capital is created by changes in persons that bring about skills and capabilities that make them able to act in new ways.

Social capital, however, comes about through changes in the relations among persons that facilitate action. If physical capital is wholly tangible, being embodied in observable material form, and human capital is less tangible, being embodied in the skills and knowledge acquired by an individual, social capital is less tangible yet, for it exists in the *relations* among persons. Just as physical capital and human capital facilitate productive activity, social capital does as well. For example, a group within which there is extensive trustworthiness and extensive trust is able to accomplish much more than a comparable group without that trustworthiness and trust.

### Forms of social capital

The value of the concept of social capital lies first in the fact that it identifies certain aspects of social structure by their functions, just as the concept "chair" identifies certain physical objects by their function, despite differences in form, appearance, and construction. The function identified by the concept of "social capital" is the value of these aspects of social structure to actors as resources that they can use to achieve their interests.

By identifying this function of certain aspects of social structure, the concept of social capital constitutes both an aid in accounting for different outcomes at the level of individual actors and an aid toward making the micro-to-macro transitions without elaborating the social structural details through which this occurs. For example, in characterizing the clandestine study circles of South Korean radical students as constituting social capital that these students can use in their revolutionary activities, we assert that the groups constitute a resource that aids in moving from individual protest to organized revolt. If, in a theory of revolt, a resource that accomplishes this task is held to be necessary, then these study circles are grouped together with those organizational structures, having very different origins, that have fulfilled the same function for individuals with revolutionary goals in other contexts, such as the *Comités d'action lycéen* of the French student revolt of 1968 or the workers' cells in tsarist Russia described and advocated by Lenin ([1902] 1973).

It is true, of course, that for other purposes one wants to investigate the details of such organizational resources, to understand the elements that are critical to their usefulness as resources for such a purpose, and to examine how they came into being in a particular case. But the concept of social capital allows taking such resources and showing the way they can be combined with other resources to produce different system-level behavior or, in other cases, different outcomes for individuals. Although, for these purposes, social capital constitutes an unanalyzed concept, it signals to the analyst and to the reader that something of value has been produced for those actors who have this resource available and that the value depends on social organization. It then becomes a second stage in the analysis to unpack the concept, to discover what components of social organization contribute to the value produced.

In previous work, Lin (1988) and DeGraaf and Flap (1988), from a perspective of methodological individualism similar to that used in this paper, have shown how informal social resources are used instrumentally in achieving occupational mobility in the United States and, to a lesser extent, in West Germany and the Netherlands. Lin focused on social ties, especially "weak" ties, in this role. Here, I want to examine a variety of resources, all of which constitute social capital for actors.

Before examining empirically the value of social capital in the creation of human capital, I will go more deeply into an examination of just what it is about social relations that can constitute useful capital resources for individuals.

### Obligations, expectations, and trustworthiness of structures

If $A$ does something for $B$ and trusts $B$ to reciprocate in the future, this establishes an expectation in $A$ and an obligation on the part of $B$. This obligation can be conceived as a credit slip held by $A$ for performance by $B$. If $A$ holds a large number of these credit slips, for a number of persons with whom $A$ has relations, then the analogy to financial capital is direct. These credit slips constitute a large body of credit that $A$ can call in if necessary—unless, of course, the placement of trust has been unwise, and these are bad debts that will not be repaid.

In some social structures, it is said that "people are always doing things for each other." There are a large number of these credit slips outstanding, often on both sides of a relation (for these credit slips appear often not to be completely fungible across areas of activity, so that credit slips of $B$ held by $A$ and those of $A$ held by $B$ are not fully used to cancel each other out). The El Khalili market in Cairo, described earlier, constitutes an extreme case of such a social structure. In other social structures where individuals are more self-sufficient and depend on each other less, there are fewer of these credit slips outstanding at any time.

This form of social capital depends on two elements: trustworthiness of the social environment, which means that obligations will be repaid, and the actual extent of obligations held. Social structures differ in both these dimensions, and actors within the same structure differ in the second. A case that illustrates the value of the trustworthiness of the environment is that of the rotating-credit associations of Southeast Asia and elsewhere. These associations are groups of friends and neighbors who typically meet monthly, each person contributing to a central fund that is then given to one of the members (through bidding or by lot), until, after a number of months, each of the $n$ persons has made $n$ contributions and received one payout. As Geertz (1962) points out, these associations serve as efficient institutions for amassing savings for small capital expenditures, an important aid to economic development.

But without a high degree of trustworthiness among the members of the group, the institution could not exist—for a person who receives a payout early in the sequence of meetings could abscond and leave the others with a loss. For example, one could not imagine a rotating-credit association operating successfully in urban areas marked by a high degree of social disorganization—or, in other words, by a lack of social capital.

Differences in social structures in both dimensions may arise for a variety of reasons. There are differences in the actual needs that persons have for help, in the existence of other sources of aid (such as government welfare services), in the degree of affluence (which reduces aid needed from others), in cultural differences in the tendency to lend aid and ask for aid (see Banfield 1967) in the closure of social networks, in the logistics of social contacts (see Festinger, Schachter, and Back 1963), and other factors. Whatever the source, however, individuals in social structures with high levels of obligations outstanding at any time have more social capital on which they can draw. The density of outstanding obligations means, in effect, that the overall usefulness of the tangible resources of that social structure is amplified by their availability to others when needed.

Individual actors in a social system also differ in the number of credit slips outstanding on which they can draw at any time. The most extreme examples are in hierarchically structured extended family settings, in which a patriarch (or "godfather") holds an extraordinarily large set of obligations that he can call in at any time to get what he wants done. Near this extreme are villages in traditional settings that are highly stratified, with certain wealthy families who, because of their wealth, have built up extensive credits that they can call in at any time.

Similarly, in political settings such as a legislature, a legislator in a position with extra resources (such as the Speaker of the House of Representatives or the Majority Leader of the Senate in the U.S. Congress) can, by effective use of resources, build up a set of obligations from other legislators that makes it possible to get legislation passed that would otherwise be stymied. This concentration of obligations constitutes social capital that is useful not only for this powerful legislator but useful also in getting an increased level of action on the part of a legislature. Thus, those members of legislatures among whom such credits are extensive should be more powerful than those without extensive credits and debits because they can use the credits to produce bloc voting on many issues. It is well recognized, for example, that in the U.S. Senate, some senators are members of what is called "the Senate Club," while others are not. This in effect means that some senators are embedded in the system of credits, and debits, while others, outside the "Club," are not. It is also well recognized that those in the Club are more powerful than those outside it.

### Information channels

An important form of social capital is the potential for information that inheres in social relations. Information is important in providing a basis for action. But acquisition of information is costly. At a minimum, it requires attention, which is always in scarce supply. One means by which information can be acquired is by use of social relations that are maintained for other purposes. Katz and Lazarsfeld (1955) showed how this operated for women in several areas of life in a Midwestern city around 1950. They showed that a woman with an interest in being in fashion, but no interest in being on the leading edge of fashion, used friends who she knew kept up with fashion as sources of information. Similarly, a person who is not greatly interested in current events but who is interested in being informed about important developments can save the time of reading a newspaper by depending on spouse or friends who pay attention to such matters. A social scientist who is interested in being up-to-date on research in related fields can make use of everyday interactions with colleagues to do so, but only in a university in which most colleagues keep up-to-date.

All these are examples of social relations that constitute a form of social capital that provides information that facilitates action. The relations in this case are not valuable for the "credit slips" they provide in the form of obligations that one holds for others' performances or for the trustworthiness of the other party but merely for the information they provide.

### Norms and effective sanctions

When a norm exists and is effective, it constitutes a powerful, though sometimes fragile, form of social capital. Effective norms that inhibit crime make it possible to walk freely outside at night in a city and enable old persons to leave their houses without fear for their safety. Norms in a community that support and provide effective rewards for high achievement in school greatly facilitate the school's task.

A prescriptive norm within a collectivity that constitutes an especially important form of social capital is the norm that one should forgo self-interest and act in the interests of the collectivity. A norm of this sort, reinforced by social support, status, honor, and other rewards, is the social capital that builds young nations (and then dissipates as they grow older), strengthens families by leading family members to act selflessly in "the family's" interest, facilitates the development of nascent social movements through a small group of dedicated, inward-looking, and mutually rewarding members, and in general leads persons to work for the public good. In some of these cases, the norms are internalized; in others, they are largely supported through external rewards for selfless actions and disapproval for selfish actions. But, whether supported by internal or external sanctions, norms of this sort are important in overcoming the public goods problem that exists in collectivities.

As all these examples suggest, effective norms can constitute a powerful form of social capital. This social capital, however, like the forms described earlier, not only facilitates certain actions; it constrains others. A community with strong and effective norms about young persons' behavior can keep them from "having a good time." Norms that make it possible to walk alone at night also constrain the activities of criminals (and in some cases of noncriminals as well). Even prescriptive norms that reward certain actions, like the norm in a community that says that a boy who is a good athlete should go out for football, are in effect directing energy away from other activities. Effective norms in an area can reduce innovativeness in an area, not only deviant actions that harm others but also deviant actions that can benefit everyone. (See Merton [1968, pp. 195–203] for a discussion of how this can come about.)

### Social structure that facilitates social capital

All social relations and social structures facilitate some forms of social capital; actors establish relations purposefully and continue them when they continue to provide benefits. Certain kinds of social structure, however, are especially important in facilitating some forms of social capital.

#### Closure of social networks

One property of social relations on which effective norms depend is what I will call closure. In general, one can say that a necessary but not sufficient condition for the emergence of effective norms is action that imposes external effects on others (see Ullmann-Margalit 1977; Coleman 1987). Norms arise as attempts to limit negative external effects or encourage positive ones. But, in many social structures where these conditions exist, norms do not come into existence. The reason is what can be described as lack of closure of the social structure. Figure 1 illustrates why. In an open structure like that of figure l(a), actor $A$, having relations, with actors $B$ and $C$, can carry out actions that impose negative externalities on $B$ or $C$ or both. Since they have no relations with one another, but with others instead ($D$ and $E$), then they cannot combine forces to sanction $A$ in order to constrain the actions. Unless either $B$ or

FIGURE 1: NETWORK WITHOUT (a) AND WITH (b) CLOSURE

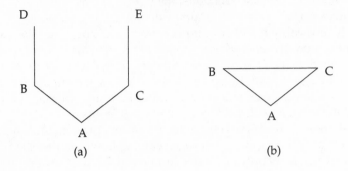

(a)                                    (b)

*C* alone is sufficiently harmed and sufficiently powerful vis-à-vis *A* to sanction alone, *A*'s actions can continue unabated. In a structure with closure, like that of figure l(b), *B* and *C* can combine to provide a collective sanction, or either can reward the other for sanctioning *A*. (See Merry [1984] for examples of the way gossip, which depends on closure of the social structure, is used as a collective sanction.)

In the case of norms imposed by parents on children, closure of the structure requires a slightly more complex structure, which I will call intergenerational closure. Intergenerational closure may be described by a simple diagram that represents relations between parent and child and relations outside the family. Consider the structure of two communities, represented by figure 2. The vertical lines represent relations across generations, between parent and child, while the horizontal lines represent relations within a generation. The point labeled *A* in both figure 2(a) and figure 2(b) represents the parent of child *B*, and the point labeled *D* represents the parent of child *C*. The lines between *B* and *C* represent the relations among children that exist within any school. Although the other relations among children within the school are not shown here, there exists a high degree of closure among peers, who see each other daily, have expectations toward each other, and develop norms about each other's behavior.

The two communities differ, however, in the presence or absence of links among the parents of children in the school. For the school represented by figure 2(b), there is intergenerational closure; for that represented by figure 2(a), there is not. To put it colloquially, in the lower community represented by 2(b), the parents' friends are the parents of their children's friends. In the other, they are not.

The consequence of this closure is, as in the case of the wholesale diamond market or in other similar communities, a set of effective sanctions that can monitor and guide behavior. In the community in figure

FIGURE 2: NETWORK INVOLVING PARENTS *(A, D)* AND CHILDREN *(B, C)* WITHOUT (a) AND WITH (b) INTERGENERATIONAL CLOSURE

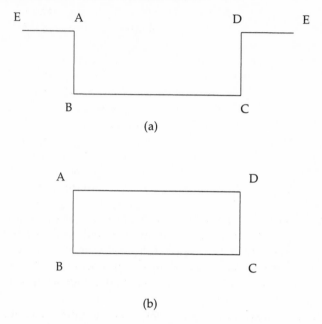

2(b), parents *A* and *D* can discuss their children's activities and come to some consensus about standards and about sanctions. Parent *A* is reinforced by parent *D* in sanctioning his child's actions; beyond that, parent *D* constitutes a monitor not only for his own child, *C*, but also for the other child, *B*. Thus, the existence of intergenerational closure provides a quantity of social capital available to each parent in raising his children—not only in matters related to school but in other matters as well.

Closure of the social structure is important not only for the existence of effective norms but also for another form of social capital: the trustworthiness of social structures that allows the proliferation of obligations and expectations. Defection from an obligation is a form of imposing a negative externality on another. Yet, in a structure without closure, it can be effectively sanctioned, if at all, only by the person to whom the obligation is owed. Reputation cannot arise in an open structure, and collective sanctions that would ensure trustworthiness cannot be applied. Thus, we may say that closure creates trustworthiness in a social structure.

### Appropriable social organization

Voluntary organizations are brought into being to aid some purpose of those who initiate them. In a housing project built during World War II in an eastern city of the United States, there were many physical problems caused by poor construction: faulty plumbing, crumbling sidewalks, and other defects (Merton, n.d.). Residents organized to confront the builders and to address these problems in other ways. Later, when the problems were solved, the organization remained as available social capital that improved the quality of life for residents. Residents had resources available that they had seen as unavailable where they had lived before. (For example, despite the fact that the number of teenagers in the community was smaller, residents were more likely to express satisfaction with the availability of teenage babysitters.)

Printers in the New York Typographical Union who were monotype operators formed a Monotype Club as a social club (Lipset, Trow, and Coleman 1956). Later, as employers looked for monotype operators and as monotype operators looked for jobs, both found this organization an effective employment referral service and appropriated the organization for this purpose. Still later, when the Progressive Party came into power in the New York Union, the Monotype Club served as an organizational resource for the Independent Party as it left office. The Monotype Club subsequently served as an important source of social capital for the Independents to sustain the party as an organized opposition while it was out of office.

In the example of South Korean student radicals used earlier, the study circles were described as consisting of groups of students from the same high school or hometown or church. Here, as in the earlier examples, an organization that was initiated for one purpose is available for appropriation for other purposes, constituting important social capital for the individual members, who have available to them the organizational resources necessary for effective opposition. These examples illustrate the general point, that organization, once brought into existence for one set of purposes, can also aid others, thus constituting social capital available for use.

It is possible to gain insight into some of the ways in which closure and appropriable social organization provide social capital by use of a distinction made by Max Gluckman (1967) between simplex and multiplex relations.[2] In the latter, persons are linked in more than one context (neighbor, fellow worker, fellow parent, coreligionist, etc.), while in the former, persons are linked through only one of these relations. The central property of a multiplex relation is that it allows the resources of one relationship to be appropriated for use in others. Sometimes, the resource is merely information, as when two parents who see each other as neighbors exchange information about their teenagers' activities; sometimes, it is the obligations that one person owes a second in relationship $X$,

---

[2]   I am especially grateful to Susan Shapiro for reminding me of Gluckman's distinction and pointing out the relevance of it to my analysis.

which the second person can use to constrain the actions of the first in relationship Y. Often, it is resources in the form of other persons who have obligations in one context that can be called on to aid when one has problems in another context.

## Social capital in the creation of human capital

The preceding pages have been directed toward defining and illustrating social capital in general. But there is one effect of social capital that is especially important: its effect on the creation of human capital in the next generation. Both social capital in the family and social capital in the community play roles in the creation of human capital in the rising generation. I will examine each of these in turn.

### Social capital in the family

Ordinarily, in the examination of the effects of various factors on achievement in school, "family background" is considered a single entity, distinguished from schooling in its effects. But there is not merely a single "family background"; family background is analytically separable into at least three different components: financial capital, human capital, and social capital. Financial capital is approximately measured by the family's wealth or income. It provides the physical resources that can aid achievement: a fixed place in the home for studying, materials to aid learning, the financial resources that smooth family problems. Human capital is approximately measured by parents' education and provides the potential for a cognitive environment for the child that aids learning. Social capital within the family is different from either of these. Two examples will give a sense of what it is and how it operates.

John Stuart Mill, at an age before most children attend school, was taught Latin and Greek by his father, James Mill, and later in childhood would discuss critically with his father and with Jeremy Bentham drafts of his father's manuscripts. John Stuart Mill probably had no extraordinary genetic endowments, and his father's learning was no more extensive than that of some other men of the time. The central difference was the time and effort spent by the father with the child on intellectual matters.

In one public school district in the United States where texts for school use were purchased by children's families, school authorities were puzzled to discover that a number of Asian immigrant families purchased *two* copies of each textbook needed by the child. Investigation revealed that the family purchased the second copy for the mother to study in order to help her child do well in school. Here is a case in which the human capital of the parents, at least as measured traditionally by years of schooling, is low, but the social capital in the family available for the child's education is extremely high.

These examples illustrate the importance of social capital within the family for a child's intellectual development. It is of course true that children are strongly affected by the human capital possessed by their parents. But this human capital may be irrelevant to outcomes for children if parents are not an important part of their children's lives, if their human capital is employed exclusively at work or elsewhere outside the home. The social capital of the family is the relations between children and parents (and, when families include other members, relationships with them as well). That is, if the human capital possessed by parents is not complemented by social capital embodied in family relations, it is irrelevant to the child's educational growth that the parent has a great deal, or a small amount, of human capital.[3]

I will not differentiate here among the forms of social capital discussed earlier, but will attempt merely to measure the strength of the relations between parents and child as a measure of the social capital available to the child from the parent. Nor will I use the concept in the context of the paradigm of rational action, as, for example, is often done in use of the concept of human capital to examine the investments in education that a rational person would make. A portion of the reason for this lies in a property of much social capital not shown by most forms of capital (to which I will turn in a later section): its public goods character, which leads to underinvestment.

Social capital within the family that gives the child access to the adult's human capital depends both on the physical presence of adults in the family and on the attention given by the adults to the child. The physical absence of adults may be described as a structural deficiency in family social capital. The most prominent element of structural deficiency in modern families is the single-parent family. However, the nuclear family itself, in which one or both parents work outside the home, can be seen as structurally deficient, lacking the social capital that comes with the presence of parents during the day, or with grandparents or aunts and uncles in or near the household.

Even if adults are physically present, there is a lack of social capital in the family if there are not strong relations between children and parents. The lack of strong relations can result from the child's

---

[3]    The complementarity of human capital and social capital in the family for a child's development suggests that the statistical analysis that examines the effects of these quantities should take a particular form. There should be an interaction term between human capital (parents' education) and social capital (some combination of measures such as two parents in the home, number of siblings, and parents' expectations for child's education). In the analysis reported, here, however, a simple additive model without interaction was used.

embeddedness in a youth community, from the parents' embeddedness in relationships with other adults that do not cross generations, or from other sources. Whatever the source, it means that whatever *human* capital exists in the parents, the child does not profit from it because the *social* capital is missing.

The effects of a lack of social capital within the family differ for different educational outcomes. One for which it appears to be especially important is dropping out of school. With the *High School and Beyond* sample of students in high schools, table 1 shows the expected dropout rates for students in different types of families when various measures of social and human capital in the family and a measure of social capital in the community are controlled statistically.[4] An explanation is necessary for the use of number of siblings as a measure of lack of social capital. The number of siblings represents, in this interpretation, a dilution of adult attention to the child. This is consistent with research results for measures of achievement and IQ, which show that test scores decline with sib position, even when total family size is controlled, and that scores decline with number of children in the family. Both results are consistent with the view that younger sibs and children in large families have less adult attention, which produces weaker educational outcomes.

Item 1 of table 1 shows that, when other family resources are controlled, the percentage of students who drop out between spring of the sophomore year and spring of the senior year is 6 percentage points higher for children from single-parent families. Item 2 of table 1 shows that the rate is 6.4 percentage points higher for sophomores with four siblings than for those with otherwise equivalent family resources but only one sibling. Or, taking these two together, we can think of the ratio of adults to children as a measure of the social capital in the family available for the education of any one of them. Item

---

[4]  The analysis is carried out by use of a weighted logistic model with a random sample of 4,000 students from the public schools in the sample. The variables included in the model as measures of the family's financial, human, and social capital were socioeconomic status (a single variable constructed of parents' education, parents' income, father's occupational status, and household possessions), race, Hispanic ethnicity, number of siblings, number of changes in school due to family residential moves since fifth grade, whether mother worked before the child was in school, mother's expectation of child's educational attainment, frequency of discussions with parents about personal matters, and presence of both parents in the household. The regression coefficients and asymptotic standard errors are given in the Appendix table Al. An analysis with more extensive statistical controls, including such things as grades in school, homework, and number of absences, is reported in Hoffer (1986, table 25), but the effects reported in table 1 and subsequent text are essentially unchanged except for a reduced effect of mother's expectations. The results reported here and subsequently are taken from Hoffer (1986) and from Coleman and Hoffer (1987).

TABLE 1: DROPOUT RATES BETWEEN SPRING, GRADE 10, AND SPRING, GRADE 12,
FOR STUDENTS WHOSE FAMILIES DIFFER IN SOCIAL CAPITAL, CONTROLLING FOR
HUMAN CAPITAL AND FINANCIAL CAPITAL IN THE FAMILY[a]

| | Percentage Dropping Out | Difference in Percentage Points |
|---|---|---|
| 1. Parents' presence: | | |
| Two parents | 13.1 | } 6.0 |
| Single parent | 19.1 | |
| 2. Additional children: | | |
| One sibling | 10.8 | } 6.4 |
| Four siblings | 17.2 | |
| 3. Parents and children: | | |
| Two parents, one sibling | 10.1 | } 12.5 |
| One parent, four siblings | 22.6 | |
| 4. Mother's expectation for child's education: | | |
| Expectation of college | 11.6 | } 8.6 |
| No expectation of college | 20.2 | |
| 5. Three factors together: | | |
| Two parents, one sibling, mother expects college ... | 8.1 | } 22.5 |
| One parent, four siblings, no college expectation ... | 30.6 | |

[a] Estimates taken from logistic regression reported more fully in Appendix table Al.

3 of table 1 shows that for a sophomore with four siblings and one parent, and an otherwise average background, the rate is 22.6 percent; with one sibling and two parents, the rate is 10.1 percent—a difference of 12.5 percentage points.

Another indicator of adult attention in the family, although not a pure measure of social capital, is the mother's expectation of the child's going to college. Item 4 of the table shows that, for sophomores without this parental expectation, the rate is 8.6 percentage points higher than for those with it. With the three sources of family social capital taken together, item 5 of the table shows that sophomores with one sibling, two parents, and a mother's expectation for college (still controlling on other resources of family) have an 8.1 percent dropout rate; with four siblings, one parent, and no expectation of the mother for college, the rate is 30.6 percent.

These results provide a less satisfactory test than if the research had been explicitly designed to examine effects of social capital within the family. In addition, table Al in the Appendix shows that another variable that should measure social capital in the family, the frequency of talking with parents about personal experiences, shows essentially no relation to dropping out. Nevertheless, taken all together, the data do indicate that social capital in the family is a resource for education of the family's children, just as is financial and human capital.

## Social capital outside the family

The social capital that has value for a young person's development does not reside solely within the family. It can be found outside as well in the community consisting of the social relationships that exist among parents, in the closure exhibited by this structure of relations, and in the parents' relations with the institutions of the community.

The effect of this social capital outside the family on educational outcomes can be seen by examining outcomes for children whose parents differ in the particular source of social capital discussed earlier, intergenerational closure. There is not a direct measure of intergenerational closure in the data, but there is a proximate indicator. This is the number of times the child has changed schools because the family moved. For families that have moved often, the social relations that constitute social capital are broken at each move. Whatever the degree of intergenerational closure available to others in the community, it is not available to parents in mobile families.

The logistic regression carried out earlier and reported in table A1 shows that the coefficient for number of moves since grade 5 is 10 times its standard error, the variable with the strongest overall effect of any variable in the equation, including the measures of human and financial capital in the family (socioeconomic status) and the crude measures of family social capital introduced in the earlier analysis. Translating this into an effect on dropping out gives 11.8 percent as the dropout rate if the family has not moved, 16.7 percent if it has moved once, and 23.1 percent if it has moved twice.

In the *High School and Beyond* data set, another variation among the schools constitutes a useful indicator of social capital. This is the distinctions among public high schools, religiously based private high schools, and nonreligiously based private high schools. It is the religiously based high schools that are surrounded by a community based on the religious organization. These families have intergenerational closure that is based on a multiplex relation: whatever other relations they have, the adults are members of the same religious body and parents of children in the same school. In contrast, it is the independent private schools that are typically least surrounded by a community, for their student bodies are collections of students, most of whose families have no contact.[5] The choice of private school for most of these parents is an

---

[5]    Data from this study have no direct measures of the degree of intergenerational closure among the parents of the school to support this statement. However, the

(*Note continues on the following page.*)

individualistic one, and, although they back their children with extensive human capital, they send their children to these schools denuded of social capital.

In the *High School and Beyond* data set, there are 893 public schools, 84 Catholic schools, and 27 other private schools. Most of the other private schools are independent schools, though a minority have religious foundations. In this analysis, I will at the outset regard the other private schools as independent private schools to examine the effects of social capital outside the family.

The results of these comparisons are shown in table 2. Item 1 of the table shows that the dropout rates between sophomore and senior years are 14.4 percent in public schools, 3.4 percent in Catholic schools, and 11.9 percent in other private schools. What is most striking is the low dropout rate in Catholic schools. The rate is a fourth of that in the public schools and a third of that in the other private schools.

Adjusting the dropout rates for differences in student-body financial, human, and social capital among the three sets of schools by standardizing the population of the Catholic schools and other private schools to the student-body backgrounds of the public schools shows that the differences are affected only slightly. Furthermore, the differences are not due to the religion of the students or to the degree of religious observance. Catholic students in public school are only slightly less likely to drop out than non-Catholics. Frequency of attendance at religious services, which is itself a measure of social capital through intergenerational closure, is strongly related to dropout rate, with 19.5 percent of public school students who rarely or never attend dropping out compared with 9.1 percent of those who attend often. But this effect exists apart from, and in addition to, the effect of the school's religious affiliation. Comparable figures for Catholic school students are 5.9 percent and 2.6 percent, respectively (Coleman and Hoffer 1987, p. 138).

The low dropout rates of the Catholic schools, the absence of low dropout rates in the other private schools, and the independent effect of frequency of religious attendance all provide evidence of the importance of social capital outside the school, in the adult community surrounding it, for this outcome of education.

A further test is possible, for there were eight schools in the sample of non-Catholic private schools ("other private" in the analysis above) that have religious foundations and over 50 percent of the student body of that religion. Three were Baptist schools, two were Jewish, and three

---

one measure of intergenerational closure that does exist in the data, the number of residential moves requiring school change since grade 5, is consistent with the statement. The average number of moves for public school students is .57; for Catholic school students, .35; and for students in other private schools, .88.

TABLE 2: DROPOUT RATES BETWEEN SPRING, GRADE 10, AND SPRING, GRADE 12, FOR STUDENTS FROM SCHOOLS WITH DIFFERING AMOUNTS OF SOCIAL CAPITAL IN THE SURROUNDING COMMUNITY

|  | *Public* | *Catholic* | *Other private schools* |
|---|---|---|---|
| 1. Raw dropout rates | 14.4 | 3.4 | 11.9 |
| 2. Dropout rates standardized to average public school sophomore[a] | 14.4 | 5.2 | 11.6 |
|  |  | *Non-Catholic Religious* | *Independent* |
| 3. Raw dropout rates for students[b] from independent and non-Catholic religious private schools |  | 3.7 | 10.0 |

a. The standardization is based on separate logistic regressions for these two sets of schools, using the same variables listed in n. 5. Coefficients and means for the standardization are in Hoffer (1986, tables 5 and 24).
b. This tabulation is based on unweighted data, which is responsible for the fact that both rates are lower than the rate for other private schools in item 1 of the table, which is based on weighted data.

from three other denominations. If the inference is correct about the religious community's providing intergenerational closure and thus social capital and about the importance of social capital in depressing the chance of dropping out of high school, these schools also should show a lower dropout rate than the independent private schools. Item 3 of table 2 shows that their dropout rate is lower, 3.7 percent, essentially the same as that of the Catholic schools.[6]

The data presented above indicate the importance of social capital for the education of youth, or, as it might be put, the importance of social capital in the creation of human capital. Yet there is a fundamental difference between social capital and most other forms of capital that has strong implications for the development of youth. It is this difference to which I will turn in the next section.

### Public goods aspects of social capital

Physical capital is ordinarily a private good, and property rights make it possible for the person who invests in physical capital to capture the benefits it produces. Thus, the incentive to invest in physical capital is not depressed; there is not a suboptimal investment in physical capital

---

6   It is also true, though not presented here, that the lack of social capital in the family makes little difference in dropout rates in Catholic schools—or, in the terms I have used, social capital in the community compensates in part for its absence in the family. See Coleman and Hoffer (1997, chap. 5).

because those who invest in it are able to capture the benefits of their investments. For human capital also—at least human capital of the sort that is produced in schools—the person who invests the time and resources in building up this capital reaps its benefits in the form of a higher-paying job, more satisfying or higher-status work, or even the pleasure of greater understanding of the surrounding world—in short, all the benefits that schooling brings to a person.

But most forms of social capital are not like this. For example, the kinds of social structures that make possible social norms and the sanctions that enforce them do not benefit primarily the person or persons whose efforts would be necessary to bring them about, but benefit all those who are part of such a structure, For example, in some schools where there exists a dense set of associations among some parents, these are the result of a small number of persons, ordinarily mothers who do not hold full-time jobs outside the home. Yet these mothers themselves experience only a subset of the benefits of this social capital surrounding the school. If one of them decides to abandon these activities—for example, to take a full-time job—this may be an entirely reasonable action from a personal point of view and even from the point of view of that household with its children. The benefits of the new activity may far outweigh the losses that arise from the decline in associations with other parents whose children are in the school. But the withdrawal of these activities constitutes a loss to all those other parents whose associations and contacts were dependent on them.

Similarly, the decision to move from a community so that the father, for example, can take a better job may be entirely correct from the point of view of that family. But, because social capital consists of relations among persons, other persons may experience extensive losses by the severance of those relations, a severance over which they had no control. A part of those losses is the weakening of norms and sanctions that aid the school in its task. For each family, the total cost it experiences as a consequence of the decisions it and other families make may outweigh the benefits of those few decisions it has control over. Yet the beneficial consequences to the family of those decisions made by the family may far outweigh the minor losses it experiences from them alone.

It is not merely voluntary associations, such as a PTA, in which underinvestment of this sort occurs. When an individual asks a favor from another, thus incurring an obligation, he does so because it brings him a needed benefit; he does not consider that it does the other a benefit as well by adding to a drawing fund of social capital available in a time of need. If the first individual can satisfy his need through self-sufficiency, or through aid from some official source without incurring an obligation, he will do so—and thus fail to add to the social capital outstanding in the community.

Similar statements can be made with respect to trustworthiness as social capital. An actor choosing to keep trust or not (or choosing whether to devote resources to an attempt to keep trust) is doing so on the basis of costs and benefits he himself will experience. That his trustworthiness will facilitate others' actions or that his lack of trustworthiness will inhibit others' actions does not enter into his decision. A similar but more qualified statement can be made for information as a form of social capital. An individual who serves as a source of information for another because he is well informed ordinarily acquires that information for his own benefit, not for the others who make use of him. (This is not always true. As Katz and Lazarsfeld [1955] show, "opinion leaders" in an area acquire information in part to maintain their position as opinion leaders.)

For norms also, the statement must be qualified. Norms are intentionally established, indeed as means of reducing externalities, and their benefits are ordinarily captured by those who are responsible for establishing them. But the capability of establishing and maintaining effective norms depends on properties of the social structure (such as closure) over which one actor does not have control yet are affected by one actor's action. These are properties that affect the structure's capacity to sustain effective norms, yet properties that ordinarily do not enter into an individual's decision that affects them.

Some forms of social capital have the property that their benefits can be captured by those who invest in them; consequently, rational actors will not underinvest in this type of social capital. Organizations that produce a private good constitute the outstanding example. The result is that there will be in society an imbalance in the relative investment in organizations that produce private goods for a market and those associations and relationships in which the benefits are not captured—an imbalance in the sense that, if the positive externalities created by the latter form of social capital could be internalized, it would come to exist in greater quantity.

The public goods quality of most social capital means that it is in a fundamentally different position with respect to purposive action than are most other forms of capital. It is an important resource for individuals and may affect greatly their ability to act and their perceived quality of life. They have the capability of bringing it into being. Yet, because the benefits of actions that bring social capital into being are largely experienced by persons other than the actor, it is often not in his interest to bring it into being. The result is that most forms of social capital are created or destroyed as by-products of other activities. This social capital arises or disappears without anyone's willing it into or out of being and is thus even less recognized and taken account of in social action than its already intangible character would warrant.

There are important implications of this public goods aspect of social capital that play a part in the development of children and youth. Because the social structural conditions that overcome the problems of supplying these public goods—that is, strong families and strong communities—are much less often present now than in the past, and promise to be even less present in the future, we can expect that, ceteris paribus, we confront a declining quantity of human capital embodied in each successive generation. The obvious solution appears to be to attempt to find ways of overcoming the problem of supply of these public goods, that is, social capital employed for the benefit of children and youth. This very likely means the substitution of some kind of formal organization for the voluntary and spontaneous social organization that has in the past been the major source of social capital available to the young.

### Conclusion

In this paper, I have attempted to introduce into social theory a concept, "social capital," paralleling the concepts of financial capital, physical capital, and human capital—but embodied in relations among persons. This is part of a theoretical strategy that involves use of the paradigm of rational action but without the assumption of atomistic elements stripped of social relationships. I have shown the use of this concept through demonstrating the effect of social capital in the family and in the community in aiding the formation of human capital. The single measure of human capital formation used for this was one that appears especially responsive to the supply of social capital, remaining in high school until graduation versus dropping out, Both social capital in the family and social capital outside it, in the adult community surrounding the school, showed evidence of considerable value in reducing the probability of dropping out of high school.

In explicating the concept of social capital, three forms were identified: obligations and expectations, which depend on trustworthiness of the social environment, information-flow capability of the social structure, and norms accompanied by sanctions. A property shared by most forms of social capital that differentiates it from other forms of capital is its public good aspect: the actor or actors who generate social capital ordinarily capture only a small part of its benefits, a fact that leads to underinvestment in social capital.

# Appendix

TABLE A1: LOGISTIC REGRESSION COEFFICIENTS AND ASYMPTOTIC STANDARD ERRORS FOR EFFECTS OF STUDENT BACKGROUND CHARACTERISTICS ON DROPPING OUT OF HIGH SCHOOL BETWEEN SOPHOMORE AND SENIOR YEARS 1980–82, PUBLIC SCHOOL SAMPLE

|  | $b$ | $SE$ |
|---|---|---|
| Intercept | −2.305 | .169 |
| Socioeconomic status | −.460 | .077 |
| Black | −.161 | .162 |
| Hispanic | .104 | .138 |
| Number of siblings | .180 | .028 |
| Mother worked while child was young | −.012 | .103 |
| Both parents in household | −.415 | .112 |
| Mother's expectation for college | −.685 | .103 |
| Talk with parents | .031 | .044 |
| Number of moves since grade 5 | .407 | .040 |

*Source:* Hoffer (1986).

# References

Baker, Wayne. 1983. "Floor Trading and Crowd Dynamics." In Patricia Adler and Peter Adler, eds., *Social Dynamics of Financial Markets*, pp. 107–28. Greenwich, Conn.: JAI.

Banfield, Edward. 1967. *The Moral Basis of a Backward Society.* New York: Free Press.

Becker, Gary. 1964. *Human Capital.* New York: National Bureau of Economic Research.

Ben-Porath, Yoram. 1930. "The *F*-Connection: Families, Friends, and Firms and the Organization of Exchange." *Population and Development Review* 6: 1–30.

Black, R. D. C., A. W. Coats, and C. D. W. Goodwin, eds. 1973. *The Marginal Revolution in Economics.* Durham, N.C.: Duke University Press.

Blau, Peter. 1964. *Exchange and Power in Social Life.* New York: Wiley.

Coleman, James S. 1986a. "Social Theory, Social Research, and a Theory of Action." *American Journal of Sociology* 91: 1309–35.

———. 1986b. *Individual Interests and Collective Action.* Cambridge: Cambridge University Press.

————. 1987. "Norms as Social Capital." In Gerard Radnitzky and Peter Bernholz, eds., *Economic Imperalism*, pp. 133–55. New York: Paragon.

Coleman, J. S., and T. B. Hoffer. 1987. *Public and Private Schools: The Impact of Communities*. New York: Basic.

DeGraaf, Nan Dirk, and Hendrik Derk Flap. 1988. "With a Little Help from My Friends." *Social Forces*, vol. 67 (in press).

Festinger, Leon, Stanley Schachter, and Kurt Back. 1963. *Social Pressures in Informal Groups*. Stanford, Calif.: Stanford University Press.

Geertz, Clifford. 1962. "The Rotating Credit Association: A 'Middle Rung' in Development." *Economic Development and Cultural Change* 10: 240–63.

Gluckman, Max. 1967. *The Judicial Process among the Barotse of Northern Rhodesia*, 2d ed. Manchester: Manchester University Press.

Gouldner, Alvin. 1960. "The Norm of Reciprocity: A Preliminary Statement." *American Sociological Review* 25: 161–78.

Granovetter, Mark. 1985. "Economic Action, Social Structure, and Embeddedness." *American Journal of Sociology* 91: 481–510.

Hoffer, T. B. 1986. *Educational Outcomes in Public and Private High Schools*. Ph.D. dissertation. Department of Sociology, University of Chicago.

Homans, George. 1974. *Social Behavior: Its Elementary Forms*, rev. ed. New York: Harcourt, Brace & World.

Katz, E., and P. Lazarsfeld. 1955. *Personal Influence*. New York: Free Press.

Lenin, V. I. (1902) 1973. *What Is To Be Done*. Peking: Foreign Language Press.

Lin, Nan. 1988. "Social Resources and Social Mobility: A Structural Theory of Status Attainment." In Ronald Breiger, ed., *Social Mobility and Social Structure*. Cambridge: Cambridge University Press.

Lipset, Seymour, M. Trow, and J. Coleman. 1956. *Union Democracy*. New York: Free Press.

Merry, Sally, E. 1984. "Rethinking Gossip and Scandal." In Donald Black, ed., *Toward a General Theory of Social Control*, Vol. 1, *Fundamentals*, pp. 271–302. New York: Academic.

Merton, Robert K. 1968. *Social Theory and Social Structure*, 2d ed. New York: Free Press.

————. n.d. "Study of World War II Housing Projects." Unpublished manuscript. Department of Sociology, Columbia University.

Schultz, Theodore. 1961, "Investment in Human Capital." *American Economic Review* 51 (March): 1–17.

Ullmann-Margalit, Edna. 1977. *The Emergence of Norms*. Oxford: Clarendon.

Williamson, Oliver. 1975. *Markets and Hierarchies*. New York: Free Press.

————. 1981. "The Economics of Organization: The Transaction Cost Approach." *American Journal of Sociology* 87: 548–77.

Wrong, Dennis. 1961. "The Oversocialized Conception of Man in Modern Sociology." *American Sociological Review* 26: 183–93.

# Defining social capital: an integrating view[1]

**Ismail Serageldin** and **Christiaan Grootaert**
*World Bank*

*The paper argues that different, but mutually reinforcing, types of social capital coexist in society. Consequently, an integrating view is needed on the definition and measurement of social capital that bridges the distinctions in the literature between micro- and macroinstitutional social capital in formal and informal institutions, and in horizontal and vertical associations. The paper also argues that, for a given country at a given time, there exists an "appropriate" level and composition of social capital, based on complementarities with other forms of capital.*

## Social capital and sustainability

Social capital is best studied in the context of the contribution it makes to sustainable development. Building on this view, this paper puts forth two propositions that will hopefully help integrate the widely different definitions of social capital and facilitate the measurement and operational application of the concept. The immediate advantage of seeing social capital in this context is that sustainable development is a widely accepted concept. It appeals to the public at large and conveys a sense of continuity and concern for the environment and for children—but it does not imply that the economy must stagnate or living standards need to fall.

The first formal definition saw sustainable development as "[meeting] the needs of the present without compromising the ability of future generations to meet their own needs" (Brundtland Commission 1987, p. 43). While philosophically attractive and simple, this definition raises difficult operational questions. Given the variations in living standards within and across countries, defining needs in a meaningful and coher-

---

[1] This paper draws on earlier work on social capital by the authors. See especially Serageldin (1996a) and Grootaert (1996).

ent way is virtually impossible. We have therefore tried to operationalize the definition by referring to the *stock of capital* that underlies the generation of income and welfare.

In an earlier paper, Serageldin (1996b) puts forth an especially promising approach that views sustainability as opportunity. This notion leads to a second definition: "Sustainability is to leave future generations as many opportunities as we ourselves have had, if not more" (Serageldin 1996b, p. 3). This approach views opportunity, in economic terms, as expanding the capital stock. In economics and finance, the idea of depleting capital to create an income stream is simply unacceptable, because income based on capital depletion is unsustainable.[2] Capital and capital growth are the means of providing future generations with the opportunities we have had—provided that capital is defined on a per capita basis to account for the needs of the burgeoning global population. Sustainability as opportunity thus means that future generations must be provided with as much or more capital per capita than the current generation.

The composition of the capital left to the next generation can differ from the composition of the current stock, however. Thus, defining sustainability as opportunity highlights the importance of looking at a stock variable (wealth) as well as a flow variable (income). The approach requires distinguishing among different kinds of capital (produced assets, natural capital, human capital, and social capital) and recognizing that they are both complements and substitutes.

## Key features of "sustainability as opportunity"

Defining sustainability as opportunity requires looking beyond traditional measures of sustainability to existing stocks of wealth, genuine saving rates, and human and social capital. It also posits three levels of sustainability—weak, sensible, and strong.

■ *Existing stocks.* Income measures have traditionally focused on flows. But no corporation runs its affairs using only cash flow and income statements, ignoring balance sheets and net worth. Countries need to behave more like corporations and analyze existing stocks.

■ *Genuine saving.* Adjusting national accounts for depreciation of all classes of assets has little effect on trends in traditional income measures. However, similar adjustments to gross investment data pro-

---

[2]   This notion goes to the heart of the definition of income given by Nobel Laureate Sir John Hicks: "The maximum value a person can consume during a week, and still expect to be as well off at the end of the week as at the beginning."

vide important signals on saving and investment. A measure based solely on gross investment as a percentage of GNP can mask major variations in genuine saving. For example, a constant level of gross investment of 15–18 percent of GNP for Latin America translates into a positive genuine savings rate of 7 percent in 1969 but a negative rate of 2–3 percent in 1982 (Pearce and Atkinson 1993).

■ *Human and social capital.* "Back of the envelope" calculations show that in 192 countries (except for a few raw materials exporters), human and social capital equals or exceeds natural capital and produced assets combined (World Bank 1995). (See figure 1.) Produced assets, or human-made capital, represents only 16–20 percent of the wealth of most of the countries. Yet most current economic policies focus on this small group of assets. A more recent comparison based on better data and using purchasing power parity conversion factors provides stronger evidence of the importance of human and social capital, although it found a smaller gap between rich and poor countries (World Bank 1997).

■ *Level of sustainability.* Sustainability as opportunity has several levels—weak, sensible, and strong—depending on how strictly the concept of maintenance, or nondeclining capital, is applied (Pearce and Atkinson 1993).

1. Weak sustainability means maintaining current levels of total capital without regard to its composition (natural, human-made, social, or human). This scenario implies that the different kinds of capital are perfectly interchangeable, at least within the boundaries of current levels of economic activity and resource endowment.

2. Sensible sustainability means maintaining capital intact while also considering its composition. Thus, oil may be depleted as long as the receipts are invested in another type of capital (human, for instance). Under this scenario, countries seek to set the minimum level of each type of capital that is necessary to allay concerns about substitutability. Monitoring ensures that development does not promote the decimation of one kind of capital in favor of another. This recognizes that human-made and natural capital are to a large extent substitutes but also that they are complements—and that, to function fully, a country requires a mix of all four types.

3. Strong sustainability means maintaining the different kinds of capital separately, keeping the stock of each intact. Thus, re-

FIGURE 1: COMPOSITION OF WORLD WEALTH BY INCOME GROUP (PERCENTAGE OF TOTAL)

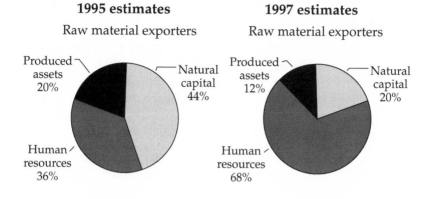

**1995 estimates**                    **1997 estimates**

Raw material exporters            Raw material exporters

Produced assets 20% — Natural capital 44% — Human resources 36%

Produced assets 12% — Natural capital 20% — Human resources 68%

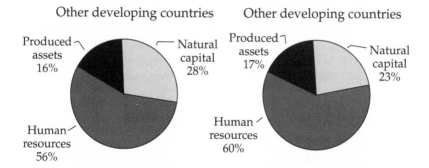

Other developing countries        Other developing countries

Produced assets 16% — Natural capital 28% — Human resources 56%

Produced assets 17% — Natural capital 23% — Human resources 60%

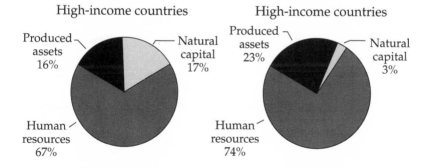

High-income countries             High-income countries

Produced assets 16% — Natural capital 17% — Human resources 67%

Produced assets 23% — Natural capital 3% — Human resources 74%

*Source:* World Bank 1995, 1997.

ceipts from oil (natural capital) are invested in sustainable energy production rather than in another asset. This scenario assumes that natural and human-made capital are not really substitutes but rather complement each other in most production functions. For instance, a sawmill (human-made capital) is worthless without a forest (natural capital). The same logic argues that reductions in one kind of educational investment should be offset by investments in another, not by investments in roads.

### Definitions of social capital

The previous section showed that the sum of human and social capital exceeds that of produced and natural capital in many countries (figure 1). But while the concept of human capital is by now well accepted, the concept of social capital is not. A "glue that holds societies together" (Serageldin 1996a, p. 196) is generally recognized as necessary to a functioning social order, along with a certain degree of common cultural identifications, a sense of "belonging," and shared behavioral norms. This internal coherence helps to define social capital. Without it, society at large would collapse, and there could be no talk of economic growth, environmental sustainability, or human well-being—as Somalia, Yugoslavia, and Rwanda painfully illustrate. More positively, social capital can be identified indirectly in countries where similar stocks of natural, produced, and human capital have turned in very different economic performances. It can also be seen in regions or cities within the same country and even in communities within regions or cities. The examples that follow show how social capital contributes to economic growth.

*East Asia.* Conventional factors such as investments in human and physical capital and technology only partially explain the high growth rates of the East Asian "miracle" economies. These governments have also invested in social capital by creating policies that provide an enabling environment for growth. Institutional arrangements and organizational designs that enhance efficiency, facilitate the exchange of information, and promote cooperation between government and industry characterize this environment (World Bank 1993; Stiglitz 1996).[3]

*Northern Italy.* In a study of Italy, Putnam, Leonardi, and Nanetti (1993) argue that the large number of voluntary associations among people in

---

[3] There are dissenting views on the role of social capital in the growth rates of the East Asian economies. Some authors argue that increased mobilization of resources—that is, increases in labor force participation rates, education, and investment in physical capital—explain most or all of the growth (Krugman 1994). Other observers, relying on endogenous growth models, argue that low income inequality (which characterizes the East Asian economies) has been an important stimulus to growth (Birdsall, Ross, and Sabot 1995). For a recent review and interpretation of the evidence, see Stiglitz (1996).

Northern Italy explains the region's economic success. These associations provide the north with the social capital that the south, where the associations are far less common, does not have.

*Somalia.* After the fall of Somalia's government in 1991, the country was plagued with civil disorder and declining incomes. An exception was the port city of Boosaaso, where a local warlord supported by local residents organized a security force and a council of clan elders. With this investment in social capital, trade flourished and incomes increased (Buckley 1996).

*India.* In the state of Gujarat, violent confrontations between local people and government officials over forest management led to economic stagnation. But once the communities were mobilized and joint forest management was instituted, conflicts declined and land productivity and village incomes rose (Pathan, Arul, and Poffenberger 1993). In this case, the investment in social capital was a joint effort by local governments and communities.

Examples of social capital are easier to provide than one specific definition. The term is used differently depending on the field of study, for instance. In the literature of political science, sociology, and anthropology, *social capital* generally refers to the set of norms, networks, and organizations through which people gain access to power and resources that are instrumental in enabling decision-making and policy formulation.[4] Economists add to this focus the contribution of social capital to economic growth. At the microeconomic level, they view social capital primarily in terms of its ability to improve market functioning. At the macroeconomic level, they consider how institutions, legal frameworks, and the government's role in the organization of production affect macroeconomic performance.

The most famous and in some ways most narrowly defined concept of social capital is Putnam's (Putnam 1993; Putnam, Leonardi, and Nanetti 1993). Putnam views social capital as a set of "horizontal associations" among people who have an effect on the productivity of the community. These associations include "networks of civic engagement" and social norms. Two assumptions underlie this concept. The first is that networks and norms are empirically associated; and second, that they have important economic consequences. In this definition, the key

---

[4] Coleman (1988) has been attributed with introducing the term "social capital" into the sociological literature. He defines it as a "social structure [that] facilitates certain actions of actors within the structure" (p. 598). Similar to this definition is Etzioni's (1988) concept of "social collectivities," or "major decisionmaking units, often providing the context within which individual decisions are made" (p. 186). In economics, Loury (1977) introduced the concept of social capital in an analysis of racial inequality to describe the social resources of ethnic communities. More generally, economists have argued that aspects of social capital, such as institutions, have always been present in economic analysis.

feature of social capital is that it facilitates coordination and cooperation for the mutual benefit of the members of the association (Putnam
1993).[5]

Coleman (1988, p. 598) puts forth a second, broader concept of social
capital. Coleman sees social capital as "a variety of different entities,
with two elements in common: they all consist of some aspect of social
structure, and they facilitate certain actions of actors—whether personal
or corporate actors—within the structure." From the outset, this definition broadens the concept to include vertical as well as horizontal associations and the behavior of other entities, such as firms.[6] This wider
range of associations covers both negative and positive objectives.
Coleman states explicitly that "a given form of social capital that is valuable in facilitating certain actions may be useless or even harmful for
others" (Coleman 1988, p. 598). In fact, this view of social capital captures not only social structures at large but the ensemble of norms governing interpersonal behavior.

A third, still more encompassing view of social capital includes the
social and political environment that enables norms to develop and
shapes social structure. In addition to the largely informal horizontal
relationships included in the first concept and the vertical hierarchical
organizations of the second, this view encompasses formalized institutional relationships and structures, such as governments, political regimes, the rule of law, court systems, and civil and political liberties.
(See box 1.)

The impact of this more broadly defined concept of social capital
on macroeconomic outcomes has been investigated by North (1990)
and Olson (1982). They argue that differences in per capita incomes
across countries cannot be explained by the per capita distribution
of productive resources (land and natural resources, human capital,
and produced capital, including technology). Institutions and other
forms of social capital, along with public policies, determine the returns a country can extract from its other forms of capital. Olson argues that low-income countries, even those with a large resource base,
cannot obtain large gains from investment, specialization, and trade.
These countries are limited by a lack of institutions that enforce con-

---

[5]   While this concept of social capital was originally limited to associations having positive effects on development, it has recently been relaxed to include groups
that may produce undesirable outcomes, such as rent-seekers (for instance, the
Mafia in Southern Italy, and militias).
[6]   This concept of social capital is closely related to the treatment of firms and
other hierarchical organizations in institutional economics, which sees the
organization's purpose as minimizing transaction costs (Williamson 1985, 1993).
Vertical associations are characterized by hierarchical relationships and the un-
even distribution of power among members.

Box 1. Three Views on Social Capital: Common Features

The three views on social capital progressively broaden the concept. The first includes mostly informal and local horizontal associations, while the second adds hierarchical associations. The third interpretation builds on the first two, adding formalized national structures such as government and the rule of law. The three views have several common features:

■ All link the economic, social, and political spheres. They share the belief that social relationships affect and are affected by economic outcomes.

■ All focus on relationships among economic agents and the ways in which formal and informal organizations of these agents can improve the efficiency of economic activities.

■ All imply that desirable social relationships and institutions have positive externalities. Since individuals cannot appropriate these externalities, agents tend to underinvest in social capital, creating a role for public support.

All recognize not only the potential social relationships create for improving development outcomes but also the possibility that these same relationships can have negative effects. The outcome depends on the nature of the relationship (horizontal versus hierarchical), preexisting norms and values, and the wider legal and political context.

tracts impartially and secure long-term property rights—and by misguided economic policies.

## The effects of social capital

There is growing evidence that social capital can have an impact on development outcomes, including growth, equity, and poverty alleviation (Grootaert 1996). Associations and institutions provide an informal framework for sharing information, coordinating activities, and making collective decisions. Bardhan (1995) argues that what makes this informal model work is peer monitoring, a common set of norms, and sanctions at the local level.

### Sharing information

Formal and informal institutions can help avert market failures related to inadequate or inaccurate information. Economic agents often make inefficient decisions because they lack needed information or because one agent benefits from relaying incorrect information to another. (Credit or employment applications are good examples of the latter.) In other circumstances, optimal decisions may be difficult to make because of uncertainty and the response of other agents to that uncertainty. Institutions can help disseminate adequate, accurate information that allow market players to make appropriate, efficient decisions. Group-based lending schemes are a case in point. These schemes—from tontine (informal saving circles) in West Africa to the Grameen Bank in Bangladesh—work because members have better information on each other than banks do.

Information problems can be particularly severe in capital markets. Japan and Korea have responded to such problems by developing "deliberation councils," which manage competition among firms for credit and foreign exchange. The process is transparent, encouraging cooperative behavior and information sharing among firms by removing incentives for rent-seeking behavior (World Bank 1993; Campos and Root 1996). The rule of law and a well-functioning court system (elements of social capital in its broadest definition) also help reduce uncertainty in capital markets by enforcing contracts. The contracting parties thus receive advance information about the penalties for noncompliance. In the absence of effective courts, many informal associations internalize this policing role for their members. Diamond merchants, who often base deals involving millions of dollars worth of diamonds on a handshake, present a striking example. Failure to deliver on a deal irrevocably leads to expulsion from the group, and all members are aware of this fact. Unfortunately, this mechanism also works for groups pursuing undesirable outcomes, so that mafias function efficiently as well.

### Coordinating activities

Uncoordinated or opportunistic behavior by economic agents can also lead to market failure. Such behaviors lie behind the failure of many irrigation projects. Because these projects often lack formal or informal (social) means of imposing equitable agreements for sharing the water, some farmers use water needed by others or fail to contribute to maintenance. Effective social capital in the form of water user groups can overcome such problems (Meinzen-Dick and others 1995; Ostrom 1995). These associations reduce opportunistic behavior by creating a framework within which individuals interact repeatedly, enhancing trust among members (Dasgupta 1988).[7]

---

[7]    This *backward-looking* motivation for trust has been discussed in the social psychology literature. Trust can also be *forward-looking*, based on the perception of retaliation for untrustworthy behavior.

*Making collective decisions*

Collective decision-making is a necessary condition for the provision of public goods and the management of market externalities. It is one of the basic rationales behind the notion of government. But like governments, local and voluntary associations do not always effectively maximize their ability to make collective decisions. The extent to which they do depends not only on how well they address the problems of information-sharing but on the degree of equity that prevails. Local institutions are more effective at enforcing common agreements and cooperative action when the assets are distributed relatively equitably and benefits shared equally. On the local level, then, efficiency and equity go together. Sharing provides an incentive for improved coordination in the management of local public goods, increasing productivity for everyone.

This microeconomic focus on markets is only part of the story. Market outcomes are also influenced by the macroeconomic environment and the political economy. The latter can be enabling, enhancing the effects of formal and informal civil associations (as has arguably been the case in the East Asian success stories). But the macro environment can also damage or undo the effects of local-level social capital. Where there are good governance, well-functioning courts, and freedom of expression, local associations thrive and complement the functions of macroinstitutions. But where these are absent or function poorly, local institutions may try to substitute for them, resulting in more stress and fewer economic benefits. Just as it makes little sense to assess an investment project without looking at the sector and relevant macroeconomic policy environment, it makes little sense to consider local associations in isolation. What is needed is a balanced view of the role of the central state and local-level institutions. This point suggests that the three definitions of social capital are not really alternative views but complementary aspects of the same concept.

## Social capital: an integrated view

The distinctions drawn in the literature among the three definitions are largely artificial and unnecessary. We argue that an integrated view of social capital is an important step toward measuring and operationalizing the concept. Such a view is based on the recognition that the four types of capital can coexist and are in fact needed to maximize the impact of social capital on economic and social outcomes. This complementarity applies not only across but within the types of capital. Physical capital provides a good example. The production process depends on different types of physical capital that work together (for example, machines that produce goods, factories that house machines, and roads that transport workers to factories and goods to market). Likewise, limited substitution possibilities exist across and within types of capital.

Stone, Levy, and Paredes (1992) illustrate the complementarity between micro- and macrolevel social capital and the limits to substitution in their comparison of the garment industries in Brazil and Chile. Brazil has a complex regulatory system, with laws that are often inconsistent and very expensive courts. Businesses have learned to rely on informal alternatives in their day-to-day transactions with customers and suppliers, especially when credit is involved. Brazilian garment entrepreneurs have worked out an effective informal credit information system that places a premium on an untarnished reputation. Nevertheless, contracts remain insecure and are frequently renegotiated, even up to the moment of delivery. The entrepreneurs have therefore adopted risk-reducing strategies—such as producing only standard items and reducing the size of orders—that ultimately hinder expansion.[8]

In contrast, Chile's relatively simple legal system and consistent enforcement of contracts have made the contracting process more secure, so that few contracts are renegotiated and the default rate on loans has dropped. The comparison suggests that the extent to which informal associations can replace the rule of law and a formal court system is limited, underscoring the importance of the role of macrolevel social capital in making business possible and especially of the government's role in providing an enabling environment that is simple, transparent, and consistent.

Complementarity between micro- and macrolevel social capital not only influences economic outcomes but has a mutually strengthening effect. Macroinstitutions can provide an enabling environment for microinstitutions to develop and flourish. In turn, local associations help sustain regional and national institutions and give them a measure of stability. The key measures of successful interaction between the two levels of institutions are shared values and norms and mutual trust. These can be expressed in the recognition and acceptance, at both levels, of a common entity (which could be the state itself) or a common objective (such as peace or economic progress) (figure 2a). Switzerland, where the cantons joined in a confederation that supported the common objective of creating a sovereign state, offers an example of successful micro- and macrolevel interaction—in fact, the modern Swiss state may well be represented by figure 2b. Local institutions are not initially required

---

8    A study of Peru shows that the sheer complexity of laws and regulations can undermine their effectiveness and provide economic agents with strong disincentives to adhere to formality (Soto 1989). In Peru, the complexity of the legal framework has led to the shifting of economic transactions to an informal sector that is not protected by formal law but is functional, thanks to informal substitutes.

to share norms among themselves, other than the norm that is also common to the macro institution. But cohesion is likely to improve (through bonding and overlapping norms at the local level) as institutions work toward a common objective. This mutually reinforcing interaction between the micro- and macrolevels increases the stock of social capital.

Sometimes micro- and macrolevel institutions fail to develop shared norms or overcome distrust (figure 3a). Such a situation is likely to be unstable and to deteriorate until all bonds are broken (figure 3b). If the key norm in question relates to basic human respect, the outcome is civil strife or war, as in Yugoslavia. If the distrust is in the economic sphere, the result is economic setback, as in Québec.

Among the factors that determine whether a positive (figure 2) or negative (figure 3) scenario prevails is the macroscale framework and the extent to which it is both enabling and perceived by the microscale institutions to be legitimate, representative, and fair. The relationship between formal and informal institutions also needs to be considered. At the local level, formal government and other institutions interact with a dense set of informal networks, associative frameworks, and voluntary associations. These interactions help define the constraints on and the scope of individual, household, and group activities.

The quality of the institutions themselves is also important. The abilities and effectiveness of the institutions at the macro- and microlevels (and in the formal and informal spheres) influence outcomes. Institutions need values, but they also need organizational and management capacity and communication and technical skills in order to act effectively upon these values. This observation provides an entry point for donors, at least in the positive scenario portrayed in figure 2. Support for capacity-building and training can improve institutions and promote social capital to make the positive interaction more efficient.

The transition economies of Eastern Europe and the former Soviet Union provide a dramatic instance of the importance of constructive interaction between macro- and microlevel social capital and the costs of the absence of such interaction. The sudden disappearance of government from many social and economic functions has eroded trust, forcing people to rely on local networks and informal associations. Rose (1995b) creates the "new democracies barometer" to measure this phenomenon. He notes that people have withdrawn from the "official" economy and begun to rely on multiple informal economies to satisfy most needs. Informal activities include growing food, repairing houses, and helping friends in return for needed assistance. In a well-functioning market economy, these activities may be hobbies (and helping out may reflect friendship), but in the transition economies, this "social economy" has developed out of necessity. In Ukraine, for example, three-fourths of the households are involved in such activities (Rose 1995a). In Russia, the transition has led to what Rose calls an "hourglass society" (Rose

FIGURE 2: POSITIVE INTERACTION BETWEEN MACRO- AND MICROINSTITUTIONS

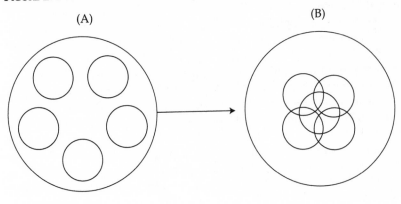

(A)                                    (B)

*Source:* Authors.

FIGURE 3: NEGATIVE INTERACTION BETWEEN MACRO- AND MICROINSTITUTIONS

(A)                                    (B)

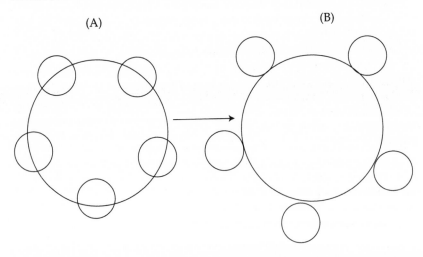

*Source:* Authors.

1995c). At the base is the "rich" social life of most Russians, consisting of strong informal networks based on trust among friends and face-to-face interactions. At the top is another "rich" social life and the political life of the elite, who compete with each other for power and wealth. The links between the base and the top are limited and characterized by a general distrust of the elite. Not even one in three Russians expects fair treatment from the police or their municipal offices (the post office is the most trusted institution). Sustainable development is unlikely in

Russia without a change for the better in the linkages between micro- and macrolevel institutions.

The process by which interactions between micro- and macrolevel social capital develop is dynamic. A good example is the gradual replacement, in the course of successful development, of informal associations and networks with formal administrative structures and impersonal market mechanisms. Large anonymous markets are more efficient than networks because the "best" buyer or seller may not be part of a network. If the development path is supported by a solid court system and a mechanism for enforcing contracts, anonymous markets will over time replace the "named" transactions within networks (that is, whereby the number of agents in each network is small and they know each other by name). In this situation, all participating economic agents gain.[9]

We suspect that, in principle, complementarity among different levels and types of social capital can be recognized and readily accepted. Capturing this complementarity empirically is not so straightforward, however. Should the shift from informal to formal networks be registered as declining or increasing social capital—or as a steady total amount, with one-for-one substitution among "units" of social capital? An initial step in measuring social capital could be to aggregate the indicators that have been developed at the micro- and macrolevels in an index that resembles the Human Development and Physical Quality of Life indexes. For microindicators, there are the Putnam-type examples of associational activity used by Narayan and Pritchett (1996). For macroindicators, there are the cross-country analyses of Knack and Keefer (1995, 1996) and Klitgaard and Fedderke (1995) and the macroinstitutional and trust indicators used by Rose (1995a, 1995b, 1995c). Indicators for the same country can in principle always be aggregated (abstracting from the usual issue of weighing component indexes).

Measuring complementarity or the feedback process between social capital at the micro- and macrolevels—particularly determining whether the process is additive or multiplicative—is even more difficult. The index suggested in the previous paragraph assumes an additive process. Conceptually, it is not difficult to describe a multiplier- or exponent-type process in the context of a production function, and social capital can be factored into the equation in much the same way as technology. In this case, certain types of social capital enter the process additively, but others have multiplier effects. The

---

9  Under the narrow definition of social capital, this phenomenon registers as a decline in social capital. But using the broader concept, the same phenomenon emerges as the substitution of one form of social capital (the rule of law) for another (horizontal associations).

empirical estimation of such a function is still a distant objective, but a conceptual start can be made by thinking through what mathematical form the function will take. Theoretical conceptualization then guides the empirical investigation, and the results of the empirical research feed back to the theoretical constructs and help validate, reject, or refine them.

## Appropriate social capital

The recognition that all different types of social capital are necessary to produce optimal results (and can in fact be mutually reinforcing) has a further implication—namely, that an "optimal mix" of types of social capital exists. This paper posits that the optimal mix is defined in terms of an objective function and that the obvious candidate is the maximization of economic outcomes—a process described by the macroeconomic production function and constrained by resource endowments.

This proposal is akin to arguing that we can identify an "appropriate technology" for a given country that will maximize returns to the other factors of productions. It takes into account the nature of complementarity and substitution across these factors. A nuclear reactor, for instance, is not appropriate technology in a country that lacks the human capital to manage and maintain it. In practice, appropriate technology is not identified with formal economic models but is based on ad hoc insight and a thorough knowledge of a country. The same is true for appropriate social capital, which also enhances the efficiency of the combination process of the other factors of production. In Putnam's words, "Social capital enhances the benefits of investment in physical and human capital" (1993, p. 36). In other words, it is not just an input into the production function but, like technology, a shift factor (or exponent) of the entire production function.

The key to determining what constitutes appropriate social capital is data—on both the composition and the level of the total stock. This information needs to be assessed in light of the other types of available capital in a country. We think that the most useful way to advance this notion is to undertake case studies in selected countries where a good bit of information on microinstitutions is already available. These case studies would investigate the interaction of the institutions with other organizations and levels of government and determine which economic processes they affect (as well as the levels and types of human, physical, and natural capital involved). However, to be truly useful in the context of this discussion, the case studies must be guided by a methodological framework that facilitates the measurement and analysis of findings and assesses testable hypotheses.

## Summary and conclusions

This paper argues for an improved understanding of social capital by putting forth two propositions. First, it suggests that the distinctions drawn in the literature by competing definitions of social capital are largely artificial and unnecessary. They detract from the fact that different types of social capital coexist and can be mutually reinforcing. We propose an aggregate formulation (if not a single index) of social capital and a continuing investigation into the additive and multiplicative nature of the interactions among the different types of social capital. Second, we argue that there is an appropriate level and composition of social capital for a given country at a given time. This level takes into account complementarities with other types of capital. Its composition is likely to change over time, but the total should increase through accumulation.

We hope that the discussion of the two propositions advances our understanding of how social capital contributes to economic and social outcomes. While these proposals introduce new demands on both conceptualization and measurement, they also open the door to bringing together data sources and approaches to data collection.

## References

The word *processed* describes informally reproduced works that may not be commonly available through libraries.

Bardhan, Pranab K. 1995. "Research on Poverty and Development— Twenty Years after Redistribution with Growth." Paper prepared for the Annual Bank Conference on Development Economics, May 1–2, 1995. World Bank, Washington, D.C.

Birdsall, Nancy, D. Ross, and R. Sabot. 1995. "Inequality and Growth Reconsidered: Lessons from East Asia." *World Bank Economic Review* 9(3): 477–508.

Brundtland Commission (World Commission on Environment and Development). 1987. *Our Common Future.* New York: Oxford University Press.

Buckley, Stephen. 1996. "Somalis Make City Thrive amid Anarchy— Amid Anarchy in Somalia, Port City Thrives on Community Efforts." *Washington Post*, March 3, A01.

Campos, José Edgardo L., and Hilton L. Root. 1996. *The Key to the Asian Miracle: Making Shared Growth Credible.* Washington, D.C.: Brookings Institution.

Coleman, James. 1988. "Social Capital in the Creation of Human Capital." *American Journal of Sociology* 94 (Supplement): S95–S120.

Dasgupta, Partha. 1988. "Trust as a Commodity." In Diego Gambetta, ed., *Trust: Making and Breaking Cooperative Relations*. Oxford: Blackwell Limited.

Etzioni, Amitai. 1988. *The Moral Dimension: Towards A New Economics.* New York: The Free Press.

Grootaert, Christiaan. 1996. "Social Capital: The Missing Link?" In *Monitoring Environmental Progress—Expanding the Measure of Wealth*. Washington, D.C.: World Bank.

Klitgaard, Robert, and Johannes Fedderke. 1995. "Social Integration and Disintegration: An Exploratory Analysis of Cross-Country Data." *World Development* 23(3): 357–69.

Knack, Stephen, and Philip Keefer. 1995. "Institutions and Economic Performance: Cross-Country Tests Using Alternative Institutional Measures." *Economics and Politics* 7(3): 202–27.

———. 1996. "Does Social Capital Have an Economic Payoff? A Cross-Country Investigation." World Bank Policy Research Department, processed. World Bank, Washington, D.C.

Krugman, Paul. 1994. "The Myth of Asia's Miracle." *Foreign Affairs* 73(6): 62–78.

Loury, Glen. 1977. "A Dynamic Theory of Racial Income Differences." In P. A. Wallace and A. LeMund, eds., *Woman, Minorities, and Employment Discrimination*. Lexington, Mass.: Lexington Books.

Meinzen-Dick, Ruth Suseela, Richard Reidinger, and Andrew Manzardo. 1995. *Participation in Irrigation*. Environment Department Participation Series. Washington, D.C.: World Bank.

Narayan, Deepa, and Lant Pritchett. 1996. "Cents and Sociability: Household Income and Social Capital in Rural Tanzania." Environment Department, processed. World Bank, Washington, D.C.

North, Douglass Cecil. 1990. *Institutions, Institutional Change and Economic Performance*. New York: Cambridge University Press.

Olson, Mancur. 1982. *The Rise and Decline of Nations: Economic Growth, Stagflation, and Social Rigidities.* New Haven: Yale University Press.

Ostrom, Elinor. 1995. "Incentives, Rules of the Game, and Development." In M. Bruno and B. Pleskovic, eds., *Annual Bank Conference on Development Economics 1995.* Washington, D.C.: World Bank.

Pathan, R., N. Arul, and M. Poffenberger. 1993. "Forest Protection Committees in Gujarat—Joint Management Initiatives." Reference Paper No. 8 prepared for Sustainable Forest Management Conference. Sponsored by the Ford Foundation, Delhi.

Pearce, David, and G. Atkinson. 1993. "Capital Theory and the Measurement of Sustainable Development: An Indicator of Weak Sustainability." *Ecological Economics* 8: 99–123.

Putnam, Robert D. 1993. "The Prosperous Community—Social Capital and Public Life." *The American Prospect* 13: 35–42.

Putnam, Robert D., R. Leonardi, and Raffaella Nanetti. 1993. *Making Democracy Work: Civic Traditions in Modern Italy.* Princeton: Princeton University Press.

Rose, Richard. 1995a. "Adaptation, Resilience and Destitution—Alternative Responses to Transition in Ukraine." *Problems of Post-Communism* (November/December): 52–61.

———. 1995b. "New Russia Barometer IV—Survey Results." Studies in Public Policy No. 250. University of Strathclyde, Glasgow.

———. 1995c. "Russia as an Hour-Glass Society: A Constitution without Citizens." *East European Constitutional Review* 4(3): 34–42.

Serageldin, Ismail. 1996a. "Sustainability as Opportunity and the Problem of Social Capital." *The Brown Journal of World Affairs* 3(2): 187–203.

———. 1996b. *Sustainability and the Wealth of Nations—First Steps in an Ongoing Journey.* Environmentally Sustainable Development Studies and Monographs Series No. 5. Washington, D.C.: World Bank.

Soto, Hernando de. 1989. *The Other Path: The Invisible Revolution of the Third World.* New York: Harper and Row.

Stiglitz, Joseph E. 1996. "Some Lessons from the East Asian Miracle." *World Bank Research Observer* 11(2): 151–77.

Stone, Andrew W., Brian Levy, and Richardo Paredes. 1992. "Public Institutions and Private Transactions: The Legal and Regulatory Environment for Business Transactions in Brazil and Chile." Policy Research Working Paper No. 891. World Bank, Washington, D.C.

Williamson, Oliver E. 1985. *The Economic Institutions of Capitalism—Firms, Markets, Relational Contracting.* New York: The Free Press.

———. 1993. "The Economic Analysis of Institutions and Organizations—In General and with Respect to Country Studies." Economics Department Working Paper No. 133. OECD (Organisation for Economic Co-operation and Development), Paris.

World Bank. 1993. *The East Asian Miracle.* New York: Oxford University Press.

———. 1995. *Monitoring Environmental Progress—A Report on Work in Progress.* Washington, D.C.

———. 1997. *Expanding the Measure of Wealth—Indicators of Environmentally Sustainable Development.* Washington, D.C.

# Formal and informal institutions

Joseph E. Stiglitz
*World Bank*

*Social capital—including tacit knowledge, a collection of networks, an aggregation of reputations, and organizational capital—can be interpreted in the context of organizational theory as a social means of coping with moral hazard and incentive problems. As a society develops economically, its social capital must adapt as well, allowing the interpersonal networks to be partially replaced with the formal institutions of a market-based economy, such as a structured system of laws imposed by representative forms of governance. This process may initially involve a depletion in the overall level of social capital, but eventually leads to the creation of a different type of social capital, in which social relations are embedded in the economic system, rather than vice versa. Despite its complexity, we can make several observations about it: First, even if it is not directly mediated by the market system, social capital is clearly affected by (and in turn affects) the market economy. Secondly, since history matters, sequencing reforms correctly matters a great deal. And finally, community-produced social capital need not necessarily be superior to state-produced social capital, and in some cases is not. Recognizing social capital and acknowledging an important public role for its provision, it should be noted, does not specify who should undertake that role. The answer to that question requires further research and reflection.*

Social capital is a concept with a short and already confused history. Since Coleman's (1988) use in the context of education, the concept has evolved a great deal. I want to approach the subject from the perspective of organization theory and ask four questions:

- Viewing society in its entirety as an organization, what does organization theory have to tell us about social capital?

- What does this analysis allow us to see about the relationship between social capital and markets? In particular, to what extent can "social capital" or social institutions more broadly make up for deficiencies in the market economy?

■ What can we say about the evolution of social institutions and the development of social capital over time? In particular, is there reason to believe that there may be, at certain stages of development, an undersupply of social capital?

■ If lack of social capital is a common characteristic of developing economies, we should be as concerned about its progress as we are about increasing human and physical capital. What can be done to improve the social capital of a society, to accelerate its formation? In particular, is there reason to believe that devolution and a movement to greater participation is likely to prove beneficial?

These are all broad questions, and I can only sketch an answer to each in this paper.

### Organization theory and social capital

Our society comprises a myriad of organizations. In recent years, the nature and performance of these organizations have come under increasing scrutiny. This is one of the most successful areas of interdisciplinary research, bringing together psychologists, sociologists, and economists. Among the organizations that economists have studied most closely are firms. The market value of a firm typically exceeds by a considerable amount the value of its physical assets and the human capital that is attached to the firm. Accountants call this capital "good will," but it is, I think, closely akin to what many of us think of as social capital.

Understanding the sources of this capital provides insights into the nature of social capital. There are, I think, at least four distinct aspects:

First, social capital is tacit knowledge; it is partly the social glue that produces cohesion but also a set of cognitive aptitudes and predispositions. For example, college kids who are now in U.S. universities are overwhelmingly computer-literate and share the "Internet culture." This is not the case, I venture to say, with college kids in Ethiopia—not even with many retired U.S. university professors. So, the cohort of college students in the United States share some tacit knowledge, which is part of their "social capital." It is capital because it takes time and effort to produce (it has an opportunity cost) and it is a means of production.

Second, social capital may be thought of as a collection of networks, what sociologists used to call the "social group" into which one is socialized or aspires to be socialized. When I am with one of my social groups I know how to behave, I know whom to call, I know what is expected and how it is measured. The problem, of course, is that I may belong simultaneously to many social groups and they may have incompatible rules. So there is a need for hierarchy in rules, for a metaorganizing device—and I will return to this in a moment.

Third, social capital is both an aggregation of reputations and a way to sort out reputations. Individuals invest in reputation (an implicit form of capital) because it reduces transactions costs and it helps break barriers to entry in a variety of production and exchange relations.

Finally, social capital includes the organizational capital that managers have developed through their styles of administration, incentives and command, their labor practices, hiring decisions, systems of dispute resolution, style of marketing, and so on. While economists focus on incentive mechanisms, there has been increasing attention to how organizations offset preferences through processes of affiliation that could alter these incentive mechanisms.

Thinking about social capital from the organizational perspective helps one focus on its nonmarket aspect: most activity within a firm is not mediated by standard market mechanisms. Yet what goes on within the firm is clearly closely linked with what goes on outside the firm, with the firm's environment. There is thus a close link between markets and social capital. Much of what I want to explore here is the relationship between the two.

### Social capital and the market economy

One way to think about these issues is through rational choice theory: If we want to improve our organizations we should redress the incentives, hence behavior, by perfecting the instruments that match individual effort with individual gain through competitive market mechanisms. But, as I noted earlier, what goes on inside the organization is often, at best, only imperfectly mediated by market mechanisms. Typically there are reasons, such as those suggested by Coase (1937), related to transactions costs, that make the inside of firms closer to organizations than to markets. More recent discussions have focused on one particular manifestation of transactions costs—information costs.

Some economists have viewed organizations as providing efficient solutions to resource allocation mechanisms (for example, in the presence of these transactions costs). Economists such as Douglass North, Oliver Williamson, and Ronald Coase have developed an institutional perspective that argues that societies are generally efficient.

Could it be that there are dysfunctional social institutions? Obviously, there are: Colombia today would be better off without the narcotics trafficking, as would be the United States, Mexico, and so forth, provided they could each enjoy the same level of income without it, or nearly so. That is the catch—it is easy to show that, in partial equilibrium a given institution appears to be suboptimal. And it is easy to trace in these partial equilibrium models a particular inefficiency to particular problems, such as lack of property rights. The mantra holds that once property rights are appropriately assigned, the system will find an efficient equilibrium.

But, remarkably, all of this has been based on a matter of assertion and faith; there are few analytic results. On the contrary, it is possible to show that in fact Candide was wrong, that this is not the best of all possible worlds. Indeed, it is surprising that what I shall for short call the Chicago hypothesis has had such influence, because it has never been much more than an assertion. We know how difficult it is to establish that the market economy is Pareto efficient. Why should there be any presumption that the Nash equilibrium within and among nonmarket organizations has any optimality properties? Yet many economists have thought of social capital—and more broadly, social institutions—as making up for deficiencies in the market economy, as filling the gaps left by markets.

### Moral hazard, markets, and reciprocity

I will refer to a model presented in Arnott and Stiglitz (1991) to illustrate these issues. The discussion will show that while in some circumstances social institutions can indeed improve upon market institutions, in other cases, they can actually make matters worse.

All social systems must find ways to deal with moral hazard and incentive problems, and market systems deal with these in special ways. Consider the case of car insurance. We are used to a market for insuring cars. One way the market responds to moral hazard is to provide only partial insurance, since individuals then have some incentive to take care to avoid an accident. The implication is that, as a result, people can buy less insurance than they may wish to have. To get what is missing they may choose to enter into nonmarket mutual insurance agreements. Marriage may be thought of as one such mechanism: the wife implicitly (sometimes explicitly!) insures the husband and vice versa.

As social scientists, can we develop a normative position on this arrangement? Is it socially optimal? It turns out that it may very well not be. Whatever the other merits of marriage, it is not the best way to provide car insurance; not unless husband and wife can monitor each other perfectly and both agree to this monitoring system and the sanctions it implies. That is to say, not unless they have a very peculiar marriage in which they recognize that their utility not only is interdependent but is *fully interdependent*, they never cheat and always act as if one's utility is dependent on the other's effort to avoid accidents.

Why is nonmarket insurance suboptimal? Because for market insurance to work efficiently it must be the case, as I mentioned earlier, that the quantity of insurance provided by the insurance company is less than the quantity of insurance demanded. Otherwise some drivers would be reckless—they would not have the same incentive to avoid accidents entirely, because they are fully protected from the consequences of their actions (ignoring, for the moment, the incentive to prevent injury to self and others). Now the insurance company knows that the husband and the wife offer each other *some* nonmarket insurance, albeit imperfectly. So their response is to reduce further the quantity of insurance offered. In the end the same quantity of insurance exists; some provided by the market (the insurance company), and some by the family (nonmarket). But it exists at a higher cost because the insurance company can pool its risks more extensively than can the husband-and-wife team; thus its cost is lower.

In this example, the nonmarket insurance is harmful and dysfunctional. The equilibrium without nonmarket insurance cannot be improved upon, and if it were possible, it would be desirable to outlaw the provision of nonmarket insurance. The provision of nonmarket insurance does not enhance the risk-sharing capabilities of the economy. Rather, such insurance crowds out market insurance. It is less effective than market insurance since it is provided individually; in addition, the simultaneous provision of market and nonmarket insurance violates exclusivity (the need for insurers to limit the quantity of insurance)— which typically creates negative externalities that cannot be internalized and thus lead to higher costs.

What is going on in this story? The example vividly illustrates the functionalist fallacy: the fact that an institution (nonmarket insurance) has a clearly identifiable function (to improve risk-sharing by supplementing the rationed insurance provided by the market) does not mean that it actually performs that function. Several other nonmarket institutions may be dysfunctional. An important research issue is to understand better the situations in which nonmarket institutions are dysfunctional. At the same time, Arnott and Stiglitz (1991) showed that nonmarket institutions could be complementary to market institutions. If—and it is a big if—the monitoring and enforcement conditions I described earlier were valid, then the market's performance would actually be enhanced by the nonmarket institutions, since the reduction in moral hazard behavior induced by the within-family monitoring has a spillover to the market.

## Social capital and development

My third question was: What can we say about the evolution of social capital and social institutions? Typically, institutions (organizations) develop an internal coherency that is not too dissonant with the external environment they must face. When it becomes too dissonant, then institutions change. The fact that institutions seem to respond to their environment is one of the factors that have misled some observers to think of them as efficient. But just as one can show that, as a matter of equilibrium, social institutions may or may not improve upon the market equilibrium; there is no presumption that evolutionary processes have any strong optimality properties. Unfortunately, this is a subject on which I cannot expand here. What I do want to do is to comment on certain aspects of the evolution of social capital in the process of development, and in doing so begin to answer my fourth question: Should we care about the accumulation of social capital?

Clearly at least one important function of what we have come to call "social capital" is to complement or substitute for market-based exchange and allocation. Clearly too, it interacts with, and influences, market exchange. And it may be that there is a pattern in this complementarity and interaction—one that can be described as an inverted U-shape relationship between the density of social capital and the level of development.

Early on in the development of market economies, when markets are thin and incomplete, a thick network of interpersonal relations functions to resolve the allocative and distributive questions. Especially when the scale of the organization is relatively small, the system works reasonably well: in some cases, the principal can directly supervise the agent; in others, there are social mechanisms that induce agents to monitor each other. Peer monitoring is a good example of collective mutual monitoring. It creates an interdependence between the agents, who are simultaneously producers and monitors. A good example is a university department. A faculty member's utility depends not only on his or her salary, performance, reputation, and working conditions, but also directly on the department's and university's reputation. Furthermore, the individual's salary, performance, reputation, and working conditions all depend to some extent on the department's quality. For these reasons, faculty members have a strong incentive to monitor one another's performance, which they do through peer review. Direct monitoring, peer monitoring, and reputation all have a critical role for controlling moral hazard—and moral hazard is more frequent in nonmarket-based forms of organization. For example, in some developing countries, loans are often made to groups of individuals; the members of a group then have an incentive to monitor each other.

Change itself serves to weaken some aspects of social capital: old networks get destroyed, and a past that contains rapid upheaval may reduce incentives to invest in reputation mechanisms.

The initial impact of the markets' development and deepening is that some of this network of interpersonal relations gets dispensed with and destroyed. The value of personal relations—and with it the value of social capital—declines. Contracts imbedded in a reasonably well-functioning legal framework dispense with intrapersonal means of dispute resolution and enforcement. The observation has been made often, and it is important, that if the State is weak or oppressive, social networks assume importance for producing and enforcing "credible commitment," for designing, implementing, and enforcing all sorts of formal and informal contracts. In this case the "public function" is decentralized and idiosyncratic, "community-based" and community-ruled—a web of horizontal relationships. But as the modern capitalist State matures, representative forms of governance with a clear hierarchical structure and a system of laws, rules, and regulations enforced by traditions replace the "community" as the guardian of social, business and personal contracts—and as the sole agent with a preemptory right to the use of force. The point is simple: one form of "social capital" is partly replaced by what might be thought of as another, an effective Webbehan bureaucracy that either substitutes or complements it in accomplishing the same sort of things—nonmarket allocation and distribution.

In advanced market economies there seems to be a restructuring and deepening of social capital, not in the form of "rules and regulation" to substitute or complement the market and the state but in the form of *tacit knowledge*. Markets and institutions are deep but so are the complexities of production and exchange. The production line is replaced by quality control circles in which workers are in a better position to monitor their coworkers than are employers. Partnership arrangements (which encourage monitoring) substitute for vertically integrated conglomerates. Large bureaucracies develop "cultures" and even "languages" of their own—dense webs of interpersonal tacit knowledge that are key to their success. Social capital is restructured and adapted to specific circumstances, distinct from areas in which the market and the state can deliver more efficiently.

Thus, the evolution I have described reflects a marked change in the interrelationship between market and nonmarket institutions. This has been characterized as a change from a situation in which economic activity is embedded in social relations, to one in which social relations are embedded in the economic system. This change is not uniform across the world, nor is it ever complete.

## Investment in social capital

Now for my final question: Should we do anything to promote social capital and, if so, what? There is a huge literature on the importance of credible commitment for successful exchange and, as Dasgupta (1999) observes, "I trust" (that is, a credible commitment) is something riddled with externalities (she trusts you, now you trust me, so she now trusts me, and so on). It is akin to a public good, thus it is undersupplied. Trust can obviously be produced: Trust is based on reputation and reputation is acquired on the basis of consistent behavior over time, regarding which consistency has value and is the product of human actions. There is an immediate implication: there is a "public" role in the provision of trust.

But saying that there is a public role does not in itself give us much guidance in thinking about how that role should be performed. Interventions in organizations are far more complex than interventions in markets, through which we have learned how to use Pigouvian taxes to correct for market failures. Our earlier discussion provides some background for four preliminary observations:

First, changing the external environment may provide a context that motivates a change in the social capital. We noted early that institutions develop an internal coherence that is not too dissonant with the external environment they must face. Large changes in the external environment (for instance, the opening up to international markets) can effect a large transformation in the society—for instance, a transformation from an inward-looking society into an outward-looking one.

Second, because institutions may be inefficient, and inefficient institutions may persist, it is important to get things right, or as right as possible, the first time around. History matters.

Third, since history matters, how we sequence reforms can matter, and matter a great deal.

The fourth issue is far more complicated: it concerns decentralization in the production of social capital. I said earlier that there was a role for the public provision of trust, or more broadly, in the production of social capital. But "public" here does not have to be state-produced; it could be produced by the community. Trust is a component of social capital and we could agree that much of what we call social capital is not state-produced. In fact, today, many think of "community trust" as a superior good to public trust. But, obviously, this need not be the case. Social networks are necessarily personalized, and as such, they are exclusive—otherwise they would not be social networks (Dasgupta 1999). And the disadvantageous exclusionary elements to community trust are not present in the concept of citizenship, which is—and should be—far more inclusive.

There is social progress in moving from a society ruled by mutually exclusive groups to one that aspires to be ruled by citizens, hopefully through democratic forms of representation. Moreover, there is progress in moving from group-based to market-based participation. Groups are perforce particularistic and discriminatory. The market is anonymous and, if it functions reasonably well, it responds equally to all with equal amounts of purchasing power. The market is a more powerful and just form of participation. Whenever we can introduce markets *with competition* in the provision of collective goods and services, it has been argued that we tend to produce superior outcomes. This was, of course, Tiebout's (1956) great insight.

Tiebout's conjecture went further and argued that decentralization, that is, "voting with one's feet," was an efficient solution to the provision of collective goods and services. But this link cannot be firmly established. Like many such insights, including that of Adam Smith's, it should be subjected to close scrutiny, and when that is done, there is a less compelling case than there seems to be at first blush.

This is another instance, like Coase's conjecture (1960), in which we have generalized a simple intuition and taken the result as a matter of faith. Some years ago, I subjected Tiebout's hypothesis to the same close scrutiny that Coase's conjecture and the functionalist fallacy had been subjected to. I showed that the failures of decentralized provision of even local collective goods are even more marked than the decentralized provision of private goods, and there are, in addition, a host of political economy issues that arise. Indeed, it is precisely in these political economy issues in which our understanding is weakest, though they lie behind much of the current force for devolution. It is precisely these forces in the U.S. context that disturb me. Again, the lesson to be learned for policy is one of circumspection: decentralization has, I believe, strong virtues but we must learn its limits as well as its strengths.

A real disaster may happen when states are powerful enough to disrupt an existing local cooperative status but not capable enough to replace it with anything functional and less arbitrary. Examples here abound and they are powerful reminders of the potentially destructive role of otherwise well-intended development projects. But the other extreme is equally as likely. Latin America has a tradition of oligarchic self-rule and, at least historically, a more powerful central government is known for acting to counterbalance reactionary local forces. We do not want to forget that when associations are organized around provincial economic interests, they rarely contribute to overall economic efficiency or equity. *The outcome of participation depends on the incentives of participants and the issues in question.* And the structure of participation is a factor as well.

### Conclusion

I will conclude with four propositions that I hope I have been able to establish here:

(a) Social capital is a very useful concept, but an extremely complex one, in which different perspectives have much to contribute. I believe that the organizational perspective in particular provides a useful frame.

(b) There are reasons to believe that the composition, quality, and quantity of social capital of a society are not necessarily optimal.

(c) Social capital is affected by, and affects, the development process.

(d) There is an important public role in the enhancement of social capital, but who should undertake that public role, and how it should be done, are questions that will need a great deal more thought.

## References

The word *processed* describes informally reproduced works that may not be commonly available through libraries.

Arnott, Richard, and Joseph E. Stiglitz. 1991. "Moral Hazard and Nonmarket Institutions: Dysfunctional Crowding Out or Peer Monitoring?" *American Economic Review* 81 (March): 179–90.

Coase, R. H. 1937. "The Nature of the Firm." *Economica*, pp. 386–405.

————. 1960. "On the Problem of Social Cost." *Journal of Law and Economics*, Vol. 3: 1–44.

Coleman, James S. 1988. "Social Capital in the Creation of Human Capital." *American Journal of Sociology* 94 (Supplement): S95–S120.

Dasgupta, Partha. 1999. "Economic Development and the Idea of Social Capital." Processed, Faculty of Economics, University of Cambridge.

Tiebout, C. M. 1956 (1988). "A Pure Theory of Local Expenditures." In Martin Ricketts, ed., *Neoclassical Microeconomics*, Vol. 2, Schools of Thought in Economics Series, No. 3. Aldershot, Hants, U.K.: Edward Elgar Publishing; and Brookfield, Vermont: Gower Publishing.

# Institutional Analysis

# Creating and harnessing social capital

**Anirudh Krishna**
*Cornell University*

*A rare conundrum is presented to social scientists and development practitioners by Putnam and his associates. Even though social capital in their conception is clearly associated with higher institutional performance, it does not follow that investing in social capital will improve performance. Societies that do not inherit a high level of social capital are condemned, this view indicates, to having low rates of economic growth.*

*This deterministic and pessimistic conception of social capital can be retained only by maintaining a fairly restrictive set of assumptions. In addition to assuming an invariant stock of social capital, it is also necessary to assume that stock is connected with a fixed and invariable level of flow. Flows of benefits can be enhanced, however, even in cases in which the stock of social capital remains fixed. Through purposive action, aimed at altering the expectations they have about each others' actions, members of any society can improve the prospects for mutually beneficial collective action—even within a relatively short period of time.*

*A strategy for purposive action is suggested by considering social capital in two distinct, though related, dimensions. While Institutional Capital refers to the structural elements—roles, rules, procedures, and organizations—that facilitate mutually beneficial collective action; Relational Capital refers to the values, attitudes, norms, and beliefs that predispose individuals toward cooperation with others. Depending on where weaknesses exist in any particular situation, purposive action can be fashioned to bolster either Institutional or Relational Capital. Examples of development practice are drawn on to illustrate an appropriate strategy for creating or harnessing social capital in specific situations.*

A rare conundrum is presented to social scientists and development practitioners by Putnam, Leonardi, and Nanetti (1993). Even though social capital in their conception is clearly associated with higher institutional performance, it does not follow from their view that investing in social capital will improve performance. Social capital, they claim, is a legacy of long periods of historical development. Present generations cannot add productively to their inherited stock of social capital, definitely not in the short run. Thus, societies are condemned to live with the fruits of their inheritance. If rich in social capital, they will develop fast; if their forebears have left behind a depleted stock, then these societies will develop only extremely slowly.[1]

Seen in this way, the concept of social capital may be academically interesting but practically sterile. Faced with a low social capital setting, the development practitioner might as well pack his or her bags and go home. Nothing these practitioners or their clients can do will change what history has in store for them.

The gloomy prognosis is challenged by a number of recent empirical studies. Research done by Schneider and others (1997) shows that "the design of the institutions delivering local public goods can influence levels of social capital.... government policies can and do affect the level of social capital" (p. 91). Changing the structure and composition of school boards, the authors find, enhances significantly the level of parental involvement in a wide range of school-related activities that in turn help build social capital. Lam (1996) and Ostrom (1994) present similar conclusions about the design of irrigation systems. Ostrom demonstrates for the case of farmer-managed irrigation systems how physical and organizational characteristics of the system work as parametric conditions under which individuals make choices about collective action. Opportunities for sustained cooperation are enhanced when organizational arrangements, such as cost sharing, tend to balance the distribution of bargaining power between head- and tail-enders.

But there are other studies, as well, which reinforce opinions about the historical and evolutionary origins of social capital. Locke (1995) claims that differences in economic performance among regions in Italy are accounted for largely by inherited patterns of social interaction among firms. Trust and reciprocity among firms are higher in regions where polycentric networks are the norm than in those where inherited networks are hierarchical or fragmented. Fukuyama (1995) similarly regards trust in any society as a product of inherited and in the short term inflexible patterns of cultural inheritance.

---

[1]    "Social patterns plainly traceable from early medieval Italy ... turn out to be decisive in explaining why ... some [contemporary Italian] communities are better able to manage collective life and sustain effective institutions" (Putnam, Leonardi, and Nanetti 1993, p. 121). "The astonishing tensile strength of civic traditions testifies to the power of the past" (p. 162).

Given this mix of optimism and pessimism in the literature, what view is a development practitioner to take of the prospects for investing in social capital? How does one determine, in any given situation, *whether* it is useful to invest in social capital and how one might best go about this task?

Insofar as the optimistic studies demonstrate that social capital *has* been induced successfully in some circumstances, it would be reasonable to expect that it *can* be induced as well in other situations. But such small comfort is hardly enough. Much clearer answers are required by the thoughtful practitioner concerning both whether and how to invest. Some suggestions are offered in this context, drawing upon concepts available in the literature and real-life examples that I know of or have been personally involved with.

### Stock and flow in the conception of social capital

Social capital can be understood most simply as a category for various kinds of social assets that yield streams of benefits. These assets comprise the stock of social capital, while the benefits constitute the flow.

The beliefs one has about the nature of stock and flow directly influence the view one holds about the efficacy of investing in social capital. Two questions, in particular, are critical:

(a)  Can the stock of social capital be added to in the short run?

(b)  Are variable flows possible out of a given stock?

Concern with the second question is analogous to investigating the difference between the stock and the productivity of physical capital. A large stock can be utilized with little productive efficiency, while low stocks are often utilized with great efficiency. In the context of social capital, similarly, along with questions about stocks it is also relevant to inquire how efficiently stocks are utilized in any specific situation.

This distinction between stock and flow, between the level and productivity of the resource, is finessed in much of the available literature. In the conception of social capital made popular by Putnam, Leonardi, and Nanetti (1993), Putnam (1995, 1996), and Fukuyama (1995), the extent of flow is related directly to the level of the stock—that is, a high stock of social capital invariably results in profuse flows of benefits, while low stocks always result in impoverished flows. The connection between stock and flows is direct, proportionate and invariant. Responding to each of the two questions posed above, there are two assumptions that produce a pessimistic view:

*Assumption (a):* The stock of social capital cannot be added to in the short run.

*Assumption (b):* A given stock produces a single, invariant level of flow.

There is nothing inherently right or wrong about these assumptions. Their validity can only be ascertained by looking at empirical results.

Wade's (1994) village-level study in south India directly challenges the stock-flow assumption of the pessimists. Given the nature of the situation it faces, this view suggests, a society can bring its stock of social capital to bear more or less effectively upon the task in hand. Efficiency of usage will be higher when social purpose is well-defined and objectives are commonly agreed upon. When people in a group do not share similar views about the nature or urgency of any joint task, social capital will not be equally effectively attracted toward this task.

Investigating villages within one irrigation system in southern India, Wade and his associates found that villages that were faced with insufficient or uncertain water supply were also the ones in which farmers developed the most active organizational responses: irrigator associations backed with serviceable rules and widely accepted norms. In other villages, closer to the headwork and thus more assured of continuous water supply, villagers behaved not collectively but as atomized individuals. All of the villages investigated were within a contiguous area, sharing a common history and similar social and cultural features. Since they did not differ significantly from each other in any feature other than water demand and supply, it is reasonable to conclude that villages that felt a greater need for cooperation were also the ones in which such cooperation was achieved. Demand led to its own supply.

What made it possible for tail-end villages to behave differently from their head-end neighbors? Given that tail-end and head-end villages are separated from each other by at most just a few kilometers, and are thus culturally and historically similar, what are the implications for stocks and flows of social capital?

To resolve the puzzle, either one acknowledges variable flows [question (b) above], or one is forced to rethink one's assumptions relating to historical evolution of the stock [question (a)]. It is hard to explain, otherwise, how institutional responses lined up so perfectly with the intensity of the problem faced by different villages. Wade's example shows clearly that the pessimists cannot simultaneously hold both their assumptions (a) and (b). One or another of these assumptions has to go, thereby yielding space for more optimistic expectations.

It hardly matters which of these two assumptions is jettisoned. The practical significance of either admission is similar: social capital can either be created [discarding assumption (a)] or its flows harnessed [dropping (b)] even within the short run. The development practitioner is not really concerned about this distinction. So long as social capital *can* be brought to bear upon the task in hand, it matters little whether this is a stock or a flow transaction. Admitting either variable flows or variable stocks, therefore, one is much farther along the way toward addressing the *how* questions: how, in practice, does one *engage* social capital while resolving important problems of a joint or collective nature?[2]

Acknowledging either variable stocks or flows is helpful as well in another sense. It helps us break free of an essentialist notion of culture. Implicitly (in the case of Putnam) and explicitly (for Fukuyama) we are exposed to a conception of "more trusting" and "less trusting" cultures, enveloping entire regions and even countries.[3] While such a static notion of culture may drive home the analysts' point; it makes little sense practically. As Swidler (1986) and Johnson (1996) show, "culture" is not something uniquely defined and invariate in any society. Different and competing conceptions of culture coexist at all times in all societies. Some of these conceptions may be more supportive of generalized trust than others. Assigning any simplified index of culture or trust to an entire society is not free of problems.

Trust and cooperation, which form the core of social capital, exist in some form in all societies. The scope of trust may be narrow—that is, people may trust only a small circle of family members and immediate relatives—but people everywhere know how to trust. Limitations arise from not always knowing *whom* one can trust and *how much* one should trust them. The task of building up social capital lies, therefore, in extending previously narrow expectations of mutual trust to produce more positive-sum outcomes for all. Expectations concerning how one should behave, how others will behave, and how others expect one will behave influence how each of us will behave in any given situation. When these diverse expectations are convergent and complementary, cooperation can result. When expectations are disparate, dissimilar, and detached from one another, cooperation becomes more difficult. Engaging social capital is tantamount, therefore, to building up appropriate expectations.[4]

---

[2]  Though, as I point out in a later section, admitting variable flows is qualitatively different in conceptual terms from acknowledging variable stocks, the practical effect of this distinction is minimal.

[3]  Fukuyama speaks of "high-trust societies with plentiful social capital—Germany, Japan and the United States [excluding inner-city neighborhoods]" and compares these with "relatively low-trust societies such as Taiwan, Hong Kong, France and Italy" (Fukuyama 1995, p. 30). Societal trust is culturally determined and "traditional religious or ethical systems ... constitute the major institutionalized sources of culturally determined behavior" (p. 36). "Where the regional soil is fertile [with trust]," Putnam, Leonardi, and Nanetti (1993) claim, "the regions draw sustenance from regional traditions, but where the soil is poor, the new institutions are stunted" (p. 182).

[4]  Klandermans (1984, p. 585) believes that participants in collective action are influenced by at least three sets of expectations:

"(a) expectations about the number of participants;

  (b) expectations about one's own contribution to the probability of success; and

  (c) expectations about the probability of success if many people participate."

Often it is not cultural or cognitive preconceptions that limit expectations leading to trust. Available institutional avenues, reflecting past or prevailing structural conditions, act as limitations on how far one can extend the ambit of trust. Southern Italians may be less trusting not simply because of their Catholic culture, but because the structural conditions for participating in state activities have been far less supportive and beneficial historically than those in the northern part of that country.[5] Having an institutional foundation for cooperation helps reinforce expectations of supportive behavior, thereby strengthening whatever cultural traits may have led to cooperation in the first place. Without the institutional supports, the same cultural traits may disappear. Societal traits are neither so rigid nor so essentially dissimilar from other societal experiences as to be compartmentalized away into some isolated category.

The act of enhancing flows from social capital depends, therefore, on attending—in addition to the cultural dimension—also to the structural dimension of social capital, a distinction highlighted by Uphoff in a subsequent chapter. In the next section of this paper, two forms of social capital are discerned, each corresponding to one of these two dimensions. With the help of a few examples, I show how social capital of each type can be developed and engaged to assist with ongoing development efforts. I underplay the distinction between stock and flow in the next section, returning to this theme in the subsequent section.

### Two forms of social capital: institutional and relational capital

Consider the following example. Someone's house or barn burns down at night and people of the neighborhood come together the next day to help the afflicted family rebuild the structure. This kind of collective action can be found among diverse social groups in all parts of the world. What is interesting to examine, however, is the causal force that leads people to behave in this way.

Two alternative constructions are possible. It may be, first of all, that there is a well-recognized leadership within the neighborhood. Receiving information about the unfortunate event, community leaders direct community members to gather at the site, bringing along whatever tools and implements and building material they might possess.

Alternatively—and this is the second construction of the sequence of events—there are no clear roles for organizing such actions in this community. Motivated, instead, by norms of what is appropriate behavior—that it is only right and proper and that one is expected to help out any one of their community who is faced with a similar situation—people collect spontaneously and assist with the rebuilding.

---

[5]    For a cogent and instructive discussion of the interaction between structure and cultural practice, see Tarrow (1995).

Thus the same outcome can come about in two different ways. In the first case, the basis of collective action is *institutional*: persons who are acting in accepted and well-recognized roles of leadership direct the community to act together. Collective action in the second case is based on norms and beliefs; it has a *cognitive*, and not an institutional, basis.

The first manifestation of social capital is an example of what I would call Institutional Capital, and the second, an example of Relational Capital. The difference between the two forms of social capital is not merely academic. Though in the present example there is no difference in outcome, marked differences are likely to exist in the potential that each pure form has for assisting cooperative action in other spheres of community action. Either form can give rise to collective action, as we have seen, but each form supports a different range of such actions.[6]

Institutional Capital is structured. Rules and procedures exist to guide individuals' behavior, supervised by people acting out well-recognized roles. Relational Capital is more amorphous and also more diffuse. This distinction parallels that which is made between specific and generalized patterns of exchange (Cook 1990).

Institutional Capital is, by itself, not easily fungible. Clear rules and procedures, devised to deal with one issue area, may serve little purpose when the group turns to deal with some other collective concern (Ostrom 1990; Coleman 1988). No doubt, groups that manage to solve one problem collectively will be encouraged to tackle other problems as well. In all cases, however, purposeful efforts will be required to recraft rules and procedures, more particularly when substantially dissimilar organizational responses are needed to deal with the new area. If norms of diffused reciprocity are practiced in the community, then the process of working out new rules becomes so much easier. Institutional Capital works best, thus, when it goes side by side along with Relational Capital.

And vice versa. People in a community may share strong feelings of trust and mutual goodwill, but structures and roles will usually be required to translate individual attitudes and values into coordinated, goal-oriented behaviors. These structures may not always be formal or even readily visible, but some agreed-upon commitments, explicit or implicit, are usually necessary for individual actions to add up to collective results. Implicit though well-understood rules of coordinated behavior—what Schelling (1960) terms "focal points"—are almost a minimal requirement.

Institutional and Relational Capital are unlikely to be found empirically in their pure form; mixed manifestations are more likely. Cooperative response in any given situation is most likely to flow from some

---

[6] Institutional and Relational Capital are related, respectively, to Uphoff's structural and cognitive dimensions of social capital.

combination of Institutional and Relational Capital.[7] Both Institutional and Relational Capital are required to sustain social capital and to make it broad-based. Thus, each form of Social Capital needs to be complemented by the other (see table 1).

The two extreme manifestations serve as analytical categories, which enable us to construct a typology of different forms of social capital likely to be found in practice. This allows us to look separately at the independent effect of networks (Institutional Capital) and norms (Relational Capital).[8] Classifying a given situation on the two axes suggested by these dimensions also points the investigator toward appropriate remedial measures (figure 1).

While situations that fall within cell (1) are the most hopeful, and those in cell (4) the least, both of these cells are seen mostly as representing ideal types. That these are constructed polar types, and not valid empirical categories by themselves, is obvious when one looks at any real-world situation. All societies show some, if only a few, instances of coordinated or cooperative behavior. Even though manifestations of co-operation in any given society may be sparse—confined, for example, merely to agreeing to drive on the same side of the road or to show more consideration to insiders rather than to outsiders—it is hard to find an example of a society in which cooperation and coordination are entirely nonexistent.[9] The two ideal-typical situations must be seen, therefore, as constructed types that mark opposite ends of a continuum. Most

---

[7]    Berman (1997) shows how dispositions toward trust and association are influenced by structural factors, even within the short term. Speaking of late-nineteenth century Germany, she comments: "The *granting of Universal suffrage* encouraged a wide variety of groups to form organizations in order to give themselves a voice in the political sphere ... *the prolonged economic downturn* that began in the late 1870s highlighted the vulnerability of different groups.... During the following two decades almost all sectors of German society engaged in a frenzy of organizational activity.... *The fight over protectionism* was certainly a key reason for the emergence of new associations" (p. 409, emphasis mine).

[8]    Putnam, Leonardi, and Nanetti (1993) underplay the analytical distinction between structural and cognitive elements. They expect that norms and networks will exist together in mutually reinforcing patterns. In general, horizontally organized networks are expected to assist cooperation, while vertical relationships inhibit it—regardless of context.

[9]    The most often cited case of zero cooperation, Banfield's study of the "amoral society," suffers from lack of causal specificity. It is not clear which way the causal arrows point: from lack of cooperation to poor economic development, or in the reverse direction. Banfield is himself not clear about the direction of causation. Concluding his analysis, he observes that "it must be acknowledged, too, that the Montegrano economy would not develop dramatically even if the villagers cooperated like bees.... the sad fact is that Montegrano's isolation and relative lack of resources give it a comparative disadvantage which no amount of cooperation can overcome" (Banfield 1958, p. 166).

TABLE 1: Two Forms of Social Capital

| | *Institutional capital* | *Relational capital* |
|---|---|---|
| *Basis of collective action* | Transactions | Relations |
| *Source of motivation* | Roles | Beliefs |
| | Rules and procedures | Values |
| | Sanctions | Ideology |
| *Nature of motivation* | Maximizing behavior | Appropriate behavior |
| *Examples* | Markets, legal framework | Family, ethnicity, religion |

*Source:* Berman (1997).

FIGURE 1: A Classificatory Scheme

**Relational capital**

|  | | Strong | Weak |
|---|---|---|---|
| **Institutional capital** | Strong | (1)<br><br>*High social capital*<br><br>Task: extend scope of activities | (2)<br><br>*"Strong" organizations*<br><br>Task: legitimation, intensification |
|  | Weak | (3)<br><br>*"Traditional" associations*<br><br>Task: introduce rules, procedures, and skills | (4)<br><br>*Anomic, atomistic, or "amoral"*<br><br>Task: assist development of structures and norms |

typical and interesting are the situations that fall within cells (2) and (3). Our previous work involving successful cases of rural development allows us to suggest examples and strategies corresponding to each of these situations.[10] The two-dimensional typology suggests how cases can be classified and strategies conceived for analyzing the extent and types of social capital.

*Building institutional capital on a relational capital base*

Many situations involving rural development are notable for the presence among villagers of traditional norms of association. These norms can be found embodied alternatively in tribal groups, village councils, caste associations, self-help groups, or other similar congrega-

---

[10] These cases are presented in Krishna, Uphoff, and Esman (1997), and Uphoff, Esman, and Krishna (1998).

tions. Depending on how they are engaged by program managers, these norms of association can assist or inhibit the task of building social capital.

A good example of a successful strategy in these circumstances is the self-help rural water supply program, started in Malawi in the late 1960s. Rather than either bypassing traditional village chieftains or allowing them to dominate decisions, program managers chose to elicit new forms of organization. They sought the blessing and support of the traditional leaders, who headed the advisory committee for the program. However, committees in charge of day-to-day planning and task management operated under a new leadership elected by the people. This decentralized leadership was responsible for ensuring that labor tasks were apportioned fairly among all households, and not on the basis of some traditional rank or privilege.

Similarly, the Six-S, an assisted self-reliance group, which operates over a very wide area of Sahelian Africa, has built upon traditions of labor-sharing and cooperation, especially among the youth of these villages.[12] It persuaded village youth to direct their efforts toward building productive infrastructure, both physical and social.

These groups have reconfigured themselves into a closer alignment with residential patterns and a greater sharing of tasks; group leadership is by rotation among members; and activities are selected through a process of discussion and voting. Group representatives get together at federation meetings, during which each group's funding proposal is discussed and then voted on by the assembly. Proposals are evaluated on the basis of the proposing group's prior preparation, the resources it will contribute, and its past record. In addition to funds, groups also get technical advice. One of their members is trained to keep accounts, which are discussed by the group "in the sunlight." These innovations in organizational procedures have not only helped reinvigorate traditional bonds of association among villagers, they have also substantially enhanced their capacity for collective action over a much wider range of activities.[11]

Both in Malawi and in Six-S, people have built institutional capacity atop a base of relational capacity, a strategy that has proven to be immensely successful. Traditional forms of relationship have been modi-

---

[11]  In addition to Krishna, Uphoff, and Esman (1997), see also Ouedraogo (1977) for a discussion of Six-S.

[12]  Established in 1977, Six-S is a multi-national support organization assisting self-help efforts of thousands of voluntary village groups organized into unions across large parts of Francophone West Africa. By the late 1980s, this organization was serving almost a million people organized into 3,000 groups, located in more than 1,500 villages, and federated into 75 unions, spread across Burkina Faso, Mali, and Senegal, with expansion to serve village groups in Niger, Togo, the Gambia, and Guinea Bissau.

fied considerably, and new organizational devices have been introduced. Institutional capital has been built up, and relational capital has been modified to meld with it.

Not equally successful, in our view, are those cases in which preserving the integrity of traditional relationships has been given overriding priority. One instance that could be cited is of ORAP (Organization of Rural Associations for Progress), a Zimbabwean NGO (nongovernmental organization). Perhaps because of ethnic conflict, widespread in the early years, or because of the organization's origins in Zimbabwe's civil war period, ORAP's leaders continued through the organization's initial few years to resist any "modernizing" changes. Organization at all levels continued to remain highly informal and protected. Neither new accounting systems nor any other changes requiring significant input from "outsiders" were introduced for a long time.[13]

Both internal and donor agency evaluators were unimpressed by the results achieved during this period. Internal reports pointed to the need for "grafting technical planning skills and procedures onto the cultural milieux, skills base, and social structure of rural communities, without compromising the aspirations of these communities[; this] remains the crucial test of ORAP's success."[14] ORAP has completed these tasks with considerable success, becoming a well-known NGO both at home and abroad.

### Institutional capital without relational capital

The Kenya Tea Development Authority (KTDA) was hailed in the 1960s and early 1970s as an exemplar of what a crop development and marketing agency should be.[15] Set up by the Kenyan government in 1964, KTDA grew steadily to become the largest producer and marketer of tea in the world. Within a few years of its formation, KTDA became a fully integrated tea manufacturer, wholesaler, and retailer. Almost all the senior positions were filled by Kenyans, and very few expatriates remained to advise them on specific technical activities.

Though it worked efficiently for a number of years, there was little sense of ownership for the KTDA system among farmers themselves. All its structures, processes and personnel were put in place by the Authority, and personnel at all levels looked upward for direction and support. Farmers elected representatives to the Tea Committees and thus had some voice in management. But rather than having real decision-making powers, these committees were limited to an advi-

---

[13] See Corson (1994) for an account of ORAP in its earlier years. Also see Nyoni (1987).

[14] ORAP (1992, p.1).

[15] Lamb and Mueller (1982), Paul (1982), Uphoff (1986), Leonard (1991).

sory and a consultative role, explaining to farmers the rationale for centrally decided policies and (less frequently) conveying upward the views of farmers.

Being dependent on the goodwill of the government, the KTDA system began a precipitous decline in the early 1980s just as withdrawal of political support coincided with declining world prices. The worst sufferers—namely, the farmers themselves—were also the ones who had the least influence over the system as it had been erected. With interactions among stakeholders based almost entirely on their positions within the formal structure, any weakening of this structure translated automatically into a corresponding decline in performance.

Contrast this situation with the case of Six-S, which had structures being modified over time to reflect changing tasks. Structures could be altered easily in this case because they themselves were not the critical or the only integuments of the organization. In addition to structure, members were also united by bonds of mutual trust and affection. Both structure and norms changed, but change in each was made easier because of accompanying strengths along the other dimension. KTDA's stock of social capital was mostly single-dimensional, thus social capital in this case was more precarious and less sustainable. It could not easily imbue the organization with resilience by itself.

Other examples exist but these should be enough to illustrate the two types of social capital and what it means to have more of one type of social capital without having enough of the other. I would repeat, however, that although these two dimensions are analytically distinct, they are likely to be complementary and associative in practice. Addressing the issue of social capital formation in two-dimensional terms enables us to enrich the emergent conception, to assess and measure a wide range of field situations, and to construct appropriate strategies of intervention.

## Rationality, cognition, and social capital

Beginning to conceive of social capital as not a linearly scaleable but as a two-dimensional phenomenon captures some of the richness of the underlying dynamic. Both purely rationalist and purely culturalist explanations have struggled to explain the emergence and sustainability of collective action. Rationalists posit restrictive conditions and a narrow range of circumstances supporting collective action, thereby predicting much less cooperation than is actually observed in practice. Rationalists who broaden the scope for cooperation do so, implicitly or explicitly, by implanting terms in their argument terms such as path dependence, goodwill, reputation, and dense communications, which basically have a culturalist origin. Similarly, more sophisticated culturalist explanations conceive not so much of any primordial, immutable, and constitutive culture but of culture as it is constantly being made and unmade through the knowledgeable practices of persons acting purposively toward particularistic goals, whether individually or in groups.

Empirical results support the view that behavior is rarely either entirely instrumental or purely emotion—or habit—driven. For instance, Knoke (1988) demonstrates that participation in collective action can arise not only from rational choice but can also be brought about by the other two sources of motivation: (a) affective bonding (that is, emotional attachments to other persons and groups), and (b) normative conformity (in other words, adherence to standards of conduct grounded in socially instilled values about principled behavior). The broad operation of normative and affective inducements in addition to rational choice is validated by the author's empirical data,[16] which reveal that "purely selective benefits ... tend to attract apathetic members, while the public goods of normative inducements are among the strongest factors motivating member involvements.... members of all types of associations seem willing to engage in 'sacrificial' actions whose results may well benefit others more than themselves" (Knoke 1988, p. 326).

Finkel, Muller, and Opp (1989) provide another empirical demonstration of how rationalist and culturalist motivations combine in practice. They show that individuals act in concert when subjective beliefs of high group efficacy are combined either with (a) a belief in the "unity principle" ("participation of everyone is necessary to have a chance of obtaining the public good") or with (b) a sense of duty (everyone must "do what we can rationally will that everyone else should do"). Individual rationality—perceptions of group and personal efficacy—combines interactively in the authors' model with culturalist predispositions (the unity principle and sense of duty). Using survey data from Germany to test their model, Finkel, Muller, and Opp conclude as follows: "In contrast to the assumptions of the conventional rational choice model, many individuals believe that they *are* personally influential in providing public goods. Many individuals, further, believe—and act on—the unity principle, which stipulates illogically that all group members are necessary for group success.... Finally, individuals appear to act on the basis of moral obligations and feelings of duty" (p. 900; emphasis in the original).

These empirical findings resonate with the emergent conception of social capital. Drawing together both rational and cultural streams of

---

[16] Knoke tests his hypotheses with the help of interview data from 8,746 respondents belonging to 47 different associations, randomly selected from a master list of United States national mass membership organizations, including professional societies, recreational organizations, and women's associations (National Association Study data).

individual motivation, social capital can bridge the gap that divides the rationalist from the sociological view of the world.[17]

The two-dimensional framework presented above is an attempt to represent how social capital can be treated conceptually as a pleasing synthesis of rationalist and culturalist views. It allows us to view separately what can be discerned as two components of social capital, here termed Institutional and Relational Capital.

The empirical question remains: how is each component best built up? It is also important to know how, in this context, each component is best conceived—as stock or as flow? While more empirical work will reveal the conception most appropriate to each specific set of situations, some preliminary guidance can be taken from the literature presently available.

That the process of building social capital is incremental is almost universally accepted. What needs to be fleshed out some more is how the two forms of social capital interact with each other over time.

Hechter (1987) suggests a multistage process for building group solidarity. People who need credit and insurance agree to join together in groups, especially when, as in premarket societies, credit and insurance are not openly available to all individuals. Having joined together to obtain private goods, however, members must devise membership criteria and monitoring and sanctioning procedures. These rules and procedures get institutionalized over time. Internalizing rules and procedures, members moderate behaviors so that these correspond to the expectations others have. This buildup of social capital—of formal rules and mutual expectations—facilitates extending group activities to other previously unexplored areas.

Sabel's (1994) conception focuses examination of process on the nature of discourse. Social capital builds up, in this view, as a result of "discursive institutions," in which all actors commit themselves to ongoing negotiations based on a shared understanding of common goals. "Discrete transactions among independent actors become continual, joint formulations of common ends in which the participants' identities are reciprocally defining.... discussion is precisely the way by which parties come to reinterpret themselves and their relation to each other by elaborating a common understanding of the world" (p. 138).

The cognitive dimension (culture) and the structural dimension (formal rules) are not just important in this view; they are *mutually reinforcing*. What actors "want and what they regard as legitimate means to getting it are powerfully shaped by what the groups into which they are born and raised indicate as desirable and legitimate in taking their world for granted.

---

[17] On the disparity between the rationalist and the sociological view see Smelser and Swedberg (1994).

But in contrast to the sociological view, in the world of learning by monitoring this moral guidance is neither precise nor persuasive enough to determine action. Individuals must interpret the general rules and expectations to bring them to bear on their actual situation. These reinterpretations proceed through argumentative encounters in which the individual attempts to establish an equilibrium between his or her views and social standards by recasting both. It is this reflexive capacity to embrace different forms of self-expression that defines persons as individuals and creates new interpretative possibilities for society" (Sabel 1994, p. 156).

Cognition and structure come together in an intertwined strand of explanation. Furthermore, while stock and flow are both important, they are not independent of each other. The critical conception is that of *process*. The idea of engaging social capital is not exclusively one of building a stock or of harnessing a flow (alternative conceptions that I explored earlier); the winning plan consists of getting the process right, of arranging a fit between stock *and* flow. And this process is two-dimensional, with each of structure and culture reacting with the other.

This is sufficiently complex in concept to require illustration by example. In the following section, I draw upon the example of a development program with which I was closely associated, directing the enterprise for its first three years.

## Watershed development in Rajasthan, India

The Rajasthan Watershed Development Program was commenced in 1990. Managed by a newly established multidisciplinary government department—the Department of Watershed Development and Soil Conservation—the program was introduced in order to tackle widespread and chronic insecurities in the availability of food, fodder, and firewood in the state.

Livelihood insecurity has been a constant feature of Rajasthan's semi-arid to arid landscape, becoming even more pronounced in recent years. Only 13 percent of Rajasthan's area has access to any assured source of irrigation. Mean annual rainfall is low and highly variable. Agriculture is the major occupation of almost 80 percent of the population, with animal husbandry playing a critical role in protecting against the uncertainties inherent in rain-fed crop production. The pressure of increasing population (2.5 percent per year, implying a doubling of population every 28 years) places a great strain on natural resources. Cattle population has been increasing even faster, leading to intense biotic pressure on grazing lands. Diminishing production from common and forest lands has led to a temporal decline in the availability of fodder and firewood. Wide annual variations around the trend result in frequent drought, which produces shortages of food, fodder, and water and temporary outmigration of human and cattle populations—creating a permanent situation of severe strain on food, fodder, and energy security.

The Department is currently managing program activities in over 250 watersheds, together covering almost half a million hectares. Given the large and dispersed area they have to attend, full-time staff are rather thinly spread on the ground. They are complemented by paraprofessionals (village persons selected and trained by the Department) and by *users committees*—committees of between four to seven persons who have been elected by the residents of a village.

Users committees (UCs) in each watershed have primary responsibility for program activities related to common lands. The initial objective behind assisting the establishment of these committees was to provide village communities with a forum for discussing problems related to common lands as well as a management committee for resolving these problems. Common lands are the principal source of fodder and firewood in all dryland areas where the work of watershed development has been taken up, yet prior to the program few if any villages had established formal arrangements for common land management.[18] The work that is performed by users committees, therefore, fills an important gap and targets an important community need. Users Committees of some areas have taken additional tasks upon themselves (for example, contracting to do drainage line treatment), but UCs in all areas are exclusively responsible for work on common lands.

In most villages, Department staff did not come across any existing organizations engaged in common land management, so they had to enthuse village residents to create new organizations. In the first year, 1991, villagers were hesitant and watchful, but by 1993, over 30,000 hectares of common land were being fenced and developed yearly. In addition to improved varieties of grass and legumes, over a million trees were planted on common lands to serve as a common pool of firewood. Tree species were selected by the UCs, which themselves contracted to have seedlings raised in decentralized village nurseries. Members of UCs and the nursery raisers were trained in technical aspects by program staff.

Three-year survival rates of trees in a sample of 17 village common lands ranged from a high of 89 percent to a low of 56 percent. Fodder yields in the same villages went up from three to ten times. These are no mean achievements in an area where water is available only during the three monsoon months, and where collective pasture management and tree planting have been notable for their absence. Readers can get a fuller account of this case in Krishna (1997).

---

[18] Formal and informal arrangements did exist in some villages in days gone by, but over the last 40 or 50 years, these arrangements have ceased to operate. In almost all villages, common lands are in a state of neglect characterized by overgrazing and overfelling, with no replanting or protection being undertaken. For a more comprehensive discussion of these issues, see Jodha (1986) and Brara (1992).

What is of importance to this discussion of social capital is the evidence that social capital—embodied in functioning and legitimate Users Committees—was not available ready-made to the program and that it was developed, actually quite quickly, in the course of program implementation.

What is important, too, is the step-by-step process of development, almost along the lines suggested by Hechter and Sabel.[19] In the first step, village residents came together to discuss the situation and to arrive at a common definition of the problem. They agreed to set apart tracts of common lands, and to prohibit grazing of animals on these lands. In the second step, the elected UC, in association with department staff, drew up a plan of development and presented it for approval to the assembly of villagers. Once approval was obtained, the UC, in the third step, set about collecting the local share of costs (10 percent), which could be paid by individual members either in cash or in the form of labor. The UC had to devise a method for allocating these costs among residents—for instance, deciding whether better-off members should pay the same amount as the less affluent.[20] In the fourth step, the UC designated a subcommittee to incur expenditures. Accounts were presented regularly and publicly. The committee also had to develop a strategy for protecting the grass sown on these lands, mainly from stray animals but also from willful defaulters. As a fifth step, the UC had to devise a formula for sharing the harvest (the first grass crop is harvested just three to five months after sowing). In the sixth step, they decided what to do with the proceeds, in case they had decided earlier to charge a fee for fodder collection. Finally, the plan of action must be revised on a continuing basis, with new activities taken up and old activities modified or abandoned. In between, the UC must renew itself through elections every year (or sometimes two); it must keep in contact with Department staff and other public officials; and it must make efforts to keep villagers' interests alive in the program.

Not all of these steps were taken at the same time and none were implemented equally successfully in all villages. Villagers who recognized the importance of the program and who realized that only a collective solution could work and those able to set up their UCs earlier were able to advance faster on the first few steps, benefiting from both the Relational and Institutional forms of social capital. In cases in which the first steps were completed effectively to mutual satisfaction, villagers became both more willing to work with one another (Relational)

---

[19] This is quite similar to the process of farmer organizations in the case of Gal Oya, Sri Lanka. See Wijayaratna and Uphoff (1997).
[20] The Department has not prescribed any standard pattern or policy for cost- or benefit-sharing. An open-ended exploratory approach was adopted, thus different sharing methods have been developed by villages.

and, given a functioning UC, also more able to do so (Institutional). Relational and Institutional Capital developed in tandem, each a result of the discursive institution, represented by the ongoing discourse of collectively undertaken common land development, and embodied structurally in UC roles and rules.

The critical external intervention was the introduction of this discourse among villagers. Though the presence of staff and the prospect of funds was the trigger and the incentive for the discourse—which probably would not have been initiated otherwise, at least not so systematically—it was as discourse generators more than as resources that staff played the major role. Funds and specialist staff form part of every development program, but often these tend to replace and suppress local resources and local decision-making. Participation is facilitated not just when outsider staff is more receptive to local opinion, but when such staff assists local residents in building up *institutions*, including rules and norms, structures and attitudes, which undergird local efforts to identify problems, assess alternative solutions, and implement those that are selected. Institutions developed to deal with one set of problems can be helpful for taking on the next set. Reproducing the Hechter dynamic, UCs in many villages have taken on additional activities—seed provision, fodder banks, poultry development, and so on—going beyond their original role of common land management. The Rajasthan case presents an interesting site for a research study.[21]

The methodological consequence of this exposition is the following: social capital is not something whose significance can be judged finally at any single point in time. Social capital may be either developing or depleting, and the direction of flow is as important to discern as the level of stock.[22]

---

[21] Uphoff and I are currently engaged with this enterprise. Not all villages developed equally effective Users Committees, and not all performed equally well in the program, and not all UCs diversified activities beyond watershed development. Even among contiguous villages there is a range of variation in program performance and a visible, though not equally easily measured, variation in UC effectiveness. One way to make the case for or against social capital is to relate the two indexes to each other—do villages with high program performance indicators also have the more effective UCs? Another interesting question requires establishing the correlates of UC effectiveness. What characteristics are shared among villages with high performing UCs and not shared among those villages whose UCs were not so effective? Following these methods, we can assess the importance of a social capital–based explanation relative to other explanations accounting for program performance, such as having more commercialization and modernization, greater relative need for watershed development, better quality of departmental staff, and so on. We expect to have some results available within a year.

[22] Putnam, Leonardi, and Nanetti (1993) make a similar point when they speak of virtuous and vicious cycles. The difference between their conclusions and mine lies in our different depiction of process. While they expect that a virtuous cycle

Stock and flow interact with one another in complex ways, which are as yet not entirely well understood. Observing instances of collective action in rural Latin America, Hirschman (1984) noted that repertoires of collective action developed in the past get revived if an appropriate stimulus is presented. What is an appropriate stimulus in any given setting can best be determined after assessing the institutional and the relational elements of social capital.

## Conclusion

In any society there are multiple issue areas, some of which show evidence of high social capital while others are low on this characteristic. How far expectations have been coordinated within any given realm of human coexistence will indicate how much cooperation is observed within that realm. In cases in which behaving in a coordinated manner assumes a high degree of legitimacy, we find that high social capital is in evidence. In other cases, of instrumental reasoning taking precedence over appropriate behavior, social capital is less easily come by, though it is still not entirely ruled out, at least not in the future. Since mixed motives, involving both self-regarding and other-regarding motives, are more common than purely instrumental or purely other-regarding motives, the situation when low capital is in evidence is not as hopeless as it may at first appear.

The task in these cases is to show to the participants, first, how coordinated behavior can improve upon the benefits individuals expect to achieve; second, to devise the structures (organizations) and norms that support the required coordinated behavior; and third and most important, to institutionalize these structures and norms in such a way that the desired form of behavior becomes institutionalized, or customary. Behavior coordinated by custom, by a norm of appropriateness, is a better guarantee of sustained cooperation, than is behavior backed by individual calculation. The ideal situation, of course, is when each type of logic gives rise to the same form of behavior.

It took the genius of Adam Smith to show that in a perfectly functioning market, what is individually good for one is also collectively good for all. Thus the logic both of self-seeking and other-regarding behavior points toward similar action by the individual placed within such a perfect market situation. The polar opposite of this situation is indicated by the parable of the commons (Hardin 1968) in which one person's gain equals another person's loss. Real-life situations lie, as always, between these two extremes. Persons can have regard both for their own welfare and that of others. Indeed, this is the typical case. What matters in any

---

will exist only when the stock of social capital is also high; I do not anticipate stock and flow to be connected so rigidly to each other.

given case is how the individuals concerned view their situation—that is, as more or less zero-sum or as roughly positive-sum.

The task of building social capital lies in altering the representation of the situation that any individual has such that zero-sum images give way to positive-sum perceptions. The avenues available for this enterprise fall into two distinguishable types—institutions and relations—that can effect the desired change in attitudes and behavior. How to do so in any given situation is at present only vaguely known. Operationally grounded investigations rather than definitional finesse will prove more helpful in addressing these and related issues.

## References

Banfield, Edward C. 1958. *The Moral Basis of a Backward Society*. Chicago: The Free Press.

Berman, Sheri. 1997. "Civil Society and the Collapse of the Weimar Republic." *World Politics* 49 (April): 401–29.

Brara, Rita. 1992. "Are Grazing Lands 'Wastelands'? Some Evidence from Rajasthan." *Economic and Political Weekly* (Bombay), February 22.

Coleman, James S. 1988. "Social Capital in the Creation of Human Capital." *American Journal of Sociology* 94 (Supplement): S95–S120.

Cook, Karen S. 1990. "Exchange Networks and Generalized Exchange: Linking Structure and Action." In Bernd Marin, ed., *Generalized Political Exchange: Antagonistic Cooperation and Integrated Policy Circuits*, pp. 215–30. Boulder, Colo.: Westview.

Corson, Catherine A. 1994. *The Organization of Rural Associations for Progress in Zimbabwe: A Case Study of a People's Movement as a Development Agent*. M.P.A. thesis, Cornell Institute for Public Affairs, Ithaca, New York.

Finkel, Steven E., Edward N. Muller, and Karl-Dieter Opp. 1989. "Personal Influence, Collective Rationality, and Mass Political Action." *American Political Science Review* 83(3): 885–903.

Fukuyama, Francis. 1995. *Trust: The Social Virtues and the Creation of Prosperity*. New York: The Free Press.

Hardin, Garrett. 1968. "The Tragedy of the Commons." *Science* 168: 1243–48.

Krishna 91

Hechter, Michael. 1987. *Principles of Group Solidarity.* Berkeley and Los Angeles: University of California Press.

Hirschman, Albert O. 1984. *Getting Ahead Collectively: Grassroots Experience in Latin America.* New York: Pergamon Press.

Jodha, N. S. 1986. "Common Property Resources and the Rural Poor in Dry Regions of India." *Economic and Political Weekly* (Bombay), July 5.

Johnson, James. 1996. "Why Respect Culture?" Paper presented to the Toronto Chapter of the Conference for the Study of Political Thought. Unpublished manuscript.

Klandermans, Bert. 1984. "Mobilization and Participation: Social-Psychological Expansions of Resource Mobilization Theory." *American Sociological Review* 49(5): 583–600.

Knoke, David. 1988. "Incentives in Collective Action Organizations." *American Sociological Review* 53(3): 311–29.

Krishna, Anirudh. 1997. "Participatory Watershed Development and Soil Conservation." In Anirudh Krishna, Norman Uphoff, and Milton J. Esman, pp. 255–72.

Krishna, Anirudh, Norman Uphoff, and Milton J. Esman, eds. 1997. *Reasons for Hope: Instructive Experiences in Rural Development.* West Hartford, Conn.: Kumarian Press.

Lam, Wai Fung. 1996. "Institutional Design of Public Agencies and Coproduction: A Study of Irrigation Associations in Taiwan." *World Development* 24(6): 1039–54.

Lamb, Geoffrey, and Linda Mueller. 1982. *Control, Accountability, and Incentives in a Successful Development Institution: The Kenya Tea Development Authority.* World Bank Staff Working Papers Number 550. World Bank, Washington, D.C.

Leonard, David K. 1991. *African Successes: Four Public Managers of Kenyan Rural Development.* Berkeley and Los Angeles: University of California Press.

Locke, Richard M. 1995. *Remaking the Italian Economy.* Ithaca: Cornell University Press.

Nyoni, Sithembiso. 1987. "Indigenous NGOs: Liberation, Self-Reliance, and Development." *World Development* Vol. 15, Supplement.

ORAP (Organization of Rural Associations for Progress). 1992. Second Three-Year Development Plan: 1993–1995. Harare, Zimbabwe: ORAP.

Ostrom, Elinor. 1990. *Governing the Commons: The Evolution of Institutions for Collective Action.* Cambridge (UK): Cambridge University Press.

———. 1994. "Constituting Social Capital and Collective Action." *Journal of Theoretical Politics* 6(4): 527–62.

Ouedraogo, Bemard Ledea. 1977. *Les Groupements Pre-Cooperatifs au Yatenga.* Paris: Centre de Recherches Cooperatives.

Paul, Samuel. 1982. *Managing Development Programs: The Lessons of Success.* Boulder, Colo.: Westview.

Putnam, Robert D. 1995. "Bowling Alone: America's Declining Social Capital." *Journal of Democracy* 6 (January): 65–78.

———. 1996. "The Strange Disappearance of Civic America." *The American Prospect* 24 (Winter): 34–48.

Putnam, Robert D., Robert Leonardi, and Raffaella Y. Nanetti. 1993. *Making Democracy Work: Civic Traditions in Modern Italy.* Princeton: Princeton University Press.

Sabel, Charles F. 1994. "Learning by Monitoring: The Institutions of Economic Development." In Neil J. Smelser and Richard Swedberg, eds., *Handbook of Economic Sociology*, pp. 137–65. Princeton: Princeton University Press.

Schelling, Thomas C. 1960. *The Strategy of Conflict.* Cambridge, Mass.: Harvard University Press.

Schneider, Mark, Paul Teske, Melissa Marschall, Michael Mintrom, and Christine Roch. 1997. "Institutional Arrangements and the Creation of Social Capital: The Effects of Public School Choice." *American Political Science Review* 91(1): 82–93.

Smelser, Neil J., and Richard Swedberg. 1994. "The Sociological Perspective on the Economy." In Neil J. Smelser and Richard Swedberg, eds., *Handbook of Economic Sociology*, pp. 3–26. Princeton: Princeton University Press.

Swidler, Ann. 1986. "Culture in Action: Symbols and Strategies." *American Sociological Review* 51: 273–86.

Tarrow, Sidney. 1995. "Making Social Science Work across Space and Time: A Critical Reflection on Robert Putnam's *Making Democracy Work*." *American Political Science Review* 90(2): 389–97.

Uphoff, Norman Thomas. 1986. *Local Institutional Development: An Analytical Sourcebook with Cases*. West Hartford, Conn.: Kumarian Press.

Uphoff, Norman Thomas, Milton J. Esman, and Anirudh Krishna. 1998. *Reasons for Success: Learning from Instructive Experiences of Rural Development*. West Hartford, Conn: Kumarian Press.

Wade, Robert. 1994. *Village Republics: Economic Conditions for Collective Action in South India*. San Francisco: Institute for Contemporary Studies.

Wijayaratna, C. M., and Norman Uphoff. 1997. "Farmer Organization in Gal Oya: Improving Irrigation Management in Sri Lanka." In Anirudh Krishna, Norman Uphoff, and Milton J. Esman, pp. 166–83.

# The formation of social capital

Jonathan H. Turner
*University of California*

*A sociological analysis of the types of social capital produced at the macro-, meso-, and microlevels of social organization is presented. General sociological theory is used to present ideal-typical portrayals of those social forces generating social capital that can sustain long-term, national-level economic development. These ideal-typical portrayals are, however, qualified by analyses of types of social capital in actual empirical systems that can work at cross purposes with, or undermine, efforts to create new forms of social capital that can fuel national economic development. The goal of the paper is to present, admittedly at a very high level of abstraction, "checklists" of new and older forms of social capital so that the viability of potential investment strategies at the macro-, meso-, and microlevels of social organization can be assessed.*

The concept of "social capital" represents the latest approach for a sociology of economic development. Older developmental models of modernization, especially the ones devised by functional sociologists addressing stages of societal evolution (for example, Parsons 1964, 1966), have long been rejected, only to be resurrected in tandem with the concept of social capital being applied to an ever greater number of social forces influencing economic development. With notable exceptions (for example, Woolcock 1997), however, efforts to redefine sociological variables as "social capital" alongside other forms of capital—that is, human, natural, and physical capital—tend to pour "old sociological wine" into the "new and smaller bottles" of economics (for example, Coleman 1988). For certain purposes, narrow views of social capital as "social networks" (Burt 1992) or as civic associations (for example, Putnam 1993; Putnam, Leonardi, and Nanetti 1993) are perhaps useful, but if integration of sociological knowledge into economic thinking is to occur, we need a broad conception of social capital. Indeed, we may have to exhume the long-dead functionalist theories, bring them back to life, and combine their enduring insights with other modes of sociological reasoning.

In this chapter, a very general sociological perspective on social capital will be proposed. For some, this approach will seem too inclusive and too abstract, but if sociological insights are to be properly employed, we must at least look at the range of ideas that might prove useful for those interested in making decisions about investments in social capital. My definition of social capital is, therefore, broad: *those forces that increase the potential for economic development in a society by creating and sustaining social relations and patterns of social organization.* These forces operate at macro-, meso-, and microlevels of analysis. That is, social capital is formed (a) as a population becomes organized to meet basic and fundamental needs for production, reproduction, regulation, and coordination (the macroinstitutional level); (b) as corporate units organize human capital and as categoric units generate social distinctions influencing how members of a society are treated (the mesolevel); and (c) as social encounters in the form of face-to-face interaction unfold within corporate and categoric units (the microlevel).

These levels *of analysis* are just that: levels of analysis. They represent ways of looking at the ebb and flow of social activity; and each level gives us a somewhat different picture of how social capital is formed. Because actual reality is not divided into levels, analysis at one level is inevitably embedded in the other two (Granovetter 1985). From a top-down perspective, the ways that a population meets fundamental needs for survival in an environment (the macroinstitutional level) constrain the types of corporate and categoric units that can be built as well as constraining the flow of face-to-face encounters. From a bottom-up vantage point, corporate and categoric units are sustained by face-to-face interactions, while macroinstitutional forces are constructed from corporate and categoric units. Figure 1 summarizes this embeddedness of forces exposed at the macro-, meso-, and microlevels of analysis.

How, then, do we get a conceptual handle on the operation of these forces and their effects in forming social capital? To explore this I will construct an "ideal type" at each level of analysis, indicating the nature of the social capital that can be generated. These ideal types represent, of course, a utopian view of forces stimulating economic development, but they do provide an analytical yardstick to compare actual societies against—in terms of how much, if any, of the social capital necessary for development they reveal. I visualize these ideal types as a kind of "check-list" with which the empirical particulars of any society can be compared. I also provide a real-world "checklist" of what I view as older forms of social capital that can undermine the formation of newer forms necessary for sustained national development. Much of this "older" social capital is what typically exists in a developing society; and it can provide social capital for local development, but I would argue that for

FIGURE 1: THE EMBEDDEDNESS OF MACRO-, MESO-, AND MICROLEVEL SOCIAL FORCES

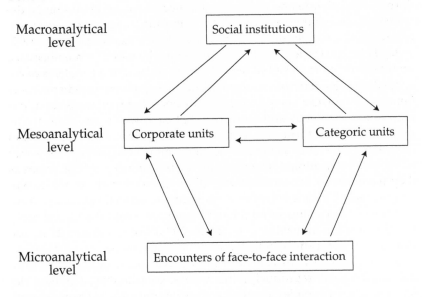

Source: Author.

sustained national-level development, this older social capital will need to be replaced by the newer forms flowing from analytical features presented in the ideal types.

An exercise such as this invites the criticism of previous functional evolutionary models, as well as early studies of "modernization"—which were so prominent three decades ago (for example, McClelland 1961) that the "western ideal" is being used as the template against which all other societies are being assessed. To some extent this is a reasonable criticism, but it can be taken too far. For the fact remains that development in a capitalist world system will, indeed, have to reveal many of the features of western capitalism, adopted and adapted to the unique historical and contemporary circumstances of a society. The advantage of focusing on social capital, as opposed to previous conceptualizations of the developmental stages, takeoff points, or "critical" social or psychological needs and dispositions, is that we can see the forces influencing development as *variables*, revealing different values and configurations. Development can be encouraged or discouraged at national, local, and regional levels depending on the particular mix of social capital formed. This kind of analytical approach thus allows us to avoid a western-centric view of economic development, while at the same time recognizing that development is, in the current world system, going to be capitalist.

## Macrolevel analysis: the dynamics of institutional differentiation

Surprisingly, there is no consensus on what a social institution is, despite the fact that the term "institution" is widely used in the social sciences. From a variety of works on the topic (for example, Turner 1972, 1997), I employ the term *institution* to denote the way that members of a population are organized in order to face fundamental problems of coordinating their activities to survive within a given environment. Functional sociologists all emphasized institutions and then went about formulating basic needs and requisites that each was seen to meet. The problems in this form of analysis are well documented (Turner and Maryanski 1979), but as long as we take a more selectionist view—that is, existing institutional structures are the product of selection forces as they have forced humans individually and collectively to meet challenges posed by the external environment as well as by the internal environment of ongoing social relations—we can avoid the logical problems of most functional theories (Turner 1996). For it is reasonable to see institutions as means by which members cope—by design, experimentation, or chance—with such basic problems as securing resources from the environment, reproducing the species, coordinating activities, defending against enemies, maintaining social control, and so on. Because institutions resolve such fundamental problems, they have some special characteristics: the norms regulating activities within institutional contexts are well known and heavily infused with value standards about what is right and proper, giving them a moral character and inviting sanctions for their violation (Turner 1997, pp. 1–15).

### The differentiation of institutional spheres

The first element in my ideal typical portrayal of society is the differentiation among five basic institutional spheres: (a) kinship, (b) religion, (c) economy, (d) polity, and (e) law. These institutional spheres must be differentiated in several respects: First, each reveals separate types of corporate units within which activities are coordinated. Second, distinctive types of categoric units placing people into socially defined categories flow out of the division of labor within corporate units. Third, distinctive sets of symbols (for example, beliefs, ideologies, myths, linguistic styles, and norms) exist in order to facilitate actions and transactions and to connect general value standards of the society as a whole to face-to-face encounters. Fourth, separate generalized media of exchange—or systems of symbols—that are used to (a) structure discourse among social actors; (b) order nonverbal expressions among social actors; (c) define the units and terms of exchange among actors; (d) develop beliefs, myths, norms, ideologies, and other symbol systems connecting value standards to the specifics of actions and transactions among actors; and (e) legitimate activities of actors, must exist for each institutional sphere. The presence of these media give an institution a certain degree of cultural autonomy from others but at the same time provides a means for exchange with individuals and corporate units from other institutional contexts (Turner 1996, pp. 162–67).

Thus, for an institutional sphere to be relatively autonomous it must be, first of all, *structurally* distinct in terms of revealing (a) types of corporate units (for example, firms for economy; families for kinship), as well as (b) corresponding categoric units (for example, "worker" in economy; "father" in family). Second it must be *culturally* distinct in terms of evidencing (a) systems of symbols translating values into norms, beliefs, and other cultural forms facilitating transactions (for example, beliefs in profit-seeking behavior in the economy; beliefs in commitments to family members); and (b) systems of generalized media of exchange (for example, money in economy; loyalty, love, and duty in the family). To the extent that a population cannot construct separate institutional spheres in these terms, economic development will be inhibited because if the institution's internal structural and cultural systems are not autonomous, outside factors such as the economy, the corporate and categoric units of other institutions, coupled with the cultural systems of these institutions, will pull activities in several, often contradictory directions. For example, if economic activity is carried out primarily in the family units of the kinship system, categoric distinctions among family members—as mothers, fathers, and children—blend into those for workers, while the systems of symbols for translating values into norms and media for conducting exchanges within and between families will be heavily influenced by love, loyalty, and duty to kin. Such overlap between economy and kinship does provide a kind of particularized social capital for organizing production and conducting exchanges, but it is not the kind of capital that will lead to larger-scale economic development in terms of profit-seeking firms hiring human capital in a labor market for money and conducting most exchanges with money.

Institutional autonomy should exist for at least the above-mentioned five institutions: kinship, religion, economy, polity, and law. Of course, development is facilitated by the autonomy of additional institutional spheres, such as education, medicine, and science, but differentiation among these five is essential. The reason for this is well known: nonkin production in corporate units and market distribution in terms of money will not realize their dynamic potential when embedded in other institutional spheres. Religion is essentially devoted to the nonsecular realm; while general values contained within religious dogma can provide standards for elaboration within the economic sphere, as Weber (1904–1905) argued for Protestantism, they cannot provide the detailed prescriptions or generalized media necessary for highly dynamic economic activity. Similarly, kinship can be a successful way of organizing economic activity when other, more purely economic structures are absent (for example, in rural areas of extremely poor countries) or not available to certain social categories (that, for example, are victims of ethnic discrimination), but it is limiting in its capacity to increase macrolevel development beyond certain economic niches. Polity as the house of power can turn economic activities toward narrow goals, from supporting the privilege of elites to war-making, none of which facilitates the development of physical, human, and natural capital toward robust economic development; and so, operation of the economy must, to some degree, have autonomy from diffuse and arbitrary political demands. In place of arbitrary use of power must come a legal system that enjoys sufficient institutional autonomy, or what Niklas Luhmann (1982, pp. 90–137) has called "sovereignty"— the right to create laws specifying rights, duties, and obligations in all institutional spheres and to legislate laws as new points of dispute and problems of coordination and control arise. Indeed, as explored below, law becomes an increasingly important institution for managing problems within and between the individuals and corporate units inhabiting other institutional spheres (Turner 1980).

Yet, institutional autonomy alone is insufficient for increasing economic development. The degree to which differentiation penetrates all layers and regions as well as the profile of institutional spheres is also an important factor, as explored below.

*The degree of successive penetration of institutional differentiation*

As Peter Blau (1977, 1994) has emphasized, it makes a great deal of difference if patterns of differentiation penetrate into successive layers of a society. If a pattern of institutional differentiation—for instance, among economy, polity, and law—exists only at the national level of societal organization but does not penetrate down to regional and local levels, the social capital generated by such differentiation will be far less effective in promoting economic development. If traditional patterns of institutional fusion or overlap among, for example, economic activities, kinship, and community persist at the same time that a dynamic market-driven economy, polity, and legal system operate in larger urban areas or key points of import and export, older forms of social capital will impede the penetration of the newer forms inhering in institutional differentiation. There are, however, always pressures for the new social capital being created by institutional differentiation to be adopted at local levels, but traditional ways of organizing economic activity can be especially difficult to unseat if people in the townships and villages of the outlying regions of a society do not trust the stability and buying power of money, do not see the political regime as legitimate or trustworthy, and do not perceive that there is real sovereignty and impartiality in the legal system. Under these conditions, older forms of organizing activities, including economic activities, will be used to insulate members of the population from what are perceived to be both alien and unreliable ways of organizing social life; and when this kind of balkanization occurs, old and newer forms of social capital work at cross purposes.

As a practical matter of where to invest resources, a dilemma emerges. If local networks built from kin and village media of exchange, norms, and beliefs are used for small development projects, these projects have the effect of increasing per capita income and reinforcing the very institutional arrangements that long-term development will have to disrupt, change, and indeed, eliminate. By contrast, investments in the national economy, current political regime, and legal system may have little immediate effect on improving the life of the rural poor, thereby increasing their reliance on, and trust in, those older forms of social capital that might delay or sabotage the penetration of new types of social capital.

### The profile and structure of key institutional spheres

For economic development to be maximized, each institutional sphere must evidence a particular profile in the structure of its corporate and categoric units as well as in the cultural symbols used to facilitate transactions within and between institutional spheres. Let me review each of the five institutions in terms of the ideal-typical features it should reveal.

*Kinship.* While extended families and larger kin structures organized in terms of a descent rule do represent a form of social capital, such capital will almost always be localized and particularized—that is, tied to localities and the corporate-categoric units organizing family activity. Moreover, this capital will work to maintain the primacy of diffuse family norms and media of exchange built from symbols emphasizing love, loyalty, and duty to kindred. As such it will work to decrease kin members' willingness to enter as autonomous actors into labor markets and, once they are there, to sell their labor power for a more neutral medium of exchange such as money; and even when they may be forced to do so, these actors' orientations will focus on the larger kin unit and the diffuse obligations that inhere in such units. Thus, in the end, national development is facilitated by more isolated nuclear kin units, with adult members oriented to selling their labor in impersonal markets and developing their skills in ways to strike a better bargain when entering labor markets. This shift in orientation makes the family a consumption rather than production unit; and it involves a "psychology of commodification"—or selling oneself as an object for money and for viewing transactions outside the family in terms of less effective media of exchange such as money and authority. To the degree that such nuclearization does not occur, structural and cultural roadblocks to long-term development are created, even when these roadblocks provide social capital for local and short-term economic activity.

Thus, inhering in the nuclearization of family, and the associated shifts in orientations of its members, are important sources of social capital revolving around the willingness to leave categoric distinctions, systems of cultural symbols, and generalized media of exchange in kin groups—and adopt the categoric distinctions, cultural symbols, and media of other institutional spheres. And once actors can make this transition, they become more willing and able to (a) see themselves as an autonomous object in labor markets, (b) subject themselves to the inherently competitive nature of such markets operating in accordance with the laws of supply and demand and to abide by the decision on "price" generated by market forces, (c) commodify themselves for the purposes of work, and (d) use nonfamilial generalized media such as money and rational-legal authority for organizing nonkin transactions. Of course, as will be explored later, people's ability and willingness to develop and use this kind of social capital depends on the strength of kinship networks and on the perceived benefits of developing and investing this capital, which in turn is dependent on whether they trust labor markets and corporate units to provide benefits exceeding those of kin networks.

*Religion.* As a system of structures and beliefs concerned with the sacred and supernatural, the ritual practices used to sustain these beliefs will, in the end, need to become segregated from productive and distributive units within the economy, from decision-making structures of polity and law, and even from many secularized activities in a nuclearized kinship system. Religion can still provide highly generalized value premises, but these need to become extremely abstract so that they apply to the ever-increasing diversity of secular activities, mediated by money and authority. And so, to the degree that maintaining the authority of the supernatural, sustaining traditional texts and rituals, and orienting actors toward nonsecular concerns are carried to nonreligious institutions, religion can work to impede economic development.

*Economy.* It is useful to separate the productive and distributive forces in an economy (Turner 1996, 1997). Production revolves around gathering resources and converting them into useable goods and commodities, while producing those services necessary for gathering, conversion, and distribution to occur. Distribution involves (a) developing the physical infrastructure for moving people, materials, and information about a society (for example, roads, communications, ports, airports) and (b) differentiating those markets necessary for the exchange of goods and services. Efforts at development often focus on infrastructural needs because these physical or human-made capital investments can encourage the expansion of market systems. To a degree, this is true, but infrastructural development does not automatically lead to market expansion and differentiation. Market differentiation depends on a complex set of factors, the most important of which are described below:

First, the significance of money as a form of social rather than just physical capital must be recognized (Simmel 1907; Braudel 1982; Turner 1996). For development to occur, money must be trusted as a generalized medium of exchange, such that its ability to secure and transfer value is relatively stable. Thus, if inflation is high, it is difficult for individual and collective actors to trust money as a medium by which value is transferred; and to the extent that this distrust leads actors to use alternatives to money or to use the money of another society, the development of markets will be hindered.

In a related vein, actors must be willing to abandon other generalized media of exchange (for example, love, loyalty, piety, traditional authority, and so on) in many of their transactions and to accept the inevitability of commodification. If actors are not oriented to defining value in terms of money, they will be less willing to orient their actions in terms of utilities assessed in terms of money. And without this willingness to commodify an ever-growing number of spheres of social life, limits are placed on the volume and diversity demand generated for goods and services. Such commodification depends, of course, on the stability of money as a medium of exchange but it also depends on the partitioning of alternative media of exchange from calculations of value—at some point, a commodification invades actors' more personal spheres and has, no doubt, many of the dehumanizing effects dramatized by critical theorists such as Habermas (1973); and yet, without a willingness to push the limits of commodification, market development will be arrested.

Money has unique properties in that it transfers value and, indeed, can be used to increase value by expanding the options of actors to individualize their needs as these translate into market demand. Other media tend to confine value to particular spheres, whereas money is more neutral and can create value in virtually all spheres of human activity (Simmel 1907). But this unique characteristic of money, when compared to other media, assumes that people are willing to individualize their tastes and desires and that they are willing to depersonalize social relations by mediating them with a "cold" and morally "neutral" medium such as money. This willingness depends upon the pull of other institutional spheres and the media by which transactions in these spheres are conducted—and upon the isolation and vulnerability people feel when they define their well-being by the purchasing power of money.

To have and use money, then, depends on a highly complex set of attitudes and orientations by actors. When these exist, money serves not only as a physical capital but *as a form of social capital* because it ensures that actors will use and invest their money in an increasing number of relationships and that they will come to define their happiness in terms of values established by money.

A second factor in the expansion and differentiation of markets revolves around the activities of polity in assuring the stability of money. Polity employs power and authority as its medium of exchange, but it must usurp and use money to finance its operations; and the way in which this usurpation occurs is critical in the formation of social capital. If polity simply taxes its population to the point that little surplus capital for investment outside the needs of political regimes is available, then money cannot become an important source of social capital. If polity prints more money, thereby destabilizing currencies, then the requisite sense of trust in money (and polity as well) cannot become a source of social capital. In contrast, if polity recognizes that its own legitimacy depends on the availability and stability of currency to bestow value, then this recognition becomes an important source of social capital, because polity becomes committed to viewing the purchasing power of money as symbolically important in maintaining its capacity to regulate society. And because money is a more neutral medium of exchange than other media, it lowers the intensity of those symbols by which polity seeks to justify its right to engage binding decisions for the society as a whole (compare the "cool" qualities of money, for example, with rule by religious doctrines, traditional ways of doing things, or personal charisma).

A third feature of market processes revolves around their differentiation, both horizontally and vertically. If money is accepted as a generalized medium of exchange in a wide variety of transactions and if its purchasing power is maintained by polity, then exchange moves beyond local markets, or, alternatively, local markets can become integrated with national markets. Exchange is limited as long as transactions—even those employing money and particularly those employing other media such as duty and loyalty—are conducted in local markets that are somewhat detached from national markets and regulated by agents whose legitimacy resides in local networks. Once money is consistently employed and the diverse offerings of national (and global) markets can be made available to outlying subpopulations, a movement away from more traditional patterns of exchange based on use of nonmonetary media in dense network systems and toward more impersonal and neutral exchanges is initiated. As a consequence of this movement, trust is increasingly transferred from actors in local networks—and the particularized symbols and media by which such networks are maintained—to the purchasing power of money, per se, and to those other institutional spheres, such as law and polity, by which this more cosmopolitan sense of trust is sustained. As this transition is made, other market instruments made possible by money, such as credit, become viable; and as credit is used, commitments to those actors in the economy itself, such as banks and other credit-creating agencies as well as those in other institutional spheres—for example, polity and law—increase, thereby decreasing the salience and power of local networks. These processes must, I believe, be viewed as a source of social capital because they involve a willingness to invest in money as a medium of exchange. If these investments bring benefits to actors, they become ever more willing to expand their investments in money, markets, and the institutions such as polity and law that monitor market processes.

These forces, once initiated, lead to the vertical differentiation of markets in the sense that the instruments of exchange in one market, such as money, credit contracts, stocks, mortgages, bonds, and the like, become themselves the very commodities exchanged in another market, or what Collins (1990) has termed "meta-markets." Thus, the trust implied by the use of money, credit, or other financial instruments creates a broader level of trust among those exchanging these instruments in metamarkets. This more diffuse trust across horizontally and vertically differentiated markets implies an increased faith in the ability of actors within the economy and other institutional spheres, especially polity and law, to monitor and sanction commitments and obligations. This kind of escalating trust and the commitments it implies to corporate actors within the economy (for example, banks, brokerage houses, stock exchanges) and the monitoring and sanctioning capacities of polity and law all represent a form of social capital that extends social relations beyond kin and local networks. Thus, once again, what might be considered physical or liquid capital has the capacity to generate social capital—in that corporate and individual actors begin to have a more diffuse sense of trust in the corporate units of economy, polity, and law. This kind of diffuse sense of trust makes individuals more willing to invest their money, time, and emotional commitments in activities extending beyond kinship, community, and local networks; and as such, diffuse trust in the economic sphere becomes important in stimulating the market demand necessary for national-level economic development.

Thus, the pattern of market differentiation becomes particularly important in generating social capital. As actors develop the commitments involved in commodifying their selves and actions in terms of money, as polity and law see their legitimacy as dependent on sustaining the purchasing power of money, and as markets differentiate horizontally and vertically in ways that expand and extend trust, important sources of social capital are developed. In societies in which money is not trusted, in which actors in polity and law do not see their stake in sustaining the purchasing power of money, and in which markets beyond those in local communities are not seen as trustworthy, social capital cannot be effectively developed beyond communities and networks whose monitoring and sanctioning are conducted by local agents and actors. Without the willingness to trust economic actors and key agents in the political and legal arenas, the diffuse trust needed for national economic development cannot be developed.

The other key force in economy, production, is obviously related to these distribution processes. Production cannot expand without market differentiation, especially differentiation in terms of money and the financial instruments that money makes possible, and without the willingness of actors to invest their money and trust in market demand. Conversely, markets and the distributive infrastructure are unlikely to expand without the capacity of corporate actors within the productive sphere to create outputs of goods and services. Production of goods and services involves considerable social capital beyond the entrepreneurial capacity of coordinating technology, human-made or physical capital, and human capital for production and distribution. Such entrepreneurship promotes long-term economic development when it leads to certain structural characteristics in corporate units. Some of the most important of these are briefly examined below.

First, the organization of production and distribution involves the creation of corporate units revealing a division of labor in which human capital is paid by an extrinsic reinforcer such as money. Human capital must, therefore, be willing to accept selling itself at a labor market and building its relationship to employers as an exchange of work for money. To the degree that other media of exchange such as duty or loyalty emerge, these must be toward employers rather than kin-based networks and other corporate units outside the workplace; and to the extent that this is not the case, the scale and efficiency of corporate units is compromised.

Second, the division of labor among workers who are compensated with money is held together by an authority system in which active monitoring and sanctioning of activities occur. Such systems must be accepted as trustworthy and legitimate if they are to be effective, and they must rely upon nonkin, noncommunal, nonreligious bases of legitimation. What, then, is this basis? Max Weber (1922) saw it as "rational-legal" authority, but we need to indicate what it is about rational-legal authority that makes it a source of legitimation. Such authority depends on the perception by human capital that agents involved in monitoring and sanctioning do so in order to sustain or increase the efficiency of the organization in meeting its production goals (even if workers are not happy with these goals). If, however, authority is seen as personalistic, vindictive, punitive, and otherwise unrelated to production goals, the authority system will not generate the generalized trust in rational-legal authority that is vital for efficient organization of corporate units. Thus, when human capital is able to accept rational-legal authority in organizations as legitimate, this acceptance becomes a source of social capital, not just for the production of the goods and services in economic organizations, but in all organizations in other institutional spheres relying on rational-legal authority.

This shift in orientation away from kin-, community-, religious-, and tradition-based authority becomes essential in order to create the diffuse trust in economic actors as well as in those actors in the polity and the legal system that are essential to economic development.

Third, corporate units involved in productive and distributive processes must coordinate activities through formal rules. One set of rules is the entrance and exit rules of the organization—when one joins and leaves the organization. These rules involve considerable social capital because they depend on commitments by human capital to suspend for a specified amount of time and in a particular place their other obligations, their use of other cultural symbols, and their reliance of other generalized media of exchange (Luhmann 1982). If human capital is unwilling to do this, then the efficiency of the organization is undermined. In addition to these commitments, there is also a commitment to suspend the salience of categoric distinctions that do not correspond to the division of labor within the organization, leaving outside the organization one's concern with such categoric distinctions as religion, ethnicity, and gender. Organizations also have rules that specify how human capital is to work in relation to others and, if relevant, machine capital, and workers must be willing to accept the legitimacy of these norms and to suspend concern with those more diffuse norms used in other corporate units, such as kinship.

Fourth, organizations control social relations above and beyond those generated by formal rules and rational-legal authority. They also require that personal relations generated in face-to-face interaction do not become so particularistic that they reduce commitments to work obligations, especially with respect to abiding by formal rules and accepting systems of rational-legal authority. The emergence of such ties of solidarity among workers must exclude normative and authority systems of corporate and categoric units outside the organization, and equally important, relations of solidarity are to be aligned with the production goals of the organization.

These issues will be examined further when we turn to mesolevel forces revolving around corporate and categoric units, but the point to be made here is that the creation of corporate units for production of goods and services, including those necessary in marketing and other distributive processes, involves a dramatic shift in the way people relate to corporate units; and as individuals become able to make the transition to work for money in a division of labor structured by formal norms and systems of rational-legal authority, they produce the very social capital necessary for such organizations to function efficiently and, hence, in ways increasing the development potential of the society as a whole.

*Polity.* There are four bases of power on which all forms of government depend (Turner 1996, pp. 75–102): (a) coercive, or the use of physical force to make other actors abide by directives from agents in the polity; (b) administrative, or the use of regulatory structures to implement directives by agents in the polity and to monitor conformity to such directives; (c) material incentives, or the use and manipulation of valued material resources, including money, to induce actors to abide by directives from agents in polity; and (d) symbolic, or the use and manipulation of systems of cultural symbols, including generalized media of exchange, to convince actors to abide by directives from agents in the polity. Governments vary in terms of the relative use of these four bases of power; and depending on the mix of these bases, markedly different types of governmental systems emerge. If any one—or two bases—is used disproportionately, polity will prove inviable in the long run and ineffective in promoting economic development. Thus, the way these bases of power are consolidated becomes a source of social capital. In addition to the consolidation of power around a particular mix of the four bases of power, centralization of power—that is, concentration of decision-making among a small set of agents within the polity—will also vary. Centralization, per se, increases consolidation, especially around the administrative base, but the pattern of centralization varies enormously in terms of the relative mix of bases on which it is built.

What degree of centralization and what pattern of consolidation among the bases of power increase the development potential of a society? Much depends, of course, on the demographics of the population, the history of a society, the geopolitical situation faced by polity, and the current institutional structure, but there is a range of variation beyond which polity will undermine the development of social capital in other institutional spheres.

Let me first address the issue of centralization of power. Development can occur under conditions of high centralization, in cases in which power is concentrated in the hands of relatively few decision-making agents and in which democratic election of decision-makers is nonexistent or only a public ritual. But in the long run—and even in the short run in developing societies with a previous history of authoritarian rule—centralization of power, coupled with democratic elections of at least some crucial decision-makers, makes government even more effective in promoting development. Centralization brings coherence into decision-making, puts in place administrative structures to enable decisions to be carried out at the local level, creates a system of managed incentives for actors to pursue certain activities, and backs up nonconformity with coercion or, at least, with threats of coercion. Democracy provides correctives to arbitrary, corrupt, and authoritarian rule, while stimulating a host of symbols, media of discourse in the political arena, and protections for dissent supported by the legal system that legitimate political decision-making. Indeed, rapidly developing parts of the world, such as in China and South Asia, will need to expand democracy in order to sustain their rapid development because the more prosperity depends on market dynamism, the more accustomed actors in such markets become to having the freedom to choose among options; and eventually, this kind of orientation extends to political freedoms and political demands. What is critical, then, is what Luhmann (1982, pp. 141–89) has termed a distinctive "arena of politics" in which it is safe to discuss and debate alternative policies and to which political decision-makers must pay some attention, even when they are not elected officials. In this way, individualized tastes stimulated by market forces do not create a dramatic disjuncture between what is possible economically and what is possible politically. When this disjuncture becomes too large, the symbolic base of power for a political regime is undermined, thereby lessening the level of trust in political agents that is essential to development. Thus, the ideal pattern of centralization would involve the state's (a) possessing monopoly on the use of coercive power but rarely using it except in short-term strategic situations; (b) evidencing moderately high degrees of administrative centralization so that directives are coherent but, at the same time, avoiding the tendencies to micromanage the activities of individuals and corporate units in a market economy; (c) having its decision-makers selected from an arena of politics or, at the very least, from among those who are responsive to this arena; (d) relying heavily on the use of material incentives, through direct subsidies or tax expenditures, to encourage certain activities by individual and collective actors in the economy; and (e) relying almost exclusively on law rather than threats of coercion, micromanagement in the administrative arena, religion, or intense personal charisma to legitimate its right to make binding decisions. Western political democracies score high on this profile of centralization, and it can be argued that this is one of the reasons that their economies have been so dynamic over the last one hundred years.

Turning now to the issue of consolidation among the four bases of power, the most ideal form is balance among the bases. In this ideal scenario, coercion is rarely used, and used only strategically and episodically when needed; administrative regulation is, at best, only moderate and confined mostly to monetary policy, protections for actors in markets, and infrastructural development and maintenance; material incentives are used extensively but still very strategically, being employed primarily for encouraging the development of physical, social, and human capital formation; and legitimating symbols are lodged in traditions and an autonomous legal system enjoying considerable "sovereignty" from the polity as a whole. This pattern of consolidation promotes what can be termed diffuse legitimacy that gives polity the right to make binding decisions, even when actors may disagree with the specific of many decisions. This diffuse legitimacy is furthered when a clear arena of politics enables actors to vent their more specific points of disagreement; and as they are allowed to do so, this dialogue in the political arena generates increased trust in government.

As with the corporate units organizing production and distribution, those involved in the centralization and consolidation of power need to reveal a rational-legal profile, relying on labor markets for recruitment, using money and authority as dominant media for transactions, excluding other media and normative systems with entrance-exit rules, codifying formal rules that specify work obligations, regulating face-to-face interactions to ensure that patterns of informal solidarity, monitoring, and sanctioning are aligned with the goals of the organization, and creating formal systems of monitoring and sanctioning that step in when informal monitoring and sanctioning prove inviable. Moreover, such units must exclude categoric distinctions generated from the division of labor in communities and kin groups. Under these conditions, individuals and corporate units in nonpolitical institutional spheres will develop trust in governmental organizations, and those working in these organizations will perceive that their activities should be devoted to sustaining this trust.

*Law.* Legal systems consist of (a) bodies of rules specifying rights, duties, and obligations of actors, (b) procedures for developing new rules, (c) agents for mediating and adjudicating disputes, deviance, and other points of tension among actors in terms of law, and (d) agents enforcing conformity to rules and outcomes of adjudicative processes (Turner 1997, pp. 185–90). As such, a legal system employs a generalized media of imperative coordination—in other words, it uses rules carrying moral and coercive authority that regulate and coordinate actions, transactions, and exchanges among agents operating in other institutional spheres (Parsons and Smelser 1956). Without the development of a legal system that has these capacities for imperative coordination, societal complexity and development are limited because there is no mechanism standing outside each institutional sphere to coordinate activities.

Economic development also depends on a positivistic legal system that enjoys considerable sovereignty. While the legislative and coercive functions of a legal system overlap with polity, it is essential that the laws, procedures for adjudicating disputes before the laws, and decision-makers within the system of courts all have autonomy from polity. To the extent that they do not have such autonomy, law will not be seen as universalistic, courts will not be seen as fair mediators of justice, and officials of the court will not be seen as impartial. Moreover, unless law is positivistic and can change to fit new circumstances, it will not be seen as flexibly relevant to the problems faced by actors in various institutional spheres. Additionally, as Luhmann (1972, 1982) has pointed out, the legal system itself must engage in considerable "self thematization" in which the premises of law itself, particularly procedural law, are constantly debated much as political issues are examined in a distinctive arena of politics. Under these conditions, individual and corporate actors will perceive the legal system as trustworthy in imperatively coordinating activities; and as actors develop a generalized trust in the mediating capacities of the legal system, they will also develop a trust in legislative and enforcement arms of this system overlapping with polity. This trust thus becomes social capital that is invested in the political-legal system and the operation of productive and distributive processes of the economy.

*Priorities among institutional spheres*

From the narrow perspective of development, per se, some institutional spheres need to become dominant over others during the process of institutional differentiation. The corporate units, categoric distinctions, media of exchange, and systems of symbols within the economic, political, and legal spheres must become dominant over kinship and religion. If the corporate units, categoric distinctions, generalized media, and systems of symbols within kinship and religion deeply penetrate and permeate economy, polity, and law, then the ideal profile for these three critical institutional spheres cannot be reached and development will be arrested. For, if kinship and religion exert too much influence, new media of exchange revolving around money, rational authority, and imperative coordination cannot produce extended and diffuse trust in (a) markets, polity, and law, (b) rational-legal corporate units, (c) categoric distinctions tied to the division of labor in rational-legal corporate units and, (d) new forms of administration, regulation, control, and mediation.

Tables 1 and 2 summarize the basic line of argument developed above. In these and subsequent tables, the middle column represents the social capital generated by the ideal-typical portrayal summarized in the left column. The right column presents real-world restrictions that can limit the formation of new forms of social capital summarized in the middle column. The left and right columns—that is, ideal type and the real world restrictions, respectively—are portrayed as a "checklist" in this sense: by checking to see how a particular society fares on these checklists, the opportunities and obstacles to development can be highlighted. By performing this exercise, options for investments in development are suggested. If the real-world restrictions listed in the right column are prominent, however, development strategies are limited—primarily to local infrastructural projects that can raise standards of living and per capita income, which perhaps in the very long run can provide a base for more national-level development. In contrast, if at least some of the ideal conditions listed in the left column are met, or can be met, then investment should focus on these and, thereby, on those forms of social capital listed in the middle of the tables.

One problem with social capital at this macrostructural level revolves around the difficulty of manipulating it. Such capital is so embedded in

*(continued on p. 119)*

TABLE 1: THE FORMATION OF SOCIAL CAPITAL AND INSTITUTIONAL DIFFERENTIATION

| Checklist of ideal macrostructural characteristics | New forms of social capital generated | Checklist of real-world constraints imposed by older forms of social capital |
|---|---|---|
| Structural differentiation among economy, polity, law, kinship, and religion, especially with respect to: | | |
| (1) Autonomy of institutional spheres from each other. | Capacity to separate generalized media of exchange, belief, norms, and authority systems of diverse institutions, thereby freeing economy. | Generalized media of exchange, values, beliefs, norms, and systems of authority from kinship and religion do not allow for separation of economy, polity, and law. |
| 2) Penetration of structural differentiation to local levels. | Capacity to develop economic, political, and legal systems in local and rural areas along same paths as in large cities and at the national level. | Local communal forms and institutional structures resist penetration of economic, political, and legal structures operating at the national level, especially if the latter are not trusted. |
| (3) Domination of all other institutional spheres by economy, polity, and law. | Reduces capacity of media of exchange, beliefs, norms, and authority systems of institutions outside economy, polity, and law from influencing economic development. | Media of exchange, beliefs, norms, and authority system of kinship and religion, and the social networks on which they are sustained, do not allow for domination by economy, polity, and law. |
| (4) Distinctiveness of organizational units in institutional spheres, with respect to: | Facilitates development of distinctive organizational units, structured along rational-legal lines, when: | Organizational units and network structures of kinship, religion, and community see rational-legal units as threats, because: |

(Continued on next page.)

111

TABLE 1 (*continued*)

| Checklist of ideal macrostructural characteristics | New forms of social capital generated | Checklist of real-world constraints imposed by older forms of social capital |
|---|---|---|
| a. nature of incentives for actors to participate in units; | a. money is the dominant incentive for participation by actors, stimulating development of labor markets; | a. money erodes traditional incentive system, and traditional nonmarket ways to allocate human capital; |
| b. symbolic media used to mediate actions and transactions; | b. money is the measure of value in transactions, encouraging commodification; | b. money erodes other measures of value that do not commodify; |
| c. content of belief systems as they translate value premises into imperatives for activities of incumbents; | c. value premises are translated into systems of formal rules and systems of authority for structuring the division of labor; | c. formal rules erode power of informal rules, lodged in traditional networks; |
| d. nature of rule system, or norms, for specifying how incumbents are to act; and | d. system of rules is formal and universalistic; and | d. formal and universalistic rules are seen to erode informal and particularistic agreements; and |
| e. nature of authority systems for monitoring and sanctioning conformity to norms. | e. authority is rational in its emphasis on realizing goals of organization. | e. rational authority undermines all other, more traditional bases of authority. |
| (5) Diversity of categoric unit formation, especially with respect to: | Diversity of categoric distinctions increases tolerance for new distinctions based on development of economy, polity, and law, thereby: | Traditional categoric distinctions operate to decrease tolerance of new distinctions, because: |

a. emergence of new categoric distinctions beyond those of traditional kinship, religion, and stratification; and

b. emergence of categoric distinctions corresponding to the expanding division of labor in new types of corporate units.

a. breaking hold of kinship, religion, and ascriptive stratification to define social categories; and

b. shifting key categoric distinctions to the emerging division of labor in rational-legal organizational units.

a. kinship, religion, and traditional stratification are embedded in values, beliefs, norms, authority systems, media of exchange and networks that resist change and support the status quo; and

b. kinship, religion, and traditional stratification see new distinctions corresponding to the division of labor in rational-legal organizational units as threatening to the integrity of traditional values, beliefs, norms, authority systems, media of exchange, and networks, thereby mobilizing efforts to reduce the threat.

*Source:* Author.

TABLE 2: THE FORMATION OF SOCIAL CAPITAL AND THE PROFILE OF INSTITUTIONS

| Checklist of ideal institutional profiles | New forms of social capital generated | Checklist of real-world constraints imposed by older forms of social capital |
|---|---|---|
| (1) Kinship: | Nucleation of kinship produces the following sources of social capital: | Maintenance of strong kinship ties, particularly more extended networks, maintained by descent rules and by use of generalized media revolving around love, duty, and loyalty to kin can have the following effects on formation of new types of social capital: |
| a. nucleated, with weak descent and residence rules; | a. willingness to leave family unit and enter labor markets, mediated by more neutral media of exchange, especially money but rational-legal authority and formal rules as well; | a. unwillingness to enter labor markets mediated by money and to submit to nonkin systems of authority and rules; |
| b. nuclear units primarily involved in consumption rather than production; | b. willingness to commodify self, nonfamilial social relations, and most objects in terms of money; | b. unwillingness to use money as a measure of self and as the medium for developing social relations inside and outside of formal organizations; |
| c. generalized media of exchange confined to relations in nuclear unit and to relatively few additional kin; and | c. willingness to abide by entrance and exit rules of formal organizations and, thereby, to suspend use of values, beliefs, norms, and media of exchange in kinship systems; and | c. unwillingness to abide by entrance and exit rules of rational-legal organizations and to suspend use of kin-based media of exchange; and |
| d. categoric distinctions associated with division of labor in family not considered relevant beyond the kin unit. | d. willingness to use division of labor in economic units as relevant categoric distinctions for most nonkin activities. | d. unwillingness to abandon traditional categoric distinction; |

(2) Religion:

Segregation of religion from institutional spheres, particularly economy, polity and law, produces the following sources of social capital:

Failure to segregate religion, both beliefs and ritual practices, can have the following effects on the formation of new types of social capital:

a. segregated structurally in time and space from other institutional spheres;

a. ability to develop and use secular, rational-legal corporate units for organizing most institutional activity outside of kinship and practice of religious rituals;

a. erosion of secular bases for forming corporate units using rational-legal authority and secular rules;

b. values, beliefs, norms, and generalized media of exchange confined to practice of religious rituals in segregated religious structures;

b. ability to employ ethically neutral media of exchange such as money, secular authority, and formal rules in organizing activities in corporate units;

b. inability to deploy fully the use of money, secular power and authority, and secular rules to organizational activities;

c. generalization and abstraction of religious values in ways making it possible to redefine and specify them through secular beliefs to diverse institutional spheres; and

c. ability to secularize religious values and to refashion them so as to provide value premises for building rational-legal organizational units; and

c. inability to secularize fully value premises and their translation into more secular beliefs and norms for building rational-legal units; and

d. reduction in salience of religious affiliation as a paramount categoric distinction.

d. ability to use other criteria, especially those based upon the nonkin division of labor, for making key categoric distinctions.

d. superimposition of religious categories on the rational-legal division of labor, thereby imposing a strong negative externality on the smooth functioning of labor markets, secular divisions of labor, and authority systems for coordinating labor.

(Continued on next page.)

115

**TABLE 2.** (Continued)

| Checklist of ideal institutional profiles | New forms of social capital generated | Checklist of real-world constraints imposed by older forms of social capital |
|---|---|---|
| (3) Economy: | Structuring of economic activity in terms of rational-legal organizational units using money as the dominant medium of exchange and complex markets generates the following types of social capital: | Failure, or inability, to structure the economy in terms of rational-legal corporate units, money as the dominant medium of exchange, and complex market systems erodes new forms of social capital in the following ways: |
| a. organization of production and distribution in rational-legal organizational units, revealing certain key properties: | a. capacity to generate organizational complexity and size in coordinating division of labor, along several dimensions: | a. the complexity of transactions, and the size of productive and distributive units, becomes restricted because: |
| 1. entrance-exit rules specifying the time, place, and media of exchange to be utilized, while specifying those values, beliefs, norms, and media of exchange that cannot be utilized; | 1. entrance-exit rules diminish effects of particularistic media of exchange, while assuring that formal rules, authority, beliefs, and norms focus on the goals of production; | 1. the lack of entrance-exit rules reduces the capacity to exclude media of exchange from other institutional spheres; |
| 2. reliance on a labor market and credentials of human capital in selecting incumbents; and | 2. use of labor market and systems of credentialing skill increases likelihood that human capital and requirements of the division of labor are matched; and | 2. the inability to use market systems and credentials decreases the ability of economic units to match human capital with the requirements of a more complex and rational division of labor; and |

3. reliance on money, rational-legal authority, and formal rules for coordinating activities and structuring inducements to human capital.

b. development of distributive infrastructure that is autonomous from infrastructures needed to sustain activities in other institutional spheres; and

c. development of market systems for distribution of goods and services in ever-widening spheres of social activity, and revealing the following properties:

1. the use of money as the medium of exchange in all transactions;

2. trust in the stability of money to bestow value, a trust backed up by commitments from polity;

3. use of money, rational-legal authority, and formal rules creates incentives for human capital that reinforce entrance-exit rules and lead to an efficient division of labor.

b. separate distributive infrastructure increases autonomy of economic actors from demands of other institutional spheres; and

c. development of market systems creates social capital along a number of fronts:

1. use of money enables actors to neutralize exchange relations, while excluding noneconomic media of exchange and segregating nonsecular values, beliefs, and norms from economic transactions;

2. trust in the purchasing power of money and its capacity to bestow value makes actors more willing to abandon more particularistic media of exchange;

3. other, more particularistic and nonrational systems of inducements work to undermine the power of entrance-exit rules and the efficiency of the division of labor.

b. when the distributive infrastructure is controlled by local kin networks, community elites, and other more localized systems, limits are placed on national-level market and productive forces; and

c. when market systems remain local, and detached from national production and distribution, they limit the formation of social capital by:

1. introducing nonmonetary media of exchange and systems of values, beliefs, and norms that restrict the range of potential transactions among actors;

2. preventing full trust in money as an alternative to other generalized media and the local networks built upon traditional values, beliefs, and norms;

*(Continued on next page.)*

TABLE 2. (Continued)

| Checklist of ideal institutional profiles | New forms of social capital generated | Checklist of real-world constraints imposed by older forms of social capital |
|---|---|---|
| 3. high levels of horizontal differentiation of markets, extending into ever-increasing number of spheres of social life and encouraging high levels of commodification of persons, objects, and social relations; and | 3. horizontal differentiation of markets encourages actors to develop trust in the capacity of money to bestow value in ever wider spheres of social relations and to individualize their needs and tastes in ways not allowed by other media of exchange, while making them willing to commodify and evaluate themselves in terms of money. Such changes escalate market demand and, thereby, promote development; and | 3. limiting the extent of market demand to a narrow range of goods and services; and |
| 4. high levels of vertical differentiation of metamarkets, creating diffuse trust across a wide and deep set of potential market transactions and developing in actors a willingness to be positionally and psychologically mobile networks. | 4. vertical differentiation creates a more diffuse sense of trust in market processes to bestow gratification, thereby making actors positionally and psychologically mobile because they are willing to invest resources beyond local markets and support. | 4. creating distrust and suspicion of money and markets beyond the networks supporting local traditions, thereby making individuals less positionally and psychologically mobile. |

*Source:* Author.

118

large-scale institutional processes that investments in development become prohibitively extensive and expensive. Still, some options are available—for example, investing in monetary stability, rational-legal corporate units, and penetration of national markets into local areas.

These problems of changing institutional-level processes through specific and limited investment strategies are, I imagine, one of the reasons that much development effort focuses on the mesolevel, as we explore next, but since the mesolevel is constrained by macroinstitutional processes, investment strategies must be alerted to the kinds of institutional forces in which corporate and categoric units are embedded.

## Mesolevel forces: the dynamics of corporate and categoric units

Social institutions are built from corporate and categoric units, as well as from the face-to-face interactions that occur within the encounters made possible by the structure of corporate and categoric units. We cannot, however, view social institutions as simply the sum of their respective corporate and categoric units, because institutions are emergent phenomena that, once differentiated into distinctive spheres, limit the nature and operation of their constituent components. For example, when a clearly differentiated economy exists, revealing distinctive productive organizations and dynamic markets, this system constrains the kinds of corporate units that can exist and the nature of categoric distinctions that can be made. Indeed, the existing system creates the resource niches in which corporate units must compete (Turner 1996; Hannan and Freeman 1989; McPherson and Ranger-Moore 1991); and when viewed in this way, institutional systems set the parameters within which selection processes work to generate certain kinds of corporate and categoric units. And this institutional constraint increases as the systems of relationships within polity and law become interwoven into those of the economy.

Yet, having said this, corporate and categoric structures reveal their own dynamics; and it is for this reason that these mesolevel units are often considered the best candidates for intervention by those seeking to encourage economic development. We should begin our ideal typical conceptualization of the mesolevel social universe by first reviewing the basic kinds of corporate and categoric units that would facilitate economic development.

With respect to *corporate* units, there are two basic kinds: (a) *organizational units*, which create a division of labor among individuals in order to pursue ends and goals; and (b) *spatial units*, which distribute people and organizational units in space. Examples of organizational units are firms, kin groupings (clans, moieties), voluntary associations, governmental agencies, and other relatively enduring structures revealing a division of labor for the pursuit of ends, whereas examples of spatial units include city, district, village, county, and region.

With respect to *categoric* units, these all involve distinguishing members of subpopulations in terms of some characteristic or set of characteristics and, then, using these to define the members of this subpopulation as distinctive, and on the basis of these definitions, treating them differently. Age (and its elaboration into age cohorts and categories) and sex (and its elaboration into gender distinctions) have been universal categories through human history, but with societies after hunting and gathering came additional categoric distinctions based on territory, religion, ethnicity, and social class.

Thus, mesolevel of analysis involves (a) the investigation of the ways that corporate units are organized, (b) the different kinds of categoric units that become salient to members of a population, and (c) the relationships between the two (Hawley 1986). Let me begin with organizational corporate units, moving next to spatial corporate units and, then, to key categoric units.

### Organizational corporate units

Development ultimately involves the differentiation of institutional spheres, giving each a certain degree of autonomy and enabling each to construct distinctive organizational forms. For development to proceed, kin units must move toward a more nuclear profile. It makes relatively little difference as to the form of religious organizational units, whether they are small or larger bureaucratic cults; the only key condition is that these organizational forms be excluded from economic, political, and legal organizational structures. The crucial condition for development, then, is for the organizational units within the economic, political, and legal system to have considerable autonomy from other institutional systems and, moreover, for each to reveal organizational forms that approximate Weber's portrayal of rational-legal bureaucracy. What are some of the critical features of such bureaucracies? Extending my earlier discussion, the most important features are reviewed below.

First, the organizations in this institutional triad of economy, polity, and law must all use their own and the other two's dominant generalized media of exchange. That is, transactions and actions must all be conducted in terms of money, power and authority, and imperative coordination. Other media of exchange must be subordinate to these and, if used in transactions, must be aligned with the way money, power, and imperative coordination are employed.

Second, these media must be used in particular ways. Money must be the basis for recruiting members to the organization and for structuring the reward system for performance within the division of labor. Power must be converted into rational authority and must, therefore, be the basis for allocating decision-making prerogatives, for giving directions, for monitoring conformity to directives and rules, and for imposing sanctions in the name of achieving organizational goals in an efficient manner. Imperative coordination must be translated into a codified set of formal rules, specifying entrance-exit conditions for human capital, indicating the precise nature of tasks and duties to be performed at each level and position in the organization, and applying expectations equally for those incumbent in a particular position (that is, universalism).

Third, encounters of face-to-face interactions within the organization will inevitably generate sentiments and use other media of exchange, such as loyalty, friendship, and social approval. These must produce commitments among human capital that are aligned with the goals of the organization and that support the rule and authority systems. This "informal system" of relations is particularly effective if it can produce a highly valuable joint good—sociality, friendship, and approval, for example—that is reinforcing to members, since members will then monitor and sanction free-riding in ways that reduce the need to use (and high costs in so using) the formal authority system (Olson 1965; Hechter 1987).

The same can be said for informal relations that develop in organizations such as voluntary associations and clubs, and that operate outside the formal boundaries of economic, political, and legal organizational forms. The types of particularized social capital—informal networks, contacts, gossip, friendships, information—that emerge in these outside contacts must also be loosely aligned with the goals of the organizations in economy, polity, and law. Even kinship networks can operate this way, although these generally tend to introduce generalized media of exchange that subvert formal organizational goals. Thus, organizational forms in the environment of rational-legal organizations in the economic, political, and legal spheres must not pull the loyalties and commitments of key decision-makers too far from their commitments to formal organizational goals; instead, they should be used to facilitate the realization of these goals.

Whether directly involved in production and distribution or performing supportive functions in making binding decisions (polity) and providing imperative coordination (law) for these productive and distributive processes, rational-legal organizational systems are important for economic development. They exclude or subordinate generalized media of exchange that could lower the efficiency of the organization or that could encourage corruption and graft. Of course, no rational-legal organizational form in the real world could meet this ideal of using only money, authority, and imperative coordination to organize the division of labor, but this ideal gives us a yardstick for calibrating and comparing actual organizational forms in a society.

Rational-legal organizations also generate social capital by virtue of structural equivalences among such organizations. For, as organizations employ the same media of exchange, such as money and authority, to organize human capital in a division of labor, this equivalence of structure allows individuals at similar locations in different organizations to have convergent experiences, to develop common outlooks and, as a result, to possess the capacity to move from one organization to another without having to relearn *how* to perform.

Table 3 summarizes the details of the arguments presented above. As was done for macroinstitutional forces, a checklist of characteristics generating new forms of social capital is presented, as is a checklist of older forms of social capital that restrict the formation of those newer forms. To the degree that the features listed on the left side of the table exist in a society, investments in such structures will promote the types of social capital listed in the middle column. But in most developing societies, the real-world constraints arrayed on the right undermine and deplete these new forms of social capital.

### Spatial corporate units

Populations are distributed in space, and this distribution reflects the number and nature of corporate units that partition space and, thereby, create geographical boundaries in which self-governance occurs. What emerges in any society, then, is a *system* of villages, townships, cities, and metropolitan areas that are spread across larger spatial units such as states, counties, districts, areas, and regions. For our purposes in building an ideal type, it is reasonable to ask: What properties of this system would most facilitate development?

First, the geographical units would need to constitute an integrated and coherent system in which (a) jurisdictional boundaries among spatial units are clear and supported by law; (b) administrative structures within boundaries are rational-legal in their organizational forms; (c) administrative rights and obligations are specified by law; (d) governance by administrators is subject to influence by vested interests and public opinion; and (e) infrastructural developments are sufficient to ensure relatively easy movements of information, materials, and people among spatial units. When spatial units constitute a system revealing these features, the similarity of structure and the connections among them enable economic, legal, and political actions to flow readily from place to place, uninterrupted by local cultural forces, local power brokers, and local bodies of law and tradition. This kind of integration and coherence, then, represents an important form of social capital because it facilitates the dispersion and adoption of economic changes, political directives, and new means of imperative coordination with law.

Second, the geographical units would reveal some diversity in the relative size, such that in addition to large cities or metropolitan regions, there would be middle-sized cities linked to smaller townships. Gradations in city size, as well as their proportionate dispersion across all parts of a society's territory, provide a system of linkages from small through intermediate to

TABLE 3: THE FORMATION OF SOCIAL CAPITAL IN ORGANIZATIONAL UNITS

| Checklist of ideal characteristics of corporate units | New forms of social capital generated | Checklist of real-world constraints imposed by older forms of social capital |
|---|---|---|
| Organizational units structure the division of labor in the economic, political, and legal institutional sphere in ways that increase: | | |
| (1) Organizational autonomy from the units in other institutional spheres. | Autonomy of organizational units enables them to build structures tailored to the distinctive problems of a particular institutional sphere, while segregating these structures from domination by other institutional systems not conducive to economic development. | Penetration or overlap among organizations meeting institutional needs infuses values, beliefs, norms, and generalized media not appropriate for development of rational-legal units, while superimposing networks that are not appropriate for development of rational-legal systems. |
| (2) Rational-legal structures in which: a. use of money, power, and imperative coordination are the dominant media of exchange; | Money, power, and imperative coordination are media that increase the capacity to build complex structures organizing relatively large pools of human capital; | To the extent that media from kinship, community, religion, and personal networks erode the salience and use of money, rational power, and imperative coordination by formal or universalistic rules, the complexity of organizational units is limited, as is their efficiency; |

(Continued on next page.)

TABLE 3. *(continued)*

| *Checklist of ideal characteristics of corporate units* | *New forms of social capital generated* | *Checklist of real-world constraints imposed by older forms of social capital* |
|---|---|---|
| b. money is the media used for recruiting human capital to organizational units and for constructing the incentive systems ensuring performance by human capital; | Money neutralizes other media of exchange, quantifies assessments of value, encourages labor market development, and provides a standardized reinforcer for manipulating incentives within and between organizations; | Nonmonetary media are not generalizable, not easily quantified, not convertible beyond the networks in which they are produced; and to the extent that they limit the use of money, they reduce the capacity to develop labor markets and standardized reinforcers in organizing human capital; |
| c. power is converted into rational authority and is perceived to operate in ways increasing the efficiency of coordinated activities in realizing organizational goals; | Power translated into authority facilitates the coordination of the division of labor in terms of media of exchange tied to the goals of the organization rather than the characteristics of actors or their personal relations, thereby neutralizing the effects of more particularistic media inside and from outside the organization; | If authority is dependent on personal characteristics of actors, and on their location in networks and units outside an organization, then authority cannot be used to build large, complex, and efficient divisions of labor in pursuit of narrow goals; |
| d. imperative coordination is translated into a set of formal and universalistic rules specifying entrance-exit conditions, performance obligations of human capital, and lines of authority; | Coordination by formal, universalistic rules gives "sovereignty" to rules as existing outside persons and personalities, thereby providing a way to structure the division of labor on an efficient basis that does not rely on personal or particularistic media of exchange; | Rules that are not sovereign, that operate above and beyond specific actors and actions, that are not formal, and that are not universalistically applied cannot generate large, complex, flexible, and efficient organizational units, because they are too embedded in traditions, particularistic networks, and media not conducive to forming rational systems of authority or monetary measures of value; |

124

| | | |
|---|---|---|
| e. encounters of face-to-face contact within a rational-legal organization that use media of exchange other than money, power, and imperative coordination remain aligned with organizational goals; and | Aligned interpersonal encounters create a highly valued intrinsic reinforcer, giving actors incentives to conform to norms and to monitor and sanction each other's conformity to formal rules and systems of authority; and | Nonaligned interpersonal encounters generate knowledge and emotional dispositions that weaken conformity to rules, acceptance of authority, incentives based on monetary rewards for performance, or pursuit of organizational goals; and |
| f. encounters of face-to-face contact outside a rational-legal organization that use media of exchange other than money, power, and imperative coordination will either be isolated from the organization by entrance-exit rules or, if not isolated, aligned with organizational goals. | Aligned interpersonal encounters outside the organization create informal systems, with their own monitoring and sanctioning, that can facilitate meeting organizational goals. | Nonaligned networks of personal relations outside an organization create informal systems that challenge the appropriateness of money as a measure of value, the appropriateness of formal rules, and the acceptance of rational authority. |
| (3) Patterns of structural equivalence in the form and operation of rational-legal organizational units. | Structural equivalence around a division of labor structured in terms of rules, authority, and money gives human capital transferable skills, outlooks, orientations, and dispositions. | Older patterns of structural equivalence—such as kin and community structures—are less transferable, because they are organized by nonrational authority, less formal rules, and particularistic media of exchange. |

*Source:* Author.

very large, and vice versa. Movements of goods and services through markets, and migrations of individuals, can be more readily achieved under these conditions because there is less discontinuity between smaller and larger communities. Moreover, when mid-sized cities exist, development can target these in ways that can often spill over to smaller townships (creating opportunities for work and less intimidating exposure to new forms of social capital) and, at the same time, provide economic (for example, markets, organizational forms) and infrastructural bases (for example, roads, ports, communications, plants, and facilities) for macrolevel economic, political, and legal processes.

When a society reveals one or two large cities and many small township systems, however, this discontinuity often creates problems in connecting events in large urban cores to the outlying population because there is no intermediate system of markets, organizations, administrative agencies, and legal agents to facilitate the flow of goods and services, the implementation of political directives, or the codes of the legal system. Additionally, when such discontinuity between large and small spatial units occurs, migration patterns often produce large, shantytown masses in substandard housing around the core cities. These masses have come to seek opportunities that do not exist, but that might have been available if there had been moderate-size cities near their townships and villages. When migration patterns involve large-scale movements from isolated village-township structures to large urban areas, migrants bring with them cultural systems that do not prepare them for integration into the larger urban core, draining physical capital for social control and social services that could otherwise be used to finance economic development.

Third, the patterns of institutional differentiation evident at the larger and mid-sized cities need to penetrate into smaller villages and townships, thereby reducing discontinuity in economic, political, and legal processes between large and small spatial units. To the extent that there is discontinuity, smaller community structures will present obstacles to full national development, although such communities can be organized successfully for local development projects.

Development is encouraged, then, by a system of spatial units, varying in size, revealing isomorphism or structural equivalence in their administrative structure, evidencing similar institutions and organizational forms within institutional spheres, and being connected by a well-developed distributive infrastructure. Under these conditions the social capital generated by institutional processes can more readily penetrate outlying areas and, as a consequence, accelerate development in these areas. And, at the same time, development in outlying areas can provide the economic and infrastructural base for national-level development. Table 4 summarizes this ideal-typical system of spatial units, while indicating how older types of social

TABLE 4: The Formation of Social Capital in Spatial Units

| Checklist of characteristics of spatial units | New forms of social capital generated | Checklist of real-world constraints imposed by older forms of social capital |
|---|---|---|
| (1) The extent to which spatial units form an integrated system of community forms, along the following lines: | Systemic nature of community forms increases capacity to move information, resources, materials, and people, while providing the administrative capacity to coordinate such movements and to use them to promote economic development: | The less coherent and integrated the system of communities, the more likely will the effects of development in one area to be disconnected to that in another, creating vast differences in the degree of development across a society—which, in turn, discourages national economic development and promotes inequalities and the resulting tensions between regions and communities: |
| a. clarity of jurisdictional boundaries supported by law; | Legally sanctioned boundaries reduce the chances of territorial disputes, which could deplete human, social, and physical capital available for development; legally sanctioned boundaries also provide a judicial infrastructure and framework within which development can proceed; | Disputes over territory tend to make appeals to traditions, kinship, and other highly volatile media of exchange—which, in turn, escalate the intensity of conflict and, thereby, deplete the amount of physical and social capital available to development; |

(Continued on next page.)

TABLE 4. (continued)

| Checklist of characteristics of spatial units | New forms of social capital generated | Checklist of real-world constraints imposed by older forms of social capital |
|---|---|---|
| b. rational-legal administrative organizational units within spatial units coordinating activities; | Rational-legal administration of communities provides the administrative infrastructure for development by virtue of employing money, authority, and rules for organizing development efforts, as well as for redressing disputes as they arise; | Traditional forms of community leadership, and the networks on which they are built, often find the conversion to rational-legal development threatening to their interests, leading them to sabotage efforts to develop administrative structures or, at the very least, to render them less effective by virtue of imposing traditional authority, rules, and media on top of newer administrative forms of social capital; |
| c. administrative rights and obligations that are specified by written laws emanating from autonomous legal system; | Autonomous legal system sanctioning of administrative rights and obligations gives corporate actors in economic spheres assurances of their rights to engage in activities within communities; | Traditional systems of rules within kinship, community, or religion may challenge authority and autonomy of laws from an external legal system; |
| d. high capacity for public and vested interests to influence administrative decisions; and | Democratic election of decision-makers ensures that the administrative infrastructure in communities is responsive to the economic demands of individuals and organizational units; and | Traditional community and kin leaders often find electoral politics threatening to their interests, leading them to oppose local administrative structures in which key decision-makers are elected and responsive to the interests of publics or new types of organizational units involved in economic development; and |

| | | |
|---|---|---|
| e. developed infrastructure for moving of people, materials, and information within and between spatial units. | Infrastructural development within and between communities allows labor to move to labor markets, while providing the physical structures necessary for the creation, spread, and expansion of productive and marketing operations. | New infrastructural developments almost always dismantle traditional categoric and organizational units, and as a result, new infrastructural developments are often opposed by those who fear that these will destroy traditional interests and privileges. |
| (2) Diversity and dispersion of varying-sized spatial units linked together by infrastructural development. | Systems of varying-sized units from small (villages or townships) through intermediate-sized urban centers, to large cities provide an infrastructure of progressive linkages for moving people, materials, and information, while also providing sites for linking markets across large territories. | Interconnected systems of spatial units ensure that traditional categoric and organizational units that once structured social life will be disrupted, as human capital leaves and as new categoric and organizational forms move in, leading efforts to block connections to larger urban centers. |
| (3) Institutional penetration of economy, polity, and law from largest to smallest spatial units in all parts of a society's borders. | Organizational and categoric unit penetration down into local communities increases likelihood that smallest spatial units will be plugged into national-level economy, polity, and legal system in ways that make each of these institutional spheres more viable, and especially more viable in pushing economic development. | Penetration of economy, polity, and law will often be resisted by local communities because they introduce media of exchange and organizational forms that threaten traditional elites' network structures and corporate forms giving them power, authority, and privilege. |

*Source:* Author.

capital can impede the production of the social capital necessary for sustained and national-level development.

## Categoric units

In an idealized world geared only toward economic development, categoric distinctions would correspond to major divisions in labor. These differences in the skills and related attributes of human capital would be established by an educational sphere that, in essence, would grade human capital in terms of types and levels of skill and, as a result, provide the credentials that would be bought and sold in a frictionless labor market. And, as the developing economy demanded new types of labor, these too would be translated into demand in a labor market for new categories of human capital. Such classifications would indeed produce "class" distinctions but these would be based on the value of skills for the organizational units structuring employment opportunities.

Outside of hunting and gathering societies, the western political democracies come as close to this ideal as any society, although considerable ascription on the basis of gender, ethnicity, and social class categories remains—ascription not based on requirements of the division of labor or the abilities of individuals but, rather, upon traditional kinship and stratification systems. When family or class background, gender, or ethnicity determine access to positions in key institutional spheres or in the educational system providing the credentials necessary to gain access to employment, individuals in these categories are denied money and the resources it can buy as well as honor and prestige, authority and power. These inequalities partition the pool of human capital and, in so doing, prevent those who could potentially contribute to escalated production from even getting a chance. At times, discrimination can force members of excluded categories to develop their own human and social capital, as is the case with "middleman minorities" or "ethnic entrepreneurs" (Light and Karageorgis 1994; Portes and Landolt 1996), but this kind of niche activity rarely leads to macrolevel development because the human and social capital contained in these niche-oriented economic activities is still partially segregated from the core economy. For when such human and social capital is so segregated, it is not available as an investment in the full range of economic activity necessary for sustained development.

Inequalities arising from categoric distinctions and social discrimination also create tensions between those who have access to these resources and those who do not; and these tensions, often erupting into episodes of violence or feeding escalating rates of crime and deviance, dramatically raise the costs to polity and law for monitoring and social control. As these costs increase, investments in physical and human capital decline, and as a consequence, development stagnates while polity and agents in the legal system mobilize to reduce or suppress intercategory conflicts or acts of deviance caused by frustrations over discrimination.

As these social control functions of polity and law escalate, they will bias the consolidation of power toward the coercive-administrative side and away from use of material incentives and reliance on cultural symbols, including the generalized media of exchange in economy (money and its stability), power (and its legitimation as rational authority), and law (imperative coordination by universalistic rules); and as acts of repression and other forms of social control harden categoric boundaries, a polity and its increasingly less autonomous legal system become locked into a cycle of deterioration that revolves around social control—more intercategoric tension, and more repressive social control.

Thus, the more categoric distinctions and associated inequalities deviate from the incentives used to recruit and promote individuals in rational-legal organization in economy, polity, law, and other institutional systems, the greater will be the depletion of all forms of capital because corporate unit activity in polity and law will incur costs unrelated to economic development and, thereby, reduce not only the amount of money available for investments in physical and human capital but also the level of organizational resources or social capital available for investment in economic development. Thus, what becomes critical is the magnitude of the disjuncture between the requirements of the division of labor organized in rational-legal corporate units and the socially constructed divisions of people into categories restricting opportunities to gain access to valued resources such as money, prestige, and authority.

Categoric distinctions always shape the flow of face-to-face interaction in encounters, both those inside organizational units and outside in the public sphere. Categoric units influence the flow of interpersonal encounters by determining who interacts with whom, as well as how they interact. If categoric distinctions involve considerable inequality in the respective resources of interactants from different social categories, then encounters will involve highly stylized and ritualized sequences of deference and demeanor rituals—so as to lower the monitoring costs of superordinates for assuring that proper deference is given and also to lower the conformity costs of subordinates for engaging in demeanor that confirms their inferiority (Goffman 1967; Collins 1975). Yet, no matter how ritualized such encounters are, they still impose high costs. One cost is the emotional energy used to emit the proper deference and demeanor rituals; and the more energy expended on such rituals, the less it is available for other activities. Thus, when a division of labor revolving around rational-legal rules and authority in organizational units has extraorganizational categoric distinctions that must be honored in face-to-face interactions, the alignment between encounters and the goals of the organization is disrupted, as actors' emotional energies are spent upholding categoric distinctions. Another cost is equality, which forces individuals to spend some portion of their time pursuing behaviors unrelated to their jobs; and moreover, inequalities create tensions, making smooth coordination difficult as resentments lead to conflicts and as conflicts, once initiated, take on a life of their own and consume individuals' time and energy. Even a rational authority system presents this problem, and this is why it is so important that authority be seen by members of the organization as facilitating the pursuit of organizational goals. When it does not—and such is especially likely to be the case if extraorganizational status systems are superimposed on rational authority or if such systems operate at cross purposes to rational authority— then the level of social capital is lowered because coordinated efforts become sidetracked from achieving organizational goals.

Thus, in an ideal organizational world, the only categoric distinctions would be those produced by the division of labor and authority system in rational-legal organizations; however, those revolving around authority must be downplayed so that super- and subordinates do not deflect too much energy monitoring, sanctioning, and abiding by inequalities in authority. Indeed, the ideal situation is one in which the formal authority system is hardly noticeable because actors at any given level of authority generate intrinsic and jointly produced goods—such as social approval, friendship, and solidarity—that increase their commitments to the organization. Under these conditions monitoring and sanctioning from the formal authority system can be relaxed as individuals positively reinforce each other for their conformity to rules and contributions to meeting organizational goals.

Thus, to the extent that the efficiency of organizational units is considered to be a form of social capital, the interpersonal forces by which this organizationally generated social capital is produced become very important. Categoric distinctions are one of the important bases for defining what kinds of face-to-face interactions occur, and how they unfold; and when these become too prominent or are misaligned with the formal rules and authority system of organizations, the level of social capital produced at the micro- and mesolevels is reduced. Table 5 summarizes these lines of argument.

Interpersonal processes reveal their own dynamics, above and beyond the categoric distinctions that people in a society make and the organizational structures in which they interact. Before completing our review of a utopian society, then, we need to examine the dynamics of this microlevel social universe.

### Microlevel social forces: the dynamics of interpersonal behavior

Erving Goffman (1967) made a useful distinction between what he termed "focused" and "unfocused" interaction. *Focused* interaction occurs in "en-

TABLE 5: THE FORMATION OF SOCIAL CAPITAL IN CATEGORIC UNITS

| Checklist of characteristics of categoric units | New forms of social capital generated | Checklist of real-world constraints imposed by older forms of social capital |
|---|---|---|
| Categoric units are constructed in such a way that the following conditions prevail: | | |
| (1) The division of labor within rational-legal, as well as between types of rational-legal units in diverse institutional spheres, provides the basis for all major categoric distinctions in society; | Provides a nonascriptive basis for social categories, and a basis that facilitates the operation of labor markets in terms of relevant work skills and the internal operation of organizational units in terms of social categories corresponding to the division of labor and authority system of rational-legal units; | Ascriptive distinctions by gender, race and ethnicity, and strata in old stratification systems continue to remain salient and to apportion opportunities for gaining access to positions in corporate units, thereby restricting the pool of qualified human capital and undermining the operation of open labor markets and rational-legal organizational units; |
| (2) The division of labor within and between rational-legal organizational units in the economic, political, and legal spheres, as well as those spheres supplying technology or human capital (for example, science and education), dominates in the formation of categoric units; and | Provides nonascriptive basis for selecting human capital in labor markets and for promoting human capital within rational-legal organizational units essential to economic development; | Ascriptive and categoric distinctions unrelated to the division of labor and the efficient operation of rational-legal organizational units continue to determine access to opportunities in labor markets, or to operate as a substitute for open labor markets, while determining the basis for promotion of human capital in organizational units, thereby undermining the efficiency of those units most essential to economic development; and |

(Continued on next page.)

TABLE 5. (continued)

| Checklist of characteristics of categoric units | New forms of social capital generated | Checklist of real-world constraints imposed by older forms of social capital |
|---|---|---|
| (3) All encounters of face-to-face interaction within rational-legal organizational units are structured in terms of categoric distinctions corresponding to the division of labor and authority system of these rational-legal units. | Ensures that microlevel interactions among human capital reinforce relevant distinctions corresponding to the division of labor within rational-legal organizational units. | Distinctions from other corporate and categoric units (for example, gender, ethnicity, region of origin, country of origin, family class position) remain salient and distort episodes of interaction in ways creating expenditures of ritual energy unrelated to task performance in the division of labor; such distinctions also highlight points of tension and conflict, thereby reducing the efficiency of rational-legal organizations. |

*Source:* Author.

134

counters" that evidence a number of important features: a single visual and cognitive focus of attention; a mutual and preferential openness to verbal communication; a heightened mutual relevance of acts; an eye-to-eye ecological huddle; maximized mutual perception and monitoring; an emerging "we" feeling of solidarity and corresponding flow of emotions; a ritual and ceremonial punctuation of openings, closings, entrances, and exits from the ecological huddle; and a set of procedures, typically couched in rituals, for corrective compensation for deviant acts or breaches to the flow of interaction. In contrast to this kind of focused interaction in encounters, unfocused situations feature a mutual awareness of others' presence in public places that do not involve a close ecological huddle, eye-to-eye contact, prolonged sequences of talk, a mutual openness to communication, or an emergent "we" feeling and attendant emotional arousal. People's abilities to move in and out of encounters, while moving about in public space in ways that maintain order, can be seen as a form of social capital. Without the interpersonal ability and agility to engage in both focused and unfocused interactions, the social order would soon crumble.

Yet, beyond this generalized interpersonal social capital, we need to examine the dynamics of focused interactions in encounters that, typically, are lodged within organizational units and that invoke and sustain important categoric distinctions. When encounters occur, two basic types of interpersonal social capital are produced. (1) interpersonal emotional arousal; and (2) interpersonal knowledgeability. Let me begin with emotional social capital and, then, turn to the interpersonal knowledgeability as social capital.

### Emotional social capital in encounters

If an interaction has proceeded smoothly, sentiments revolving around the primary emotional complex of satisfaction and happiness are aroused in varying degrees of intensity, whereas if the interaction has been tense and conflictive, more negative emotional complexes—aversion-fear, assertion-anger, or disappointment-sadness—are likely to be activated. More positive emotions are aroused when individuals feel that their conception of themselves, or self, has been confirmed, when they sense that they have received payoffs, both extrinsic and intrinsic, proportionate to their status and investments, and when they sense that others can be trusted to behave in predictable and reliable ways (Turner 1988). The positive emotions generated under these conditions can become a jointly produced and consumed good, especially as encounters are iterated over time. When the emotional mood of the encounter becomes, itself, a joint good that is consumed, intrinsic payoffs in the form of sociality, solidarity, positive sentiments, attachments to others, and other associative emotional states become ever more important in relation to any extrinsic payoffs, such as money.

This kind of emotional social capital is generated when individuals become dependent on the contexts within which encounters are embedded, with dependence increasing when the face-to-face network of relations is dense, the costs for leaving the organizational units within which emotion-generating encounters occur are high, and the amount of information about alternatives to current encounters is low. The great benefit of such emotionally charged and iterated encounters is that they reduce the costs of formal monitoring and sanctioning, *if* the emotions generated are aligned with the goals of the more inclusive organization in which they are embedded. For as intrinsic reinforcers become highly rewarding, the participants in the encounter will themselves monitor and sanction each others' conformity to informal normative expectations; and individuals will become motivated to perform roles in ways that meet formal norms because they enjoy the positive sanctions and emotions that arise as a result of their iterated interactions.

Emotional social capital has a unique feature that is typical of most types of social capital: to consume it is to produce it. That is, when individuals consume the positive emotions given off by others, they also produce these emotions because the process of accepting approval, friendship, and sociality also generates these positive emotions. This is why interactions can increase the emotional stakes rapidly: the joint good is not depleted in consumption but, instead, augmented—at least up to the point of fatigue, satiation, or marginal utility. Conversely, inherent in this self-escalating cycle are the reasons that, once severely breached, the emotional mood of an interaction can turn toward the negative side and quickly unravel: if negative emotions such as anger, fear, or disappointment are aroused, they swiftly escalate into negative externalities unless corrective repair rituals are immediately offered. And if negative emotions rise, they deplete the more positive emotional capital that had been accumulated.

Thus, in an ideal world oriented only to efficiency of production, emotional social capital is produced and consumed in ways that reinforce formal norms, systems of authority, and organizational goals. Moreover, episodes of anger, fear, and disappointment are quickly repaired so that they do not deplete the positive emotional capital accumulated in the many daily encounters that ultimately make up the social structure of the organization. Under these conditions, human capital is willing to perform roles with maximum emotional commitment and, hence, efficiency. Of course, this kind of alignment of interpersonally generated emotional social capital with the requirements of organizational units rarely occurs, for several reasons:

First, formal rules and authority systems involved in monitoring and sanctioning always hold out the prospects of negative sanctioning which, inevitably, will interrupt the buildup of positive emotional energy in encounters; and if formal monitoring and sanctioning are intrusive, the emotions aroused from face-to-face encounters of subordinates will involve elements that run against the norms, authority systems, and goals of the formal organization. Indeed, the emerging emotional social capital will often be used as a defensive measure to protect and insulate human capital from the formal system of authority.

Second, human capital almost always brings into the formal organizational system emotional social capital produced and consumed in other social encounters lodged in alternative organizational units, such as kin networks, social clubs and organizations, and even spatial units such as villages or towns. As this emotional social capital is consumed in the encounters among human capital, it is also produced; and its production provides alternative intrinsic reinforcers to the extrinsic payoffs of a formal system, while blocking the formation of emotional social capital more aligned with organizational goals. Such processes are particularly likely to ensue if employment is not secure, thereby making human capital unwilling to commit its emotional resources to organizational goals.

### Knowledgeability as social capital in encounters

All interactions involve efforts by individuals—typically revolving around their use of rituals or stereotyped sequences of gestures—to establish their respective roles, to confirm their sense of self, to categorize each other and situations, to establish frames for delimiting what is to be excluded and included in the interaction, to assert and accept validity claims that they themselves and others are behaving appropriately and sincerely, and to develop normative agreements about how they and others are to behave (see Turner 1988). The processes through which these efforts occur are complex, but for our purposes, we really only need to understand that a great deal of interaction involves creating a store of knowledge about roles, norms, categories, frames, and validity claims. If these can be agreed upon, then the interaction can begin to produce the emotional interpersonal capital in terms of the dynamics examined above; but this knowledgeability is itself an important form of social capital.

If individuals understand and agree on their respective roles, their categorizations of each other and the situation, their frameworks for deciding what is to be included and excluded in the encounter, their respective claims as acting sincerely and appropriately, and their understandings for what each is expected to do, they have the necessary resources to sustain the interaction. Moreover, as noted above, agreement on such matters of knowledgeability is itself a positive reinforcer, arousing positive emotional energies. Conversely, if an agreement cannot be reached, the interaction will be charged with dissociative emotional energy.

In an ideal universe geared solely toward efficient production, the organizational structure establishes this necessary knowledgeability by formally specifying roles, norms, frames, categories, and modes for expressing validity claims. And, in this ideal universe, human capital would suspend alternative stocks of knowledgeability from other organizational units. Again, in the real world, this kind of alignment of organizational structure and the interpersonal knowledgeability rarely occurs, for a number of reasons:

First, the process of interaction itself will elaborate organizationally imposed knowledgeability with idiosyncratic and particularistic knowledgeability produced and consumed by individuals as they come to understand (a) the stylistic touches that each person brings to a role, (b) the more personal and intimate categorization of others, (c) the movement of frames to increasingly personal perceptions of others, (d) the redefinition of what it means to be sincere and to act appropriately, and (e) the elaboration of formal norms into an informal system that only partially embodies formal requirements and expectations. There is no way to stop this creation of particularistic knowledgeability, short of making humans into machines or cyborgs.

Second, human capital always brings to formal organizations knowledgeability from other encounters outside the organization and uses elements of this knowledgeability to build alternatives to that imposed by the organization. Indeed, the building up of emotional social capital and the informal system of relations within an organization typically draws on knowledgeability gained in other encounters, such as those revolving around friendship or kinship. And, as is the case with emotional social capital, interpersonal knowledgeability using roles, frames, norms, categories, and modes for expressing sincerity and appropriateness of behavior are progressively more likely to be imported into a formal organization when human capital does not feel that its place is secure.

Thus, microlevel interpersonal processes systematically generate emotional moods and stocks of knowledgeability that operate as social capital, in at least this sense: these interpersonal processes are resources that are developed and invested in creating and sustaining interpersonal relations. They are essential to the viability of encounters; and meso- and macrolevel social forces ultimately depend upon this viability. The difficult problem in mobilizing these interpersonal resources is their degree of alignment with the system of rules and authority in formal organizations pursuing productive goals. This alignment problem is less severe when kin and other local communal corporate units organize production, but with the expansion and differentiation of production away from older corporate forms, the problem of aligning particularistic emotional commitments and knowledgeability to the productional goals of rational-legal organizations grows.

This alignment problem poses dilemmas for those seeking to invest in social capital. If efforts are made to utilize traditional corporate units— kinship and village systems, for example, and the social networks that these generate—then mobilizing interpersonal social capital (that is, emotional commitments and knowledgeability among those engaged in iterated focused encounters) is straightforward: seek out the most central nodes in the networks as well as the densely related nodes forming cliques in networks and, then, attempt to piggyback developmental projects on the emotional ties and knowledgeability produced and consumed in focused interactions among individuals.

There are, however, problems with this strategy. One is that the interpersonal social capital being used for development goals is particularistic and, thereby, tied to specific individuals in local kin and communal units. In other words, it is not the kind of social capital that can be generalized and used to form productive social relations outside the units in which it is consumed and produced. Such particularism places limits on how extensive development goals can become above and beyond the local area or region.

For more extensive and dynamic development, investment must eventually be made in more generalized interpersonal social capital, or interpersonal skills that can be used in organizational units in which (a) formal rules and rational authority systems organize the division of labor, (b) impersonal labor markets select and deploy human capital, and (c) extrinsic reinforcers such as money attract and retain human capital. Such investments would seek to develop interpersonal social capital along several lines. First, individuals must be willing to sell themselves in a labor market and, in the process, redefine their self in terms of a neutral medium of exchange such as money. Second, individuals must be willing to leave emotional attachments and knowledgeability behind and, instead, pursue new nonkin, noncommunal emotional attachments and knowledgeability. Third, they must have emotional experience in, and knowledge about, how to participate in encounters structured by formal systems of rules and authority directed to narrow goals of productive efficiency. And fourth, they must be willing to develop and consume interpersonal social capital compatible with and constrained by the formal system of rules and authority. If these conditions can be met, then it is at least possible to align microlevel social forces with those at the meso- and macrolevel. This basic argument is summarized in table 6.

## Conclusions

Social capital is formed at many different levels of societal organization; and it is important to recognize this fact when considering investment strategies for increasing the level of social capital available to a society. In this chapter, various types of social capital have been highlighted at

TABLE 6: THE FORMATION OF SOCIAL CAPITAL IN ENCOUNTERS

| Checklist of characteristics of encounters | New forms of social capital generated | Checklist of real-world constraints imposed by older forms of social capital |
| --- | --- | --- |
| Face-to-face interactions among individuals in rational-legal organizational units produce: | | |
| (1) Emotional social capital revolving around: | Emotional arousal, per se, increases commitments and energy in performing tasks: | Emotional arousal can also increase commitments and energy for nonperformance of tasks. |
| a. positive emotions built from the basic primary emotion of satisfaction-happiness; | Positive emotional arousal is highly reinforcing and increases commitments to, and energy for, tasks; | Emotional arousal need not be positive, and when built from negative emotions, deflects energy from task performance; |
| b. positive emotions aligned with the requirements of the division of labor and goals of organizational units; and | Positive emotional energy aligned with division of labor and organizational goals increases commitments of human capital to performance of tasks and to behaviors directed toward realizing organizational goals; and | Emotional energy, whether positive or negative, may not always be aligned with the division of labor of rational-legal organizations; instead particularistic emotions aligned with alternative divisions of labor in other corporate units and categoric distinctions may dominate task performance; and |
| c. positive emotions as a jointly produced and consumed good that provides intrinsic reinforcement, such that: | Positive emotions as a joint good provide an alternative basis for reinforcement, above and beyond extrinsic reinforcers such as money and authority, and make individuals even more committed and energetic in performance of tasks: | Positive emotions as a joint good can provide alternatives for extrinsic reinforcers, but make individuals committed and energetic in activities not aligned with the formal rules, authority system, or goals of rational-legal organizations: |

1. individuals monitor and sanction each other for free-riding in the production and consumption of this intrinsic good; and

2. the production and consumption of the intrinsic joint good, as well as informal monitoring and sanctioning, are aligned with the formal norms, system of authority, and goals of rational-legal organizational units.

(2) Knowledgeability revolving around:

a. the restrictions and mandates of the division of labor, norms, and goals of rational legal organizational units, particularly with respect to their agreements over:

Monitoring and sanctioning of production and consumption of intrinsic joint good provide a supplemental and, when extensive, more efficient alternative to monitoring and sanctioning by formal authority; and

Alignment of informal monitoring and sanctioning with formal norms, systems of authority, and goals of rational-legal organizations reduces the need for formal monitoring and sanctioning, while at the same time increasing commitments and energy in the performance of tasks.

The production of informal agreements over respective roles, self-presentations and confirmations, frames, validity claims, and norms provides the essential resources for all interactions to proceed; and when the production of this knowledgeability is done within the formal norms, requirements of the division of labor, and authority system, and when this knowledgeability is aligned with the goals of the organization, it increases the resources available for social relations that in turn improve the efficiency of human capital:

Extensive informal monitoring and sanctioning of free-riding in production and consumption of an intrinsic joint good can, when not aligned with the division of labor in rational-legal organizational units, require even more formal monitoring and sanctioning by authority, thereby increasing costs to organizational units; and

Misalignment of informal system with norms, authority systems, and organizational goals not only increases costs of formal monitoring and sanctioning, but when sanctions are deployed and used, they raise the negative emotional energy among human capital—which further escalates the costs of monitoring and sanctioning, while reducing commitments of human capital to task performance.

Interactions always generate idiosyncratic and particularistic knowledge, regardless of the formal organizational constraints. This knowledgeability will always, to some degree, be misaligned with formal rules, authority systems, and organizational goals; and to the degree that such misalignment is produced, the resources used by human capital to sustain their social relations will lower the efficiency of their task performance, and as a result, increase the costs for more formal monitoring and sanctioning of conformity to formal rules and the requirements of the division of labor:

(Continued on next page.)

TABLE 6. (*continued*)

| Checklist of characteristics of encounters | New forms of social capital generated | Checklist of real-world constraints imposed by older forms of social capital |
|---|---|---|
| 1. the respective roles of human capital and the style with which they are played; | Consensus over knowledgeability is, per se, a positive reinforcer, and when it arouses positive emotions, it sets into motion the emotional processes delineated above under (1) (in the left column). | If the knowledgeability of human capital comes from outside the rational-legal organizational unit and builds on resources from kin, friendship, and communal social relations, the probability of misalignment escalates, generating lower efficiency, while imposing additional costs for formal monitoring and sanctioning; and |
| 2. the way in which the self-conceptions of human capital are displayed and confirmed; | | |
| 3. the boundaries of frames being imposed on the flow of interaction; | | If emotional arousal is built from idiosyncratic and particularistic characteristics of the human capital in encounters, or if it is imported past the entrance-exit rules of a rational-legal organization from outside social relations, emotional processes will work against organizational efficiency; and if formal sanctioning and monitoring are used too extensively, negative emotions will be aroused, further eroding commitments to organizational goals and efficiency of task performance. |
| 4. the modes of expressing validity claims over the sincerity and appropriateness of respective behaviors; and | | |
| 5. the normative agreements that are to regulate the flow of interaction. | | |

*Source:* Author.

142

the macro-, meso-, and microlevels of social organization; and while these are all embedded in each other, each level produces its own unique types of social capital. Let me close this analysis by indicating the problems and prospects of investment at these three levels.

One strategy is to piggyback development projects on the social networks, media of exchange, norms, traditional authority systems, kinship structures, values, and beliefs of local systems. This strategy can work, as long as developmental goals are modest; and it can raise per capita incomes and living standards for those involved. However, the social capital at this level of social organization is particularistic and not easily generalized beyond the local setting. As a result, it is not likely to be useful in longer-term, national-level economic development, except to the extent that short-term, local projects can provide an infrastructural base for integrating outlying areas of a society into the national economy.

Another strategy is to invest in mesolevel units of organization, such as villages, towns, and cities as well as the organizational units operating within these spatial units. Many of the same problems that occur in microlevel investments will be repeated in mesolevel investments, since the social capital of organizational and spatial units is typically particularistic and not readily generalizable to national development goals. To the extent that a mesolevel strategy is pursued, it should involve a concerted effort to displace particularistic social capital with rational-legal organizational forms, since the latter can provide a more adequate base for integrating national and local economies. If mesolevel investments piggyback on particularistic social capital, then per capita incomes and living standards may rise, but not in a way that always facilitates national-level economic development.

A third strategy is to invest at the macroinstitutional level, but this kind of investment is expensive and often too comprehensive to be viable. How does a bank, for example, change an entire political or legal system? Investments at this level are thus difficult to make, despite the fact that, if successful, they can have far-reaching effects on economic development. A more practical strategy is to invest in specific organizational units within the economy, polity, and legal systems; here, the goal should be to convert these into increasingly more rational legal forms, since in the long run, it is this kind of organization that will be necessary for sustained development.

The tables presented in this chapter offer a checklist of potential opportunities and roadblocks to developing the kind of social capital that can sustain long-term, national-level development. By assessing the existence of forces listed down the left column and comparing their strength relative to the forces down the right column of each table, the viability of various development strategies becomes evident. Using the tables to suggest investment strategies is, of course, only as good as the capacity to translate the rather abstract terms of the tables into empirical indicators for a given society. If there is to be a next step in the analysis that I have offered here, it is to find ways to make this translation to real empirical cases. If such translations are successful, then it becomes possible to develop highly specific and unique investment strategies for a particular society.

## References

Blau, Peter M. 1977. *Inequality and Heterogeneity: A Primitive Theory of Social Structure.* New York: Free Press.

———. 1994. *Structural Contexts of Opportunities.* Chicago, Ill.: University of Chicago Press.

Braudel, Fernand. 1982. *Wheels of Commerce. Civilization and Capitalism, 15th–18th Century.* New York: HarperCollins.

Burt, Ronald. 1992. *Structural Holes.* Cambridge, Mass.: Cambridge University Press.

Coleman, James S. 1988. "Social Capital in the Creation of Human Capital." *American Journal of Sociology* 94 (Supplement): S95–S120.

Collins, Randall. 1975. *Conflict Sociology.* New York: Academic Press.

———. 1990. "Market Dynamics as the Engine of Historical Change." *Sociological Theory* 8: 111–35.

Goffman, Erving. 1967. *Interaction Ritual.* Garden City, New York: Anchor.

Granovetter, Mark. 1985. "Economic Action and Social Structure: The Problem of Embeddedness." *American Sociological Review* 91: 481–510.

Habermas, Jurgen. 1973 [1976]. *Legitimation Crisis.* London: Heinemann.

Hannan, Michael T., and John Freeman. 1989. *Organizational Ecology.* Cambridge, Mass.: Harvard University Press.

Hawley, Amos. 1986. *Human Ecology: A Theoretical Essay.* Chicago, Ill.: University of Chicago Press.

Hechter, Michael. 1987. *Principles of Group Solidarity.* Berkeley, Calif.: University of California Press.

Light, Ivan, and S. Karageorgis. 1994. "The Ethnic Economy." In N. J. Smelser and R. Swedberg, eds., *The Handbook of Economic Sociology*. Princeton, New Jersey: Princeton University Press.

Luhmann, Niklas. 1972 [1985]. *A Sociological Theory of Law*. London: Routledge.

———. 1982. *The Differentiation of Society*. New York: Columbia University Press.

McClelland, David C. 1961. *The Achieving Society*. New York: Free Press.

McPherson, J. Miller, and J. Ranger-Moore. 1991. "Evolution on a Dancing Landscape: Organizations and Networks in Dynamic Blau Space." *Social Forces* 70: 19–42.

Olson, Mancur. 1965. *The Logic of Collective Action*. Cambridge, Mass.: Harvard University Press.

Parsons, Talcott. 1964. "Evolutionary Universals in Society." *American Sociological Review* 29: 339–57.

———. 1966. *Societies: Evolutionary and Comparative Perspectives*. Englewood Cliffs, New Jersey: Prentice Hall.

Parsons, Talcott, and Neil J. Smelser. 1956. *Economy and Society*. New York: Free Press.

Portes, Alejando, and P. Landolt. 1996. "The Downside of Social Capital." *The American Prospect* 26: 18–21.

Putnam, Robert. 1993. "The Prosperous Community—Social Capital and Public Life." *The American Prospect* 13: 35–42.

Putnam, Robert, R. Leonardi, and R. Nanetti. 1993. *Making Democracy Work: Civic Traditions in Modern Italy*. Princeton, New Jersey: Princeton University Press.

Simmel, George. 1907 [1990]. *The Philosophy of Money*. Boston: Routledge.

Turner, Jonathan H. 1972. *Patterns of Social Organization: A Survey of Social Institutions*. New York: McGraw-Hill.

———. 1980. "Legal System Evolution: An Analytical Model." In W. M. Evan, ed., *The Sociology of Law*. New York: Free Press.

————. 1988. *A Theory of Social Interaction.* Stanford, Calif.: Stanford University Press.

————. 1996. *Macrodynamics: Toward a Theory on the Organization of Human Populations.* New Brunswick, New Jersey: Rutgers University Press.

————. 1997. *The Institutional Order.* New York: Longman.

Turner, Jonathan H., and Alexandra Maryanski. 1979. *Functionalism.* Menlo Park, Calif.: Benjamin-Cummings.

Weber, Max. 1904–5 [1958]. *The Protestant Ethic and the Spirit of Capitalism.* New York: Scribners and Sons.

————. 1922 [1968]. *Economy and Society.* Totowa, New Jersey: Bedminister Press.

Woolcock, Michael. 1997. "Social Capital and Economic Development: A Critical Review." *Theory and Society*, forthcoming.

# Getting things done in an antimodern society: social capital networks in Russia

Richard Rose
*Centre for the Study of Public Policy*
*University of Strathclyde, Glasgow*

*While some capital networks are used to produce goods and services in every society, their form is distinctive in an "antimodern" society—that is, a society characterized by organizational failure and the corruption of formal organizations. In response, individuals can invoke networks that involve informal, diffuse social cooperation—begging or cajoling public officials, using connections to "bend" rules, or paying bribes that break rules. When formal organizations of state and market do not work, those who rely solely on formal organizations become socially excluded, since they have no other network to fall back on. The paper draws on the author's specially designed nationwide Russian social capital survey of spring 1998, which asked people about the networks they use to compensate for organizational failure in different situations. Consistent with James Coleman's assumption, it finds major variations in tactics from one situation to another.*

Social capital is not a new phenomenon; networks of people who come together for the production of goods and services are an inevitable feature of all societies, ancient or modern. But what makes a modern society distinctive is the predominance, in both the market and the state sectors, of social capital in the form of large, impersonal bureaucratic organizations operating according to the rule of law (Weber 1968), such as IBM, commercial airlines, social security agencies, and universities. Even though informal networks can supplement or at times substitute for formal bureaucratic organizations, in modern societies they are of much less importance than in a traditional or premodern society (compare Polanyi 1957; Rose 1986).

But what is the role of social capital networks in an "antimodern" society permeated by organizational failure (in other words, a society in which formal organizations are numerous and important but often fail to operate impersonally, predictably, and in accord with the rule of law)? Is this paralleled by "social failure"—that is, individuals displaying "amoral familism" and refusing to cooperate? (Compare Banfield 1958.) If social capital networks exist, are they substitutes for discredited formal organizations? Or do they penetrate formal organizations to correct for their shortcomings or to reinforce "antimodern" features by allocating goods and services through favoritism and bribery?

An antimodern society is complex; formal organizations are an integral part of activities central to the lives of every household, to the economy and the polity. But these organizations fail to operate as in a modern society (table 1). Instead of responding to signals from prices and laws, rules are bent or broken by politics, bribes, and personal contacts. The system is semitransparent or opaque rather than transparent and the rule of law is an excuse for rigidity or rent-seeking rather than a guide to conduct. The result is uncertainty, which clouds calculations and expectations. An antimodern system can be effective in, for example, putting a man on the moon or developing nuclear weapons, but its output is achieved in spite of the chronic inefficiencies of the system.

In terms of output, physical capital, and the human capital of its population, Russia appears to be a modern society. Nearly everyone in the labor force has at least a secondary education, three-quarters of the population is urban, and telecommunication and transport link a population dispersed across 11 time zones. To describe post-Communist societies as in "transition" focuses much more attention on the goal than on the point of origin. However, the Russian state and markets remain influenced by the antimodern Soviet legacy. In the past, ideological mobilization by the party-state drove individuals to seek refuge in private and unofficial networks. Russians created both a repertoire of "second economies" and a "second polity" (Grossman 1977; Gitelman 1984, p. 241), using social networks to insulate themselves from intrusive organizations and, when forced to engage, to exploit formal organizations. The networks were not destroyed by the collapse of the Soviet Union; to a substantial degree, Russians continue to rely on a variety of "unmodern" networks to get by amidst the turbulence of transformation. However,

TABLE 1: COMPARING MODERN AND ANTIMODERN SOCIETIES

| Societal features | Modern | Antimodern |
|---|---|---|
| Operation | Complex | Complex |
| Signals | Prices, laws | Rules, politics, bribes, personal contacts |
| Openness | Transparent | Translucent, opaque |
| Rule of law | Yes | Rigidity modified by waivers |
| Cause and effect | Calculable | Uncertain |
| Output | Efficient | Inefficient |
| Effectiveness | Yes | Usually but not always |

Source: As discussed in Rose (1996), p. 244 and following pages.

the persistence of such networks is a formidable barrier to Russia's transition from an antimodern to a modern society (compare Rose 1993).

Understanding societies distant from Weber's ideal-type modern society or Putnam, Leonardi, and Nanetti's (1993) civic democracy is necessary if theories of social capital are to be sufficiently robust to apply in many parts of the world where rule of law, impersonal and efficient bureaucratic organizations are not dominant, and social capital networks may be used against an antimodern state. This paper presents empirical evidence from a specially designed nationwide Russian social capital survey that examines the varied tactics people adopt in one situation or another to substitute for or subvert organizational failings in an antimodern society.

### Contrasting approaches to social capital networks

Social capital is defined here as the stock of formal or informal social networks that individuals use to produce or allocate goods and services. In common with other definitions, this emphasizes that social capital is about recurring relationships between individuals.

*Networks both informal and formal.* Social networks of an *informal* nature are face-to-face relationships between a limited number of individuals who know each other and are bound together by kinship, friendship, or propinquity. Informal networks are "institutions" in the sociological sense of having patterned and recurring interaction. Lacking legal recognition, full-time officials, written rules, and their own funds, they are not formal organizations. Even if networks have a formal identity, such as a choir or a rural cooperative, face-to-face networks tend to be horizontal and diffuse, and an individual's reputation for helpful cooperation more important than cash payments and bureaucratic regulations. The characteristic output of informal networks is a small-scale do-it-yourself service such as help with house repair or child care or providing information and contacts to deal with an unfamiliar situation. Most outputs are unrecorded in national income accounts. Many are incalculable, being based on affection or obligation within a family, extended family, or friendship network (see Rose, Mishler, and Haerpfer 1998, p. 91 and following pages).

*Formal* organizations are rule-bound, bureaucratic, and they have a legal personality and secure revenue from the market or the state. A formal organization can have individuals as its members (for example, a professional association of doctors), or its members can be organizations (for example, an association of hospitals). However, the links between actual individuals and organizations of organizations are intermediated many times—for example, the relation between the managers of a joint stock firm and its nominal owners. Formal organizations are a necessary part of a *modern* society, for it requires impersonal bureaucratic organizations of state and market that can routinely produce complex goods such as automobiles, and services such as university education (compare Woolcock 1998, p. 169 and following pages). The literature on corporatist cooperation between government ministries, enterprise associations, and trade unions emphasizes the dominance of formal organizations in a modern society. Individuals are mobilized as followers and joining an association may be a condition of operating a business or practicing a trade. Schmitter (1995, p. 310) goes so far as to argue that "organizations are becoming citizens alongside, if not in the place of, individuals."

There are many links between informal and formal organizations, both horizontal (a family books a holiday from a travel organization) or vertical (individuals can have informal relations in their union branch, which is affiliated to the district and regional levels and a distant national headquarters). Nevertheless, a leading institutionalist, Douglass North (1990, p. 36) has argued:

> In the modern Western world, we think of life and the economy as being ordered by formal laws and property rights. Yet formal rules in even the most developed country make up a small (although very important) part of the sum of constraints that shape choices. In our daily interactions with others, whether within the family, in eternal social relations or in business activities, the governing structure is overwhelmingly defined by codes of conduct, norms of behavior, and conventions.

However, a formal organization cannot behave like individuals interacting informally, for its employees are officials of a rule-bound formal organization. An informal network has fewer resources and rules but more flexibility and, in the literal sense, more sympathy than a formal organization.

The relationship between informal social capital networks and formal organizations is contingent. Informal networks can have positive consequences within formal organizations, and even more in the interstices between formal organizations, as in Edmund Burke's statement that soldiers fight for their platoon rather than for a bureaucratic military organization. But in the Soviet Union, our case study for an antimodern society, informal and formal networks often contradicted each other. Uncertainties arising from the behavior of formal organizations encouraged the formation of informal horizontal networks that individuals could use to insulate themselves from exploitative organizations. When individuals were caught up in activities of formal organizations, they could "debureaucratize" their relations, relying on personal contacts, barter, or bribes to get what they wanted (see Ledeneva 1998). Mutual cooperation was based on the morality of face-to-face groups that Max Weber characterized as *Binnenmoral*; the complement was "outsider morals" (*Aussenmoral*) that justified the exploitation of formal organizations. Russia today continues to suffer from a "missing middle" of organizations linking informal grass roots networks and modern organizations, and the gap is sometimes filled by antimodern enterprises run by former nomenklatura officials or by *Mafiya* organizations (compare Shlapentokh 1989, p. 4 and following pages; Hedlund and Sundström 1996).

*Three alternative approaches.* For empirical analysis of the production of goods and services, James S. Coleman (1990, p. 302) offers an appropriate political economy framework. Social capital is defined in *situational and instrumental* terms. Individuals use networks in order to produce a tangible flow of goods and services, such as minding another person's child or finding a job. Because social capital is instrumental, it is an endogenous feature of social relations. However, the type of network needed varies from one situation to another. To claim a pension involves interaction with officials in a large bureaucratic organization, whereas organizing a church social event depends on personal networks. A joint stock company, a Grameen bank, and agricultural cooperatives are positive examples of the instrumental use of social capital to produce goods and services. Ignoring rules to do favors for friends or taking a bribe in return for allocating public property are examples of networks misallocating goods, that is, breaking the rules governing state and market in a modern society.

Empirically, situational theories of social capital predict that *an individual relies on a heterogeneous set of social capital networks, depending on the incentives and constraints affecting how things can get done in a given situation.* Because of the variability of networks and users from one situation to another, social capital cannot be reduced to a single unit of account and aggregated into a summary statistic characterizing the whole of society. The aggregation barrier is not due to the "ghost" or residual nature of social capital networks, but because their characteristics tend to be situation-specific.

An alternative approach treats social capital as *social psychological or cultural beliefs and norms*—or in Inglehart's (1997, p. 188) phrase, "a culture of trust and tolerance in which extensive networks of voluntary associations emerge." Networks are a consequence of people trusting each other rather than trust emerging as a byproduct of association (but see Dasgupta 1988). People who trust each other interact to form associations in situations ranging from choirs and sports groups to the workplace, and thereby become more trusting.[1] In Inglehart's view, "social

---

[1] Inglehart's definition is cited because he avoids the mistake of conflating different elements in the causal chain, as Putnam (1997, p. 31) does in defining social capital as "features of social life—networks, norms and trust—that facilitate cooperation and coordination for mutual benefit," thus making it impossible to use the term to construct a cause-and-effect model of the relation between networks, norms, and trust.

capital [that is, trust] plays a crucial role in both political and economic cooperation." Social capital not only spills over from one situation to another, but also "spills up," creating large-scale representative institutions such as political parties important in *Making Democracy Work*, the title of Putnam's pioneering reinterpretation of Italian political culture.[2] It also encourages the formation of large formal organizations of state and market.

Because social capital is seen as a generalized predisposition to cooperation and trust, this leads to the empirical prediction: *There is consistency in networks chosen by an individual from one situation to another, even though there may be a wide dispersion of social capital between individuals within a society.* It is deemed possible to measure an individual's quantum of social capital by assessing his or her disposition to trust other people or major institutions of society—or by adding up the individual's participation in voluntary associations. Research may then focus on why some people or cultures are more trusting than others. These are valid social psychological questions, but they are different from the "bottom line" concern with the production of goods and services in particular situations—which is the core of Coleman's political economy approach.

Fukuyama's (1995, p. 26 and following pages) study of "social virtues and the creation of prosperity" has a Durkheimian emphasis on culture as the source of trust and cooperation. Fukuyama cites cross-cultural differences in social capital to explain cross-national differences in forms of economic organization—specifically, a predisposition toward firms based on family and kinship in societies such as France, and against those in which there are strong ties to impersonal corporations, for example, Japan. Empirically, the culture theory hypothesizes *homogeneity in social capital between individuals within a society, including consistency from one situation to another.*

There has been limited empirical resolution of differing theoretical approaches because the demand for empirical indicators far exceeds the supply. Even in data-rich OECD (Organisation for Economic Co-operation and Development) countries, the debate about whether social capital is increasing or decreasing is being conducted with fragmentary evidence collected for other purposes (compare Putnam 1997; Ladd 1996; Jackman and Miller 1998). Readily available evidence tends to be attitudinal data about trust or membership figures in organizations, even though their validity as indicators is challenged (see, for example, Baumgartner and Walker 1988; Fukuyama 1997, pp. 127–31).

---

[2] While Tocqueville is often cited as a pioneer of this approach to social capital, this is historically anachronistic. When he wrote *Democracy in America* in the 1830s, associations were primarily local, voluntaristic, and face to face, for more than 90 percent of Americans lived in communities of less than 2500 people without any of the facilities for communication that integrate individuals and communities in a modern industrial society.

## The situational character of social capital

Even in an antimodern society there is no escape from becoming involved with organizations to obtain education, health care, housing, and
employment. What do Russians do? If social capital networks are culturally determined, a single anecdote about a society would suffice. If
social capital is based on individual trust, then assessing the disposition
of individuals on this score would be sufficient to understand networks.
However, even if every individual behaved the same within a culture or
each individual relied on a generalizable stock of trust in different situations, this could only be demonstrated by systematically collecting evidence about behavior in different situations.

The social capital data analyzed here comes from a questionnaire specially designed to identify the networks that Russians turn to in everyday situations; it was used to interview 1,904 adult Russians face to face
in a multistage, randomly stratified sample covering the whole of the
Russian Federation, with 191 primary sampling units widely dispersed
in both urban and rural areas. Fieldwork by VCIOM (the Russian Center for Public Opinion Research) took place between March 6 and April
13, 1998 (for sample details, see Rose 1998, p. 72 and following pages).
The questionnaire drew on the experience of six previous New Russia
Barometer surveys since January 1992 (for details, see www.strath.ac.uk).

In selecting situations to ask about, the first criterion was that they
should affect a majority of households rather than be minority interests
such as singing in a choir or bowling. The situations asked about include concerns of every adult, whatever their economic status—food,
housing, protection from crime on the streets and at home, income security, health, and governance. In addition, questions were asked about
situations involving a substantial portion of the population: care and
education of children for the 44 percent with children, employment-
related networks for those in the labor force, and getting paid a pension
for those in retirement.

Second, to determine the extent to which Russians can or cannot rely
on formal organizations to operate as in a modern society, the questionnaire described situations in which formal organizations were major
sources for the delivery of goods and services, such as hospital treatment, education and employment. Asking about the delivery of goods
and services that the respondent, family members, or friends and neighbors use provides much evidence with greater face validity than questions about trust in distant national institutions for which television and
press are the primary media of information.[3]

---

[3] A battery of questions about trust in macroinstitutions of society showed that
a majority of Russians distrust every major institution of their society, especially
representative institutions of governance (Rose and Mishler 1998).

Third, in each situation the focus was on the production of particular goods or services, such as house repair, or on their allocation or misallocation—for example, expediting the delivery of an entitlement such as unpaid wages, or securing university admission for a youth whose grades did not entitle him or her to a place. The question left open whether or not an individual relied on a modern organization to produce what was required, or expected to turn to one informal network or another. Giving proper scope to the role of formal networks avoids the anthropological fallacy of treating every relation as "outside" modern structures; it also avoids the formalist fallacy of assuming that organizations actually represent the people on whose behalf they claim to speak. The Social Capital survey found that in Russia, 80 to 90 percent do not belong to any voluntary association.[4]

*Alternative tactics for getting things done.* In the ideal-type modern society, people do not need a repertoire of tactics for dealing with formal organizations; bureaucratic organizations are predictably expected to deliver goods and services to individuals as citizens and customers. To invoke Weber, modern organizations operate like a vending machine: a person inserts an entitlement or money and the expected good or service is delivered. In a modern society we do not think it unusual if electricity is supplied without interruption and regularly billed, an airline ticket booked by phone is ready to pick up at the airport, or a pension is paid routinely each month. If people use informal networks this choice is not a vote of no confidence in state and market organizations.

But what if modern organizations do not work in the ideal-type way? Given the centrality of money incomes in a modern society, the inability of organizations to pay wages or a pension due is an appropriate indicator of the extent of organizational failure in Russia. The Social Capital survey found that less than two in five Russians routinely receive the wage or pension to which they are entitled (figure 1). Wages are more likely to be paid late to employees of such public sector organizations as the military, education, and state enterprises than to employees in the private sector. Moreover, pensions, a state responsibility that is easy to routinize in a modern society, are even more likely to be paid late than wages.

---

[4]   In reply to direct questions, less than 5 percent of Russians said they belong to a sports, music, or arts club, housing or neighborhood association, or a political party (Rose 1998, p. 60). Altogether, 91 percent are not members of any of the face-to-face organizations often described as the building blocks of a civic democracy. Even when associational involvement is expanded to include those attending church at least once a month (4 percent) and union members who trust local union leaders to represent their interests (8 percent), the proportion of Russians completely outside institutions of civil society remains very high— 79 percent.

FIGURE 1: REGULARITY OF INCOME

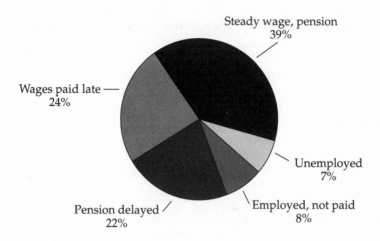

Steady wage, pension
39%

Wages paid late —
24%

Unemployed
7%

Pension delayed /
22%

Employed, not paid
8%

Notes: Steady Income: Always employed (C5.1a) AND wages never late (C5.1b), Or Pensioner AND pension paid on time (C0.3).
Unemployed: Positive reply (C5.1a).
Wages paid late: Always employed AND wages delayed (C5.1d).
Employed, not paid: Always employed AND wages not paid (C5.1d).
Pension delayed: Pensioner AND pension delayed (C0.3).
Source: New Russia Barometer Survey VII (1998). Fieldwork by VCIOM; number of respondents: 1,904.

Confronted with organizational failure, individuals have a choice between a variety of alternatives. Informal networks can substitute for the failure of modern bureaucratic organizations. Additional tactics include trying to personalize relations with impersonal bureaucrats or using connections or bribery in an attempt to get bureaucrats to violate rules; or fatalistically accepting that nothing can be done. In each module of the questionnaire, respondents were asked a series of questions about what they had done or would do or advise a friend to do to get something done in a familiar situation—including reliance on an organization to do what it is supposed to. For each situation, a multiplicity of tactics was offered. The answers show which network or networks Russians rely on and the extent to which tactics vary with the situation (for illustrations, see table 2; for full details, see Rose 1998).[5]

---

[5]  A similar approach, described as "working the output side," was used in the Soviet Interview Project to study the behavior of emigrants from the late Brezhnev period (see DiFranceisco and Gitelman 1984, p. 611). The logic is parallel to Greif's (1994, p. 915) emphasis on the importance of understanding beliefs that represent an "individual's expectations with respect to actions that others will take in various contingencies," a situational approach phrased in cultural language.

TABLE 2: ALTERNATIVE TACTICS FOR GETTING THINGS DONE

| Trusting that modern organizations work | Involved percent |
|---|---|
| *Public sector allocates by law* | |
| Police will help protect house from burglary | 43 |
| Social security office will pay entitlement if you claim | 35 |
| *Market allocates to paying customers* | |
| Buy a flat if it is needed | 30 |
| Can borrow a week's wage from bank | 16 |
| *Seeking informal alternatives* | |
| *Respondent engages in nonmonetized production* | |
| Grow food | 81 |
| Can borrow a week's wage from a friend | 66 |
| *Personalizing* | |
| *Respondent begs or cajoles officials controlling allocation* | |
| Keep demanding action at social security office to get paid | 32 |
| Beg officials to admit person to hospital | 22 |
| *Engaging in antimodern tactics* | |
| *Respondent reallocates in contravention of the rules* | |
| Use connections to get a subsidized flat | 24 |
| Pay cash to doctor on the side | 23 |
| *Adopting passive, socially excluded attitude* | |
| *Respondent believes that nothing can be done to:* | |
| Get into hospital quickly | 16 |
| Get pension paid on time (pensioners only) | 24 |

*Note:* New Russia Barometer Survey VII from Rose (1998). Fieldwork by VCIOM; number of respondents: 1,904.
*Source:* Author.

In almost every situation, when the Social Capital survey asked Russians about getting things done by nominally modern organizations, a majority did not expect to obtain what they wanted with vending machine efficiency. The only set of organizations that a majority expect to work as they should are food shops; 74 percent think the shops charge prices as marked, and go to shops regularly. While this may appear obvious in a modern society, in Russia this is a novelty, for in the old command economy food stores allocated goods by a combination of queuing, the black market, and arbitrary fiat. Only two-fifths have confidence in the police providing protection from house burglars, and a third rely on social security offices to pay entitlements.

In a modern society, the "meganetwork" of the *market* offers an alternative to the failure of government organizations to all who have a sufficient income. In Russia, choosing what you want from competing shops is a novelty. The great majority have sufficient money to pick and choose their food in the marketplace, and stores now regularly have ample stocks of food to sell. However, when larger sums are involved, the proportion that is able to turn to the market falls precipitously. Less than one in three respondents expect to have enough financial resources to consider buying a house, and only one in six reckon they could secure a bank loan.

Individuals can refrain from dealing with modern organizations by *substituting production by a nonmonetized informal network.* Having experienced chronic food shortages in shops of the old regime, four-fifths of Russian households, including a big majority of city dwellers, continue to grow some food for themselves (compare Rose and Tikhomirov 1993). While only one in four Russians has any savings and a big majority of the unemployed do not receive a state unemployment benefit, most Russians can draw on informal networks of social capital for cash. A total of 66 percent report that they could borrow a week's wages or pension from a friend or relative. In a developing society such informal networks can be described as premodern, but in the Russian context they are evidence of "demodernization," means of avoiding the consequences of the failings of large bureaucratic organizations. Even though such activities do not turn up in national income accounts, they are nonetheless real to those who rely on them.

When a formal organization does not deliver and an individual cannot substitute the market or an informal network, three different types of network can be invoked to "debureaucratize" dealings with an organization, that is, to find a way to make it produce goods and services. A person can try to *personalize* his or her relationship, begging or cajoling officials to provide what is wanted. Since the great majority of Russians do not expect to get paid an unemployment benefit when they file a claim, the most common tactic is to personalize the claim, pestering officials until it is paid. This is not a retreat into premodern informal networks but a stressful attempt to compensate for the inefficiencies of bureaucratic organizations by taking a step backwards into a premodern relationship in which individuals pleaded for benefits.

The behavior of organizations in Soviet times encouraged Russians to adopt *antimodern* tactics. The Social Capital survey found that 68 percent thought that to get anything done by a public agency in Soviet times you had to know people in the party. It was even more widely assumed that you had to have connections, a network of friends extending to friends of friends or even friends of friends of friends; in the words of the folk saying, "Better a hundred friends than a hundred roubles." The Russian concept of *blat* usually refers to using connections to misallocate benefits, as they are invoked to get an official to "bend" or break rules (compare Berliner 1957, p. 182 and following pages; Ledeneva 1998, p. 37 and following pages). The practice of using *connections*—that is, asking for favors on the basis of being part of a "circle" (*svoim*) or network—is also found today. For example, 24 percent endorse this method as the way to get a government-subsidized flat.

The introduction of the market has increased opportunities for overt corruption, that is, the payment of cash to get officials to break rules to the benefit of a recipient. Nine-tenths of Russians think corruption is now based on cash payments rather than party ties, but the expectation that the rule of law is not followed is constant. Taxation provides an excellent example, for the capacity to collect taxes is a defining characteristic of the modern state. Russia has yet to meet this requirement; there are estimates that half of anticipated state revenue is not collected— and some that is collected is "levied" rather than paid by modern means. The great majority of Russians see taxation in antimodern terms. Among employed persons, only 41 percent say that taxes are deducted when their employer pays wages.[6] A majority, 56 percent, say that there is no need to pay taxes if you do not want to do so, for the government will never find out; and 77 percent believe that a cash payment to a tax official would enable a person to evade payment of taxes claimed (figure 2). Altogether, five-sixths of Russians think that taxes can be evaded; they differ only in whether the best tactic is not to pay at all or that a "tip" to a tax official is needed to avoid legal obligations.

FIGURE 2: EASE OF TAX EVASION

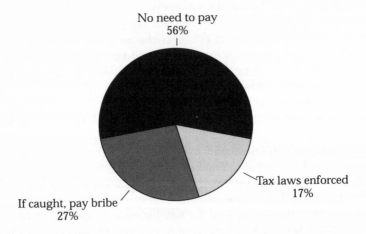

*Source:* New Russia Barometer Survey VII (1998). Fieldwork by VCIOM; number of respondents: 1,904.

---

6   Only 5 percent say that no taxes are deducted; 54 percent say that they do not know whether taxes are deducted. A separate study is required to determine what proportion of taxes deducted are paid into the appropriate public fund.

While Russians feel that "they" are corrupt, a majority usually do not say that they would pay a bribe to get things done, and those who would pay a bribe or use *blat*, while normally substantial, are usually not an overwhelming majority.

The assumption that "everybody is doing it," whatever "it" is, ignores the fact that resources for getting things done are not equally distributed throughout a society, and networks are exclusive as well as inclusive. The concept of *social exclusion* (Room 1995) is apt to characterize the position of individuals lacking networks to secure everyday goods and services. As an indicator of exclusion, for each situation the Social Capital survey offered the statement: "Nothing can be done." By this standard, a *big majority of Russians are not socially excluded*—in other words, they are not unable to draw on some form of social capital when problems arise in everyday situations (figure 3). The majority able to rely on at least one network to get things done varies from 60 percent to more than 90 percent.[7] The minority that feels helpless is largely composed of a group that faces nonpayment of wages, an indication that the enterprise itself is short of money, and pushing or bribing will be of no avail. Helplessness is limited in the face of a pension error because a majority believes that writing a letter to the pension office will get a mistake rectified. Hardly any Russian thinks nothing that can be done to protect their home from crime.

Organizational failure is not a sign that nothing works—but that *organizations do not work as in a modern society*. When a formal organization fails to operate routinely, individuals can invoke a variety of social capital networks to get things done. The networks vary from one situation to another, often for reasons related to the structure of the situation. There is far more scope for informal cooperation in house repair than in hospital treatment; more scope for using bribery or connections to obtain a flat as opposed to other needs; and growing vegetables is a straightforward method to produce food.

In every situation, a variety of networks is applicable—and Russians differ in their choice. Whatever the situation, some people will rely on the public bureaucracy to deliver goods and services, while others rely on informal do-it-yourself cooperation, personalistic cajoling of bureaucrats, or antimodern bending or breaking of rules—and if the situation makes it feasible, some turn to the market.

---

[7]   When Russians are asked how much control they have over their lives, on a scale with 1 representing no control at all and 10 a great deal, the mean reply is almost exactly in the middle—5.2. Only 7 percent place themselves at the bottom, feeling without any control of their lives.

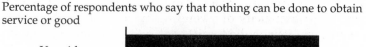

FIGURE 3: MEASURES OF SOCIAL EXCLUSION IF ORGANIZATION FAILS

Percentage of respondents who say that nothing can be done to obtain
service or good

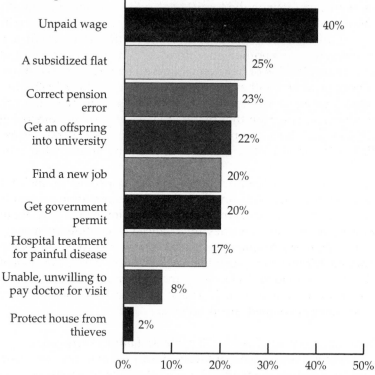

*Source:* New Russia Barometer Survey VII (1998). Fieldwork by VCIOM; number of
respondents: 1,904.

## Redundancy in the face of uncertainty

At first glance, variations in the choice of networks appear to offer support to the social psychological theory that individuals differ greatly in
their social capital. While Russians clearly differ in tactics they pursue
in any one situation, there is no reason to expect that this is attributable
to an exogenous given such as a generalized disposition to trust or distrust other people. It is unreasonable to expect an individual to rely on
only one tactic in all situations, since there are incentives and opportunities for an individual to pursue different tactics in different circumstances. A person can also invoke more than one network to get something done.

Uncertainty is the bane of an antimodern society. The presence of formal organizations is evidence that goods and services can be produced, but their infirmities are a warning that they will not be provided with the automaticity of a vending machine. In such circumstances people can rely on the logic of *redundancy*, maintaining links with more networks than are normally necessary so that if one fails another can be invoked. Insofar as networks differ in their efficacy from one situation to another, an individual who has a varied set of networks multiplies his or her nonredundant contacts, so that if one tactic does not work another may be tried (compare Burt 1992, p. 17 and following pages). Even if redundancy appears inefficient, it can also be effective, ensuring that by one means or another something will get done. In effect, the pathologies of formal organizations externalize onto individuals significant costs in obtaining what they want.

Job search is a classic example of redundancy; people can look for work by a multiplicity of means. Economic transformation has made Russians insecure; more than three-fifths in employment worry about losing their job. Yet these anxieties are balanced by confidence in being able to find another job; almost two-thirds think they could do so. Redundancy contributes to this confidence. Four-fifths have some idea of what they would do to find a job and a majority can call on at least two different networks in a job search. The alternatives, and the frequency with which they are named, are as follows:

*Informal networks:* Ask friends (50 percent), family (11 percent).
*Market networks:* Approach employers directly (33 percent); read "help wanted" advertisements (23 percent); move to another city (3 percent).
*Public organization:* Go to an employment bureau (19 percent).
*Antimodern:* Offer a payment to the manager (1 percent).
*Excluded:* Don't know (20 percent).

Most unemployed Russians are thus able to proceed on a trial-and-error basis to search until they find a new job.

Another example of redundancy arises among individuals worried about thieves breaking into their house—and with some reason, since 30 percent have had friends burglarized in the past year and 7 percent have had their own house burglarized. When offered a list of six things that might be done to make a house safer, an overwhelming majority play safe, endorsing more than one measure. The median Russian endorses four of the following six actions.

*Informal networks:* Make sure someone is usually in the house (83 percent).

*Antimodern:* Keep a fierce dog (74 percent); have a knife or gun handy
   (54 percent).
*Public organization:* Complain to the police (43 percent).
*Market:* Move someplace safer to live (20 percent).
*Excluded:* Nothing can be done (2 percent).

Multiple networks are instrumental in satisfying, that is, trying a number of different ways of getting something done until satisfaction is produced (Simon 1997, 421 and following pages). Health care provides a good illustration of a satisfying use of networks, since what is needed changes radically with the physical intensity of discomfort. In the past year, 42 percent of Russians had no need to invoke any health care network, since they had not felt ill. Of those who did feel ill at some point in time, a third did not think it necessary to visit a doctor, staying home and treating their aches with a home remedy. If they required medical treatment, seven-eighths of the respondents say that they would rely on state services, a clinic near their home, or one connected with their place of work. Only 5 percent said that they would use connections to get a doctor, and 3 percent indicated that they would pay for private treatment. Only one in eight of those who went to a doctor for treatment said that they had to make a side payment for this notionally free service.

However, when the level of dissatisfaction rises, few Russians accept the bureaucratic rule: Wait your turn. When asked what a person with a painful disease should do if a hospital says that treatment will not be available for some months, only one in six say nothing can be done. The most frequently cited tactic for queue jumping is antimodern; using connections to get hospital treatment promptly is endorsed by 44 percent and offering a tip to officials by 23 percent. The proportion ready to buy a "free" service under the table is greater than the fifth who would turn to the market to buy private treatment legally. A begging personal appeal to officials was endorsed by 22 percent; it can be tried at no expense. The tactics endorsed are not mutually exclusive: a person in pain could proceed sequentially, first begging a hospital to speed things up, then turning to connections, and if that did not work, offer a cash payment. Only if all three tactics failed would a person be left with the stark choice of waiting in pain or borrowing the cash to pay for expensive private treatment.

The great majority of Russians have a portfolio of social capital networks combining different types of resources (compare Rose 1993; 1998, p. 27). The commonest portfolio appears to be *defensive*; a person tries a modern organization and, if this fails to produce satisfaction, falls back on informal social networks as a substitute. The portfolio is defensive—it is a form of retreat or insulation from modern society. As long as do-it-yourself informal networks suffice, a person need not be anxious about the shortcomings of the country's formal organizations. An enterprising person can combine *modern market and antimodern networks*, getting some things done by buying them in the market, while achieving other goals by buying the services of officials in government agencies or using connections. While most Russians do not have enough to rely solely on what money can buy, there is a middle class with a significant amount of disposable income; in 1998 a total of 37 percent reported having a video cassette recorder, a preeminent hard currency consumer durable. The use of *connections* is likely to be much influenced by coincidence: the occupations of relatives and relatives by marriage, neighbors, schoolmates who have gone diverse ways and so forth. Nearly everyone will have connections in some situations but not in others.

In an antimodern society, vulnerability is greatest when the only network in an individual's portfolio is the entitlement of citizens to goods and services of public sector organizations, since these cannot be depended on to deliver routinely. When organizations fail, the vulnerable are effectively pushed into the ranks of the socially excluded. The above indicates that *social exclusion* tends to be situation-specific. The great majority of Russians do lack a network in a few situations, but very few Russians are consistently without any network that enables them to get things done.[8]

### How typical is Russia?

Many Sovietologists have argued the uniqueness of Russia (see, for example, Keenan 1986), and cultural and path-determined theories of social capital stressed by Putnam, Leonardi, and Nanetti (1993) and Inglehart (1997) imply that Russia ought to be unique. Insofar as this is the case, then the above evidence is of limited general significance. However, theories of command and of market economies and of democratization and undemocratic rule assume commonalities across cultures. The spread of the Communist system from Moscow made it relevant to upwards of 400 million people in Europe. Substantial elements of Marxism such as collectivist agriculture have appeared also in 33 countries across Africa, Central America, and Asia. If China is included, the total population subject to Communist one-party rule and a nonmarket economy rises to 1.5 billion (compare World Bank 1996).

According to the Freedom House (1998, p. 605) ranking of political regimes, Russia is in the middle, being classified as "partly free" along with countries such as Brazil, Mexico, and Sri Lanka. On measures of transitions toward a market economy, some place Russia as average or slightly above average, that is, between the post-Communist regimes of

---

[8]   Across ten different situations, only 18 percent of Russians say that nothing can be done in a majority of situations and only 4 percent feel excluded in four-fifths of situations.

Central Europe and former Soviet regimes in Central Asia (Karatnycky, Motyl, and Shor 1997, p. 7). More relevant here are international ratings on corruption: the 1997 Transparency International rating of 52 countries ranks Russia fourth-highest in corruption (compare Sachs and Pistor 1997).

Generalizability from Russia can be examined with comparable data from the Centre for the Study of Public Policy nationwide sample surveys in Ukraine, the Czech Republic, and the Republic of Korea (see Rose and Haerpfer 1998; Shin and Rose 1997). In each country a limited number of comparable questions were asked about getting things done in four situations: gaining admission to a university, getting a subsidized flat, securing a government permit, and obtaining prompt hospital treatment for a painful disease. Insofar as Russia is unique, responses should differ greatly from the other three countries. And to the extent that responses reflect the experience of dictatorship, they should be similar in all four countries. If networks reflect the consequences of a command economy, then Russians, Ukrainians, and Czechs should be similar and differ from Koreans. In addition, Koreans can claim uniqueness here because they have an Asian culture. And insofar as the pathologies of the Soviet experience are distinctive, then Russians and Ukrainians should differ from Czechs as well as Koreans.

Consistently, Russians and Ukrainians appear similar. In both societies the most frequently recommended tactic to get a flat, a government permit, or prompt hospital treatment, is antimodern, such as a cash payment to officials or using connections; for university admission it is the second most frequently mentioned tactic (table 3). Few Russians and Ukrainians think that nothing can be done when formal organizations fail; four-fifths have some sort of network to invoke in every situation. Except for paying a tutor for a youth with exam difficulties, the market is of secondary importance in both Russia and Ukraine. People socialized in the former Soviet regime rarely see pleading with bureaucrats as useful.

The impact of the Soviet Union on Russians and Ukrainians is confirmed by their consistent differences from Czechs. Former Soviet citizens are four times more likely than Czechs to turn to antimodern behavior to get a youth into university; two to three times as likely to use corruption or connections to get a better flat; almost twice as likely to break the law if they are having trouble getting a government permit; and up to twice as likely to use antimodern methods to get prompt hospital treatment. Furthermore, the distinctiveness of Czechs is not a consequence of passivity: Czechs tend to be less likely to think that nothing can be done than do former Soviet citizens. Big differences arise because Czechs are more likely to rely on the market or to personalize and plead with bureaucrats to expedite their demands. This suggests that the heirs of the Habsburg tradition, while often dilatory or obstructive, are not corrupt to the degree of former Soviet officials, an interpretation sup-

TABLE 3: STRATEGIES IN RESPONSE TO PROBLEMS WITH PUBLIC SERVICES

| | *Strategy* | | | |
|---|---|---|---|---|
| | *Antimodern connections* | *Personal connections* | *Market* | *Passive stance* |
| 1. Getting into university without good enough grades | | | | |
| Russia | 33 | 6 | 39 | 22 |
| Ukraine | 31 | 3 | 45 | 21 |
| Czech Republic | 7 | 2 | 72 | 18 |
| Korea | 3 | 2 | 37 | 57 |
| 2. Actions to get a better flat when not entitled to publicly subsidized housing | | | | |
| Russia | 45 | n.a. | 30 | 25 |
| Ukraine | 34 | 10 | 28 | 27 |
| Czech Republic | 14 | 23 | 48 | 15 |
| Korea | 8 | 13 | 64 | 15 |
| 3. Action if an official delays issuing a government permit | | | | |
| Russia | 62 | 18 | n.a. | 20 |
| Ukraine | 61 | 18 | n.a. | 21 |
| Czech Republic | 35 | 46 | n.a. | 19 |
| Korea | 21 | 45 | n.a. | 34 |
| 4. Getting treatment for a painful disease when hospital says one must wait for months | | | | |
| Russia | 57 | 13 | 11 | 19 |
| Ukraine | 39 | 12 | 34 | 15 |
| Czech Republic | 24 | 31 | 31 | 14 |
| Korea | (not applicable; no government health service) | | | |

n.a. Not applicable.
*Note:* New Korea Barometer 1997 (N:1,117) from Shin and Rose (1997); New Democracies Barometer V 1998 (N:1,017) from Rose and Haerpfer (1998); Russia Social Capital survey 1998 (N:1,908) from Rose (1998).
*Source:* Author.

ported by the relative superiority of the Czech Republic to Russia and Ukraine on Transparency International ratings.

Koreans are distinctive in being passive, saying that nothing can be done about the actions of government officials. While education is highly valued, Koreans also accept decisions of university admissions officials; 57 percent think that nothing can be done to reverse a refusal of admission. Similarly, 34 percent think that one must wait for a government permit to be issued and not break the law to expedite matters; Koreans advise at most writing a letter begging an official to take action. The absence of a European-style welfare state means that the operation of a public hospital system is not a concern for Koreans.

Instead of highlighting the distinctiveness of Asian values, table 3 indicates that the Soviet experience is most likely to foster antimodern social capital networks. The point is underscored by similarities between Koreans and Czechs being greater than between Czechs and former

Soviet citizens. In the readiness to use antimodern networks to get a flat, there is a difference of 31 percentage points between Czechs and Russians compared with a 6 point difference with Koreans. There is a 26 percentage point difference between Czechs and Russians in readiness to use antimodern networks to get a university place, and no significant difference between Czechs and Koreans. Similarly, there is a 27 percentage point difference between Czechs and Russians in relying on antimodern tactics when they are having difficulties in getting a government permit, and less than half that difference with Koreans.

The impact of the Soviet Union on social networks reflects the impact of mobilizational efforts under its totalitarian system (compare Linz 1975). A totalitarian society was full of organizations seeking to mobilize compliance with the regime's dictates. If anything, it was "overorganized," using bureaucratic commands and ideological coercion in efforts to make people do what the regime wanted. But it was simultaneously "underbureaucratized," in that the rule of law did not apply and the system encouraged people to create informal networks as protection against the state and to circumvent or subvert its commands. Such a "dual society" of formal versus informal networks was far more developed in the Soviet Union, where it had been in place for more than 70 years, than in the Czech Republic.

The significance of totalitarianism as being against Asian values is underscored by evidence from Shi's (1997, pp. 53, 268) "bottom up" picture of how Chinese people get things done, based on a survey in Beijing just before the Tiananmen Square massacre. Nine-tenths did not passively accept the directives of government. Instead, people formed networks to allocate goods and services to themselves rather than to others with whom they were in competition. The networks were not used to change laws—which was neither possible nor necessary—for most Chinese laws are vague (Shi 1997, p. 316, footnote 23). Individuals used networks or *guanxi* to influence the implementation of central directives by "antimodern" tactics familiar to students of the Soviet system (Shi 1997, p. 69, 121, and following pages). The broad similarities of Chinese and Soviet behavior emphasize the impact of political context on the formation of social capital networks. A totalitarian or "*post*totalitarian" legacy of mobilizational coercion encourages more persisting antimodern behavior than a "normal" Korean-style dictatorship. All undemocratic regimes, even those that superficially appear modern, offer more incentives to retreat or subvert formal organizations than do the institutions of an established democracy and market economy.

## Implications for theory and practice

Understanding the significance of social capital requires attention to networks in specific situations. This is logical because the output of the network depends on the situation—for example, networks that are used to maintain health produce different outputs than networks that produce food or house repairs. The above evidence confirms Coleman's proposition that social capital networks differ greatly between situations.

There is no single numeraire or "silver bullet" formula making it possible to sum all forms of social capital into a single index number. To make "trust in people" a proxy indicator ignores the possibility that this trust may encourage informal networks used to substitute for or insulate against repressive or failing organizations of state and market. Organizational memberships cannot be used as a proxy of social capital networks either, for national leaders may not be trusted to represent all their diverse members. For example, the Russian Social Capital survey found that while 53 percent of employees said that they were members of a trade union, less than half (that is, 22 percent of all workers) trusted their local union leader to look after their interests, and less than 11 percent trusted national union officials to look after their interests.

Paradoxically, it may be easier to measure social exclusion or nonparticipation in networks. But individuals should not be labeled as excluded or included on the basis of a single proxy indicator, such as income or education, and it should not even be assumed that exclusion is cumulative from one situation to another. The great majority of Russians appear to be "outside the loop" in some situations, but not in a majority of instances. Less than 1 percent claim to have a network for every situation, and only 6 percent claim to have tactics to get things done in all but one situation. Consistent lack of network resources is even rarer; less than 1 percent feel excluded from every situation, and little more than 1 percent from all situations but one. In addition to being situational, exclusion from effective networks may be a phase in the life cycle—for example, young people not yet having a steady job or elderly widows living alone with few interpersonal connections. To the extent that this is the case, the problems will tend to be egalitarian, insofar as every citizen is similarly at risk at a given stage of the life cycle.

Organizational failure in Russia often reflects the combination of too many regulations—and too little adherence to bureaucratic norms. A surfeit of rules imposes delays and unresponsiveness as different public agencies must be consulted. Individuals must then invest an unreasonable amount of time in pleading and pushing against bureaucrats to compensate for organizational inefficiencies. If bureaucrats offer to waive obstructive regulation in return for a bribe, this delivers a service—but in an antimodern way. The result is popular ambivalence about the rule of law. A total of 71 percent of Russians say that the national government is a long way from representing the idea of a law-governed state (*prayovoye gosudarstvo*). But if this were to come about, it would not be entirely welcome, for 62 percent of Russians think that laws are often very hard on ordinary people. Rather than being subject to the enforcement of these harsh laws, 73 percent endorse the belief that the laws can be softened by their nonenforcement (compare Sajo 1998).

The classic Schumpeterian solution to the failure of government to deliver as it should is to throw the rascals out at a general election and give the opposition a chance to show what it can do. The new Russian regime empowers the electorate to choose a president, and the Duma is an elected assembly, albeit one that lacks the capacity to hold the executive accountable. But what is to be done if a sequence of elections simply results in the "circulation of rascals," as one unpopular government is replaced by another that appears no better? At this point, a society has reached the limit of what elections can achieve (compare Rose, Mishler, and Haerpfer 1998, chapter 10).

Where antimodern practices are rampant, the immediate need is not to change the values and attitudes of the mass of the population; it is to change the way the country is governed. A first step is to reduce the number of regulations that create rent-seeking opportunities—for example, allocating goods and services to favored connections, or accepting bribes—for agencies. A second step is for governors to change their behavior. The networks described above are not a consequence of popular demand but of what individuals have learned from trying to work the institutions of an "antimodern" regime, in which officials at all levels, including elected officials, are implicated. If post-Communist governors want people to rely less on personalistic or antimodern tactics, they should reform public sector organizations that reward individuals for using social capital against the modern state.

## References

Banfield, Edward C. 1958. *The Moral Basis of a Backward Society*. Glencoe, Ill.: Free Press.

Baumgartner, F. R., and J. L. Walker. 1988. "Survey Research and Membership in Voluntary Associations." *American Journal of Political Science* 32(4): 908–28.

Berliner, Joseph. 1957. *Factory and Manager in the USSR*. Cambridge, Mass.: Harvard University Press.

Burt, Ronald S. 1992. *Structural Holes: The Social Structure of Competition*. Cambridge, Mass.: Harvard University Press.

Coleman, James S. 1990. *Foundations of Social Theory*. Cambridge, Mass.: Harvard University Press.

Dasgupta, Partha. 1988. "Trust as a Commodity." In Diego Gambettta, ed., *Trust: Making and Breaking Cooperative Relations*, pp. 49, 72. Oxford: Basil Blackwell.

DiFranceisco, Wayne, and Zvi Gitelman. 1984. "Soviet Political Culture and 'Covert Participation' in Policy Implementation." *American Political Science Review* 78(3): 603–21.

Freedom House. 1998. *Freedom in the World: Annual Survey of Political Rights and Civil Liberties, 1997–1998*. New York: Freedom House.

———. 1995. *Trust: The Social Virtues and the Creation of Prosperity*. New York: Free Press.

———. 1997. *The End of Order*. London: Social Market Foundation.

Gitelman, Zvi. 1984. "Working the Soviet System: Citizens and Urban Bureaucracies." In Henry W. Morton and Robert C. Stuart, eds., *The Contemporary Soviet City*, pp. 221–43. Armonk, New York: M. E. Sharpe.

Greif, Avner. 1994. "Cultural Beliefs and the Organization of Society." *Journal of Political Ecoomy* 102: 912–50.

Grossman, Gregory. 1977. "The Second Economy of the USSR." *Problems of Communism* 26(5): 25–40.

Hedlund, Stefan, and Niclas Sundström. 1996. "Does Palermo Represent the Future for Moscow?" *Journal of Public Policy* 16(2): 113–55.

Inglehart, Ronald. 1997. *Modernization and Postmodernization: Cultural, Economical, and Political Change in 43 Societies*. Princeton: Princeton University Press.

Jackman, R. W., and Ross A. Miller. 1998. "Social Capital and Politics." *Annual Review of Political Science*: 47–72.

Karatnycky, Adrian, Alexander Motyl, and Boris Shor. 1997. *Nations in Transit 1997: Civil Society, Democracy and Markets in East Central Europe and the Newly Independent States*. New Brunswick, New Jersey: Transaction Publishers.

Keenan, Edward. 1986. "Muscovite Political Folkways." *The Russian Review* 45: 115–81.

Ladd, Everett C. 1996. "The Data Just Don't Show Erosion of America's Social Capital." *The Public Perspective* 7(4): 1–22.

Ledeneva, Alena V. 1998. *Russia's Economy of Favours*. Cambridge (UK): Cambridge University Press.

Linz, Juan J. 1975. "Totalitarian and Authoritarian Regimes." In Fred I. Greenstein and Nelson W. Polsby, eds., *Handbook of Political Science* vol. 3: 175–411. Reading, Mass.: Addison-Wesley.

North, Douglass C. 1990. *Institutions. Institutional Change and Economic Performance*. New York: Cambridge University Press.

Polanyi, Karl F. 1957. *The Great Transformation*. Boston: Beacon Press.

Putnam, Robert D. 1997. "Democracy in America at Century's End." In Axel Hadenius, ed., *Democracy's Victory and Crisis*, pp. 27–70. New York: Cambridge University Press.

Putnam, Robert D., Robert Leonardi, and Raffaella Y. Nanetti. 1993. *Making Democracy Work*. Princeton: Princeton University Press.

Room, Graham, ed. 1995. *Beyond the Threshold: The Measurement and Analysis of Social Exclusion*. Bristol: Policy Press.

Rose, Richard. 1986. "Common Goals but Different Roles: the State's Contribution to the Welfare Mix." In Richard Rose and Rei Shiratori, eds., *The Welfare State East and West*, pp. 13–39. New York: Oxford University Press.

——. 1993. "Contradictions between Micro and Macro-Economic Goals in Post-Communist Societies." *Europe-Asia Studies* 45(3): 419–44.

——. 1996. *What Is Europe?* New York: Addison Wesley Longman.

——. 1998. *Getting Things Done with Social Capital: New Russia Barometer* VII. Studies in Public Policy No. 303, University of Strathclyde, Glasgow.

Rose, Richard, and Evgeny Tikhomirov. 1993. "Who Grows Food in Russia and Eastern Europe?" *Post-Soviet Geography* 34(2): 111–26.

Rose, Richard, and Christian Haerpfer. 1998. *New Democracies Barometer V*. Studies in Public Policy No. 308, University of Strathclyde, Glasgow.

Rose, Richard, and William Mishler. 1998. *Untrustworthy Institutions and Popular Response*. Studies in Public Policy No. 306, University of Strathclyde, Glasgow.

Rose, Richard, William Mishler, and Christian Haerpfer. 1998. *Democracy and Its Alternatives: Understanding Post-Communist Societies*. Cambridge: Polity Press and Baltimore: Johns Hopkins University Press.

Sachs, Jeffrey D., and Katharina Pistor, eds. 1997. *The Rule of Law and Economic Reform in Russia*. Boulder, Colo.: Westview.

Sajo, Andras. 1998. "Corruption, Clientelism and the Future of the Constitutional State in Eastern Europe." *East European Constitutional Review* 7(2): 37–46.

Schmitter, Philippe C. 1995. "Corporatism." In S. M. Lipset, ed., *The Encyclopedia of Democracy* vol. 1: 308–10. Washington, D.C.: Congressional Quarterly.

Shi, Tianjian. 1997. *Political Participation in Beijing*. Cambridge, Mass.: Harvard University Press.

Shiapentokh, Vladimir. 1989. *Public and Private Life of the Soviet People*. New York: Oxford University Press.

Shin, Doh C., and Richard Rose. 1997. *Koreans Evaluate Democracy: A Survey Study*. Studies in Public Policy No. 292, University of Strathclyde, Glasgow.

Simon, Herbert A. 1997. *Models of Bounded Rationality*. Cambridge, Mass.: MIT Press.

Weber, Max. 1968. *Economy and Society*. Edited by Guenther Roth and Claus Wittich. Berkeley: University of California Press.

Woolcock, Stephen. 1998. "Social Capital and Economic Development." *Theory and Society* 27(2): 151–208.

World Bank. 1996. "From Plan to Market." In *World Development Report 1996*. Washington, D.C.: World Bank.

# Social capital: a fad or a fundamental concept?*

**Elinor Ostrom**
*Center for the Study of Institutions, Population, and Environmental Change*
*Workshop in Political Theory and Policy Analysis*
*Indiana University*

*Social capital is an essential complement to the concepts of natural, physical and human capital and can be used for beneficial or harmful ends—or simply be allowed to dissipate. While all forms of capital are essential for development, none of them are sufficient in and of themselves. In this paper, I focus first on the concept of human-made capital and examine some of the essential similarities between physical, human, and social capital. In the second section, four differences between physical and social capital will be examined, including: (a) social capital does not wear out with use, but rather with disuse; (b) social capital is not easy to observe and measure; (c) social capital is hard to construct through external interventions; and (d) national and regional governmental institutions strongly affect the level and type of social capital available to individuals to pursue long-term development efforts. The third section will discuss the problem of creating social capital and present a game-theoretic analysis of how a group of farmers creates rules to allocate the benefits and costs of building and operating their own irrigation system. Empirical evidence derived from a study of 150 irrigation systems in Nepal supports the conclusions of this analysis. The last section is devoted to the policy significance of the theoretical and empirical findings presented in this paper.*

Years of development policies encouraged by donor agencies focusing on building infrastructure as the key to economic growth have made many individuals and government officials rich. Only the crumbling remains of poorly maintained roads, irrigation systems, and public facilities, however, are left today in many countries for all the billions invested. There is a serious need to rethink the overemphasis on physical

---
*   The author appreciates the continued support of the Ford Foundation and the Bradley Foundation and the outstanding editing of Patty Dalecki.

capital alone. The recent groundswell of attention in development literature to social capital is thus a refreshing and needed change (Harriss 1997; Fountain 1997; Levi 1996; Newton 1996; Narayan 1998; Putzel 1997; Sabetti 1996; World Bank 1997).

As is to be expected with any effort to introduce a new concept into policy discourse, some authors have exaggerated claims for the universal efficacy of social capital. However, some criticisms have blanketed carefully conducted analyses along with those that were rightfully in need of critical review. In other words, there has been a lot of serious work and some hoopla focusing on social capital. Some commentators think that social capital is just another fad. This is unfortunate. But, we must address the question of whether the concept will become a core foundation for our understanding of how individuals achieve coordination and overcome collective-action problems to reach higher levels of economic performance. Or, will this currently fashionable concept soon be retired to the dust heap of previous panaceas?

It is important that social capital be taken seriously and not allowed to be carried off as a fad. Social capital is an essential complement to the concepts of natural, physical, and human capital. Just as we have come to recognize that building roads and irrigation projects or providing education and training are not sufficient by themselves to enhance the economic and political growth of developing societies, social capital alone is not sufficient for development. Social capital can be used for beneficial or harmful ends or simply allowed to dissipate. While all forms of capital are essential for development, none of them are sufficient in and of themselves. Social capital shares some fundamental attributes with other forms of capital while it presents some attributes that differ. We need a much better understanding of how social capital is constituted and transformed over time.

In this paper, I will focus first on the concept of human-made capital and examine some of the essential similarities between physical, human, and social capital. The fourth type of capital—natural capital—encompasses the rich array of biophysical resource systems that are the ultimate source and storehouse of all human productivity (Jansson and others 1994). The problem of sustainable use of natural capital is itself a vitally important and immensely difficult topic that cannot be addressed in the confines of this paper. In the second section, four differences between physical and social capital will be examined: (a) social capital does not wear out with use, but rather with disuse; (b) social capital is not easy to observe and measure; (c) social capital is hard to construct through external interventions; and (d) national and regional governmental institutions strongly affect the level and type of social capital available to individuals to pursue long-term development efforts. The third section will discuss the problem of creating social capital—particularly self-organized resource governance systems. As an illustration of these processes, I will present a game-theoretic analysis of how a group of farmers creates rules to allocate the benefits and costs of building and operating their own irrigation system. I will also present empirical evidence derived from a study of 150 irrigation systems in Nepal and from in-depth case studies of efforts to improve the physical capital of irrigation systems without paying attention to the social capital of these systems. In the last section I will discuss the policy significance of the theoretical and empirical findings presented in this paper.

## The concept of human-made capital

All forms of human-made capital are created by spending time and effort in transformation and transaction activities in order to build tools or assets today that increase income in the future.[1] "People form capital when they withhold resources from present consumption and use them instead to augment future consumption [or production] possibilities" (Bates 1990, p. 153). Investments in physical capital are usually a self-conscious decision, while human and social capital may be developed as a by-product of other activities as well as purposely. The essential role of capital is everywhere acknowledged, but not always well understood. Unfortunately, capital is sometimes equated with money. Money is not capital, but rather the means by which some forms of physical, human, and social capital may be obtained. Money, like many resources, can alternatively be used for consumption or sit unused as a store of value. Many types of capital can be created without money, or with very little of it, based on the time and energy spent by individuals in building tools and facilities, learning skills, and establishing regularized patterns of relationships with others. All human-made capital involves creating new opportunities as well as exercising restraints, a risk that the investment might fail, and the possibility of using capital to produce harms rather than benefits.

### Physical capital

*Physical capital* is the stock of human-made, material resources that can be used to produce a flow of future income (Lachmann 1978).[2] Physical capital exists in a wide variety of forms including buildings, roads, waterworks, tools, cattle and other animals, automobiles, trucks, and tractors—to name just a few. The origin of physical capital is the process of spending time and other resources constructing tools, plants, facilities, and other material resources that can, in turn, be used in producing other products or future income.[3]

The construction of physical capital involves establishing physical restraints that (a) create the possibilities for some events to occur that would not otherwise occur (for example, channeling water from a distant source to a farmer's field), and (b) constrain physical events to a more restricted domain (for example, water is held within a channel rather than allowed to spread out). Thus, physical capital opens up some possibilities while constraining others. The intention to construct useful physical capital is not always fulfilled. An investment in physical capital may not generate the improved flow of future services. A new but crumbling roadway or irrigation system, or an empty building, represents a failed investment decision.

Physical capital may have a dark side and generate more harms than benefits. Investing in a weapons facility increases the quantity of physical capital existing at a particular point in time, but the product of this form of physical capital is the threat of human destruction. Even investments in the production of consumer goods can produce substantial externalities. A nuclear power plant that leaks radioactive materials, for example, is constructed in order to increase the availability of power for positive purposes but may produce more negative externalities than the net benefits generated. Physical capital cannot operate over time without human capital in the form of the knowledge and skills needed to use and maintain physical assets to produce new products and generate income. If physical capital is to be used productively by more than one individual, social capital is also needed.

### Human capital

*Human capital* is the acquired knowledge and skills that an individual brings to an activity. Forms of human capital also differ among themselves. A college education is a different type of human capital than the skills of a cabinetmaker acquired through apprenticeship training. Human capital is formed consciously through education and training and unconsciously through experience.[4] An individual who swims for the pleasure of the activity, for example, is engaging in consumption activities but also improving physical health. Health is an asset that is drawn on to achieve other goals. Some investments in human capital are not made self-consciously but result from activities engaged in primarily for other reasons. Alternatively, some individuals dislike using stationary bicycles but do so because they know that aerobic exercise is essential for sustaining future capabilities. They exercise primarily to invest in human capital and then find ways to make this activity as pleasant as possible. Thus, both self-conscious and relatively unconscious investment processes go on when building human capital.

Human capital consists of the acquisition of new capabilities as well as the learning of constraints. Learning a new language opens up different conceptions of the world. Many of the skills that individuals acquire involve the imposition of discipline on self. Like physical capital, human capital can be used for destructive purposes as well as productive ones. An individual knowledgeable in computer languages can use this skill to write programs today that help solve many problems in the future. Those who write programs to function as a virus that invades and destroys the records of others, use their human capital for destructive purposes.

### Social capital

*Social capital* is the shared knowledge, understandings, norms, rules, and expectations about patterns of interactions that groups of individuals bring to a recurrent activity (Coleman 1988; E. Ostrom 1990, 1992; Putnam, Leonardi, and Nanetti 1993). In the establishment of any coordinated activity, participants accomplish far more per unit of time devoted to a joint activity if they draw on capital resources to reduce the level of current inputs needed to produce a joint outcome. They are more productive with whatever physical and human capital they draw on, if they agree on the way that they will coordinate activities and credibly commit themselves to a sequence of future actions. In the realm of repeated coordination problems, humans frequently face a wide diversity of potential equilibria and a nontrivial problem of finding the better equilibria in the set. When they face social dilemma or collective-action situations, participants may easily follow short-term, maximizing strategies that leave them all worse off than other options available to them. Somehow participants must find ways of creating mutually reenforcing expectations and trust to overcome the perverse short-run temptations they face (E. Ostrom 1998a).

Agreements can be based on mutual learning about how to work better together. They can be based on one person agreeing to follow someone else's commands regarding this activity. Or, they can be based on the evolution or construction of a set of norms or rules that define how this activity will be carried out repeatedly over time and how commitments will be monitored and sanctions imposed for nonperformance.

Like physical capital and human capital, social capital opens up some opportunities while restricting others. A decision to establish majority rule as the decision rule for making particular collective-choice decisions, for example, opens opportunities that did not previously exist. Voting does not exist in nature, and the opportunity to vote is created by rules. On the flip side, a rule that prohibits a farmer from growing a particular water-intensive crop—rice during the dry season, for example—restrains activities to a more limited set than previously available.

There is a dark side to social capital as well as to physical and human capital. Gangs and the Mafia use social capital as the foundation for their organizational structure. Cartels also develop social capital in their effort to keep control over an industry so as to reap more profits than would otherwise be the case. An authoritarian system of government based on military command and use of instruments of force destroys other forms of social capital while building its own.

Social capital takes many different forms. Putnam, Leonardi, and Nanetti (1993) identifies social capital as involving networks, norms, and social beliefs that evolve out of processes that are not overtly investment activities. *Family structure* is considered another form of social capital. Bates (1990), for example, summarizes research on the Luo and Kikuyu of Kenya, the Bambara of Mali, and on East African pastoralists, and clearly demonstrates that different types of lineage groups create different types of property rights and access to flows of future incomes.[5] He points to the costs to individual families of belonging to extended lineages and the benefits that they obtain by spreading risk in those environments where ecological or economic variation is very high.

*Shared norms* are forms of social capital, but specific norms may have different consequences. The norm of reciprocity implies some level of symmetry among those who engage in long-term reciprocal relationships. When individuals learn to trust one another so that they are able to make credible commitments and rely on generalized forms of reciprocity rather than on narrow sequences of specific *quid pro quo* relationships, they are able to achieve far more than when these forms of social capital are not present (E. Ostrom 1998a). "In a reciprocal relationship, each individual contributes to the welfare of others with an expectation that others will do likewise, but without a fully contingent quid pro quo" (Oakerson 1993, p. 143). Thus, investments made in one time period in building trust and reciprocity can produce higher levels of return in future time periods even though the individuals creating trust and reciprocity are not fully conscious of the social capital they construct. Not all norms, however, are based on symmetric relationships. The norm of deference to elders or to those with more status or authority is based fundamentally on a concept of asymmetric relationships. Such norms may be used to generate higher returns in the future, but they may also lead to stagnation and a reluctance to build new types of enterprises. A norm such as retribution—even though it may be based on symmetry—can trigger quite destructive and escalating patterns of conflict and violence and thus be destructive of all forms of capital.

*Conventions* may be established without as much collective, self-conscious thought as is involved in creating new rules or establishing new entrepreneurial opportunities. Individuals facing a particular opportunity or problem in a specific location and time decide to handle it in a particular manner. That decision becomes a precedent for arriving at a similar agreement when a related opportunity or problem is faced again. If mutual expectations based on past behavior are fulfilled again and again, the precedent becomes a convention for how activities, costs, and benefits will be handled by individuals in the future. The convention has economic value because transaction costs are much lower when most participants already have agreed that a particular convention is appropriate and positive gains can be achieved with a low risk of breakdown (Young 1998, pp. 113–15). While the establishment of a convention occurs without formal consideration by all participants, weighing how best to act in this situation will have been made by many separate individuals, as they have faced similar situations over time. The convention evolves as a result of precedent, shared expectations, and continued behavior that is consistent with the convention.

Both evolved and self-consciously designed *rule systems* are important forms of social capital that help individuals overcome the wide diversity of social dilemmas and collective-action problems faced in all societies. Conventions alone are rarely sufficient when individuals face a social dilemma. The temptation to cheat, which does not exist in coping with coordination problems, is usually relatively difficult to overcome without more self-consciously developed agreements, monitoring arrangements, and methods for imposing sanctions on nonconformance. To create social capital in a self-conscious manner, individuals must spend time and energy working with one another to craft institutions—that is, sets of rules that will be used to allocate the benefits derived from an organized activity and to assign responsibility for paying costs (E. Ostrom 1990, 1992). Rules imply asymmetries between those assigned authority to make rules and to monitor and enforce rules. Rules also contain a reference to a sanction that can be enforced if conformance to the rule is observed by such an authority (see Crawford and Ostrom 1995). While the laws established by formal legislative, executive, and judicial bodies are an important source of the rules used by groups of individuals in productive enterprises, a large proportion of rules-in-use are created by self-organized governance systems.

Self-organizing governance systems create their own rules in millions of disparate local settings to cope with a variety of private and public problems. An extensive literature including many case studies describes institutions that have been constituted by those affected in all corners of the world (see Berkes 1986, 1989; E. Ostrom 1990; Bromley and others 1992; Fairhead and Leach 1996; Fox 1993; Fortmann and Bruce 1988; McCay and Acheson 1987).[6] Recent work on institutional analysis and institutional change begins to provide a solid theoretical foundation for understanding the conditions needed for individuals to craft or evolve their own institutions and enforce these institutions themselves (see Bates 1988; Calvert 1995; Libecap 1989; North 1990; E. Ostrom 1998b; E. Ostrom, Gardner, and Walker 1994; V. Ostrom, Feeny, and Picht 1993).

While social capital does take on many forms, there are underlying similarities among all of the diverse forms. In all forms, individuals who devote time to constructing patterns of relationships among humans are building assets whether consciously or unconsciously. Further, all forms of social capital share the following attributes:

■ Social capital is formed over time and is embedded in common understanding rather than in physically obvious structures;

■ Common understanding is hard to articulate precisely in language; and

■ Common understanding is easily eroded if large numbers of people are concerned or if a large proportion of participants change rapidly—unless substantial efforts are devoted to transmission of the common understandings, monitoring behavior in conformance with common understandings, and sanctioning behavior not in conformance with the common understanding.

These commonalities are not shared with physical capital and are the source of substantial differences between these two forms of human-made capital.

### Differences between social and physical capital

The similarities among diverse forms of social capital lead to some key differences between social and physical capital. We will discuss four key differences that include the following:

■ Social capital does not wear out with use but rather with disuse;

■ It is not easy to see and measure;

■ It is hard to construct through external interventions; and

■ National and regional governmental institutions strongly affect the level and type of social capital available to individuals to pursue long-term development efforts.

Many of these differences are due to the importance of shared cognitive understandings that are essential for social capital to exist and to be transmitted from one generation to another.

**First, social capital differs from physical capital in that it does not wear out with use but rather with disuse.** Social capital may, in fact, improve with use so long as participants continue to keep prior commitments and maintain reciprocity and trust. Using social capital for an initial purpose creates mutual understandings and ways of relating that can frequently be used to accomplish entirely different joint activities at much lower start-up costs (Putnam, Leonardi, and Nanetti 1993). It is not that learning curves for new activities disappear entirely. Rather, one of the steepest sections of a learning curve—learning to make commitments and to trust one another in a joint undertaking—has already been surmounted. A group that has learned to work effectively together in one task can take on other similar tasks at a cost in time and effort that is far less than that involved in creating an entirely new group out of people who must learn everything from scratch. The fungibility of social capital is, of course, limited. No tool is useful for all tasks. Social capital that is well adapted to one broad set of joint activities may not be easily molded to activities that require vastly different patterns of expectation, authority, and distribution of rewards and costs than used in the initial sets of activities.

If unused, social capital deteriorates rapidly. Individuals who do not exercise their own skills also lose human capital rapidly. When several individuals must all remember the same routine in the same manner, however, the probability that at least one member of a group will forget some aspect increases rapidly over time. In addition, as time goes on, some individuals enter and others leave social groups. If newcomers are not introduced to an established pattern of interaction as they enter (through job training, initiation, or any of the myriad of other ways that social capital is passed from one generation to the next), social capital dissipates through turnover of personnel. Eventually, no one is quite sure how they used to get a particular joint activity done. Either the group has to pay most of the start-up costs all over again, or forego the joint advantages that they had achieved at an earlier time.

**Second, social capital is not as easy to find, see, and measure as is physical capital. The presence of physical capital is usually obvious to external onlookers.** Health centers, schools, and roads are simple to see. Social capital, by contrast, may be almost invisible unless serious efforts are made to inquire about the ways in which individuals organize themselves and the rights and duties that guide their behavior—sometimes with little conscious thought. Even when asked, local residents may not fully describe the rules they use. Robert Yoder warns those interested in helping farmers that they must probe deeply and in nonthreatening ways to get adequate information on the rules used to allocate water and maintenance duties within irrigation systems. "Intimidated by the higher status of officials, they may fail to communicate the details of the rules and procedures they use to operate and maintain their system" (1994, p. 39). Common understanding is frequently hard to articulate in precise language, particularly when status differentials make communication difficult in the first place. If external agents of change do not expect that villagers have developed some ways of relating to one another that are productive in the setting in which they live, those who are trying to help may easily destroy social capital without realizing what they have done. If past social capital is destroyed and nothing takes its place, well-being can be harmed rather than improved by external "help."

The researcher or project workers interested in social capital cannot assume from the outside that a group has (or has not) established common understandings that enable them to rely on each other to behave in ways that are predictable and mutually productive. The presence of words on paper or a building with a name on the outside is not the equivalent of the common understandings that are shared among participants. The self-organizing processes that social capital facilitates generate outcomes that are visible, tangible, and measurable. The processes themselves are much harder to see, understand, and measure.

**Third, social capital is harder than physical capital to construct through external interventions.** A donor can provide the funds to hire contractors to build a road or line an irrigation canal. Building sufficient social capital, however, to make an infrastructure operate efficiently, requires knowledge of local practices that may differ radically from place to place. Organizational structures that facilitate the operation of physical capital in one setting may be counterproductive in another. Local knowledge is essential to building effective social capital.

Creating social capital that makes physical capital operational over the long run is something that individuals who successfully use physical capital repeatedly do, but it is not as well understood as the technology of constructing physical capital. For private sector activities, an important aspect of entrepreneurship is bringing relevant factors of production together and *relating* them effectively from one to another. Aspects of these skills are taught in schools of management and learned in the workplace through experience. The incentive to create social capital related to private enterprise is attributed to the profit motive. A great deal of what private entrepreneurs do is to create networks of relationships that increase the profits that can be obtained. The private entrepreneur then keeps the residuals from creating and sustaining social capital.[7]

The incentives and motivation *of public entrepreneurs* who provide public goods and services is not as well understood as that of private entrepreneurs. In an earlier era, the theory of bureaucracy posited public officials who ascertained the public interest and were motivated to achieve it. More recent analyses of public bureaucracies are less optimistic about the capacity of public officials to know the public interests or to undertake the least costly ways of providing and producing collective goods. Instead of being viewed as if they were automata who do what they are told to do in the most efficient way, public employees are viewed as individual actors seeking their own interests. Pursuing their own interests may or may not generate net public goods, depending on how well the rules affecting their incentives help induce high performance. Thus, simply turning over the task of creating social capital to make physical and human capital more effective to a public bureaucracy may not generate the intended results unless officials are strongly motivated to facilitate the growth and empowerment of others. The social capital created may instead be the organization of limited networks of individuals or cliques that engage in mutual reciprocity at the expense of the larger group they are supposed to be serving.

**Fourth, national and regional governmental institutions strongly affect the level and type of social capital available to individuals to pursue long-term development efforts.** Larger-scale governmental institutions can facilitate the creation of social capital by citizens trying to solve coordination or collective-action problems or make it more difficult. They facilitate the creation of social capital when considerable space for self-organization is authorized outside of the realm of required governmental action. However, when national or regional governments take over full responsibilities for large realms of human activities, they crowd out other efforts to enter these fields. When national governments take over the ownership of all forests or other natural resources or close down schools and hospitals run by religious groups in an attempt to provide all health and educational services themselves, they destroy an immense stock of social capital in short order. Rarely can this be replaced rapidly. Creating dependent citizens rather than entrepreneurial citizens reduces the capacity of individuals to generate capital.

Many local infrastructure facilities and public goods are, however, not provided either by public bureaucrats or private entrepreneurs but rather by those who directly receive the benefits of collective action. An example is the organization of an irrigation system by the group of farmers who will directly benefit from its operation (Benjamin and others 1994). When a group of potential beneficiaries contemplates providing physical capital to be jointly used in a local, public economy, they also face a lengthy process of trial-and-error social learning and of bargaining among the participants over the rules that they will use and over how to use them. Given the multitude of nested collective-action problems involved in the creation of institutions, explaining how individuals overcome these problems is not easy. Furthermore, the diverse sources of asymmetries among participants makes it even more difficult to explain how individuals solve thorny distribution problems (see Libecap 1994; Hackett, Dudley, and Walker 1994; Hackett, Schlager, and Walker 1994; Johnson and Libecap 1982; Hackett 1993). Consequently, let us examine the process of crafting rules more carefully.

### The rule-creating game: an example of constructing social capital

Thousands of farmers who need irrigation water have organized themselves in many parts of the world in order to build and maintain their own systems (E. Ostrom 1992; Tang 1992; Lam 1998). Many of these systems have survived for multiple centuries based on local knowledge regarding their construction and maintenance, and owing to the skills of local farmers in crafting institutions to overcome the many temptations involved. Farmers always face a series of collective-action problems in determining who will share in the costs of constructing and maintaining an irrigation system, how the benefits will be distributed, and how activities will be monitored so as to ensure that those who follow the rules of their self-organized governance system are not taken advantage of by those who cheat.

To illustrate how rules affect outcomes, I will analyze how farmers themselves bargain over rules.[8] When they do this successfully, they solve collective-action problems that many analysts presume cannot be solved by those involved. Thus, the analysis that follows illustrates how a collective-action problem can be analyzed when the question of institutional change is the primary focus. It also illustrates how delicately balanced rules are with the constraints and opportunities afforded by the physical infrastructure itself.[9]

*Underlying assumptions*

For farmers to consider constituting themselves into even a loose form of association to construct an irrigation system, they would need to have secure enough land tenure to believe that they can reap long-term benefits from an investment. They would need to have established a sufficient sense of community that they can engage in a full array of face-to-face relationships that value keeping promises an asset of considerable importance. Coming to a high level of common understanding (Aumann 1976) about the structure of incentives they face, the types of individuals with whom they would be interacting, and alternative ways of structuring their relationships is a prerequisite for constituting associations to undertake major, long-term collective action.[10] Knowing that individuals share a commitment to keep their promises made to a group—so long as others keep their promises as well—affects individual expectations about future behavior. Those involved also need to switch levels of action from that of a day-to-day operational situation to a rule-making situation (E. Ostrom 1990).

If the set of beliefs outlined above is not altered by experience so as to destroy the assessment made by each farmer about the beliefs that others share and the likely strategies that others will adopt, such a set of farmers would be able to construct a system and operate it for a long period of time. If the precommitment that they make by signaling their agreement is followed by behavior consistent with that precommitment, each farmer's beliefs become more certain that others will follow the agreement, including sanctioning nonconformers (Elster 1979; Schelling

1960). Given precommitments and behavior consistent with these precommitments, it is then in each farmer's interest to conform to the agreed-upon rules most of the time.[11] In other words, an agreement is successful not simply because it creates joint benefits. It is successful when those who contribute to its continuance expect net benefits for themselves and their families that are greater than the alternatives available to them.

Nothing is automatic or deterministic about such a process.[12] What is crucial is that the farmers believe that their individual long-term benefits will exceed their long-term costs, that they find a set of rules on which they can agree, and that they adopt strategies that do not constantly challenge the delicate balance of mutual expectations that they have to maintain to keep the system going over the long run. Some farmers may be left much better off than others. The less advantaged must feel, however, that they receive a positive gain from participation or they will not voluntarily participate. Individual incentives depend on farmers' expectations, the viability of the rules they have established, their consequent beliefs concerning overall net benefits, and the distribution of benefits and costs.

*Symmetric incentives*

Let us first assume that ten farmers own equal-sized plots of land on an alluvial plain. One of the farmers (who has a reputation for designing prudent and well-conceived community works) has proposed a plan to divert a previously undrained mountain stream to their area. If allocated carefully, the source could provide water for three crops for all ten farmers. The plan involves the construction of a short main canal and two branch canals that each serve five families. The farmers can obtain a low-interest loan in order to purchase some of the needed materials and they have the skills needed to do the actual construction themselves. A diversion works at the source sends water into a relatively short and uncomplicated canal that is then divided into an X Branch and a Y Branch, each serving five plots of equal size.

In order to get started with this project, the farmers need to agree about the rules that they will use to allocate (a) expected annual benefits from the project and (b) expected annual costs. No one will voluntarily contribute funds or hard work to construct an irrigation system unless they believe that their own discounted flow of future expected net benefits is larger than their share of the costs of construction. For purposes of analysis, we will treat all farmers on each branch as if they formed a single team player facing all farmers on the other branch (also conceptualized as a single team player) in a two-player bargaining game.[13] If they do not reach an agreement about the set of rules they will use, the farmers continue their practice of growing rain-fed crops. The yield that they receive from rain-fed agriculture thus constitutes the "breakdown" value for each player—in other words, what they can expect if no agreement on constructing a new system is achieved.

In this situation, there are two rules being considered: Rule I and Rule J. Both players—Branch X and Branch Y—have to agree to either Rule I or Rule J, or they will not construct the system (see Knight 1992). If they do not agree, they continue with their current rain-fed agriculture and obtain the status quo yield ($SQ_x$, $SQ_y$) from growing one crop a year. In the symmetric situation, the status quo yield is equal for both branches. If both players agree on one of the rules, each year they will receive some combination of the total annual expected benefits (B) and costs (C) associated with providing this system. Both benefits and costs are expressed in crop units.[14] Let us first assume that total annual expected benefits exceed total annual expected costs as well as the status quo yield of each branch:

$$(B - C) \geq SQ_x + SQ_y. \tag{1}$$

Each branch would most prefer a situation in which it obtained all of the benefits and none of the costs. But the other branch would never agree to such a distribution. Without agreement, no one will contribute to the construction of the systems. Rules used to allocate benefits and costs affect the proportion of benefits and costs that each side obtains. The proportion of the expected annual benefits received by Branch X will be $e^I$ if Rule I is agreed upon, and $e^J$ if Rule J is agreed upon. Similarly, the proportion of expected annual benefits received by Branch Y is given by $g^I$ or $g^J$, depending on the rule selected.

$$1 \quad e^I, e^J, g^I, g^J \quad 0 \tag{2}$$

$$e^I + g^I = 1 \text{ and } e^J + g^J = 1. \tag{3}$$

The coefficients, $f^I$, $h^I$, and $f^J$ and $h^J$ are the proportion of costs assigned to the two branches under different rules.

$$1 \quad f^I, f^J, h^I, h^J \quad 0 \tag{4}$$

$$f^I + h^I = 1 \text{ and } f^J + h^J = 1. \tag{5}$$

Let us assume that all farmers are risk-neutral (orientated neither toward taking risks nor toward avoiding them) and have equal and low discount rates that are omitted from the analysis since their inclusion would not change the results.

*Rules to allocate benefits*

Let us first focus on the authority rules that the farmers could use for allocating water. For our initial consideration of the authority rule related to benefit distribution, we will temporarily assume that cost of construction and maintenance is equally divided. Let us suppose that the farmers consider two rules.

Rule 1: All water from the main canal is allocated to Branch Y for one week and to Branch X for the next week.

Rule 2: A dividing weir constructed that permanently divides the water in half so that half of the flow of the main canal automatically flows into each branch at all times that water is present in the main branch.

The structure of this game related to these two rules (or any similar rule of equal division) is presented in figure 1. Since we are assuming for now that the share of the benefits minus the costs of the irrigation system is greater than the status quo yield for both branches (equation 1), the branches face a benign coordination situation. There are two pure-strategy equilibria in this game: both choose Rule 1 or both choose Rule 2.[15] Since communication is possible, it can be used to solve this coordination problem. Which rule is finally chosen if they come to an agreement depends on situation-dependent variables.

*Rules to allocate costs*

Now, let us focus on a second type of rule—one related to how the farmers allocate responsibilities for providing labor during construction and for the annual maintenance efforts. The rules proposed may or may not be quite so symmetric in their effect. If there were one adult son in each of the families on Branch X and no adult sons on Branch Y, someone on Y might well propose the following rule:

FIGURE 1: AN INITIAL ILLUSTRATION

|  | | **Y branch** | |
|  | | Rule 1 | Rule 2 |
| --- | --- | --- | --- |
| **X branch** | Rule 1 | $(.5B - .5C), (.5B - .5C)$ | $SQ_x, SQ_y$ |
|  | Rule 2 | $SQ_x, SQ_y$ | $(.5B - .5C), (.5B - .5C)$ |

*Source:* E. Ostrom (1994, p. 537).

Rule 3: Each family sends all its adult males for every labor day devoted to the irrigation system.

Because each family owns identical plots, this cost allocation is proportionate to the aggregate benefit accruing to each family. Someone in Branch X might, however, propose the following rule:

Rule 4: Each family sends one adult male for every labor day devoted to the irrigation system.

Assuming that either Rule 1 or Rule 2 had already been agreed upon, these proposals would result in a bargaining game such as the one found in figure 2.

Assuming that the increased yield exceeds the costs that would be imposed on Branch X under Rule 3 ($.5B - .67C > SQ_x$), both branches would be better off agreeing to either rule compared with having no system. But Rule 3 assigns a higher proportion of net benefits to Branch Y, while Rule 4 treats both branches equally. Branch Y could argue that the irrigation system was providing benefits for all households and that all adult males should pitch in. Branch X could argue that it should not have to contribute twice the amount of labor as Branch Y simply because Branch X has more adult males. There are again two pure-strategy equilibria to this game: both choose Rule 3 or both choose Rule 4. Since the results are asymmetric, however, which rule is chosen depends on the relative bargaining strength of the participants. For Branch Y to get its way, it would have to precommit itself in a credible manner to the assertion that this rule was an essential precondition to obtaining its agreement to the plan for the irrigation system.

However, Branch Y could recognize that establishing a good continuing relationship was important and that if Branch X resented being forced to agree to a rule owing to a weak bargaining situation, Branch Y might face trouble later getting Branch X to abide the agreement on a continuing basis. Even though Branch Y really thinks it is inappropriate for one-

FIGURE 2: A SECOND ILLUSTRATION

|  |  | **Y branch** | |
|  |  | Rule 3 | Rule 4 |
| --- | --- | --- | --- |
| **X branch** | Rule 3 | $(.5B - .67C), (.5B - .33C)$ | $SQ_x, SQ_y$ |
|  | Rule 4 | $SQ_x, SQ_y$ | $(.5B - .5C), (.5B - .5C)$ |

*Source:* E. Ostrom (1994, p. 538).

third of the adult males, who are benefited by the system, to sit at home while the other two-thirds do all the work, Branch Y might recognize that one adult male per household is considered a fair rule in this setting and not push this proposal to the point of a breakdown of negotiations. Further, it is unlikely that the set of rules brought forward for consideration will include only Rule 3 and Rule 4 when one branch is disadvantaged by one of the rules under consideration.

Branch X could, for example, propose Rule 5, which would make Branch Y change its absolute preference for Rule 3 over Rule 4.

Rule 5: All water from the main canal is allocated to a branch in proportion to the amount of labor that the branch provides for construction and annual maintenance.[16]

Now whether Branch Y prefers Rule 3 or Rule 4 depends on whether it is combined with Rule 5 or Rule 1 (ignoring Rule 2, which has as an identical outcome function). If the expected benefits of building the system were 100 and the expected costs were 60, the results of different configurations of rules would be:

| Rules | Branch X | Branch Y |
|-------|----------|----------|
| Rules 1 & 3 | $.50B - .67C = 10$ | $.50B - .33C = 30$ |
| Rules 1 & 4 | $.50B - .50C = 20$ | $.50B - .50C = 20$ |
| Rules 5 & 3 | $.67B - .67B = 27$ | $.33B - .33C = 13$ |
| Rules 5 & 4 | $.50B - .50C = 20$ | $.50B - .50C = 20.$ |

Once Rule 5 is introduced into the rule-making situation, Branch Y no longer finds Rule 3 essential to its interests. If combined with Rule 5, Rule 3 leaves it with the worst, rather than the best, payoff.

The process of negotiating about rules is hardly a determinant process. While it is useful to model the process as a succession of choices among two rules, the impact of each rule depends on the other rules that have already been agreed upon or are to be discussed in the future. In most constitutional processes, initial agreements to specific rules are tentative. Eventually, the participants must agree to the entire configuration of rules embodied in some form of agreement. The overall effect of one rule may change radically depending on the other rules in the set.

### Asymmetric incentives

Many variables potentially create asymmetries among the players in a choice of rules game. In the above analysis, we addressed the possibility that the amount of labor available per household could vary among the players. Now let us introduce a substantial asymmetry related to the physical world. Instead of a canal that divides into two small branches, let us assume that the canal enters from one side. Now, the first five plots receive water before the last five plots. Water is sufficient to provide an ample supply for the head-end farmers, but not for the tail-end farmers. Irrigators located at the head end of a system have differential abilities to capture water and may not fully recognize the costs others bear as a result of their actions. In addition, farmers located at the head end of a system receive proportionately less of the benefits produced by keeping canals (located next to or below them) in good working order than those located at the tail. These asymmetries are the source of considerable conflict on many irrigation systems—substantial enough at times to reduce the abilities of farmers to work together.

In a bargaining situation over the rules, farmers at the head end of a system would prefer a set of rules that allowed them to take water first and to take as much water as they needed. Farmers at the tail end of a system would oppose such an authority rule for allocating water because this would leave them with much less water. Farmers at the tail end of a system would prefer a set of rules that would enable them to take water first and as much water as they needed. Both rules are used in the field.

To the extent that head-end farmers depend on the resources that tail-end farmers mobilize to keep a main canal in good working order, the initial bargaining advantage of the head-end farmers is reduced. In other words, if the amount of resources needed to maintain the system is large, farmers at the tail end have more bargaining power relative to the farmers at the head end than had the amount of resources needed for maintenance been small.

Several physical factors affect the amount of resources needed to keep a system operating. Let us first assume that the water source serving the system is a perennial spring and that very little work is needed at the headworks to keep such a system operating. We can then posit three kinds of systems depending on the length of the main canal as illustrated in figures 3a, b, and c. In figure 3a, there is no distance between the water source and the head-enders. In figure 3b, there is a short distance; and in figure 3c, there is a long distance. The costs of maintaining these three systems will be lowest for a 3a-type of system ($C'$), higher for a 3b-type of system ($C''$), and highest for a 3c-type of system ($C'''$).

The bargaining advantage of head-enders in systems such as those illustrated in figure 3a is much stronger than in systems such as those illustrated in figure 3b or 3c. Let us illustrate this with a numerical example of the choice of rules game. Let us continue to assume that the expected benefit of the water made available, regardless of the length of the canal, is 100 units and that the labor costs of maintaining systems of the type 3a are 25 units, of type 3b are 50 units, and of type 3c are 75 units. Thus in all three systems, the expected annual benefits of water obtained are greater than the expected annual labor costs. Let us further assume that two rules were being considered in such a situation:

FIGURE 3: THREE IRRIGATION SYSTEMS WITH INCREASING COSTS OF MAINTENANCE

**3a)   $B = 100, C' = 25$**

**3b)   $B = 100, C'' = 50$**

**3c)   $B = 100, C''' = 75$**

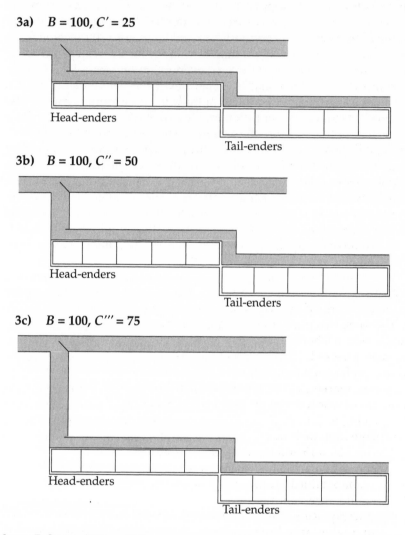

*Source:* E. Ostrom (1994, p. 544).

Rule 6: Head-end farmers are authorized to take as much water as they can put to beneficial use prior to the water being made available to tail-end farmers, and all farmers contribute labor to maintain the system voluntarily (head-enders have prior-rights rules).

Rule 7: Half of the water is allocated to the head end and half of the water to the tail end, and the labor needed to maintain the system is based on the proportion of water assigned to each set of farmers (equal split rule).

If Rule 6 were agreed upon, let us assume the head-enders would take 65 units of water per year. All labor would be contributed by the head-enders. If Rule 7 were agreed upon, the head-enders would only obtain 50 units of water per year, but would only have to put in one-half of the labor costs per year. Both head-enders and tail-enders would receive zero units of value in the situation of a breakdown.

In systems in which the cost of labor input is the lowest ($C' = 25$), there are two equilibria: both choose Rule 6 or both choose Rule 7. The head-enders would prefer Rule 6 and the tail-enders would prefer Rule 7. The head-enders would try to make a credible assertion that they will agree to Rule 6 and no other rule and refuse to engage in any further bargaining with the tail-enders. While tail-enders prefer Rule 7; Rule 6 does not leave them as disadvantaged as appears to be the case if one were to examine only the impact of the rule allocating water. Tail-enders would not contribute to the maintenance effort of the headworks. The head-enders would expect an annual return of 65 − 25 = 40. The tail-enders receive only 35 units, rather than the 37.5 ($100/2 − 25/2 = 37.5$) they could receive under an equal split. But since the tail-enders do not contribute at all to maintenance, they might even be accused of free riding in such a situation. They could, however, point to their willingness to work if and only if they obtained an equal split of the water.

The same two pure-strategy equilibria are present in a second situation, in which labor costs are 50 units. But, the preferences of the players are now reversed. Now the head-enders prefer Rule 7 while the tail-enders prefer Rule 6. And the bargaining power of the tail-enders has improved markedly. The tail-enders can credibly assert that the extra water is not worth the labor contribution. Some head-enders might end up agreeing to Rule 6. Under Rule 6, the tail-enders gain considerable advantage from their free riding on the work of the head-enders (head-enders 65 − 50 = 15 and tail-enders 35 − 0 = 35).[17]

In systems with the highest need for labor input ($C''' = 75$), head-enders cannot afford to agree to a rule that allocates them prior rights. They would receive a net loss (65 − 75 = −10) if Rule 6 were used. Consequently, Rule 7 is the only equilibrium for a choice-of-rules game involving only Rule 6 and Rule 7 in a high-cost environment. To get the labor input from the tail-enders, the head-enders would be willing to guarantee that the tail end receives a full half of the water. Thus the payoff to both segments under the high-cost condition would be 12.5 units.

*Empirical evidence*

The recently published book by Wai Fung Lam (1998), based on data from 150 irrigation systems in Nepal, provides an intriguing set of findings consistent with the game-theoretic analysis presented above. Lam finds several strong relationships between the physical attributes of irrigation systems, how the systems are governed, and three dependent variables: (a) the maintenance of the physical system, (b) the equity of water delivery, and (c) agricultural productivity. In a series of multivariant analyses (controlling for terrain, size of system, variance in farmer income and other variables), irrigation systems that have been improved by the construction of permanent headworks are in worse repair, deliver substantially less water to the tail end than to the head end of the systems, and have lower agricultural productivity than the temporary, stone-trees-and-mud headworks constructed by farmers (Lam 1998, table 5.6). In contrast, irrigation systems that are governed by the farmers themselves and those in which some sections of the canals are lined with stone or concrete are in better repair, deliver more water to the tail end of the system, and have higher agricultural productivity than unlined systems and those governed by the Nepal Department of Irrigation.[18]

It is quite intriguing that two different types of physical improvements (permanent headworks and partial lining) would have the opposite effect. And many scholars have found it hard to understand why the "primitive" irrigation systems built by the farmers themselves significantly outperform those that have been improved by the construction of modern, permanent, concrete and steel headworks (funded largely by donors and constructed by professional engineering firms). Controlling for the effect of these two physical improvements and other relevant variables, farmer-governed irrigation systems are able to achieve better and more equitable outcomes than those managed by a national agency.

Many factors contribute to these results. Most of them relate to the incentives of key participants in the finance, design, construction, operation, and maintenance of differently organized irrigation systems. On farmer-governed irrigation systems, farmers craft their own rules in processes that are similar to the stylized bargaining games presented above. These rules must counteract the perverse incentives that the farmers face given the physical and cultural setting in which they are enmeshed. The rules are frequently invisible to project planners when they design new physical systems.

In project planning, most of the effort focuses on how improving physical capital, such as creating permanent headworks, affects various aspects of the *technical* operation of a system. How these variables affect the incentives of participants is rarely explored. Unless the changes in physical infrastructure are undertaken with a consciousness that they will affect the incentives of participants—sometimes in perverse manners—projects intended to do good may generate harm instead.

Once one understands the relative strength and weaknesses of head-end and tail-end farmers, the differential impact of permanent headworks and partial lining on agricultural productivity in the Nepal context can be explained. Constructing permanent headworks reduces labor contributions dramatically. For example, in the systems analyzed by Lam, the average number of labor days per household in systems with permanent headworks is 2 days while the average is 8.5 days in systems without lining or headworks (p = .02, Lam 1998, table 5.10). Those near the headworks can obtain the primary benefit of such an investment and ignore the consequences for others. Partial lining of canals is something that the farmers themselves frequently do using local stone or may be undertaken by contractors as part of an aid effort. The primary beneficiaries of lining are those who are downstream of where the lining exists, since water loss in the lined portions is reduced. Partial lining also reduces the amount of labor time needed to keep a system in minimal repair (down to 5.3 days), but not as much as the replacement of the need to repair diversion works after major rains.

The "equalizer" in many farmer-organized systems is thus a substantial need for the contributions of resources each year by the tail-enders to keep the system well maintained. The need may stem from several physical factors including the yearly reconstruction of the headworks, the clearing and cleaning out of a long canal, or both. In those farmer-organized systems in which substantial resources are needed on a regular basis to cope with maintenance, Lain finds that rules assign water in about the same proportion as resources are mobilized, that more water is allocated to the tail, and that these systems achieve significantly higher productivity (see Lam 1998). Sweat equity can generate more equitable outcomes as well as higher levels of outcomes.

*Why external assistance that ignores social capital does not improve performance*

The above analysis allows us to understand why many effective, farmer-organized systems collapse soon after their systems have been modernized using funds provided by donors or central governments (see discussion below). Project evaluations usually consider any reductions in the labor needed to maintain a system as a project benefit. Thus, investments in modern engineering works are economically justified because of the presumed increase in agricultural productivity and the reduction in annual maintenance costs. The possibility that greatly reducing the need for resources to maintain a system would substantially alter the bargaining power of head-enders versus tail-enders is not usually considered.

Let us assume that an external donor plans to invest in a system with a physical structure and benefit-cost ratio such as that of figure 3c. Prior to investment, total benefits minus maintenance costs are equal to 25 units. The donor assumes that it is possible to raise the benefit level to

200 by teaching the farmers new agricultural techniques and by lowering the maintenance cost to 25 units through a one-time investment whose annualized value to the donor is also 25 units. Thus, the benefit-cost analysis leads the donor to make the investment since an annual benefit of 150 (200 − 25 − 25) is substantially above the 25 net annual benefits achieved prior to the planned improvement. The payoff matrix implicit in the benefit-cost analysis is illustrated in figure 4a, in which the only outcome projected is an equal distribution of a higher agricultural yield. The donor assumes that the farmers will somehow work out a scheme to share benefits as shown.

What frequently happens in practice, however, is illustrated in figure 4b. Instead of increasing benefits to 200, the system stays at 100 and the head-end farmers grab 90 units and make no investment in maintenance. Neither the head-enders nor the tail-enders are required to pay the annualized cost of the donor's investment. The tail-end farmers do not invest in maintenance and receive only 10 units of water. Rule 6 has become the default "might is right." It is not agreed upon, but rather imposed on, the tail-enders by head-enders who simply take the water.

In such systems, the head-enders can ignore the contribution to maintenance of the tail-enders because for a few years the concrete structures will operate without any maintenance. Of course, at some

FIGURE 4: PLANNED AND ACTUAL RESULTS OF SOME TYPES OF DONOR ASSISTANCE

**4a)**

|  |  | **Head end** Rule 6 | Rule 7 |
|---|---|---|---|
| **Tail end** | Rule 6 | [not in plan] | [not in plan] |
|  | Rule 7 | [not in plan] | 75, 75 |

**4b)**

|  |  | **Head end** Rule 6 | Rule 7 |
|---|---|---|---|
| **Tail end** | Rule 6 | 10, 90 | [not feasible] |
|  | Rule 7 | [not feasible] | [not feasible] |

*Source:* E. Ostrom (1994, p. 549).

time in the future, the productivity of the system will fall. If the farmers were expected to pay back the costs of the investment made in physical capital (or to pay taxes to keep the system well maintained), tail-end farmers would again find themselves in a better bargaining relationship with head-enders. A very disruptive aspect of many external assistance projects is that they appear to the farmers as if they were "free." Without any need for resources from tail-enders, head-enders can ignore the tail-enders' interests and take a larger share of the benefits.

This type of external "help" substantially reduces the short-term need for mobilizing labor (or other resources) to maintain a system each year. The calculations in the design plans, however, do not always match the results achieved. Without a realistic requirement to pay back capital investments, host government officials and the more influential farmers are motivated primarily to invest in rent-seeking activities and may overestimate previous annual costs in order to obtain external aid (Repetto 1986). Furthermore, such help can change the pattern of relationships among farmers within a system, reducing the recognition of mutual dependencies and patterns of reciprocity between head-enders and tail-enders that have long sustained the system. By denying the tail-enders an opportunity to invest in the improvement of infrastructure, external assistance may also deny those who are most disadvantaged from being able to assert and defend rights to the flow of benefits (see Ambler 1990, 1991).

*Past efforts to improve the physical capital of Nepal's irrigation systems*

Most efforts by donors and by the national government to improve the operations of the thousands of farmer-governed irrigation systems that exist in Nepal have focused on the physical capital aspect of irrigation systems and ignored social capital. To illustrate how these interventions have frequently operated in Nepal, I will draw on a study by Rita Hilton, who is now on the staff of the World Bank, analyzing the process of "improving" the Chiregad Irrigation System located in the Dang District of Nepal.[19]

The construction of the Chiregad system began in 1983 under a joint project of the United States Agency for International Development (USAID)-funded Rapti Integrated Rural Development Project and the Nepal Department of Irrigation (DOI). Construction of a system that serves between 302 and 425 hectares was completed in 1987. The new system was constructed in an area already irrigated by five irrigation systems built, governed, and managed by the farmers who owned the land served by their systems. The existence of these systems was not recognized by the DOI engineers who designed the project without consulting the farmers in the area.

A new, permanent headworks and lined main and branch canals were constructed. The field channels in the system, however, were left basically the same as those used by the five farmer-owned systems. The new construction has shown several serious design and construction flaws. The design engineers did not pay attention to the loose and sandlike soil in the region. As a consequence, the new deep-cut canals have frequently been blocked with mud and cause serious difficulties in operation and maintenance. Slides along canal alignments and poor drainage have brought on major problems at many locations of the system.

After construction, a water-users committee was formally established by the DOI as a mechanism described as one to facilitate farmers' participation in irrigation management. Irrigation officials played a dominant role in the process of forming a water-users committee. The way that a committee was established in these systems is similar to what has happened in many other agency-constructed systems in Asia: irrigation officials came to the system to summon farmers to a meeting and to inform them that a water-users committee had been established in their system. The officials simply appointed the *Pradhan Pancha* (chairman) of the local *panchayat* to be the secretary of the water-users committee, and the secretary in turn appointed other members in the committee. As a result, while the *Pradhan Pancha*—who owned no land in Chiregad's service area—was given a crucial role on the formal committee, the *aguwas* (water managers) of the five farmer irrigation systems serving the area incorporated were not even included on it.

The water-users committee was designed as a unitary organization for the entire new system. In other words, other than a committee at the system level, no formal organization was to exist at branch or field-channel levels. As the system is characterized by the existence of a number of branch canals at which communities with distinct interests are located, such a unitary institutional arrangement is highly questionable. On most farmer-governed irrigation systems of any size, branch canals are organized with their own rules and governance arrangements as well as an overall association. Some farmer-organized systems have as many as five levels of organization (Yoder 1994). The formal water-users committee rarely met and undertook few activities. During her fieldwork, Hilton (1990) found that none of the members of the users committee could provide her with information about the characteristics of the system and how the system actually operated.

The formal committee was created and recognized by DOI without any effort to understand how the prior farmer associations had been organized. Each of these farmer associations was related to a *mauja* (village) and coordinated the efforts of farmers in that village in regard to both water distribution and maintenance. The rules for each mauja differed for water distribution and for resource mobilization related to maintenance. It would appear that the farmers in each organization were able to design rules that suited the local situation. Furthermore, these organizations were strong enough initially to continue operating in a low-key manner to help with water distribution and maintenance of the system. These traditional organizations were not recognized by DOI. Consequently, their legitimacy and authority have been challenged repeatedly and are eroding.

The five farmer systems used to be able to provide adequate water to farmers located in all five maujas. After the Chiregad system was constructed, farmers in only three of these five maujas consistently received water from the new system. One mauja faces the problem of low reliability of water delivery in the monsoon season, as the canals are often damaged by floods. Another mauja faces the problem of excess water caused by poor drainage. Thus at the end of this effort to improve agricultural productivity through an investment in physical capital, a smaller service area is being served, water deliveries are unreliable, a newly established water-users committee is nonfunctional, and five farmer organizations that used to keep their systems operating well have been severely weakened. Not only is the physical capital of dubious value, a substantial reduction in institutional capital has resulted from this process. Similar processes have occurred with other government-constructed systems (Laitos 1986; Pradhan, Valera, and Durga 1993).

Chiregad is not the most extreme case in Nepal of lack of awareness of the social and physical capital that farmers have already created prior to a project. A more extreme case is the initial East Rapti Irrigation Project (ERIP) funded through credit assistance from the Asian Development Bank. ERIP was to have been initiated in 1987 to build a major diversion weir across the Rapti River and thus provide irrigation to a vast area of the terrain in the Chitwan district of Nepal. The benefits foreseen in the project plan were based on the difference between the productivity of irrigated and unirrigated land. All of the land in the project area was considered to be unirrigated. What is so remarkable about the initial project plan is that more than 85 farmer-managed systems were already providing irrigation services to most of the land in the project area (Shukla and others 1993). That project planners could overlook the irrigation activities of 85 farmer-governed systems in designing a large loan and the construction of a major system illustrates the type of blinders worn by those financing and designing major irrigation investment projects.

Fortunately, in this case, members of the Irrigation Management Systems Study Group (IMSSG) at the Institute of Agriculture and Animal Science in Chitwan had already conducted research in the area and documented the extant and relative efficiency of existing farmer-managed systems. They brought this to the attention of the donor community, which successfully challenged the appropriateness of the original plan. ERIP has now been significantly downsized. Its current objectives are to rehabilitate the existing farmer-managed irrigation system in the project area, to invest in various efforts to check stream-bank erosion, to construct better farm-to-market roads, and to construct shallow tubewells where appropriate (IMSSG 1993). Thus, the destruction of prior social and physical capital was averted because local researchers had invested time and energy studying the farmer-governed irrigation systems in the area and had excellent documentation.

While thousands of farmer-governed irrigation systems in Nepal have received no more than occasional small-scale support from external sources, those that have been the object of large, external interventions have frequently had experiences similar to that of Chiregad (or that which farmers in the East Rapti project area might have faced). The reduction in the amount of land actually served by "improved" systems—and the weakening, if not destruction, of the preexisting farmer organizations—is not unusual (Curtis 1991). Something is wrong when efforts to improve agricultural productivity by investing in physical infrastructure have the opposite result.

## The policy significance of social capital

In this chapter I have attempted to discuss the similarities and differences among the three types of human-made capital: physical, human, and social capital. Further, I have tried to establish why social capital is an essential complement to both physical and human capital. At the same time, I have also stressed that all forms of capital can be used to produce harm instead of welfare and, thus, the creation of social capital is no guarantee of increased human welfare.

While there are many forms of social capital, I focus in the last half of this chapter on the creation of social capital by self-organized resource governance systems. In particular, I presented a game-theoretic analysis of how a group of farmers might overcome the free-rider problems they face in order to devise a set of rules governing how to divide the benefits and costs of constructing and maintaining an irrigation system. The analysis shows that it is possible for farmers to overcome collective-action problems and devise rules that generate higher levels of benefits for those farmers who agree to participate in such ventures. The analysis also demonstrates that many local variables affect the specific bargaining strengths of diverse participants and the likely rule system that will emerge from such a process.

Empirical evidence drawn from a study of 150 irrigation systems, as well as from case studies in Nepal, supports the game-theoretic analysis. The empirical findings are consistent with reports about the effects of centralized, infrastructure investment in irrigation systems and watershed management that have ignored local institutions crafted by farmers in other parts of Asia.[20] Wherever extremely large sums of loan and grant funds are channeled through processes that enhance the power (and wealth) of politicians who successfully engage in rent-seeking activities, one cannot expect project plans to reflect on-the-ground conditions accurately. Wherever the engineers assigned to operations and maintenance positions hold low-status positions, are underpaid, and are not dependent on the farmers of a system for budgetary support or for career advancement, one cannot expect large, government-managed systems to perform very well. The results in Taiwan (China) and the Republic of Korea are quite different largely because the incentive systems of engineers assigned to operations and maintenance divisions reward using local knowledge and working directly with farmers (Levine 1980; Wade 1982; Lam 1995).

When farmers select and *reward* their own officials to govern and manage an irrigation system that they own and operate, the incentives faced by these officials are closely aligned with the incentives of other farmers in the system. System performance is linked to the evaluation made of the performance of the officials. In many centralized, national government systems, no such linkage is present. In cases in which the revenue received by an irrigation agency is not linked to taxes placed on the value of crop yield or the amount of water taken, the agency's budget is not even loosely linked to system performance. When fees are imposed in name only, are not an important source of revenue to the units operating and maintaining systems, and when the hiring, retention, and promotion of employees are in no way connected to the performance of a public facility, nothing offsets the dependency of citizens on insulated officials. The incentives of farmers, villagers, and officials are more important in determining performance than the engineering of physical systems.

Furthermore, the evidence that farmers can overcome local, collective-action problems when they have sufficient autonomy (either because of authorization in the formal legal system or because they live in such remote areas that no one cares about what they do), is also consistent with a substantial literature on the capacity of resource users to govern inshore fisheries, mountain commons, grazing areas, and forest resources in all parts of the world.[21] While the difficulties of sustaining long-term collective action are substantial, the benefits of creating local organizations and selecting locals as leaders who are rewarded for their performance can offset these high costs.

Instead of presuming that local users face an impossible social dilemma or collective-action problem, we are better advised to assume that it is *possible,* even though difficult, for those facing severe collective-action problems to overcome them. The greater the level and salience of the potential joint benefit and the existence of a supportive political system, the higher the probability that collective action will be undertaken. The impact of asymmetries among participants depends on the particular types of asymmetries that exist (Keohane and Ostrom 1995).

Donor agencies need to direct their efforts toward enhancing the capabilities of a larger proportion of citizens rather than simply trying to replace primitive infrastructures with modern, technically sophisticated investments. Investing substantial funds that only bolster political careers and build little at the ground level is a poor investment from a donor's perspective. It makes more sense to invest modest levels of donor funds in those local projects in which the recipients are willing to invest some of their own resources than in those projects in which the recipients are only patrons of a client looking for handouts in return for their political support. In such settings, involving users who are willing to invest some of their own resources, an infusion of external monetary capital and the construction of physical capital to complement the institutional capital on the ground may generate much larger returns. If the level of external funding gets very large without being strongly tied to a responsibility for repayment over time, local efforts at participation may be directed more at rent-seeking activities than at productive investment activities.

Entrepreneurship is not simply limited to the private sector. Local public entrepreneurs can develop a wide diversity of efficiency-enhancing solutions to local coordination and collective-action problems, even though they may not achieve full optimality, if there is an enabling environment that enhances their capacities to organize, mobilize resources, and invest in public facilities. Providing fair and low-cost conflict-resolution mechanisms, methods of achieving public accountability, and good information about the conditions of natural and constructed resource systems may be a more important task for national governments than attempting to plan and build local infrastructures throughout a country. In some cases, donors can encourage national governments to reduce the restrictions that exist in national legislation regarding the capabilities of individuals to form local associations, assess themselves to establish a common treasury, and undertake a wide diversity of local, joint projects that would benefit the association. Encouraging such groups to form associations of associations enhances their capabilities to learn from each other, exchange reliable information about what works and what does not work, and monitor the accountability of their own members.

In other words, investing in one of the strategies recommended in the *World Development Report 1994*, of giving "users and other stakeholders a strong voice and real responsibility" (World Bank 1994, p. 2), may enhance the economic benefits of investments in small- to medium-sized projects that intend to build physical capital as well as human and social capital. Investing in simple-minded, short-term projects to enhance citizen participation, by contrast, has frequently failed in the past (Sengupta 1991; Uphoff 1986). If social capital is conceptualized too casually and projects are designed to enhance "participation" without substantial changes in the structure of institutions, then the concept will become a shallow fad. One does not give stakeholders a "voice and real responsibility" by creating short-term projects that involve outsiders "organizing the farmers" in sweeping tours of the countryside. Participating in solving collective-action problems is a costly and time-consuming process. Enhancing the capabilities of local, public entrepreneurs is an investment activity that needs to be carried out over a long-term period. Changing the incentives of national, government officials so that their work enhances rather than replaces the efforts of local officials and citizens is a challenging and difficult task. And reducing the level of corruption involved in externally funded projects is an essential but daunting task (Klitgaard 1988, 1991).

Furthermore, our analytical models need to illuminate the incentives of participants whose decisions encompass multiple arenas simultaneously (Hayami and Otsuka 1993). We have misunderstood the rich network of mutual duties and benefits that common-property institutions have generated in much of the world. Recommendations to destroy these institutions are based on an assumption that the capacity to transfer ownership was the most important right in the bundle of rights potentially involved in the ownership of any resources (Schlager and Ostrom 1992). Recent studies of the evolution of indigenous land-right systems in Africa have challenged our analytical assumptions substantially (Migot-Adholla and others 1991; Berry 1993). Investments in new institutions, as well as new infrastructures, need to be based on knowledge that takes into account the multiple incentives that are generated by institutions, as they interact with social norms and the physical world in any particular setting.

We know that social capital in the form of institutions and resulting incentives is a critical factor affecting how physical and human capital affect productivity and growth. Well-developed market institutions, for example, generate incentives for private entrepreneurs to invest in physical, human, and still more social capital. The result of these investments, when matched effectively to local conditions, is substantial economic growth that is attributable to increased productivity. We also know that a polycentric public sector with specialized and general units organized at a local, regional, and national scale helps individuals to solve problems that are not effectively solved through the operation of markets (see V. Ostrom, Feeny, and Picht 1993; V. Ostrom 1991, 1997). An active and entrepreneurial public sector invests in infrastructures (roads, schools, irrigation systems, power generation, and so on) and produces public or common-pool resource goods (public health, natural resource regulation) that enhance the productivity of the private sector (E. Ostrom, Schroeder, and Wynne 1993). And the growth of a private sector can provide the income to build and maintain more infrastructures and public goods. It is these mutually reenforcing sets of relationships between private and public sector investments and activities that one can call economic development. Social capital plays as essential a role in achieving that development as physical or human capital. It does not represent, however, a quick fix that can be created by external or top-down processes. People who are facing extant coordination and collective-action problems have to have sufficient autonomy and incentives to build their own ways of working more effectively together.

## Notes

1. Transformation activities take one set of physical inputs and transform them into another set of outputs that may then be used in still further transformation activities or be finally consumed. Transaction activities are the relationships among the individuals involved that take time and energy to accomplish the transformation activities. See E. Ostrom, Schroeder, and Wynne (1993) for a detailed discussion of transformation and transaction costs involved in the provision and production of goods and services.

2. The next sections draw on E. Ostrom (1997).

3. Cattle have frequently been a major form of capital accumulation in Africa. Robin Fielder (1973, p.351; as cited in Bates 1990) notes that the Ila of Zambia often say that: "Cattle are our Bank." Fielder continues to explain:

> By this ... they mean a deposit account where their property is saved and where it will increase in value the longer it stays there. Cattle are regarded very much as shares and investments in capitalist societies.... There is no mystery about it at all: the investment is a very sound and highly rational one, and every Ila, educated or otherwise, is imbued with its sense from the time he herds his father's cattle as a small boy (1973, p. 352; as cited in Bates 1990, pp. 155–56).

4. Parents often invest in the education of their children not only to enhance their children's future income but also to enrich themselves, especially in developing countries. In Zambia, Robert Bates indicated that: "Parents paid the expenses of educating [their children], imparting sufficient skills that they could successfully compete for jobs in the cities of the Copperbelt. The costs of education were high.... But so too were the returns. For adults devoted resources to their children not only because they loved them but also because they expected later remittances of goods (soap, bedding, building materials, clothes, and pre-

pared foods) and money from children who held jobs in the towns....
Taking into account the magnitude and duration of the costs incurred in
schooling, the period of waiting for a child to gain employment, and the
subsequent magnitude and duration of the payments of remittances,
the rate of return to expenditures upon children lay in the range of eight
to ten percent" (Bates 1990, pp. 154–55).

5. The broad-based lineage structure of the Luo in Kenya, for example,
enables individuals to spread risk. "They can disperse their cattle to
family members located in contrasting settings; drought in any particular area is therefore likely to affect but a small portion of the individual's
herd. They can gain access to gardens in different ecological zones....
The lineage form of property rights thus provides insurance" (Bates 1990,
p. 158).

6. See Martin (1989/1992), *Common-Pool Resources and Collective Action*, vols. 1–2, and Hess (1996) *Common Pool Resources and Collective Action*, vol. 3, for extensive bibliographies of case studies describing institutions related to the use of common-pool resources (CPRs). These bibliographies can also be searched by accessing the Workshop web page
at: http://indiana.edu/~workshop.

7. John R. Commons (1957) stressed the difference between the plant,
on the one hand, and the going concern, on the other. The going concern
included the working rules that enabled those in the going concern to
relate to one another in a productive fashion in using a plant.

8. This section draws heavily on E. Ostrom (1996).

9. The following sections draw extensively on E. Ostrom (1994).

10. The assumptions about common knowledge are *strong* assumptions.
If participants had asymmetric and incomplete information, the results
described in this section would frequently be different.

11. It is almost impossible for farmers to follow allocation rules in all
instances. Given the stakes involved, the temptation to shirk or steal
can be enormous in some circumstances. Even in systems that have
survived for centuries, consistent evidence shows that some shirking and some stealing is a fact of life (see Weissing and Ostrom 1991,
1993).

12. Even though it is possible to discover the structure of these situations and array them as diverse games, which is done in the next section, most of these games have multiple equilibria. Which of the many

equilibria are selected depends on many factors—including the shared beliefs and conceptions held by the participants—that are localized in time and space.

13. In other words, we will not consider any within-team differences.

14. Alternatively, they could be expressed in labor units, as in the more general game-theoretic analysis presented in E. Ostrom and Gardner (1993). In either case, it is the basic production function between labor input and crop yields that enables one to use a single metric when denoting both benefits and costs. In a fully monetized economy, one would simply denote benefits and costs as a monetary unit.

15. Only pure-strategy equilibria are considered. A mixed strategy does not make sense when the alternative is a rule. However, one can model rule-breaking behavior using mixed strategies (see Weissing and Ostrom 1991, 1993).

16. This is a proportional distribution rule and would be considered an example of a "fair rule" according to many criteria such as the one proposed by Selten (1978).

17. This is an example of the "weak" exploiting the "strong" (see Olson 1965).

18. In an earlier study, the equity of water delivery was also found to be greater on the traditional, farmer-managed systems as contrasted with more "modern," agency-managed systems (E. Ostrom and Gardner 1993).

19. The information about the Chiregad system used in this analysis is based on the work of Hilton (1990, 1992) and Shrestha (1988), plus a visit to the site during the spring of 1989 by the author.

20. Bottrall (1981); Bromley (1982); Carruthers (1981); Chambers (1988); Corey (1986); Coward (1979); Easter (1985); Korten and Siy (1988); Plusquellec and Wickham (1985); Reidinger (1974); Sampath and Young (1990); Shivakoti and others (1997); Singh (1983); Wade (1985, 1988); White and Runge (1994); and Wunsch and Olowu (1995. Meinzen-Dick (1994) summarizes extensive literature from Asia, Africa, and the Americas that is highly consistent with the findings in this paper.

21. Berkes (1989); Blomquist (1992); Bromley (1991); Bromley and others (1992); Dasgupta and Mäler (1992, 1995); Eggertsson (1990); Feeny and others (1990); Fortmann and Bruce (1988); Libecap (1989); Martin

(1989/1992); McCay and Acheson (1987); Netting (1993); E. Ostrom, Gardner, and Walker (1994); V. Ostrom, Feeny, and Picht (1993); Pinkerton (1989); Sengupta (1991); Tang (1992); Thomson (1992); and Wade (1988).

## References

Ambler, John. 1990. "The Influence of Farmer Water Rights on the Design of Water-Proportioning Devices." In Robert Yoder and Juanita Thurston, eds., *Design Issues in Farmer-Managed Irrigation Systems*, pp. 37–52. Colombo, Sri Lanka: International Irrigation Management Institute.

———. 1991. "Bounding the System: Precursors to Measuring Performance in Networks of Farmer-Managed Irrigation Systems." Paper presented at the "International Workshop on Performance Measurement of Farmer Managed Irrigation Systems," Mendoza, Argentina, November.

Aumann, Robert J. 1976. "Agreeing to Disagree." *Annals of Statistics* 4(6): 1236–39.

Bates, Robert H. 1988. "Contra Contractarianism: Some Reflections on the New Institutionalism." *Politics and Society* 16: 387–401.

———. 1990. "Capital, Kinship, and Conflict: The Structuring of Capital in Kinship Societies." *Canadian Journal of African Studies* 24(2): 151–64.

Benjamin, Paul, Wai Fung Lam, Elinor Ostrom, and Ganesh Shivakoti. 1994. *Institutions, Incentives, and Irrigation in Nepal*. Burlington, Vermont: Associates in Rural Development; Decentralization, Finance and Management Project.

Berkes, Fikret. 1986. "Local-Level Management and the Commons Problem: A Comparative Study of Turkish Coastal Fisheries." *Marine Policy* 10: 215–29.

———, ed. 1989. *Common Property Resources: Ecology and Community-Based Sustainable Development*. London: Belhaven Press.

Berry, Sara. 1993. *No Condition Is Permanent: The Social Dynamics of Agrarian Change in Sub-Saharan Africa*. Madison: University of Wisconsin Press.

Blomquist, William. 1992. *Dividing the Waters: Governing Groundwater in Southern California*. San Francisco: ICS Press.

Bottrall, Anthony. 1981. *Comparative Study of the Management and Organization of Irrigation Projects*. Staff Working Paper no. 458. World Bank, Washington, D.C.

Bromley, Daniel W. 1982. *Improving Irrigated Agriculture: Institutional Reform and the Small Farmer*. Staff Working Paper no. 531. World Bank, Washington, D.C.

Bromley, Daniel W. 1991. *Environment and Economy: Property Rights and Public Policy*. Oxford: Basil Blackwell.

Bromley, Daniel W., David Feeny, Margaret McKean, Pauline Peters, Jere Gilles, Ronald Oakerson, C. Ford Runge, and James Thomson, eds. 1992. *Making the Commons Work: Theory, Practice, and Policy*. San Francisco: ICS Press.

Calvert, Randall. 1995. "Rational Actors, Equilibrium, and Social Institutions." In Jack Knight and Itai Sened, eds., *Explaining Social Institutions*. Ann Arbor, Mich.: University of Michigan Press.

Carruthers, Ian. 1981. "Neglect of O&M in Irrigation, the Need for New Sources and Forms of Support." *Water Supply and Management* 5: 53–65.

Chambers, Robert. 1988. *Managing Canal Irrigation: Practical Analysis from South Asia*. New York: Cambridge University Press.

Coleman, James. 1988. "Social Capital in the Creation of Human Capital." *American Journal of Sociology* 94 (supplement): S95–S120.

Commons, John R. 1957. *Legal Foundations of Capitalism*. Madison: University of Wisconsin Press.

Corey, A. T. 1986. "Control of Water within Farm Turnouts in Sri Lanka." In *Proceedings of a Workshop on Water Management in Sri Lanka*, pp. 25–30. Documentation Series no. 10. Colombo, Sri Lanka: Agrarian Research and Training Institute.

Coward, E. Walter, Jr. 1979. "Principles of Social Organization in an Indigenous Irrigation System." *Human Organization* 38(1): 28–36.

Crawford, Sue E. S., and Elinor Ostrom. 1995. "A Grammar of Institutions." *American Political Science Review* 89(3): 582–600.

Curtis, Donald. 1991. *Beyond Government: Organizations for Common Benefit*. London: MacMillan.

Dasgupta, Partha, and Karl Göran Mäler. 1992. *The Economics of Transnational Commons.* Oxford: Clarendon Press.

Dasgupta, Partha, and Karl Göran Mäler. 1995. "Poverty, Institutions, and the Environmental Resource Base." In Jere Behrman and T. M. Srinivason, eds., *Handbook of Development Economics, Volume III,* pp. 2171–2463. Amsterdam: Elsevier Science B.V.

Easter, K. William. 1985. *Recurring Costs of Irrigation in Asia: Operation and Maintenance.* Ithaca, New York: Cornell University Water Management Synthesis Project.

Eggertsson, Thráinn. 1990. *Economic Behavior and Institutions.* New York: Cambridge University Press.

Elster, Jon. 1979. *Ulysses and the Sirens: Studies in Rationality and Irrationality.* Cambridge (UK): Cambridge University Press.

Fairhead, James, and Melissa Leach. 1996. *Misreading the African Landscape. Society and Ecology in a Forest-Savanna Mosaic.* London: Cambridge University Press.

Feeny, David, Fikret Berkes, Bonnie J. McCay, and James M. Acheson. 1990. "The Tragedy of the Commons: Twenty-Two Years Later." *Human Ecology* 18(1): 1–19.

Fortmann, Louise, and John W. Bruce, eds. 1988. *Whose Trees? Proprietary Dimensions of Forestry.* Boulder, Colo.: Westview Press.

Fountain, Jane E. 1997. "Social Capital: A Key Enabler of Innovation in Science and Technology." In L. M. Branscomb and J. Keller, eds., *Investing in Innovation: Toward a Consensus Strategy for Federal Technology Policy.* Cambridge, Mass.: MIT Press.

Fox, Jefferson, ed. 1993. *Legal Frameworks for Forest Management in Asia: Case Studies of Community/State Relations.* Occasional Paper no. 16, East-West Center Program on Environment, Hawaii.

Hackett, Steven. 1993. "Incomplete Contracting: A Laboratory Experimental Analysis." *Economic Inquiry* 31: 278–93.

Hackett, Steven, Dean Dudley, and James Walker. 1994. "Heterogeneities, Information and Conflict Resolution: Experimental Evidence on Sharing Contracts." *Journal of Theoretical Politics* 6(4): 495–525.

Hackett, Steven, Edelia Schlager, and James M. Walker. 1994. "The Role of Communication in Resolving Commons Dilemmas: Experimental Evidence with Heterogeneous Appropriators." *Journal of Environmental Economics and Management* 27: 99–126.

Harriss, John. 1997. " 'Missing Link' or Analytically Missing? The Concept of Social Capital." Special Issue of the *Journal of International Development* 9(7): 919–49.

Hayami, Yujiro, and Keijero Otsuka. 1993. *The Economics of Contract Choice: An Agrarian Perspective.* Oxford: Clarendon Press.

Hess, Charlotte. 1996. *Common Pool Resources and Collective Action: A Bibliography,* vol. 3. Bloomington: Indiana University, Workshop in Political Theory and Policy Analysis.

Hilton, Rita. 1990. *Cost Recovery and Local Resource Mobilization: An Examination of Incentives in Irrigation Systems in Nepal.* Burlington, Vermont: Associates in Rural Development.

———. 1992. "Institutional Incentives for Resource Mobilization: An Analysis of Irrigation Schemes in Nepal." *Journal of Theoretical Politics* 4(3): 283–308.

Irrigation Management Systems Study Group (IMSSG). 1993. *Implementation of Process Documentation in ERIP.* Rampur, Nepal: IMSSG, Institute of Agriculture and Animal Science.

Jansson, AnnMari, Monica Hammer, Carol Folke, and Robert Costanza. 1994. *Investing in Natural Capital. The Ecological Economics Approach to Sustainability.* Washington, D.C.: Island Press.

Johnson, Ronald N., and Gary D. Libecap. 1982. "Contracting Problems and Regulation: The Case of the Fishery." *American Economic Review* 72(5): 1005–23.

Keohane, Robert O., and Elinor Ostrom, eds. 1995. *Local Commons and Global Interdependence: Heterogeneity and Cooperation in Two Domains.* London: Sage.

Klitgaard, Robert. 1988. *Controlling Corruption.* Berkeley, Calif.: University of California Press.

———. 1991. *Adjusting to Reality: Beyond "State versus Market" in Economic Development.* San Francisco: ICS Press.

Knight, Jack. 1992. *Institutions and Social Conflict.* New York: Cambridge University Press.

Korten, Frances F., and Robert Y. Siy, Jr. 1988. *Transforming a Bureaucracy: The Experience of the Philippine National Irrigation Administration.* West Hartford, Conn.: Kumarian Press.

Lachmann, Ludwig M. 1978. *Capital and Its Structure.* Kansas City: Sheed Andrews and McMeel.

Laitos, Robby. 1986. "Rapid Appraisal of Nepal Irrigation Systems." Water Management Synthesis Report no. 43. Colorado State University, Fort Collins, Colo.

Lam, Wai Fung. 1995. "Institutional Design and Collective Actions: A Study of Irrigation Associations in Taiwan." Paper presented at a conference on "Government Action, Social Capital Formation, and Third World Development," Cambridge, Mass., May 5–6.

———. 1998. *Governing Irrigation Systems in Nepal: Institutions, Infrastructure, and Collective Action.* Oakland, Calif.: ICS Press.

Levi, Margaret. 1996. "Social and Unsocial Capital: A Review Essay of Robert Putnam's *Making Democracy Work.*" *Politics and Society* 24(1): 45–55.

Levine, Gilbert. 1980. "The Relationship of Design, Operation, and Management." In E. Walter Coward, Jr., ed., *Irrigation and Agricultural Development in Asia: Perspectives from the Social Sciences*, pp. 51–64. Ithaca, New York: Cornell University Press.

Libecap, Gary D. 1989. *Contracting for Property Rights.* New York: Cambridge University Press.

———. 1994. "The Conditions for Successful Collective Action." *Journal of Theoretical Politics* 6(4): 563–92.

Martin, Fenton. 1989/1992. *Common-Pool Resources and Collective Action: A Bibliography*, vols. 1 and 2. Bloomington, Ind.: Indiana University, Workshop in Political Theory and Policy Analysis.

McCay, Bonnie J., and James M. Acheson. 1987. *The Question of the Commons: The Culture and Ecology of Communal Resources.* Tucson, Ariz.: University of Arizona Press.

Meinzen-Dick, Ruth. 1994. "Sustainable Water User Associations: Lessons from a Literature Review." Agriculture and Natural Resources Department, World Bank, Washington, D.C.

Migot-Adholla, Shem, Peter Hazell, Benoit Blarel, and Frank Place, eds. 1991. "Indigenous Land Rights Systems in Sub-Saharan Africa: A Constraint on Productivity?" *World Bank Economic Review* 5(1): 155–75.

Narayan, Deepa. 1998. *Voices of the Poor: Poverty and Social Capital in Tanzania.* Environmentally Sustainable Development Studies and Monograph Series, World Bank, Washington, D.C.

Netting, Robert McC. 1993. *Smallholders, Householders: Farm Families and the Ecology of Intensive, Sustainable Agriculture.* Stanford, Calif.: Stanford University Press.

Newton, Ken. 1996. "Social Capital and Democracy in Modern Europe." Paper prepared for the conference on Social "Capital and Democracy," Milan, October 3–6, 1996.

North, Douglass C. 1990. *Institutions, Institutional Change and Economic Performance.* New York: Cambridge University Press.

Oakerson, Ronald J. 1993. "Reciprocity: A Bottom-Up View of Political Development." In Vincent Ostrom, David Feeny, and Hartmut Picht, eds., *Rethinking Institutional Analysis and Development: Issues, Alternatives, and Choices,* pp. 141–58. San Francisco: ICS Press.

Olson, Mancur. 1965. *The Logic of Collective Action: Public Goods and the Theory of Groups.* Cambridge, Mass.: Harvard University Press.

Ostrom, Elinor. 1990. *Governing the Commons: The Evolution of Institutions for Collective Action.* New York: Cambridge University Press.

———. 1992. *Crafting Institutions for Self-Governing Irrigation Systems.* San Francisco: ICS Press.

———. 1994. "Constituting Social Capital and Collective Action." *Journal of Theoretical Politics* 6(4): 527–62.

———. 1996. "Incentives, Rules of the Game, and Development." In *Proceedings of the Annual World Bank Conference on Development Economics 1995,* pp. 207–34. Washington, D.C.: World Bank.

————. 1997. "Investing in Capital, Institutions, and Incentives." In Christopher Clague, ed., *Institutions and Economic Development: Growth and Governance in Less-Developed and Post-Socialist Countries,* pp. 153–81. Baltimore: Johns Hopkins University Press.

————. 1998a. "A Behavioral Approach to the Rational Choice Theory of Collective Action." *American Political Science Review* 92(1): 1–22.

————. 1998b. "Self-Governance of Common-Pool Resources." In Peter Newman, ed., *The New Palgrave Dictionary of Economics and the Law.* London: Macmillan Press, forthcoming.

Ostrom, Elinor, and Roy Gardner. 1993. "Coping with Asymmetries in the Commons: Self-Governing Irrigation Systems Can Work." *Journal of Economic Perspectives* 7(4): 93–112.

Ostrom, Elinor, Roy Gardner, and James Walker. 1994. *Rules, Games, and Common-Pool Resources.* Ann Arbor, Mich.: University of Michigan Press.

Ostrom, Elinor, Larry Schroeder, and Susan Wynne. 1993. *Institutional Incentives and Sustainable Development: Infrastructure Policies in Perspective.* Boulder, Colo.: Westview Press.

Ostrom, Vincent. 1991. *The Meaning of American Federalism: Constituting a Self-Governing Society.* San Francisco: ICS Press.

————. 1997. *The Meaning of Democracy and the Vulnerability of Democracies: A Response to Tocqueville's Challenge.* Ann Arbor, Mich.: University of Michigan Press.

Ostrom, Vincent, David Feeny, and Hartmut Picht, eds. 1993. *Rethinking Institutional Analysis and Development: Issues, Alternatives, and Choices.* 2nd ed. San Francisco: ICS Press.

Pinkerton, Evelyn, ed. 1989. *Co-operative Management of Local Fisheries: New Directions for Improved Management and Community Development.* Vancouver: University of British Columbia Press.

Plusquellec, Herve L., and Thomas H. Wickham. 1985. *Irrigation Design and Management: Experience in Thailand and Its General Applicability.* Technical Paper no. 40. World Bank, Washington, D.C.

Pradhan, Ujwal, Alfredo Valera, and Durga K. C. 1993, "Towards Participatory Management: The Case of an Irrigation System in the

Plains of Nepal." In *Advancements in IIMI's Research 1992. A Selection of Papers presented at the Internal Program Review*, pp. 233–47. Colombo, Sri Lanka: International Irrigation Management Institute.

Putnam, Robert, Robert Leonardi, and Raffaella Nanetti. 1993. *Making Democracy Work: Civic Traditions in Modern Italy.* Princeton, New Jersey: Princeton University Press.

Putzel, James. 1997. "Accounting for the 'Dark Side' of Social Capital: Reading Robert Putnam on Democracy." *Journal of International Development* 9(7): 939–49.

Reidinger, Richard B. 1974. "Institutional Rationing of Canal Water in Northern India: Conflict between Traditional Patterns and Modern Needs." *Economic Development and Cultural Change* 23(1): 79–104.

Repetto, Robert. 1986. *Skimming the Water: Rent-Seeking and the Performance of Public Irrigation Systems.* Research Report 41. World Resources Institute, Washington, D.C.

Sabetti, Filippo. 1996. "Path Dependency and Civic Culture: Some Lessons from Italy about Interpreting Social Experiments." *Politics and Society* 24(1): 19–44.

Sampath, Rajan K., and Robert A. Young. 1990. "Introduction: Social, Economic, and Institutional Aspects of Irrigation Management." In Rajan K. Sampath and Robert A. Young, eds., *Social, Economic, and Institutional Issues in Third World Irrigation Management*, pp. 1–10. Boulder, Colo.: Westview Press.

Schelling, Thomas C. 1960. *The Strategy of Conflict.* Oxford: Oxford University Press.

Schlager, Edella, and Elinor Ostrom. 1992. "Property-Rights Regimes and Natural Resources: A Conceptual Analysis." *Land Economics* 68(3): 249–62.

Selten, Reinhard. 1978. "The Equity Principle in Economic Behavior." In H. W. Gottinger and W. Leinfellner, eds., *Decision Theory and Social Ethics*, pp. 289–301. Dordrecht, the Netherlands: D. Reidel.

Sengupta, Nirmal. 1991. *Managing Common Property: Irrigation in India and the Philippines.* New Delhi: Sage.

Shivakoti, Ganesh, George Varughese, Elinor Ostrom, Ashutosh Shukla, and Ganesh Thapa, eds. 1997. *People and Participation in Sustainable Development: Understanding the Dynamics of Natural Resource Systems.* Proceedings of an international conference held at the Institute of Agriculture and Animal Science, Rampur, Chitwan, Nepal, March 17–21, 1996. Bloomington, Ind.: Indiana University, Workshop in Political Theory and Policy Analysis.

Shrestha, S. P. 1988. "Helping a Farmers' Organization: An Experience with Chiregad Irrigation Project." International Irrigation Management Institute, Kathmandu, Nepal.

Shukla, A. K., Kishor P. Gajurel, Ganesh Shivakoti, Rabi Poudel, K. N. Pandit, K. R. Adhikari, Tej B. Thapa, S. M. Shakya, D. N. Yadav, N. R. Joshi, and A. P. Shrestha. 1993. *Irrigation Resource Inventory of East Chitwan.* Rampur, Chitwan, Nepal: Irrigation Management Systems Study Group, Institute of Agriculture and Animal Science.

Singh, K. K. 1983. "Farmers' Organization and Warabandi in the Sriramasagar (Pochampad) Project." In K. K. Singh, ed., *Utilization of Canal Waters: A Multi-Disciplinary Perspective on Irrigation,* pp. 97–101. New Delhi: Central Board for Irrigation and Power, Publication no. 164.

Tang, Shui Yan. 1992. *Institutions and Collective Action: Self-Governance in Irrigation.* San Francisco: ICS Press.

Thomson, James T. 1992. *A Framework for Analyzing Institutional Incentives in Community Forestry.* Rome: Food and Agriculture Organization of the United Nations, Forestry Department, Via delle Terme di Caracalla.

Uphoff, Norman T. 1986. *Improving International Irrigation Management with Farmer Participation: Getting the Process Right.* Boulder, Colo.: Westview Press.

Wade, Robert. 1982. *Irrigation and Agricultural Politics in South Korea.* Boulder, Colo.: Westview Press.

———. 1985. "The Market for Public Office: Why the Indian State Is Not Better at Development." *World Development* 13(4): 467–97.

———. 1988. "The Management of Irrigation Systems: How to Evoke Trust and Avoid Prisoners' Dilemma." *World Development* 16(4): 489–500.

Weissing, Franz J., and Elinor Ostrom. 1991. "Irrigation Institutions and the Games Irrigators Play: Rule Enforcement without Guards." In Reinhard Selten, ed., *Game Equilibrium Models II.—Methods, Morals, and Markets*, pp. 188–262. Berlin: Springer-Verlag.

Weissing, Franz J., and Elinor Ostrom. 1993. "Irrigation Institutions and the Games Irrigators Play: Rule Enforcement on Government- and Farmer-Managed Systems." In Fritz W. Scharpf, ed., *Games in Hierarchies and Networks: Analytical and Empirical Approaches to the Study of Governance Institutions*, pp. 387–428. Frankfurt am Main: Campus Verlag; Boulder, Colo.: Westview Press.

White, T. Anderson, and C. Ford Runge. 1994. "Common Property and Collective Action: Lessons from Cooperative Watershed Management in Haiti." *Economic Development and Cultural Change* 43(1): 1–43.

World Bank. 1994. *World Development Report 1994. Infrastructure for Development*. Washington, D.C.: World Bank.

———. 1997. "Social Capital: The Missing Link?" Chapter 6 in *Monitoring Environmental Progress Expanding the Measure of Wealth*. Washington, D.C.: World Bank, Indicators and Environmental Valuation Unit.

Wunsch, James S., and Dele Olowu, eds. 1995. *The Failure of the Centralized State: Institutions and Self-Governance in Africa*. 2nd ed. San Francisco: ICS Press.

Yoder, Robert. 1994. *Locally Managed Irrigation Systems*. Colombo, Sri Lanka: International Irrigation Management Institute.

Young, H. Peyton. 1998. *Individual Strategy and Social Structure. An Evolutionary Theory of Institutions*. Princeton, New Jersey: Princeton University Press.

# Understanding social capital: learning from the analysis and experience of participation

**Norman Uphoff**
*Cornell University*

*All forms of capital represent assets of various kinds yielding streams of benefit. The "income stream" that flows from social capital is analyzed here as mutually beneficial collective action. The analysis delineates two main categories of social capital: structural (roles, rules, precedents, and procedures), and cognitive (norms, values, attitudes, and beliefs). A continuum of social capital is presented in terms of people's orientation toward positive-sum outcomes and toward positive interdependence of utility functions.*

*A case study from Sri Lanka shows how the two forms of social capital can produce substantial material benefits. Farmer organizations established under a donor project in the early 1980s produced unexpected and otherwise unobtainable rice production results in an acutely water-short season (1997) when government engineers had figured that no rice could or should be grown. By effective cooperation and by equitable sharing of scarce water, farmers achieved a better than normal crop, worth some $20 million.*

The concept of *social capital* has received impressively rapid acceptance within the community of development professionals, but it remains an elusive construct. The surge of enthusiasm reminds us of how "participation" gained much acceptance in development theory and practice during the 1970s but for many people remained abstract, more a matter of preference (or rejection) than of empirical study and application.

Concern with both of these concepts, social capital and participation, has had similar impetus. Much real-world experience had already shown that initiatives that did not take account of the human dimensions of development, including such factors as values, norms, culture, motivation, and solidarity, would be less successful than expected and intended. Indeed, it is not uncommon for development efforts ignoring these to turn into outright failures.

Development agencies in conjunction with a growing number of social scientists are trying to understand what social capital is and how it can be promoted reliably and in cost-effective ways for the sake of economic and social development. At present, social capital is more amorphous than participation, but it is also more intriguing because, if successfully understood, it offers the prospect of our being able to invest in it and thereby to create streams of benefit that justify the expenditure involved.

There is still debate whether social capital should be considered as a form of capital: whether it must be the result of some investment, (in other words, some foregone consumption); whether it must be purposefully created or can occur naturally; whether investments once created will endure or must be expected to depreciate; whether social capital should have benefits across multiple domains or will be activity-specific; and so forth.

Such questions are worth considering because they will sharpen our understanding of social capital. But they will not produce conclusive answers because social capital will not necessarily be identical with physical capital. While processes of social and physical capital formation may be analogous, they need not be exactly the same. The challenge of comprehending social capital will not be met by taking the analogy too literally. However, we should explore similarities for whatever insights these can produce.

All forms of capital can be understood as *assets* of various kinds, however they were created. Assets are things that yield streams of benefit that make future productive processes more efficient, more effective, more innovative, or simply expanded. Social capital is an accumulation of various types of social, psychological, cultural, cognitive, institutional, and related assets that increase the amount (or probability) of mutually beneficial cooperative behavior. This is behavior that is productive for others as well as for one's self. It benefits others and not just one's self, following from the Latin origins of the word "social," as discussed below.

Discussions in the literature remain inconclusive because they are based mostly on *examples* of what qualifies as social capital, rather than on some *specification* of what constitutes it. There is need for more rigorous analysis, not just description, to make theoretical and practical progress of the kind that followed from such treatment of "participation" (Cohen and Uphoff 1980). That framework is still probably the most widely used one for dealing with issues of participation in development. Something similar is needed for "social capital."

What constitutes social capital cannot be settled simply by offering a definition since definitions, while needed, offer no solution. Two hundred years ago, we could hardly have discovered what constituted physical capital simply by agreeing on how to define it. Cumulative empirical work guided by analytically coherent concepts will be needed to produce a robust understanding of a phenomenon as complex as social capital. Various definitions have been offered—see review by Serageldin and Grootaert (1997), which appears as chapter 2 in this book—but these have been more asserted than validated. We need to focus on components, relationships and results that can be evaluated in real-world development experience. Social capital needs to be addressed in terms of (a) what its constituent *elements* are, (b) what the *connections* are that exist among these, and (c) what *consequences* can be attributed to these elements and their interaction. The Biblical exhortation, "By their fruits ye shall know them," is highly relevant here.

Such a process of discovery requires subordinate conceptualization, in which the phenomena of interest are *disaggregated* in ways that lead to some tenable explanations and that indicate relationships that can be *demonstrated* in field investigations. A number of core ideas linked with social capital are worth exploring—civic culture, propensity for cooperation, collective action, mutual benefit, reduced transaction costs, solidarity, positive-sum outcomes. However, dealing with these terms by themselves represents a piecemeal exploration of associated factors rather than a systematic treatment of the subject.

Throughout the literature, two different but related categories of things are included under the rubric of social capital. Making a clear distinction between them while keeping their connection always in mind will produce some important insights into the operation of social capital as well as into its formation. This chapter first presents a conceptualization of social capital that integrates what is already known about the subject and points the way to more coherent and cumulative research. This presentation is then made more concrete by considering how social capital was created and manifested when improving irrigation management through farmer participation in Sri Lanka. The analytical framework has already been applied and demonstrated in an extensive quantified analysis of collective action for watershed conservation and development in the Indian state of Rajasthan (Krishna and Uphoff 1999).

## Understanding social capital as capital

To the standard three categories of capital in economic analysis—physical (human-made), natural, and human—is now being added a fourth, social (Serageldin 1996). These four categories are rather abstract, but each encompasses diverse sets of real things, best understood as assets. Physical capital, for example, includes highway networks, communication satellites, factories, tools, vehicles, houses, money, stocks, bonds, and other financial instruments.

What is needed for analytical purposes is not a listing of all the things that fall under different categories of capital, but rather some coherent categorization of the various factors so that we can make sense out of their heterogeneity. There are already some accepted distinctions made for the first three categories. It makes a big difference when dealing with physical capital, for example, whether one is dealing with fixed assets or fungible assets, with real property or financial instruments. Human resources are commonly categorized into skilled versus unskilled workers, or into manual versus mental labor, though this is a crude classification.

Consider how primitive our understanding and use of natural resources would be if we did not make any distinction between renewable and nonrenewable resources, lumping together forests, petroleum, fisheries, minerals, soil, and genes as if they were all basically the same. We need to remember, however, that these different categories of capital as well as subcategories are analytical rather than real. What exist are the things that are being categorized, not the categories into which they are grouped. However, making systematic and defensible distinctions among them is the most basic step toward making progress in theory and in practice.

Social capital can be understood most usefully by distinguishing two interrelated categories of phenomena: (a) **structural**, and (b) **cognitive**. These categories are as fundamental for understanding social capital, I would propose, as the distinction made between renewable and nonrenewable resources is for natural forms of capital.

The structural category is associated with various forms of social organization, particularly *roles, rules, precedents* and *procedures* as well as a wide variety of *networks* that contribute to cooperation, and specifically to mutually beneficial collective action (MBCA), which is the stream of benefits that results from social capital.

The cognitive category derives from mental processes and resulting ideas, reinforced by culture and ideology, specifically norms, values, attitudes, and beliefs that contribute cooperative behavior and MBCA.

The elements of social organization in the first category of assets *facilitate* MBCA, in particular by lowering transaction costs, having already established patterns of interaction that make productive outcomes from cooperation more predictable and beneficial. Ideas in the second category *predispose* people toward MBCA, in part because once they are widely shared they make cooperation more likely. Norms, values, attitudes, and beliefs that constitute cognitive social capital are ones that rationalize cooperative behavior and make it respectable. While it is possible in the abstract to have structural forms of social capital without cognitive ones, and vice versa, in practice, it is unlikely and difficult for either to persist without the other.

These two domains of social capital are intrinsically connected because although networks together with roles, rules, precedents, and procedures can have observable lives of their own, ultimately they all come from cognitive processes. Structural social capital assets are extrinsic and observable, while cognitive social capital assets are not. But both the social structural and cognitive realms are linked in practice (and in social science theory) by the subjective behavioral phenomena known as **expectations.**

Roles are created by expectations, and at the same time they create expectations, on the part both of (a) those persons who occupy (act according to) established and accepted roles, and (b) those persons with whom these role incumbents interact. One can say that roles and rules are objective because they are reinforced by sanctions and by incentives; but these latter sources of influence themselves depend for their effectiveness on mutual expectations, which means that objective factors have inextricable subjective underpinnings. Supporting the operation of roles and rules are procedures and precedents as secondary forms of structural social capital as discussed in an annex to this chapter.[1] Roles and their accompanying rules, precedents and procedures can be either formal or informal.

It should be pointed out, however, that norms, values, attitudes, and beliefs by creating expectations about how people *should* act, by implication create expectations about how people *will* act—for example, whether they will be cooperative or not, whether they will be generous or ungenerous. Thus what are subjective impetuses have definitely objective consequences.

*Networks,* which are patterns of social exchange and interaction that persist over time, are widely regarded as important manifestations of social capital, whether they are formal or informal. As forms of social organization, they represent structural social capital according to the categories given above. Most discussions of networks emphasize that they are held together by mutual expectations of benefit. But they are crucially sustained by expectations (that is, by norms) of reciprocity. This shows that there is an essential cognitive dimension to networks that derives from mental processes, and not just from what is exchanged.

To put the matter simply, structural forms of social capital are observable and externalized in contrast to cognitive forms. These are invisible because they are interior, within the mind, though when they are spoken of they become somewhat external. Both concurrently affect the *behavior* of persons, individually and in smaller or larger groups. Roles, rules precedents and procedures within various social structures, as well as norms and values along with their associated attitudes and beliefs, are the *mechanisms* by which social capital is built up and accumulated, stored, modified, expressed, and perpetuated, as discussed below.

Formal or informal organization with its roles, rules, precedents, and procedures, paralleled by formal or informal networks of interaction, together with norms, values, attitudes, and beliefs that are shared within a population, can have energizing and reinforcing effects, though they can also diminish depending on how people assess their results and benefits.[2] These phenomena can all be invested in to establish or increase their scope and effect; and all can depreciate in terms of the streams of benefit that they produce. Structural and cognitive phenomena that are conducive to mutually beneficial collective action are specific things that can be identified and invested in, even if they are mental more than material, giving reality to the abstract concept of social capital.

This conceptualization is consistent with ideas about social capital proposed by Coleman (1988) and Putnam, Leonardi, and Nanetti (1993). Indeed, it derived from their and others' writing on the subject. Both Coleman and Putnam include structural and cognitive elements in their definitions and analysis, but they approach social capital more descriptively than analytically. By organizing the factors that constitute social capital into two basic categories that can be made concrete and that can be studied, the formulation offered here presents social capital in terms that should be more amenable to theoretical progress as well as to measurement and evaluation.[3]

When Serageldin and Grootaert (1997) compared Coleman's and Putnam's views of social capital, they suggested that the first author more than the second "captures social **structure** at large as well as the ensemble of **norms** governing interpersonal behavior" (p. 13, emphasis added; a revised version of this article appears as chapter 2 in this volume). However, this is a matter of degree, and the differences between the two views are not great. A third view of social capital following from the work of North (1990) and Olson (1982) is characterized by Serageldin and Grootaert as treating social capital as deriving from "the social and political environment that enables **norms** to develop and shapes social **structure**" (1997, p. 13, emphasis added). We see that all three views contain the same elements and refer repeatedly to aspects of social structure and to normative (cognitive) influences, but without placing these factors into a theoretically explicit or rigorous framework.

In the literature, social capital is generally understood as having some *combination* of role-based or rule-based (structural) and mental or attitudinal (cognitive) origins. As noted already, these are related and interactive, to be sure, but they are distinguishable. Table 1 below presents in contrasting ways the main terms associated with social capital in the literature. It delineates the *complementary* factors that together produce the variety and range of assets that contribute to social capital phenomena.

These two categories of social capital are highly interdependent, as each form contributes to the other. Both affect behavior through the mechanism of expectations. Both kinds of phenomena are conditioned by experience and are reinforced by culture, *Zeitgeist* and other influences.

Both structural and cognitive forms of social capital are ultimately mental. Shared values, norms and expectations are part and parcel of all social structural arrangements. Roles and rules that are written down may appear objective, but even material influences such as the

TABLE 1: COMPLEMENTARY CATEGORIES OF SOCIAL CAPITAL

|  | *Structural* | *Cognitive* |
|---|---|---|
| Sources and manifestations | Roles and rules | Norms |
|  | Networks and other interpersonal relationships | Values |
|  |  | Attitudes |
|  | Procedures and precedents | Beliefs |
| Domains | Social organization | Civic culture |
| Dynamic factors | Horizontal linkages | Trust, solidarity, |
|  | Vertical linkages | cooperation, generosity |
| Common elements | Expectations that lead to cooperative behavior, which produces mutual benefits | |

*Source:* Author.

sanctions that are exercised by role incumbents and invoked according to rules depend for their effectiveness ultimately on cognitive processes.[4] Whether sanctions are invoked, and indeed whether they are considered sufficient to cause compliance, will be determined in the realm of thought, not simply by the nature or magnitude of what is being threatened.

At the same time, it would be wrong to say that all aspects of social capital are "only thoughts." This would miss the important fact that once ideas and purposes have been crystallized into roles, rules, networks, and other established relationships intended to catalyze certain kinds of action, the probability of such action and predictable outcomes increases by several orders of magnitude.

Social structure thus has objectified consequences even if it originates from and depends on subjective values and evaluations. Thus, it is useful to distinguish between structural and cognitive elements of social capital even though they are related and reinforcing. Not to make this distinction reduces explanatory power and also our understanding of how social capital comes into being and is sustained.

## What is "social" about social capital?

Concepts can evolve and change beyond their original meaning. But usually our understanding of something can be improved by knowing its derivation. The etymology of the word "social" should help us understand what is meant by social capital, and how it differs from other forms of capital.

The word "social" is one of the most widely and broadly used adjectives in the English language, attached to things as diverse as energy, diseases, and marketing. It is linked to the noun "society," which comes from the Latin word *socius*, which denotes "friend or comrade."[5] This indicates that what is "social" originally derived from the phenomenon of *friendship*, implying some personal attachment, cooperation, solidarity, mutual respect, and sense of common interest.

Elsewhere I have suggested that friendship can be analyzed in fairly rigorous terms using concepts from economics and game theory and drawing on the concept of utility function (Uphoff 1996, pp. 341–45, 365–67, 378–81). If people are **strangers** to one another, they are indifferent to each other's well-being. Analytically, this means that they have *independent* utility functions. They do not care whether others are better off or not and are indifferent whether their own actions help or harm others. This is the standard assumption made in most economic analysis. It was originally made to simplify analysis, but now it is often assumed to be a true description of human nature, consistent with the idea of *homo economicus* as an individual, self-interested utility maximizer.

**Friends**, by contrast, are persons whose utility functions are positively *inter*dependent, which means that they attach some value to each other's well-being. They consider themselves better off when their friends are wealthier, happier, more secure, or more respected. And finally, **enemies** are persons whose utility functions are *negatively* interdependent. Enemies derive satisfaction from their foes' misfortune and even seek to increase this for their own benefit.

As with most things, we should think in terms of *degree*, not just of kind, going beyond simple classifications. Nobody knows what minimum extent of positive interdependence is needed for society to exist or for social relations to persist. However, I would suggest that the defining characteristic for the meaning of "social" is there being *some degree of mutuality, some degree of common identity, some degree of cooperation for mutual, not just personal, benefit*. Cooperation is desirable and collective action is undertaken not just for one's own sake—that is, as purely self-interested action—but because others can benefit from it in addition to one's self.[6]

To use the language of game theory, relationships among friends are *positive-sum* because the sum total of satisfactions increases whenever anything benefits either or both of them without significantly harming the other. Friends take delight in each others' good fortune.[7] By contrast, if people are enemies, any gains have *negative*-sum effects because benefits that accrue to anyone will reduce the happiness and sense of security of all their adversaries. In between, in a world of strangers, whether or not the gains of one person represent the loss of another (a zero-sum relationship) will depend on how those gains are created. It is acceptable for strangers to gain benefit at others' expense.

Whether people are friends, enemies, or strangers can be strongly influenced by history or early socialization. This helps determine *which* persons will be regarded as friends. In the final analysis, however, friendship is a matter of individual choice. Persons can choose to value others' well-being or not. Even in recent situations as tragic and violent as those in Bosnia, Rwanda, and Kosovo, we saw many examples of persons who chose and demonstrated the path of friendship even as the institutions and culture embodying centuries of social capital accumulation were being destroyed around them.

Persons can, and often do, decide to be indifferent toward others' advancement, or even to be antagonistic toward this and to try to prevent it. When there are "social" relationships, people are, at least to some extent, *invested* in each other—that is, they attach at least some value to others' welfare, not being indifferent to this. This metaphor of investment, which is easily understood intuitively, is not a coincidental use of metaphor. It points the way toward a concrete understanding of what is involved in the creation and functioning of social capital.

It may be difficult to see this relationship partly because of our reductionist tendencies to classify things as being *either* this *or* that—considering people and relationships as being either entirely selfish or generous, for example. This conceptual predilection distracts us from discerning and assessing matters of *degree* and *directions* of change. Societies and social relationships—quite like Rome—are not built in a day, though they can be destroyed almost that fast. The realm of what is "social" is extremely complex and manifests itself along a continuum from minimal to maximal "society," with friendship, solidarity, mutuality, reciprocity, and related phenomena being manifested as matters of degree.

If people are living together, that is, not in a constant state of war and conflict, there must be some minimum of tolerance and willingness to live and let live, though there can be much exploitation and little mutual regard. The minimum condition for social capital is described in the left-hand column of table 2, which represents little interpersonal attachment and cooperation. The extreme condition, such as Turnbull (1972) described among the Ik people, is hard to imagine, let alone find. So the left-hand column is an ideal (sic) type, contrasting with the similarly rare situation of maximum social capital described in the right-hand column. Even the very benign society of the Ituri pygmies documented by Turnbull (1961) did not fully attain this level of solidarity.

Most situations are between these two extremes, somewhere along a continuum between the two middle columns in table 2. If people are not totally indifferent to each other's well-being, their society is in the range of the second column. Motivation can be highly instrumental and self-serving, with cooperation only for the sake of—and only to the extent of—personal benefit. But cooperation can create positive-sum benefits for others as well as one's self (Axelrod 1984), which can move social relationships toward, if not beyond, the third column.

TABLE 2: THE SOCIAL CAPITAL CONTINUUM

| | Minimum social capital | Elementary social capital | Substantial social capital | Maximum social capital |
|---|---|---|---|---|
| | No interest in others' welfare; seek self-interest maximization at others' expense | Interest primarily in own welfare; cooperation occurs only to the extent that it serves one's own advantage | Commitment to common enterprises; cooperation occurs to a greater extent when it is beneficial also for others | Commitment to others' welfare; cooperation is not limited to seeking one's own advantage; concern for public good |
| *Values:* | *Self-aggrandizement* respected | *Efficiency* of cooperation | *Effectiveness* of cooperation | *Altruism* regarded as something good in itself |
| *Issues:* | *Selfishness*—how can this be kept from being socially quite destructive? | *Transaction costs*—how can these be reduced to increase people's respective net benefits? | *Collective action*—how can cooperation (that is, pooling of resources) succeed and be sustained? | *Self-sacrifice*—how far should this be taken: for example, patriotism? religious zealotry? |
| *Strategy:* | Autonomy | Tactical cooperation | Strategic cooperation | Merger or submergence of individual interests |
| *Mutual benefits:* | Not considered | Instrumental | Institutionalized | Transcendent |
| *Options:* | *Exit* whenever dissatisfied | *Voice*, try to improve terms of exchange | *Voice*, try to improve overall productivity | *Loyalty*; acceptance of results if good for all in total |

| | | | |
|---|---|---|---|
| *Game theory:*<br>*Zero-sum*; but if competition is unconstrained, choices will have negative-sum results | *Zero-sum*; exchanges that are intended to maximize own benefits can have positive-sum results | *Positive-sum*; aim is to maximize own **and** others' interests to mutual advantage | *Positive-sum*; aim is to maximize common interests with own interests subordinated |
| *Utility functions:*<br>*Interdependent*, with weight given only to own utilities | *Independent*, with own utilities being advanced through cooperation | *Positively interdependent*, with some weight given to others' benefit | Positively *interdependent*, with more weight assigned to others' benefits than to one's own benefits |

*Source: Author.*

The relationships in the fourth column can be summarized in the motto of the *Three Musketeers*: "All for one, and one for all." (Recall the statement of Massachusetts Colony governor John Winthrop cited in note 7.) Such solidarity is seldom observed because it demands self-sacrifice beyond what most persons are willing to accept and sustain, however many benefits it might confer. Setting aside this most intense form of "society," there are many degrees of positive interdependence of utility functions in between the left- and right-hand columns. These represent extreme situations that can frame research and policy issues but are of less practical interest and importance than the two middle columns.[8]

Some modicum of social capital is present in the second column but even more in the third. There are some *a priori* reasons for thinking that the third would be a more productive and robust situation of cooperation and collective action, because outcomes are valued and appreciated by many persons, not just by those who contribute to them. But this situation may also be more difficult to establish and maintain, and it can be subject to its own sources of weakness.

As this is a continuum, all real situations should be seen as representing matters of *degree* rather than just of kind. One can hypothesize, for example, that to the extent some values and elements associated with the fourth column are present in the third situation, that is, if some persons are fully committed to collective well-being and are willing to make sacrifices for this, it will be more durable.

This is not a purely imagined proposition. Some of the elements of so-called "traditional" communities are associated with the more normatively interdependent and intense kinds of relationships suggested by the right-hand column such as expressed in family and kinship. The solidarity that is the essence of social relationships is usually seen most strongly in small numbers of people—families, clubs, groups, communities—although smallness is no guarantee of solidarity. Solidarity is a subjective creation, a matter of choice, and it can be observed also in large groups, even whole nations, if people identify intensely enough with each other's welfare.[9]

Social relations create value through *reciprocity*, which is closely related to *trust* (Fukuyama 1995). Many things that we want and need cannot be created simply by our own efforts. The positive effects of competition, which sets individuals (or groups) against each other, are most beneficially realized within larger frameworks of cooperation.[10] While reciprocal exchanges can be undertaken purely on a self-interested basis, their longevity and stability, and hence their productivity, will be greater to the extent that trust and confidence underlie them (Frank 1992).

While one can have the forms (structure) of society without solidarity (norms), the power and durability of social connections is greater to the extent that people are "invested" in each other, a summary statement about social capital. Social and political as well as economic relations are all more productive when people relate to each other not as strangers, and certainly not as enemies, but to some extent as friends. This reflects and reinforces trust, which in all accounts of social capital is recognized as the essential "glue" for society.

People need not be intimate acquaintances to value others' well-being, or at least not be indifferent to this. Such an orientation is the most basic requirement for "society." The values, attitudes, social structures and relationships that reinforce and reward such psychological "investment in each other" are basically what is meant when we talk about social capital. Purely self-interested cooperation represents a form or degree of social capital, but this is the weakest sort. It is not very stable because it is liable to dissolve whenever individuals think that they have put more into a role, a reciprocal relationship, an institution or a shared belief than they have gotten out of it, directly and in the short run.

### Investing in social capital

The concept of social capital is attractive to governments and development agencies in part because it could enable decision-makers to make investments that increase the efficiency and probability of success for development initiatives. If social capital is amenable to being created, it would not just explain differences in success between projects or between communities. It could contribute to success.

The understanding of social capital proposed here is consistent with an investment approach, although social capital appears more akin to natural than to physical (human-made) capital, being largely inherited from generation to generation. Structural and cognitive forms of social capital can be built up over time, though they cannot be "seeded" as simply and directly as a forest can be planted, for example. With both kinds of investment there is need for whatever is planted to "take root." Reforestation efforts can have more control over the soil, water, and nutrient conditions than social capital investors can influence the motivations and evaluations of people. The roles, rules, norms, and values that constitute social capital are not like a mineral deposit created eons ago as a fixed stock; rather there is an accretionary dynamic, more like that observed with the process of soil creation as various processes contribute to the buildup of this kind of asset. Fortunately, the building up of roles and norms need not be so slow as with soil, and networks can be established fairly quickly. Unfortunately however, social relationships and values—much like soil—can *erode* both faster and more easily than is true in the process of their formation.

Much of the creation of social organization—roles, rules, procedures, precedents, relationships—is unplanned and purposive only in small ways. Its role as social capital is mostly a by-product. These various elements of social organization aggregate into networks and associations that establish patterns for people to act together in mutually beneficial ways. How beneficial they are, and to what extent the benefits are equitably shared, will certainly vary. Organization that is purely coercive or exploitative is essentially redistributive, rather than productive; since it does not contribute to mutual benefit, it is not considered here under the rubric of social capital.

The values, norms, attitudes, and beliefs that qualify as social capital are built up over time, but can be diminished and even destroyed in fairly short order. Much as with other forms of capital, accumulation occurs usually with some expenditure, though net expenditure can be fairly small if the benefits are evident and attractive. What has been accumulated can be lost subsequently through a variety of uses or misuses.

In previous work on the subject of social organization, it was concluded that there are four basic, ubiquitous activities of organization: decision-making, resource mobilization and management, communication, and conflict resolution.[11] These four activities, or functions, are essential for mutually beneficial collective action, lowering transaction costs and increasing the probability that individual efforts in concert with others' will be efficacious.

Without roles and rules for decision-making and resource mobilization, collective action becomes more difficult and thus less likely. Facilitating communication among persons, as well as resolving any conflicts that may arise among them, is likewise needed for getting and keeping people together to accomplish things that are beyond the capability of individuals who are seeking just their own well-being. These four kinds of activities can be carried out formally or informally, and they apply for any level of social organization or between levels of organization.[12]

Creating social capital requires more than just introducing roles, since it is the *acceptance* of roles that patterns people's behavior in predictable and productive ways. A role exists when there are shared and mutual expectations about what any person in a certain role should and will do under various conditions. These expectations need to be shared by both role incumbents and those persons who interact with that role. Social organization is less costly and often more effective in cases in which cooperation is motivated by norms, values, beliefs, and attitudes that create reinforcing expectations, rather than the organizers having to gain cooperation through material incentives or coercive actions. While such incentives and actions may be involved in any complex set of social relations, if they are all that produces intended behavior, this is a very expensive way to achieve results.

Establishing rules and procedures is only a first step toward creating structural social capital. Gaining and maintaining their acceptance, with a significant if not total degree of voluntary compliance, is what makes them beneficial, by establishing both greater predictability and productivity from people's interaction. Social networks likewise represent established patterns of communication and cooperation that reduce transaction costs and thus make collective action of various sorts more feasible and profitable.

All forms of structural social capital are influenced by prior experience since precedents affect expectations about how future behavior will be rewarded, materially or nonmaterially. Enforcement and reinforcement of rules and procedures require certain expenditure of resources. These produce payoffs, penalties, or both, that make future outcomes more predictable and more beneficial. There may need to be training, which entails present cost, to make people explicitly aware of the expectations that are supposed to govern their behavior.

Interpersonal relationships that aggregate into social networks, large or small, need to be sustained by the contributions that people make to each other's welfare. The net reward over time to participants in social networks can be substantial, but achieving these benefits requires a willingness to make some sacrifices at least in the short run. More than other forms of social capital, networks clearly require investment (of time, money, information, and prestige) that can yield a benefit flow (of employment, income, sociability, knowledge, and other payoffs).

Investment in cognitive social capital is less obvious, but it clearly can involve costs. The articulation of norms and values, attitudes, and beliefs does not entail much cost, but living up to them can. Principles such as solidarity, trust and honesty will evoke little support and have little effect unless there is some confidence that others will also uphold them. This means that people must make some sacrifices to demonstrate that these norms or values are alive and well, reflecting appreciation that these values are good for individuals and for society at large. In cases in which these values are honored more in the breach than the observance, at least some individuals may nevertheless make personal sacrifices to affirm them and elevate them in public consciousness.

While such explanations of the social capital formation process are still fairly sketchy, the outlines of a theory for explaining such formation, as well as social disinvestment and decapitalization, should be reasonably clear from this analysis. Certain reinforcing kinds of behavior, especially by persons who are in positions of leadership and authority or who occupy high social status, can support structural and cognitive forms of social capital—while negative behavior can diminish others' commitment to them.

Of most relevance are norms, values, attitudes, and beliefs that support mutually beneficial collective action, through which people may be seeking their own benefit but are also interested in and willing to contribute to the benefits of others. Cooperation that is entirely contingent on one's own benefit, without regard to the welfare of others, may reflect some minimum of social capital, compared with having norms, values, attitudes, and beliefs that work against even this much cooperation. But it is a limited and brittle kind of cooperation. Most understandings of social capital entail some element of generosity toward others, not being motivated only by self-interested considerations.

Social capital is more likely to be beneficial and durable when it involves more than purely instrumental, self-serving considerations. Social capital based on *"mixed-motive" cooperation* is more productive and sustainable because it operates in a positive-sum manner. To the extent that people's thinking is based on positively interdependent utility functions—valuing others' well-being *in addition to* their own—economic, social, and political relationships will become more fruitful and long-lasting than if these are entered into only on the basis of narrow self-interest. More resources can be mobilized and put into joint ventures than will be the case if narrower calculations of individual self-interest prevail.

The roles, institutions, values, and relationships covered by Coleman's and North's definitions can be considered as social capital. But something is lost or at least foregone if our understanding of the productive potential of this construct is restricted to a self-centered vision of how and why people work together. Hirschman's interest in social energy (1984) is supported by my own observations in Sri Lanka (Uphoff 1996) and by many instructive experiences in other countries (Krishna, Uphoff, and Esman 1997). Social capital that derives from animating norms and personal relationships can accomplish much more than what the minimalist version of social capital will.

People do not operate only on the basis of self-interest *or* altruism. Generally they combine the two in a both-and way, since self-interest and altruism can coexist in people's minds and motivations. To the extent that people value others' well-being, a valid preference, they derive satisfaction from altruistic behavior even when it costs them something. Social capital arises from the human capacity to think and act generously and cooperatively. If there were not this disposition, we would see little of the phenomena associated with social capital.

Is it irrational for persons to perform voluntary community service, to accept unpaid leadership responsibilities, or to make efforts to maintain social peace and harmony around them? This depends on what people value. Norms and roles that make such behavior acceptable, even expected, are likely to contribute to higher levels of societal well-being as more efforts go into activities that benefit more persons than the individual making them. If the persons making these expenditures value such outcomes, they do not consider these activities only as a cost.

Alternatively, norms that promote only the individual pursuit of self-interest are likely to lead to the neglect and even undermining of social institutions that, once established and maintained, produce streams of benefits that enhance the welfare of many. Adopting a purely competitive stance toward others—and accepting zero-sum or, worse, negative-sum outcomes as the norm—can make such outcomes into the norm. In the absence of social capital, other resources are likely to become less productive for lack of trust, commitment, ingenuity, cooperation, reliability and other qualities that humans can either display or suppress.[13]

That structural forms of social capital are conceived and maintained for a variety of instrumental and normative considerations should be clear. The same applies for cognitive forms of social capital, ideas that predispose people toward—and support them in—cooperative behavior or collective action. Real-life situations are almost always a combination of both, though for analytical purposes, one can distinguish instrumental from normative ideas. These can be differentiated as follows, recognizing that actual motivations tend to be composite:

■ Instrumental ideas are routines and repertoires that create an *effective* culture, with shared confidence in the methods and feasibility of cooperative or collective undertakings. These are reinforced through efficiency and efficacy in the performance of such undertakings.

■ Normative ideas include values, norms, attitudes, and beliefs that create an *affective* culture, with feelings of trust and solidarity that encourage cooperative or collective undertakings. These are reinforced through ideas about legitimacy, altruism, duty, and ethical behavior.

These can be compared analytically as follows in table 3. Both categories contribute to mobilizing and sustaining cooperative behavior.

Having made this distinction, it is important to reiterate that the motivations that undergird social capital are most likely to be, and to be beneficially, mixed, drawing on some combination of both instrumental and normative considerations.

### Sources and magnitudes of benefit from social capital: analysis of a case from Sri Lanka

This discussion has been general, intended to provide concepts and principles that apply everywhere. Interest in social capital has arisen because development practitioners and researchers have observed associations between desirable developmental outcomes and the existence of social roles and networks or of certain kinds of values and norms. There are starting to be some systematic and quantified studies of such relationships, such as that by Narayan and Pritchett (1996), but they are still rather few.

TABLE 3: CONTRASTING MODES OF COGNITION AFFECTING SOCIAL CAPITAL

| *Instrumental cognition* | *Normative cognition* |
| --- | --- |
| Shared technical, organizational and operational *knowledge* that makes cooperative behavior and collective action *effective*, over and above what could be achieved through individual action. | Shared *thinking* about positive-sum relations and mutual benefits that makes cooperative behavior and collective action *attractive*, over and above its individual and instrumental value. |
| Answers questions of: *HOW to work together?* | Provides answers for the question: *WHY work together?* |
| Traditions, inertia, and habit create common expectations and role repertoires that lead to synchronization and cooperation. | Trust, solidarity and related values, norms, attitudes, and beliefs create presumptions that people should and will work together. |
| Expectations that others *WILL* cooperate create pressures to cooperate from outside one's self. Reinforcement comes from the benefits of cooperation and collective action for one's self. | Expectations about why one *SHOULD* cooperate create pressures to cooperate from inside one's self. Reinforcement comes through self-respect and satisfaction from others' benefit in addition to one's own. |

*Source:* Author.

My most extensive and intensive experience with a development project was in Sri Lanka, where the United States Agency for International Development (USAID) engaged Cornell's Rural Development Committee to work with the Agrarian Research and Training Institute (ARTI) to improve the efficiency of water management in the Gal Oya irrigation system through the introduction and operation of farmer organizations. When we started in 1980, there was no concept of social capital to inform or guide our work, and "participation" was the operative concept. We can see now, however, that our efforts created and benefited from social capital, both through establishment of water user associations and by mobilizing and reinforcing certain value orientations of cooperation and generosity that were available within the culture but were at that time not influencing behavior in the area.

Gal Oya was said by engineers and officials to be the most deteriorated and disorganized irrigation system in the country. Yet it became one of the most efficient and cooperatively managed systems, even fairly quickly, once approached with an effective plan for engaging farmers in joint system management. The efficiency of water use was doubled within two years, even before the planned physical rehabilitation was completed, through the introduction of "social infrastructure." Fairly conservative benefit-cost calculations indicated about a 50 percent rate of return on this investment in social infrastructure, similar to the rate calculated for similar investment in the Philippines, some of it by the World Bank (Uphoff 1986, pp. 27–30).

Perhaps most significant, a postproject evaluation commissioned by the International Irrigation Management Institute, four years after project completion, calculated that the production of rice per unit of irrigation water issued had increased by about 300 percent (Wijayaratna and Uphoff 1997, p. 178). While not all of this increase can be attributed to social capital, probably at least half was due to creating new roles and social relationships and to activating certain norms and attitudes—respectively, structural and cognitive forms of social capital. That social organization is a more important determinant of the higher productivity than are changes in physical structures has been shown through quantitative analysis (Amarasinghe, Sakthivadivel, and Murray-Rust 1997).

The social structures created for decision-making, resource mobilization and management, communication, and conflict resolution were a network of farmer organizations, beginning with small, informal groups (10–20 members) at field channel level. Each of these groups was headed by a Farmer-Representative (FR), chosen by consensus and serving on an unpaid basis. All of the FRs for field channels drawing water from a given distributary canal formed a distributary canal organization (DCO), which had, eventually, formal-legal status. FRs also met regularly in larger area councils, and they selected from among themselves in these councils trusted FRs to serve on a joint project management committee with engineers and other officials.

Participatory irrigation management along these lines became national policy by an act of the cabinet in 1988 (Brewer 1994), and this structure of organization became a model for all of the major irrigation schemes in Sri Lanka (those with command areas over 80 hectares). Project committees have a management committee with a farmer majority and usually a farmer chairman. Probably few other irrigation systems have organizational structures as effective and efficient as Gal Oya, but then there was less investment made in creating social capital in other schemes.

The method of investment used was to recruit, train, and deploy young persons called Institutional Organizers (IOs) as "catalysts" for collective action and formation of organizations. IOs lived in the farming communities, got to know farmers and their families on a personal basis, and encouraged problem-solving efforts, beginning quite informally. The strategy was to "work first, organize later" so as to demonstrate the benefits achievable through MBCA. This created a *demand* for local organization, rather than begin by creating a *supply* of organization for which there was no clearly felt need. This strategy has been documented in Uphoff (1996).

The creation of the role of Farmer-Representative had a dramatic transforming effect within the farming communities, manifested in more efficient and wider water distribution (Uphoff 1996, pp. 335–36 and throughout). Already within six weeks after the IOs began their work, in a water-short year when the main reservoir was only one-quarter full, farmers on 90 percent of the field channels were engaging in some combination of (a) voluntary collective cleaning of channels (some of which had not been maintained for 10 and even 20 years), (b) rotating water deliveries among users along the channel (so that tail-enders got their fair share, previously impossible), and (a) saving any water that had been issued but was not absolutely needed by farmers along a channel, donating any surplus to more needy farmers downstream. About one-sixth of authorized supply was given up in this way, with, in some cases, Sinhalese farmers giving up water to help Tamil farmers cultivating in tail-end areas.

This rapid mobilization of collective action where it had been absent before was as much a surprise to Cornell and ARTI as it was to the engineers, officials, and farmers themselves. Given the serious water scarcity, it had been anticipated that there would be more conflict rather than more cooperation. Actually, the next year's dry season began with the reservoir even lower (only one-fifth full), yet the pattern of increased cooperation continued, producing tangible benefits equitably distributed.

The FR roles created a structure of organization that reached from the field channel up to project level and was able to produce decisions, mobilize resources, facilitate communication, and resolve conflicts. It did this in ways that farmers and officials had not been able to accomplish before—and was very much appreciated. One area council chairman told me proudly, "There used to be lots of fights among farmers here over water, even murders. You can check the records of the police if you don't believe me. Now there are no more [violent conflicts]" (Uphoff 1996, p. 10). Roles that could facilitate the four activities listed above raised both the feasibility and efficacy of mutually beneficial collective action.

As or maybe more important were the norms of fairness and equity that existed in the traditional culture, heavily influenced by Buddhism, which the organizers could appeal to. Such norms were being honored more in the breach than the observance in Gal Oya, where disputes, water stealing and breaking structures were common. However, once these norms were articulated publicly and were proposed as criteria for irrigation management behavior, they were readily accepted among farmers. Their existence in the collective consciousness of Gal Oya settlers was an important form of social capital that the program could call upon to get more equitable water distribution, which contributed concurrently to greater efficiency in water use.

Specifically with regard to mobilizing resources to rehabilitate and maintain the channels, there was a tradition known as *shramadana*, which can be found also in India, Nepal, and other South Asian countries. This custom obliges people to participate in voluntary group labor to produce some community good, such as clearing a road, building a temple, or repainting or reroofing a school. Persons who contribute their labor to *shramadana* activities are believed to acquire spiritual "merit" that will benefit them in the present or in the future.

Little *shramadana* was being done when our program started in 1981, for irrigation or other purposes. Gal Oya was a settlement scheme, to which households from all over the country had been relocated in the 1950s. The usual local leadership roles that could have mobilized local labor for public benefit, including the common roles of village headman and temple priest, were either missing or weak. Structural social capital was weak, but there was some significant, even if latent, cognitive social capital to draw on.

Suggestions that farmers get together to clean clogged canals or dig new channels were easily understood and quickly taken up, given the favorable attitudes in people's minds toward this kind of collective action, sanctioned by traditional beliefs (see references to *shramadana* in Uphoff 1996). There were associated roles that people could bring into being quickly because of the level of trust the institution enjoyed—someone to collect money for refreshments, someone to assign work duties. It became quite clear to us in the field that we could not have gotten such rapid and widespread response from Gal Oya farmers without this custom already existing in people's cognitive repertoire of acceptable, indeed socially approved, behavior.

The discovery of the importance of positively interdependent utility functions was likewise quite empirical. None of my training as a social scientist prepared me for the extent of cooperation, even some examples of self-sacrificing behavior, that we observed in a place that officials had characterized as the most conflictive irrigation scheme in the country.[14]

To be sure, farmers benefited personally from their cooperation, which increased the available water supply by reducing losses and raising the efficiency of use. But they almost always indicated, when asked about the outpouring of cooperation, that part of their motivation was to help others less fortunate than themselves, once the plight of others was made a public issue, and once the organizational means (structural social capital) were in place to make generous actions effective.

By resurrecting dormant values that supported fairness and altruism, which farmers had in mind even if these were not being expressed in practice, organizers and then farmer-representatives made participation in *shramadana* a new norm. The practice came to be taken for granted as contributing labor to clean channels became normal, rather than deviant behavior. Sharing water and saving it to assist others when possible also became the norm.

When farmers were asked to explain the dramatically changed and improved management system, I expected to hear from them an enumeration of incentives and benefits. But the most frequent response was that with the new structure of organization, and the interaction it produced among farmers, they came to realize others' needs for water and this made them think about the effect of their (wasteful) actions on others. They began taking others' interests into account, rather than simply looking out for themselves. They also took satisfaction in demonstrating to engineers and officials that farmers could indeed be responsible and capable individuals. The language of friendship, among farmers and between farmers and engineers, became common, whereas before the words were of indifference or even antagonism.[15] To what extent this renewed concern for others was bolstered by the increases in production and other benefits, I cannot say. That more generous and cooperative behavior benefited individuals and their neighbors certainly made it more attractive and sustainable.

The cooperative water management practices were, in economic terminology, Pareto-optimal. By distributing water more carefully and efficiently, there could be gainers without anyone losing crop yields. There were some costs involved as this new, more intensive management system required some expenditure of time and labor. But this was compensated for in various ways, many material but some nonmaterial; many benefits were individual but some were collective.[16] Once channels were free of weeds, silt and rocks, and when each farmer got the full flow in turn for a specified period of time, seepage and conveyance losses were greatly reduced. This increased the supply of what was normally considered a scarce resource, and when turns were taken, irrigating one's field could be accomplished satisfactorily in a matter of hours rather than unsatisfactorily in a matter of days.

This required trust, which also had been in exceedingly short supply before. For the previous 30 years since the Gal Oya system began operation, it had been known mostly for conflict. Zero-sum competition for water had resulted in breakage of structures and chaotic water deliveries that produced negative-sum outcomes—almost everyone became worse off. Engineers—partly because they lacked the means, and also because they invested little effort in management—seldom adhered to the calendar of water deliveries that was announced before the start of the season. Water was supposed to run down distributary canals for a period of five days, and then was to be diverted to an alternate canal, following five-days-on, five-days-off rotation. In fact, water might be received for four days and then not for six, or entire turns could be missed.

Thus it was quite an accomplishment to get farmers to rotate water among themselves when there was not a reliable schedule for delivery. There is some objective evidence that we activated the attitude of trust, not just the general values of cooperation and generosity. During the first year, about one-fifth of the field channels in the pilot area changed their rotation plan during the season; all of these changes were from head-end-first rotations to tail-end-first, on the grounds that this would assure greater equity as well as efficiency. Given the unpredictability of water deliveries from the main system, this was most remarkable, because head-end farmers were putting their own crops at risk (although there was an understanding that if alterations in the distribution schedule were likely to shortchange head-end farmers, they would be given priority for available water).

My own explanation for what happened is not that values were changed but rather that values that existed within the culture and within the local population were activated and made more salient by the opportunities for MBCA that the IOs helped farmers fashion. There was too little time to "change" values, and besides, the IOs had not been instructed to attempt this. Instead, they initiated a participatory process of problem identification and solution through group efforts. There was cognitive social capital which was latent—lying fallow, so to speak—that could be capitalized upon, once other-regarding local leadership was mobilized to take initiative and alter the normative climate (ethos) in the communities, with supportive social structures.

More could be said about this experience with the purposeful creation of social capital, both structural and cognitive, but this would require another chapter. The experience is documented and analyzed in explanatory terms in Uphoff (1996). Cornell's and ARTI's involvement in Gal Oya ended in 1985, so the farmer organizations there have been largely on their own for more than a dozen years. They are still operating effectively (Wijayaratna and Uphoff 1997), though not always perfectly. There have been some disappointments and shortfalls, as there are in any human institution. They could have been kept and made more effective with some continuing support. Just as the "hardware" of irrigation systems needs some maintenance investments, so does the "software" of farmer organization require some ongoing investment in operation and maintenance (O&M).

That the social capital of these organizations has remained effective both structurally and cognitively can be seen from their performance during the 1997 dry season, when the water level in the main reservoir was so low that the Irrigation Department refused to authorize cultivating rice on the 65,000 acres of the Left Bank area of Gal Oya. It said that it could provide just 60,000 acre-feet of water and authorized planting only of other field crops (not rice) on 15,000 acres (Uphoff and Wijayaratna 1999).

Farmers through their organizations objected to this preemptive curtailment of cultivation. One of their leaders who was fairly educated collected data showing that there should be some inflow to the reservoir during the dry season from groundwater already in the catchment area. He also pointed out that no consideration had been given to whatever rain was likely to fall during the season even if it was not very much. He and other farmers were convinced that through their organizations they could manage whatever water became available more efficiently than the engineers estimated. Finally, they got the government members of the project management committee to agree to the cultivation of a larger area and with rice if farmers wished—though without any promises of additional water being issued from the reservoir.

Rather than trying to decide which farmers would be allocated the limited supply of water, the organizations decided to share equally whatever supply was available. (This meant that Sinhalese farmers at the head of the Left Bank system willingly shared with Tamil farmers at the tail, water that they could have monopolized because of locational advantage.) Farmers correctly predicted that there would be additional supply in the reservoir, and almost 100,000 acre-feet of water were issued; they were fortunate to have slightly better than average rainfall during the season, which added 24 inches of supply to fields. They cultivated almost 65,000 acres of rice, where it had been thought there was only enough water for 15,000 acres of other field crops, and got a better than average yield (85 to 95 bushels per acre).

The total water supply available at field level during the season was about 3.5 acre-feet, far less than the 5 to 5.5 acre-feet usually required during a dry season. (Before farmer organizations were introduced, the amount used in Gal Oya had been 8 to 9 acre-feet.) The roles, rules, procedures, and precedents that farmers could draw on thus were materially very productive, being essential for production of $20 million worth of rice where none would have been grown otherwise. The norm of equity, which became very strong among the Gal Oya farmers once they formed organizations, was also part of this productive "formula" because without it, water would not have been distributed throughout the whole Left Bank.

Governments are unfortunately still often reluctant to make investments in social capital, even though its benefits can be demonstrated. They prefer to put money and personnel into more tangible physical assets. At least the policy environment for participatory irrigation management is strongly supportive in Sri Lanka now, and few engineers would like to return to the status quo ante, before farmer organizations shared responsibility in system management.

The World Bank has had some difficulty in investing in social capital. In 1983, a Bank design team passed up an opportunity to establish farmer organizations, utilizing the IO and FR roles that we offered to introduce, in its Major Irrigation Rehabilitation Project. The team leader characterized such investment as "gold-plating," even though we showed him data demonstrating a 50 percent rate of return on the first two years of social infrastructure investment in Gal Oya. As it turned out, the project became bogged down without farmer organizations in the irrigation schemes it was rehabilitating, and subsequently it took some of our best

IOs from Gal Oya to try to "retrofit" organizations into systems that it had already physically rehabilitated. This was much less beneficial than if organizations had been put in place at the start of the project, involving farmers in the planning and implementation, not just postrehabilitation operations.

Even though by the 1990s, participatory development was strongly endorsed by the World Bank at the policy level, such thinking had not "trickled down" to the operational level. When the Bank started up a National Irrigation Rehabilitation Project in 1990, it included IOs in the design (because the Government of Sri Lanka insisted on this). But then in its hurry to start up the implementation, it started physical rehabilitation before IOs had even been recruited, let alone trained and placed in the field.[17]

Experience within the irrigation sector in Sri Lanka points out dramatically the productive potentials of structural and cognitive forms of social capital for achieving some tangible material benefits for farmers and for utilizing both physical and natural assets more efficiently. The payoffs go beyond increased production and greater water use efficiency. They include saving labor and gaining sleep. Farmers also stressed improvements in their quality of life, stating that their communities now had *ekemutekama* (a spirit of unity), which is highly valued in traditional Sinhalese culture as it is in most communities around the world.

The organizational skills that were mobilized and improved in Gal Oya were extended into other beneficial activities such as crop protection (the use of chemical pesticides was cut by one-quarter just through coordination of planting schedules to reduce staggering of crops) and savings and loan operations (to circumvent the usurious operations of private moneylenders who charged as much as 25 percent interest per month). One can see from many examples of local social organization around the world that when such capacities are developed, members utilize them for solving a broader range of problems than they tackle initially (Uphoff, Esman, and Krishna 1998, pp. 207–209). What is not known so far is the extent of fungibility of social capital, either in structural or cognitive terms. Understanding this will be one of the most useful and challenging areas of research on social capital.

The Gal Oya experience is not unique. In Krishna, Uphoff, and Esman (1997), there are many impressive examples of the creation and utilization of structural and cognitive forms of social capital. The study of social capital is just beginning, however. We need to employ concepts always in a consistent manner, with categories that are mutually exclusive and at the same time, when taken together, collectively inclusive. These are the minimal requirements for rigor. Thus far in the literature there has been little effort to meet them. With such a pretheoretical foundation, we need empirical work that moves the study of social capital beyond descriptive treatments.

### Annex: terminology and conceptualization of social capital

**I. Structural forms of social capital:** ROLES, RULES, PROCEDURES and PRECEDENTS as well as NETWORKS that facilitate mutually beneficial collective action (MBCA) by lowering transaction costs, coordinating efforts, creating expectations, making certain outcomes more probable, providing assurance about how others will act, and so on.

A. Primary forms: Though these have cognitive origins, they are relatively objective and observable:

  1.  Specific ROLES, both formal and informal, and RULES, explicit and implicit, that support the four basic functions and activities required for collective action:

      a.  Decision-making (planning, evaluation, and so on);
          [Goal attainment]
      b.  Resource mobilization and management;
          [Adaptation]
      c.  Communication and coordination; and
          [Integration]
      d.  Conflict resolution.
          [Pattern maintenance]

  2.  SOCIAL RELATIONSHIPS more generally—broad and specific patterns of exchange and cooperation that involve both material and nonmaterial goods and that facilitate MBCA on a regular or as-needed basis. These are often described, and can be analyzed, in terms of NETWORKS (network analysis).

B. Secondary forms: These are largely cognitive, though they pertain to be objective, observable relationships:

  1.  PROCEDURES: Agreed and understood processes or routines for carrying out the above activities and functions, through roles and rules in ways that make these roles and rules widely understood and accepted.

  2.  PRECEDENTS: Previous actions and outcomes that establish the validity and value of roles, rules, and procedures. Precedents increase the likelihood that people will act in certain ways and that such action will be accepted and effective.

A good example of a **structural** form of social capital is *sanctions*, which reinforce and regularize agreements and dispositions for collective action. Sanctions are produced by persons acting in the four kinds of roles listed above. They are specified by rules and are carried out according to procedures and precedents. They make cooperation more likely because others' behavior is more predictable, and they accordingly make cooperation more widespread and beneficial.

**II. Cognitive forms of social capital:** NORMS, VALUES, ATTITUDES, and BELIEFS that create and reinforce positive interdependence of utility functions and that support mutually beneficial collective action (MBCA).

A. Primary forms:

1.  Orientations toward OTHERS—how one should think about and act toward others:

    a. TRUST and RECIPROCATION—MEANS of relating to others:
       - *Norm* of reciprocation;
       - *Value* in being trustworthy;
       - *Attitude* of trust; and
       - *Belief* that others will reciprocate.

    These make cooperation and generosity *efficacious*. One can assume that others will act in a friendly, reliable way; will keep agreements, but will also act in a beneficent way even without explicit agreements. An area in which more analysis and evaluation needs to be done concerns "specific" versus "generalized" norms and behaviors of reciprocity. The first set is more intense while the latter set is broader. Both represent forms of social capital but with different effects.

    b. SOLIDARITY—ENDS of relating to others:
       - *Norm* of helping others, of "standing together," of incurring costs for benefit of some larger group, beyond immediate family or kin;
       - *Value* of maintaining solidarity among persons within larger group;
       - *Attitude* of benevolence and loyalty toward all within a larger group; and
       - *Belief* that others will uphold norm of solidarity and be willing to make some sacrifices to help others.

    These make cooperation and generosity *desirable*. One can assume that others will act in a friendly, reliable way and will be willing to make some sacrifices for the "greater good" of larger group.

2.  Orientations toward ACTION—how one should be disposed to act:
    a.  COOPERATION—MEANS of action with others:
        *   *Norm* of cooperation, working together, rather than separately;
        *   *Value* of being cooperative, working with others for common good;
        *   *Attitude* of cooperation, being willing to oblige, accommodate, accept tasks and assignments for common good; and
        *   *Belief* that others will similarly be cooperative and that cooperation will be accordingly successful.

    These create expectation that others will cooperate and make this action *efficacious*. They predispose people to seek joint solutions to problems rather than think cooperation will not occur or not be successful, making individual action preferred.

    b.  GENEROSITY—ENDS of action toward others:
        *   *Norm* of altruistic behavior, contributing to others' well-being in addition to one's own;
        *   *Value* of acting generously, recognizing that this (if reciprocated) will be beneficial for one's self, but at the same time taking satisfaction in others' well-being;
        *   *Attitude* that being generous is good, natural, beneficial, and that generous actions will be good for everyone, including self;
        *   *Belief* that others will act generously and will not take advantage of one's own generosity beyond some reasonable limit.

    These create the expectation that "virtue will be rewarded," later if not right away. These also establish *inter*dependent utility functions that produce positive-sum satisfactions. As means, TRUST and COOPERATION are interactive and interdependent and mutually reinforcing, much as are SOLIDARITY and GENEROSITY as ends.

B.  Secondary forms: Numerous norms, values, attitudes, and beliefs correspond with and reinforce these primary normative orientations, for example, honesty, egalitarianism, fairness, participation, democratic governance, and concern for the future (for example, the next generation). Little systematic analysis has been done on these as secondary forms of cognitive social capital because they have, thus far, been treated mostly descriptively, lumped together with trust and reciprocity, solidarity, cooperation, and generosity.

These primary forms of cognitive social capital listed here are the basic normative orientations that produce mutually beneficial collective action—the "income stream" that comes from social capital. These other, more specific normative orientations such as honesty are important, but they are better understood as secondary forms of social capital.

## Notes

1. This analysis has been developed jointly by Anirudh Krishna and myself. It has been operationalized in Krishna and Uphoff (1999), in which we analyzed the results of a study of 64 villages participating in a World Bank–Government of India watershed conservation program, with interviews of almost 2,400 villagers. The index of social capital that we constructed at both community and individual levels using factor analysis turned out to provide surprisingly strong explanatory power for mutually beneficial collective action, much stronger than can be obtained from usual explanations found in the literature such as relative need (Wade 1994), stratification, or modernization.

2. There may be a useful analogy here with batteries that can store electrical current. Once charged up, they yield a continuing stream of power, though they can also be run down if not recharged. Roles once established and ideas once accepted work much like this. They can be maintained, almost indefinitely, as long as some recharge is provided, matching the draw-down of current. In the social realm, successful performance that matches normative and empirical expectations has the effect of recharging both roles and ideas. Indeed, ideas, because they are not subject to the law of conservation of matter, can be sustained with extremely low levels of input and reinforcement.

3. Both Coleman and Putnam have performed a great service by putting social capital on the agenda for social scientists and development practitioners. But both have inclined more toward descriptive than explanatory treatments of the subject. Coleman considers social capital to be, for example, "a variety of different entities, with two elements in common: they all consist of some [any?] aspect of social structure, and they facilitate certain actions of actors—whether personal or corporate actors—within the structure" (1988, p. S98). This abstract formulation leaves out norms, which Coleman considers important in most of his other discussions of social capital.

Putnam includes both structural and cognitive aspects of social capital in his definition: "social capital consists of social networks

('networks of civic engagement') and associated norms that have an effect on the productivity of the community" (see Serageldin and Grootaert 1997, p. 12; see chapter 2 in this book for an updated version). But he makes no consistent distinction between these two kinds of social capital, for example, suggesting that trust, norms and networks are "all elements of social organization that improve the efficiency of society by facilitating coordinated actions" (Putnam, Leonardi, and Nanetti 1993, p. 172). Such wording, which equates social capital with social organization, has the effect of subsuming all cognitive factors under structural considerations.

Coleman's and Putnam's writings on the subject are not incorrect, only unsystematic. Approaching complex subjects more in descriptive than in analytical terms is unfortunately fairly common in the social science literature. For a similar critique, and analytical resolution, concerning the treatment of "power" in the literature, see Uphoff (1989).

4. Authority and legitimacy are intrinsically intertwined with one another. The first is a structural, role-based phenomenon, codified in laws and statutes and exercised via formal organizations, yet authority can rarely be sustained unless it is regarded as legitimate by a sufficient number of persons according to prevailing norms, beliefs, and attitudes (Uphoff 1989; Ilchman and Uphoff 1997, pp. 73–86). Both cognitive and structural elements are thus essential and almost inextricable for the process of governance.

5. This derivation applies similarly for the French word *social* and, not coincidentally, for the German equivalent, *gesellschaftlich*, which comes from the word *Gesell*, which likewise means friend or comrade.

6. This explication argues against a long and strong tradition in sociology that stems from the work of Emile Durkheim. He contrasted *Gemeinschaft* (community) with *Gesellschaft* (society), considering the first to have more "organic" links and the latter to consist of more "mechanical" connections. That there had been in Europe at the time Durkheim wrote an increase in the latter and a decline in the former is not contested. However, the original meaning of *Gesellschaft* is no less grounded in the dynamics of friendship, personal attachment, and reciprocity than is *Gemeinschaft*, which means to have things in common.

7. One of the strongest descriptions of what it means to have positively interdependent utility functions was offered by John Winthrop, first governor of the Massachusetts Bay Colony when he spoke to the Puritans as they set off to establish a new society in North America in 1630: "We must delight in each other, make others' conditions our own, rejoyce together, mourn together, labor and suffer together, always having be-

fore our eyes our community as members of the same body" (cited in Bellah 1985, p. 28).

8. This continuum was developed with similar terminology in Uphoff (1996, pp. 341–45).

9. This factor of group size has been analyzed by Mancur Olson (1965). He gives logical reasons why collective action should be observed less often in larger groups, pointing to the greater difficulty in detecting and deterring free riding, which undermines people's willingness to contribute to the creation of a public good. He is, however, assuming independent utility functions, as if all members or contributors are strangers who attach no value to others' benefits from collective action. I would suggest that the phenomenon of greater amount and durability of collective action observable with smaller groups is *not* only attributable to the greater possibilities for observing and controlling shirking, as Olson suggests. It can be ascribed also (or even more) to people in smaller groups being more "invested" in one another.

10. Adam Smith, who has given us the most powerful arguments in favor of competition, argued this in *The Theory of Moral Sentiments* 17 years before he published *An Inquiry into the Wealth of Nations* (1776). See discussion of these issues in Ormerod (1994).

11. A working group of the Cornell Rural Development Committee undertook with USAID assistance in 1984 to analyze and assess farmer participation in irrigation management. After reviewing many analyses by others (Uphoff 1986, pp. 165–67), we concluded that there are four categories of activities that are necessarily performed by all water user associations or officials and technicians (Uphoff 1986, pp. 10–11, 40, 46–53). These are actually common to all forms of social organization.

12. After identifying these four activities of organization, we realized that they are practically the same as the "pattern variables" that Talcott Parsons had previously delineated (1951) as the four basic functions necessary for the operation and preservation of social organization of any kind: goal attainment, adaptation, integration, and pattern maintenance. Our categories are less abstract than those of Parsons, but they are essentially the same.

13. Leibenstein (1965, 1976) offered some instructive ideas on how productivity can be raised by such means beyond what the efficient allocation and employment of land, labor, and capital can explain. His concept of "x-efficiency" unfortunately never gained much support within the discipline of economics, but see Weiermair and Perlman (1990). All

students of social capital would benefit from reviewing Leibenstein's ideas about "x-efficiency."

14. The senior deputy director of irrigation for water management told us before the project started that if we could make progress [with participatory management] in Gal Oya, we could make progress anywhere in Sri Lanka. The top civil servant in the district told our organizers before they began work in the field, having said that farmers in Gal Oya were very uncooperative and prone to conflict, "If you can bring even ten or fifteen farmers in Gal Oya to work together, that will be a big achievement" (Uphoff 1996, p. 6). These words were supposed to be encouraging, but organizers knew that they were supposed to get ten to fifteen *thousand* farmers organized in the next four years, making their nominal odds against success about a thousand to one. This same official within four years said in a magazine interview: "Before there were farmer organizations, out of every ten farmers I talked with, eight had problems getting water. Now I hear practically no complaints about irrigation distribution." *Desatiya*, No. 15, October 1984, p. 19 (own translation from Sinhala).

15. A summary assessment in this regard came from the chairman of the UB1 (Uhana Branch distributary canal no. 1) distributary canal organization in July 1985, who said that before the program started in 1981, referring to relations between farmers and engineers, "We were like snake and mongoose," not suggesting which was which. He added that they now worked together as friends (Uphoff 1996, p. 204).

16. One reason frequently given for satisfaction and cooperation with the new system was that "we can now sleep at night." Farmers did not need to stay in their fields all night, to protect their meager supply of water, or to steal water from others, when water was distributed to all according to an agreed-upon schedule in proportion to their fields' needs.

17. When I visited some irrigation schemes being rehabilitated under NIRP (National Irrigation Rehabilitation Project) in 1994 (as a member of a CGIAR/TAC [Consultative Group on International Agricultural Research/Technical Advisory Group] external review team for the International Irrigation Management Institute), the project manager on one scheme we visited complained about the problems he was having owing to lack of farmer participation. This could have been predicted, because the project design was not serious about structural forms of social capital, and was oblivious to cognitive forms.

## Bibliography

The word *processed* describes informally reproduced works that may not be commonly available through libraries.

Amarasinghe, Upali A., A. K. Sakthivadivel, and D. Hammond Murray-Rust. 1997. *Impact Assessment of Rehabilitation Intervention in the Gal Oya Left Bank*. Research Report 18. Colombo: International Irrigation Management Institute.

Axelrod, Robert. 1984. *The Evolution of Cooperation*. New York: Basic Books.

Bellah, Robert. 1985. *Habits of the Heart: Individualism and Commitment in American Life*. New York: Harper and Row.

Brewer, Jeffrey D. 1994. "The Participatory Irrigatory System Management Policy." *Economic Review* 20(6): 4–9. Colombo: People's Bank.

Cohen, John M., and Norman Uphoff. 1980. "Participation's Place in Rural Development: Seeking Clarity through Specificity." *World Development* 8(3): 213–35.

Coleman, James S. 1988. "Social Capital in the Creation of Human Capital." *American Journal of Sociology* 94 (Supplement): S94–S120.

———. 1990. *Foundations of Social Theory*. Cambridge, Mass.: Harvard University Press.

Frank, Robert. 1992. *Passions within Reason: The Strategic Role of Emotions*. New York: W. W. Norton.

Fukuyama, Francis. 1995. *Trust: The Social Virtues and the Creation of Prosperity*. New York: Free Press.

Hirschman, Albert O. 1970. *Exit, Voice and Loyalty: Responses to Decline in Firms, Organizations and States*. Cambridge, Mass.: Harvard University Press.

———. 1984. *Getting Ahead Collectively: Grassroots Experiences in Latin America*. New York: Pergamon Press.

Ilchman, Warren F., and Norman Uphoff. 1997. *The Political Economy of Change*. New Brunswick, New Jersey: Transaction Books. Originally published by University of California Press, 1969.

Krishna, Anirudh. 1997. "Participatory Watershed Development and Soil Conservation in Rajasthan, India." In Anirudh Krishna, Norman Uphoff, and Milton J. Esman, eds., pp. 255–72.

Krishna, Anirudh, and Norman Uphoff. 1999. *Mapping and Measuring Social Capital: A Conceptual and Empirical Study of Collective Action for Conserving and Developing Watersheds in Rajasthan, India*. Social Capital Initiative Working Paper No. 13. World Bank, Washington, D.C.

Krishna, Anirudh, Norman Uphoff, and Milton J. Esman, eds. 1997. *Reasons for Hope: Instructive Experiences in Rural Development*. West Hartford, Conn.: Kumarian Press.

Leibenstein, Harvey. 1965. "Allocative Efficiency versus 'X Efficiency.' " *American Economic Review* 56(2): 392–415.

———. 1976. *Beyond Economic Man: A New Foundation for Microeconomics*. Cambridge, Mass.: Harvard University Press.

Narayan, Deepa, and Lant Pritchett. 1996. "Cents and Sociability: Household Income and Social Capital in Rural Tanzania." Processed. World Bank, Washington, D.C.

North, Douglass. 1990. *Institutions, Institutional Change and Economic Performance*. New York: Cambridge University Press.

Olson, Mancur. 1965. *The Logic of Collective Action: Public Goods and the Theory of Groups*. Cambridge, Mass.: Harvard University Press.

———. 1982. *The Rise and Decline of Nations: Economic Growth, Stagflation and Social Rigidities*. New Haven, Conn.: Yale University Press.

Ormerod, Paul. 1994. *The Death of Economics*. London: Faber.

Parsons, Talcott. 1951. *The Social System*. New York: Free Press.

Putnam, Robert, R. Leonardi, and R. Nanetti. 1993. *Making Democracy Work: Civic Traditions in Modern Italy*. Princeton: Princeton University Press.

Serageldin, Ismail. 1996. "Sustainability as Opportunity and the Problem of Social Capital." *Brown Journal of World Affairs* 3: 187–203.

Serageldin, Ismail, and Christiaan Grootaert. 1997. "Defining Social Capital: An Integrating View." Draft, World Bank, Washington, D.C. April 3.

Turnbull, Colin. 1961. *The Forest People*. New York: Simon and Schuster.

———. 1972. *The Mountain People*. New York: Simon and Schuster.

Uphoff, Norman. 1986. *Improving International Irrigation with Farmer Participation: Getting the Process Right*. Boulder, Colo.: Westview Press.

———. 1989. "Distinguishing among Power, Authority and Legitimacy: Taking Max Weber at His Word Using Resource-Exchange Analysis." *Polity* 22(2): 295–320.

———. 1996. *Learning from Gal Oya: Possibilities for Participatory Development and Post-Newtonian Social Science*. London: Intermediate Technology Publications. Originally published by Cornell University Press, 1992.

Uphoff, Norman, Milton J. Esman, and Anirudh Krishna. 1998. *Reasons for Success: Learning from Instructive Experiences in Rural Development*. West Hartford, Conn.: Kumarian Press.

Uphoff, Norman, and C. M. Wijayaratna. 1999. "Demonstrated Benefits from Social Capital: The Productivity of Farmer Organizations in Gal Oya, Sri Lanka." Unpublished paper.

Wade, Robert. 1994. *Village Republics: Economic Conditions for Collective Action in South India*. Cambridge (UK): Cambridge University Press.

Weiermair, Klaus, and Mark Perlman, eds. 1990. *Studies in Economic Rationality: X-Efficiency Examined and Extolled*. Ann Arbor, Mich.: University of Michigan Press.

Wijayaratna, C. M., and Norman Uphoff. 1997. "Farmer Organization in Gal Oya: Improving Irrigation Management in Sri Lanka." In Anirudh Krishna, Norman Uphoff, and Milton J. Esman, eds., pp. 166–83.

# Statistical Analysis

# Economic growth and social capital in Italy

John F. Helliwell
*University of British Columbia*

and

Robert D. Putnam
*Harvard University*

## Introduction

The northern parts of Italy have been richer than the southern for several centuries, despite having been on a par at the beginning of the millennium. Recent research has shown that these differences in per capita income are matched by differences in the societal structure, with horizontal structures common in the North and hierarchical forms in the South, and by differences in the extent of civic community, citizen involvement and governmental efficiency (Putnam 1993). Other studies have shown evidence of convergence among the Italian regions, as among the sub-national regions of other European countries, in terms of the growth of real per capita incomes from 1950 to the early 1980s (Barro and Sala-i-Martin 1991). But recent data show a new divergence of regional per capita incomes, dating from 1983. In this paper we attempt to link and explain all three pieces of evidence.[1]

Our hypothesis is that some Italian regions have been able to establish and maintain higher levels of output per capita by virtue of greater endowments of social capital. However, greater openness and education levels in the past thirty years have increased the ease with which the poorer regions can emulate productivity advances elsewhere and

---

[1] Like Campiglio (1993) and SVIMEZ (1991, pp. 39–40), we find that the recent divergence dates from 1983–84. Some other accounts, especially those focusing on the gross gap between South and North, place the turning point slightly earlier (in the mid-1970s) (Baussola and Fiorito 1994, pp. 498–99, and sources cited therein).

have thus facilitated convergence in both the levels and rates of growth of regional per capita incomes. The divergence during the 1980s is especially surprising inasmuch as it came in the face of massive interregional transfer payments and other interventions by the central government aimed at reducing the North-South disparities. We hypothesize that this divergence can be traced, in part to the possibility that the increased powers of regional governments, as they came into play at the beginning of the decade, were used more effectively in those regions with more social capital. Within the framework we are testing, this divergence should be self-limiting and eventually reversing, since the increasing gap between rich and poor regions enlarges the scope for future transfer of knowledge.

We start with a brief description of our various regional measures of civic community in Italy. Then we consider a theoretical framework in which differences in social capital affect the nature and extent of economic convergence and present our estimates of the ways in which civic community and convergence appear to be jointly determining regional growth patterns in Italy. Finally, we consider the evidence of the economic effects of regional government reforms.

Italy was governed from Rome until steps were made in the 1970s to elect regional governments and subsequently to give them significant powers. In mid-1975 regionalist forces in parliament managed to secure passage of a law authorizing the decentralization of important new functions to the regions. By mid-1977 agreements were reached "...that dismantled and transferred to the regions 20,000 offices from the national bureaucracy, including substantial portions of several ministries, such as the Ministry of Agriculture, as well as hundreds of semipublic social agencies" (Putnam 1993, p. 221). Regional governments took time to exploit the new powers and to adapt to the new responsibilities. The funds expended by regional governments rose from next to nothing in 1970 to almost 10 percent of GDP by the end of the 1980s, with most of the growth taking place in the 1980s (Putnam 1993, p. 251). The watershed, if one must be found, may have been in 1981–82, after the first full round of post-devolution regional elections. By that time, interviews show that the regional councillors had become more pragmatic, less ideological, and more regionally focused in their contacts.[2] We shall attempt later in the paper to assess whether these institutional reforms had consequences for economic growth.

---

[2]    Between 1976 and 1981–82, the percentage of regional councillors who agreed that considerations should have more weight than political ones (in contemporary social and economic affairs) increased from 43 percent to 64 percent (Putnam 1993, p. 33). In the 1976 surveys, regional councillors' regional administrative contacts were twice as frequent as local ones. For the 1981–82 councillors, regional contacts were five times as frequent as local ones (Putnam 1993, p. 43).

## Social capital in Italian regions

Whether judged by how long it takes to get a phone answered at a government office, or by polls of citizen satisfaction with regional governments, there are major continuing differences among the Italian regions in how well government works. Although the nature of the available evidence has changed from one decade to the next, almost all of it supports the notion that these differences have existed for centuries. We conjecture that the differences date from the time when hired guns came into the South with authoritarian structures in hand, while the northern communities became linked instead by tower societies and other means of cooperative action involving more horizontal and open structures of government and society (Putnam 1993, esp. Ch. 5). These initial differences have been reinforced and countered in succeeding centuries, however, by many other factors, such as trading patterns and foreign occupation. The historical origins and trajectory of this North-South split remain a matter of considerable controversy (Cohen 1994; Ridolfi 1994).

Our concern in this paper, however, is not with how these differences may have become established, but with how they can be measured, and what influence they are still likely to have in the late twentieth century. We shall generally restrict our review to features that have been measured as part of the earlier research and which have been found to have explanatory power in determining the effectiveness of local government. The three variables of principal interest, all of which are explained in more detail in Putnam (1993), are:

1. Civic Community (*Civic*). This index of social capital is a composite measure of four indicators, two intended to measure the breadth and depth of civic community (newspaper readership and the availability of sports and cultural associations) and two related to the political behavior of citizens (turnout in referenda and the incidence of preference voting).[3] The four measures provide strikingly consistent results. Italians living in the nine regions from the Abruzzi south generally read fewer newspapers, have fewer sports and cultural associations, vote less frequently in referenda, and are more likely to use prefer-

---

[3] The turnout in referenda is used as a measure of citizen involvement, and hence of civic community. The incidence of preference voting in national elections is used as an inverse measure of civic community, since it is an option available to voters who choose to use it and is in fact used chiefly in regions where party labels are largely a cover for patron-client networks. Thus students of Italian politics have long used the incidence of preference voting as an index of patron-client politics (Putnam 1993, p. 94).

ential voting. The converse is the case for the northern regions. With only minor exceptions, the four indicators all rank the northern regions as more civic than the southern. However, within each of the two main regional groupings, civic community differs substantially, and the four indicators provide different rankings.

2. Institutional Performance (*Perf*). This is a composite measure of the comparative performance of regional governments. It covers twelve separate elements, ranging from the timeliness of budgets to legislative innovation (across domains ranging from preventive medical clinics to consumer protection) to direct measures of bureaucratic responsiveness (e.g. the speed and accuracy of responses to citizen requests for information about established programs). Measures on each of the twelve dimensions are combined into a single factor score for institutional performance. The dates for the assessments are over the period 1978–1985.

3. Citizen satisfaction (*Satis*). This is based on a number of large sample surveys between 1977 and 1988, in which respondents were asked how satisfied they were with the activities of their regional government. The index of satisfaction used here is the share of respondents who were 'very' or 'rather' satisfied, with the alternatives being 'little' or 'not at all' satisfied.

There are fairly tight linkages among the three variables, with the higher levels of civic community associated with higher measures of institutional performances and greater citizen satisfaction. The causal logic in Putnam (1993) runs from civic community, for which stable roots are traced back for centuries or more, to institutional performance, with this leading to greater citizen satisfaction with regional government.

### Economic growth and social capital

Those who have been struck by the persistence in Italy of systematic regional differences in everything from civic community to per capita incomes may be inclined to doubt whether convergence could be present to the extent suggested by the results of Barro and Sala-i-Martin (1991) and others, which refer more generally to income differentials among sub-national regions in Europe and the United States. The convergence literature makes a distinction between unconditional convergence, in which the degree of income dispersion lessens among countries, and conditional convergence, which reflects a tendency for income gaps to be narrowed when all other relevant variables are equal.[4] If it were possible to find evidence of either conditional or unconditional convergence, does that necessarily imply no causal economic role for the systematic differences in civic institutions and efficiency that Putnam and his colleagues have identified? We think that it is possible to lay out a theory of partial conditional convergence that leaves room for institutional differences to influence rates of growth and levels of income. Such a theory could still permit a role for conditional convergence in establishing a form of trickle-down technical progress which serves to limit the size of the income gaps in the long run between regions with differing qualities of institutions. Indeed, the idea that progress and institutional reform might be incremental and experimental, with successes copied by other regions, is reflected in some of the components of the measure of institutional performance presented above. For example, the indicators relating to reform legislation, legislative innovation, day care centers and family clinics all relate to the speed and extent to which the regions adopted laws and programs usually developed and tested elsewhere. It should be noted that although expenditures are used to define the extent of some of these activities, the amounts do not simply measure the ability to pay of the regions, since program spending on these activities is financed by the national government.

We will now be more explicit about the form of our view of partial conditional convergence. In this study, we use real GDP per capita as our measure of income per capita, since our primary emphasis is on productivity, and since in any event we do not have data accounting for regional differences in the amount and ownership of physical capital. GDP per capita can be defined as the quintuple product of some measure of cyclical capacity utilization (a ratio of actual output to what it would be at normal rates of utilization), normal output per employee, the employment rate (employment as a fraction of the active labor force), the labor force participation rate (measured as a fraction of the population of labor force age) and the fraction of the population of labor force age. Normal output per employee is in turn a function of the stocks of physical, human, and social capital and the efficiency with which they

---

[4]    We make below a further distinction between partial and complete convergence. With complete convergence, growth rates and levels move to equality in equilibrium. With partial convergence, equilibrium income levels differ by enough so that the gap-closing influence of conditional convergence is large enough to offset variables inducing divergence, so that growth rates tend to be equal while income levels are not. We assume here, consistent with the results of Helliwell and Chung (1991), Dowrick and Gemmell (1991), Coe and Helpman (1993) and others, that convergence is driven mainly by inter-regional or international flows of know-how, and not merely by differences in investment rates, the channel that is emphasized by Barro and Sala-i-Martin (1991) and Mankiw, Romer, and Weil (1992).

are used. In this study, by using GDP per capita as the variable of interest, and using measures of social capital to explain regional differences in its level and rate of growth, we are implicitly assuming that measurable differences among regions in other factors are not large, or at least are not correlated with the measures of social capital being used. Since these assumptions are unlikely to be fully met, the best way to interpret our research is as an attempt to show the total direct and indirect effects of differences in social capital, recognizing that they may appear in a variety of forms. These may include higher investment rates, higher rates of education, more efficient government services, better social institutions (e.g., operation of the civil and criminal justice systems), and more efficient operations within individual firms.

This leaves open the possibility, if we find that some measures of social capital are correlated with higher levels or rates of growth, that we have not properly identified a reduced-form system, in that causation may be running from higher levels of GDP per capita to better institutions. Our best bet for ensuring that a correlation, if found, runs from institutions to economic performance lies in the regional government reforms instituted at the end of the 1970s. These reforms may have given better institutions more scope to encourage growth. If those regions with more social capital were to experience a subsequent period of higher growth, we would have solid evidence that some significant part of any correlation linking social capital and economic growth must be attributed to causation running from social capital to economic performance. We shall follow up that line of enquiry in the next section. In the current section we set up a system that treats social capital as a determinant of the level and/or the rate of growth of income per capita. Since we do not have comparable time for regional measures of the components of physical or human capital, we use real per capita regional GDP as a composite efficiency measure, bearing in mind that it encompasses differences in natural resources, location, private capital, education levels, and public infrastructure as well as the measures of social capital that are the primary focus of our attention in this paper.[5]

---

[5] In contrast to Mankiw, Romer, and Wail (1992) and Barra and Sala-i-Martin (1991), we explicitly assume that convergence is likely to be due to inter-regional transfers of knowledge, and not to depend solely on differing physical investment rates with the same levels of productivity applicable in each region. Our broader view of convergence is consistent with a wide range of theory and evidence, including the technological transfer models of Grossman and Helpman (1991), the convergence of rates of growth of Solow residents among industrial countries found by Helliwell and Chung (1991) and Dowrick and Gemmell (1991), the role for institutions found by Keefer and Knack (1993), and the R&D spillovers found by Coe and Helpman (1993). The functional form chosen is one of those proposed by Nelson and Phelps (1966), and is also used by Eaton and Kortum (1994) in their study of technology diffusion.

If we use $A_{it}$ to represent real per capita GDP in region $i$ in year $t$, a theory of partial conditional convergence can be specified by the following equation for the rate of growth of income:

$$(1) \quad ln\,(A_{it}/A_{i,t-1}) = \delta(ln(g_{it}A^*/A_{it-1})) + \delta_{it}.$$

The first term represents a model of conditional partial convergence. If income per capita in region $i$ is less than fraction $\gamma_i$ of per capita income $(A^*)$ in some leading region with which region $i$ is in economic contact, then the fraction $\delta$ of the gap will be closed each year. If the region-specific growth rate $(\delta_{it})$ of productivity is the same as in the leading region, then eventually the level of income per capita in region $i$ will approach the fraction $\gamma_{it}$ of the level in the leading region. This is a model of partial convergence, since it accepts the possibility that the level of income in region $i$ will always be less than that in the leading region (if $\gamma_i < 1.0$), whether because of differences in natural resources, civic traditions, or whatever else may have enduring and not fully transferable impacts on economic well-being. It is a model of conditional convergence because changes in country-specific or aggregate factors, entering through changes in the $\gamma_{it}$ or $\delta_{it}$ can alter the timing, extent, and even the existence of unconditional convergence. Inter-regional differences in the quality of government may enter this framework through differences in either the $\gamma_{it}$ or $\delta_{it}$.

Conditional partial convergence ensures that, however great the regional differences in the quality of government, the equilibrium growth paths for the regions in general have different levels but equal growth rates, so long as the inter-regional differences in institutions remain constant. Whether a difference in the quality of government enters primarily as a level effect $(\gamma_{it})$ or a rate of growth effect $(\delta_{it})$ affects only the dynamics of the adjustment path, which in any event will be difficult to establish clearly, given the variety of other unspecified factors influencing regional development. If regional differences of the quality of government do not change measurably, then any attempt to separate $\gamma_i$ and $\delta_{it}$ channels will be fruitless. Since the bulk of our available measures of the structure and effectiveness of civic society in Italy are either estimates for a single year, or averages over several observation points, our estimation form for equation (1) reduces to the following cross-sectional equation attempting to explain regional differences in growth rates of per capita incomes between time $t-n$ and time $t$:

$$(2) \quad ln\,(A_{it}/A_{i,t-1}) = a_0 + a_1\,Civic + a_2 lnA_{it-n} + \varepsilon_i$$

where $a_0 = \delta(ln(A^*))$,
$\quad\quad\quad a_1 = \delta(ln(g_i)) + \delta_i$,
$\quad\quad\quad a_2 = -\delta$, and

$\varepsilon_i$ is an error term assumed to be normally distributed and uncorrelated with any measure (*Civic* is the example employed in equation (1)) used to capture the relative strength of civil society in each region.

Table 1 reports results from estimating equation (2) using the measures of civic community, institutional performance and citizen satisfaction as alternative indicators of the quality of growth-supporting institutions in the Italian regions. The regressions using the measures of civic community and institutional performance cover twenty regions, while equations using citizen satisfaction cover only the eighteen largest regions. The growth period covered is 1950 through 1990. The results in equations (i) through (iii) use ordinary least squares regression, while those in equations (iv) through (vi) are estimated by instrumental variables regression, using 1970 values for income per capita as instruments for 1950 income to avoid the risks of coefficient bias emphasized by Friedman (1992) and Quah (1993).[6] As expected, the results using instrumental variables show slightly smaller and less significant convergence effects. Nevertheless, the convergence effects are significant in all equations and the social capital effects are significant at the 1 percent level in five of the six equations. The equations combining conditional convergence with social capital effects are significantly more accurate than those based either exclusively on social capital or unconditional convergence. Estimates of the same equations on a decade-by-decade basis reveal that the good fit of the model is based almost entirely on the experience of the 1960s and 1970s, with its explanatory power being essentially zero for the 1950s and the 1980s.

The failure of convergence in the 1950s and the 1980s can be seen quite clearly by inspecting the top part of Figure 1, which shows the standard deviations of regional per capita incomes from 1950 to 1990, with gaps for the years for which we do not have suitable measures. The data show a slight increase in the dispersion from 1950 to 1960, a steady and highly significant decline from 1960 to 1983, and a sharp increase thereafter. In the absence of more observations before 1960, we shall concentrate our attention on the experience of the 1980s, especially since it may be linked to changes in the structure of regional government.

---

[6]  Alternatively, or additionally, it is possible to exploit the time series properties of relative growth rates by examining what happens to the regional dispersion of real incomes (to measure the extent of unconditional convergence, as done by Friedman (1992) and Blanchard (1991)) or to the dispersion of residuals from models explaining regional differences in terms of other variables (to examine the extent of conditional convergence, as recommended by Quah (1993)). Both methods will be used in the next section.

## Did the regional government reforms make a difference?

In this section we assess the extent to which the reforms of regional government might have contributed to the reversal of convergence during the 1980s. The top part of Figure 1 shows the time series of standard deviations of the natural logs of per capita incomes in the twenty regions, covering the 1950 to 1990 period, using the most appropriate measure for each year for which data are available.[7]

TABLE 1: EFFECTS OF SOCIAL CAPITAL ON REGIONAL GROWTH WITH CONDITIONAL CONVERGENCE

| Equation | (i) | (ii) | (iii) | (iv) | (v) | (vi) |
|---|---|---|---|---|---|---|
| No. of Observations | 20 | 20 | 18 | 20 | 20 | 18 |
| Estimation Method | OLS | OLS | OLS | IV | IV | IV |
| Dependent Variable | gr5090 | gr5090 | gr5090 | gr5090 | gr5090 | gr5090 |
| Constant | 1.395 | −.174 | −.079 | .489 | −.065 | −.872 |
| | (2.46) | (0.86) | (0.13) | (0.67) | (0.12) | (1.22) |
| *Coefficients* | | | | | | |
| lnGDP50 | −.717 | −.544 | −.456 | −.557 | −.458 | −.315 |
| | (7.14) | (6.32) | (4.17) | (4.36) | (4.77) | (2.49) |
| Civic | .172 | | | .124 | | |
| | (4.80) | | | (2.84) | | |
| Perf | | .118 | | | .096 | |
| | | (3.84) | | | (2.93) | |
| Satis | | | .096 | | | .063 |
| | | | (2.63) | | | (1.58) |
| $R^2$ | .739 | .671 | .477 | .699 | .651 | .419 |
| S.E.E. | .0848 | .0953 | .1058 | .0910 | .0980 | .1144 |

*Note:* Absolute values of *t*-statistics are in parentheses. Durbin-Watson statistics are not reported as they have no use in cross-sectional regressions unless the observations have been organized in groups to be tested for homogeneity. Equations (iv) through (vi) are estimated by instrumental variables, using 1970 values for *lnGDP* as instruments for *lnGDP50*. The dependent variable in each equation is the natural log of GDP per capita in 1990 minus the corresponding value for 1950. This normalization permits series in index form to be used comparably with those in lire, given that all observations for the same year are in the same units. The number of observations is reduced from 20 to 18 for the satisfaction equations since survey data are not available for the two smallest regions, Val d'Aosta and Molise, with populations of 115- and 328-thousand, respectively.

---

[7]  The preferred measure is real per capita GDP at market prices, but for a number of years we have instead used value-added at factor cost. The former measure includes indirect taxes, while the latter does not. We find that the measures of dispersion tend to be slightly smaller for the factor cost estimates, suggesting that average indirect tax rates are lower in the poorer regions. We have tried to allow for the varying nature and quality of the regional income measures in two ways. First, we have done some tests making use of all the alternative measures that we have been able to find, including sometimes as many as three different measures for a single

*(Note continues on the following page.)*

The trend line through the time series of standard deviations shows a significant break in 1983, as documented by the regression results reported in Table 2. With or without a break, the time series shows a significant downward trend over the 40 year period starting in 1950, although the observations for 1950 and 1960 confirm the absence of any convergence during the 1950s. In the context of our investigation of the effects of social capital and regional government reforms, it is appropriate to wonder if the increase in dispersion during the 1980s might be due to the increasing powers of the regional governments being used to greater effect in the regions with greater civic traditions.

Unfortunately, we do not have enough information about trends in institutional performance to directly test this hypothesis. However, we can at least see if the trends coincide, and then indirectly test whether the reforms in regional government are likely to have been responsible for the 1980s divergence of regional growth paths.

FIGURE 1: REGIONAL INCOME DISPERSION

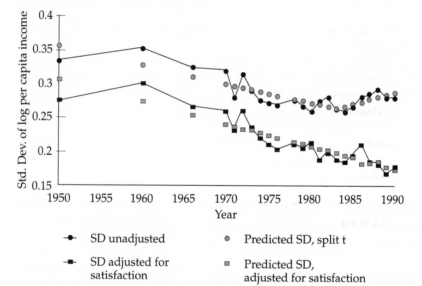

year. Second, we have in our regressions for the time series variation of income dispersion tested a variable representing years when a factor cost measure was used, to ensure than any of our other results are not affected by the unavailability of continuous series based on the name concepts of income. The results suggest that our conclusions are unaffected by the mix of income definitions.

Their timing looks fairly close. The legislation providing significant powers to the new regional governments was passed in 1977, and implementation generally followed the 1980 regional government elections. Allowing some time for the new regional government programs to be designed and implemented, and to start to affect economic growth, we might expect to find some effects on growth paths before the middle of the 1980s. If the regions with greater social capital were able to put their new powers to more effective use, we would expect to find growing (relative) citizen satisfaction and greater economic growth in those regions. Since the regions with greater social capital were already relatively rich, their greater growth would show up as a slowing or reversal of the convergence of income levels documented for the 1960s and 1970s. That is exactly what happened, as shown by the significant reversal of convergence starting in 1983, as pictured in Figure 1 and confirmed by equation (i) in Table 2.

As noted above, the lack of time series measures for the effectiveness of regional government makes it difficult to see whether it is more than coincidence that greater dispersion of incomes occurred when we expected more effective regional governments to start affecting economic

TABLE 2: ESTIMATED TRENDS IN REGIONAL DISPERSION OF PER CAPITA INCOMES, 1950–1990

| Equation | (i) | (ii) | (iii) | (iv) | (v) |
|---|---|---|---|---|---|
| No. of Observations | 23 | 23 | 23 | 23 | 23 |
| Estimation Method | OLS | OLS | OLS | OLS | OLS |
| Dependent Variable | $\sigma y$ | $\sigma$Civicres | $\sigma$Perfres | $\sigma$Satisres | $\sigma$Satisres |
| Constant | .4991 | .4416 | .4763 | .4780 | .4720 |
| | (17.63) | (14.09) | (13.43) | (14.99) | (18.66) |
| *Coefficients* | | | | | |
| Year | −.00288 | −.00448 | −.00430 | −.00343 | −.00344 |
| | (7.58) | (10.64) | (9.42) | (8.01) | (10.31) |
| Year−83, if > 0 | .00641 | .00811 | .00991 | .00062 | |
| | (3.79) | (4.32) | (4.67) | (0.33) | |
| $R^2$ | .722 | .846 | .787 | .819 | .827 |
| S.E.E. | .0135 | .0149 | .0168 | .0152 | 0.148 |
| D.W. | 1.90 | 1.48 | 1.20 | 1.82 | 1.79 |

*Note:* Absolute values of *t*-statistics are in parentheses. The dependent variable in each equation is a time series of cross-sectional standard deviations. For equation (i), the standard deviations are of per capita incomes across 20 regions. In equations (ii) and (iii) the standard deviations are of the residuals from cross-sectional equations explaining regional income differences by either civic traditions (ii) or institutional performance (iii). In equations (iv) and (v) the residuals are from equations estimated across the 18 larger regions for which data are available from the surveys of citizen satisfaction. Equation (v) differs from equation (iv) only by excluding the insignificant second time trend.

growth. We can think of two ways of proceeding. One indirect strategy is to do a series of cross-sectional regressions on the single measures of civic traditions and governmental effectiveness, and see if higher values of these measures are associated with higher dispersion of incomes during the 1980s. These tests reveal no significant trends. Thus we are not surprised, when we regress the residuals from these regressions on split time trends, as shown in equations (ii) to (iv) of Table 2, to find a significant split at the same point as for the raw measures of income dispersion.

A more direct and probably more appropriate test is provided by the measures of citizen satisfaction, available from several different years, both before and after the likely dates when the reforms would have started to affect economic growth. As shown by Putnam (1993, Figure 2.8), public satisfaction with regional government, even in 1977, was almost twice as high in the northern as in the southern regions of Italy. In both parts of the country, the subsequent increases in regional government powers apparently led to increases in citizen satisfaction, and the proportionate gap increased slightly. Further supportive evidence is that about 8 percent of southerners moved from the unsatisfied to the satisfied group between 1977 and 1988, while in the North more than 25 percent of those polled did so.

To get an idea of whether this greater perceived efficiency of regional government may have translated into higher growth in the already richer regions, we performed cross-sectional regressions of regional income differences on the most recent previous measure of citizen satisfaction. We plot the standard deviations of the residuals from these regressions in Figure 1. We then tested whether these adjusted measures of income dispersion (standard deviations of the residuals) also increased during the 1980s, and found that they did not, as can be seen by comparing equations (iv) and (v) in Table 2. More directly, the series plotted in the lower half of Figure 1 show no sign of turning upward in the 1980s, and indeed keep the same downward trend estimated for the earlier decades.[8] We interpret this result as support for the idea that at least some part of the increased dispersion of per capita incomes during the 1980s was due to changes in the relative effectiveness of regional governments, as revealed by changes in greater citizen satisfaction with their regional

---

[8]    The outlying observation for 1986 would be brought completely into line if the cross-sectional regression were based on the satisfaction survey for 1987 rather than that for 1981–82, since the standard error of the equation would drop from .214 to .186 if the 1987 survey result were used. The 1987 measure is no doubt closer to the true 1986 measure than is the 1981–82 result. However, given the risk that the satisfaction survey responses may be influenced by prior growth, we continued to use the stale 1981/82 survey results to ensure that we never use survey responses collected after the year for which the income dispersion is being calculated.

governments. We are cautious about this inference, since it is based on a fairly slender amount of evidence, and the changes in citizen satisfaction may be due in part to other factors which caused the richer regions to grow faster during the 1980s.

## Conclusion

We confirm strong convergence of per capita incomes among the Italian regions during the 1960s and 1970s, and find significant evidence that convergence is faster, and equilibrium income levels higher, in regions with more social capital, using any of three measures—an index of the extent of civic community, an index of various direct measures of the effectiveness of regional government, or surveys of citizen satisfaction with their regional governments. We also find evidence of a sharp reversal of convergence from 1983 through 1990, as indicated by increasing dispersion among regions in the levels of real per capita GDP. Since this reversal of convergence occurred when the increase in regional autonomy was expected to start affecting economic performance, we believe the regional government reforms have been in part responsible. The direct measures of citizen satisfaction with regional government show greater post-reform increases in satisfaction in the North than in the South, and the regional growth rate differences after 1983 suggest that these perceived increases in the effectiveness of regional government also led to greater economic growth. If our view of conditional convergence is valid, then this divergence will be temporary, since the larger income gaps, and the associated differences in the effectiveness of government, will offer more good examples for the lagging regions to follow and will probably increase the demands from their citizens that they should do so. Both of our conclusions are consistent with Putnam's finding of pervasive influence of longstanding regional differences in social institutions and with his survey results showing much more effective regional governments in those regions with initially higher levels of social capital. Our results confirm his view that institutions matter, while also supporting a version of conditional convergence of productivity that makes catching-up a function of the size of the productivity gap between the richer and poorer regions.

Our conclusion that the regional government reforms have been responsible, at least in part, for the reversal of convergence in the 1980s is provisional and qualified. It is provisional because no doubt other possible reasons remain to be spelled out and tested. The conclusion is qualified since only the satisfaction data provide clear indication that regions with better institutions grew faster in the aftermath of the regional government reforms. The earlier measures of civic community and government performance are not sufficient to predict which regions would have more satisfactory regional government (as seen by citizen surveys) and faster growth after 1983. The satisfaction data are more useful, since they are measured both before and after the regional government reforms were implemented, and hence have some chance of showing what effects the reforms had on the relative effectiveness of the various regional governments. Since we do not have comparable pre-reform and post-reform measures of institutional performance and social capital, determining which elements of social capital and institutional performance were most important in permitting the benefits of regional autonomy to be translated into faster growth in the 1980s remains for future research. That the increasing dispersion will be self-limiting, and possibly reversed, by the forces of conditional convergence, which should enable the poorer regions to once again start closing the gap in real incomes also remains to be confirmed.

## Notes

Helliwell is Professor of Economics at the University of British Columbia and Research Associate of the National Bureau of Economic Research. Putnam is Clarence Dillon Professor of International Affairs at Harvard University and Director of Harvard's Center for International Affairs. The research was undertaken while Helliwell was Mackenzie King Visiting Professor of Canadian Studies at Harvard. An earlier version was presented at the Eastern Economics Association Annual Meeting in Boston, March 1994. We are grateful for suggestions received there from Chris Clague, Mancur Olson and others. A subsequent presentation at the University of British Columbia also produced many helpful suggestions, and the editor has provided many helpful editorial suggestions. For assistance in collecting and interpreting regional income data, we are grateful to Luigi Campiglio and Pauliina Girsen.

## References

Barro, R., and X. Sala-i-Martin. 1991. "Convergence across States and Regions." *Brookings Papers on Economic Activity* 1991(1): 107–58.

Baussola, M., and R. Fiorito. 1994. "Regional Unemployment in Italy: Sources and Cures." *Journal of Policy Modelling*, 1994, pp. 497–527.

Blanchard, O. J. 1991. "Comments and Discussion" (on paper by Barro and Sala-i-Martin). *Brookings Papers on Economic Activity* 1991(1), pp. 159–74.

Campiglio, L. 1993. "Capitalism senza capitale: Il capitalismo italiano diversità." *Quaderni dell'Instuto di Politica Economica* n. 1. Milano: Universita Cattolica del Sacro Cuore.

Coe, D. T., and E. Helpman. 1993. "International R&D Spillovers." *NBER Working Paper* No. 4444, November. National Bureau of Economic Research, Cambridge, Mass.

Cohen, S. "La Storia secondo Robert Putnam." *Polis*, August 1994, pp. 315–24.

Dowrick, S., and N. Gemmell. 1991. "Industrialisation, Catching Up and Economic Growth: A Comparative Study across the World's Capitalist Economies." *Economic Journal*, March 1991, pp. 263–75.

Eaton, J, and S. Kortum. 1994. "International Patenting and Technology Diffusion." NBER Working Paper No. 4931, November. National Bureau of Economic Research, Cambridge, Mass.

Friedman, M. 1992. "Do Old Fallacies Ever Die?" *Journal of Economic Literature*, December 1992, pp. 2129–32.

Grossman, G. M., and E. Helpman. 1991. *Innovation and Growth in the Global Economy*. Cambridge, Mass.: MIT Press.

Helliwell, J. F., and A. Chung. 1991. "Macroeconomic Convergence: International Transmission of Growth and Technical Progress." In P. Hooper and J. D. Richardson, eds., *International Economic Transactions: Issues in Measurement and Empirical Research*, pp. 388–436. Chicago: University of Chicago Press.

Keefer, P., and S. Knack. 1993. "Why Don't Poor Countries Catch Up? A Cross-National Test of an Institutional Explanation." *IRIS Working Paper*. IRIS, College Park.

Mankiw, N. G., D. Romer, and D. N. Weil. 1992. "A Contribution to the Empirics of Economic Growth." *Quarterly Journal of Economics*, May 1992, pp. 407–37.

Nelson, R. R., and E. S. Phelps. 1996. "Investment in Humans, Technological Diffusion, and Economic Growth." *American Economic Review Papers and Proceedings*, May 1966, pp. 69–75.

Putnam R. D. 1993. *Making Democracy Work: Civic Traditions in Modern Italy*. Princeton: Princeton University Press.

Quah, D. 1993. "Galton's Fallacy and Tests of the Convergence Hypothesis." *Scandinavian Journal of Economics*, December 1993, pp. 427–43.

Ridolfi, M. 1994. "Tradizioni civiche e regioni nella storia d'Italia" (with contributions by M. Fincardi, L. Musella, G. Riccamboni, and M. Ridolfi). *Memoria e Ricerea: Rivista di storia contemporanea*, July 1994, pp. 147–76.

SVIMEZ. 1991. *Rapporto 1990 sull'economia del Mezzogiorno*. Bologna: Mulino.

# Social capital: evidence and implications[*]

**Deepa Narayan** and **Lant Pritchett**
*World Bank*

*This paper does three things. First, we present evidence from household surveys in Tanzania showing that social characteristics of villages, in particular the extent to which individuals maintain a dense network of horizontal associations, affect individual outcomes. Second, in light of this empirical evidence we examine the various definitions of social capital and the mechanisms proposed whereby social capital affects economic outcomes. Third, we examine the operational implications for governments and donors of the role of social capital in the delivery of basic services.*

## Introduction

Clarity on what social capital is, what it is not, and what it does will come from empirical research, which forces definitional and measurement issues. Our study in Tanzania focuses on measuring social capital at the community level. In this paper we do three things. First, we show that associational relationships and social norms of that existing in the villages in rural Tanzania are both *capital* and *social*. Second, we show how our empirical results on "social capital" flow into the many emerging streams of literature on social capital. Third, we show how the analysis of social capital is central to many of the emerging problems faced by development practitioners in designing institutional mechanisms for providing basic public services.

---

[*] The findings, interpretations, and conclusions expressed in this paper are entirely those of the authors. They do not necessarily reflect the views of the World Bank, its Executive Directors, or the countries they represent.

## Empirical evidence from Tanzania

We cannot examine the effects of what we *mean* by social capital, only what we *measure*. In order to investigate the topic of "social capital" a special household survey was designed to examine the link between "social capital" and village-level outcomes. The basic survey instrument, the Social Capital and Poverty Survey (SCPS), asked individuals a variety of questions to capture these aspects of village life. The SCPS was carried out in rural Tanzania in April and May of 1995 as part of a larger participatory poverty assessment exercise (Narayan 1997). While the households were chosen randomly within clusters, the sampling clusters themselves, which correspond roughly to villages in rural areas, were the same as those randomly selected for use in the 1993 Human Resource Development Survey (HRDS)—hence the SCPS and HRDS data can be matched village by village. The total usable SCPS sample is 1376 households located in 87 clusters.[1]

The survey's social capital section queried a household respondent about three dimensions of social capital: first, their membership in groups; second, the characteristics of those groups in which the households were members; and third, the individual's values and attitudes—particularly their definition, and expressed level, of trust in various groups, and their perception of social cohesion. In this work we describe the groups only briefly; a fuller description of the groups, their activities, and the results of qualitative and quantitative information from interviews and participatory data collection methods can be found in a companion paper (Narayan 1997).

The first set of questions was simply the number of groups in which an individual was a member. Table 1 lists the most prevalent groups, individuals' responses as to their "most important" group, and the groups they would join if they could join only one group. Most groups are Christian churches, mosques, the village burial society, women's groups, and the political party. The more purely economic associations (cooperatives, rotating credit groups) are much less important. In addition to questions about membership a second set of questions was asked about the characteristics of each group in which the individuals reported membership. These were grouped into five categories: (a) kin heterogeneity of membership, (b) income heterogeneity of membership, (c) group functioning, (d) group decision-making, and (e) voluntary membership.

---

[1]   The survey was implemented in two parts, a social capital module and a household module devoted primarily to measuring household expenditures, but unfortunately the second part was only administered in every other cluster. Therefore only 53 clusters have SCPS expenditure data.

TABLE 1: GROUPS IN RURAL TANZANIA, BY MEMBERSHIP AND CHARACTERISTICS

| | Group as a percent of all membership | Number of households with members | "Most important group in your life at present?" | "If you could join only one group, which one would it be?" |
|---|---|---|---|---|
| Church | 21 | 230 | 29 | 24 |
| Political party (CCM) | 17 | 195 | 10 | 3 |
| Burial society | 15 | 167 | 19 | 14 |
| Women's group | 9 | 104 | 5 | 8 |
| Muslim group | 9 | 109 | 11 | 8 |
| Farmers' group | 8 | 87 | 8 | 16 |
| Other | 21 | 252 | n.a. | n.a. |

n.a. Not applicable.
*Note:* In this table "Other" includes (with percent reporting): Youth group (7), Primary society (4), Cooperative (2), Rotating credit societies (2), Dairy and cattle (1), and Other (5).
*Source:* Narayan and Pritchett (1999).

The information on the number of groups and their characteristics was combined into an overall numerical index using a method described in Narayan and Pritchett (1999). In the construction of our proxy index for social capital we deliberately do not differentiate by type of group, as the main purpose is to examine whether groups with noneconomic functions have village-level spillover effects on economic outcomes.

Before examining the specific hypotheses about social capital, some information on the situation and activities of the people surveyed will set the context. Rural Tanzania is a clear case of arrested economic development. Tanzanians are extremely poor; the average per person consumption expenditures reported in the 1993–94 HRDS in rural areas is 50 *cents* a day ($180 per person per year).[2] Most of the population is employed in traditional agriculture, with a substantial subsistence component, as the imputed value of production for one's own consumption accounts for half of consumption expenditures. Nearly all agriculture is rain-fed and uses almost no modern inputs, is labor-intensive depending primarily on household labor, and uses only a few rudimentary tools with an almost complete lack of mechanization (table 4). The data from the HRDS confirm that the health and nutrition status of the population is extremely poor, with an infant mortality rate of 92 in 1991–92 and 47 percent of children showing signs of stunting. The government's past

---

[2] *The World Development Report* of 1995 reports Tanzania as tied with Mozambique for the lowest GNP per capita of $90.

emphasis on primary schooling means that although many adults in rural households have primary schooling and the average years of schooling completed for adults is about 4.5, very few rural residents have secondary schooling.

### Social capital and outcomes

We show that associational life is in fact social capital (or a good proxy for social capital) first by showing that it is *capital*—in the sense of augmenting incomes—and then by showing that this capital is *social*, not only in the sense of relating to a social phenomena, but also social in the economists' sense of containing spillover effects from one household to another within the village. We show also that there is an independent effect at the *village* level.

We are able to establish these effects strongly because both the SCPS and the HRDS collected data on the economic and demographic characteristics of *different* households in the *same* villages. In this way, not only can we examine the effect of our index of associational life on the households from which this data was constructed, but also show the impact of the measured associational life of one set of households on the outcomes of a *different* set of households living in the same village. Crudely put, we are able to show not only the association between person A belonging to a church group or burial society and person A's income but also the relationship between person A's membership in associations and the income of person B who lives in the same village as A.

For our indicator of incomes total consumption expenditures per person in the household were estimated, including imputations for own-produced consumption and for consumer durables (for example, housing).[3] In order to estimate the impact of social capital on incomes we first adopt a specification of the determinants of per person household expenditures that includes both individual $(Z_{ij})$ and village-level $(X_j)$ variables.[4]

A number of household characteristics are included in the regression: the average years of schooling of male and female adults (over 20) in the

---

[3] We use expenditures as a proxy for incomes (and use the terms interchangeably) for two reasons. First, when there is saving and dissaving (and especially with functioning capital markets) current expenditures are a better measure of permanent income than is current income. Second, extensive experience with household surveys has shown that it is tremendously difficult (if not impossible) to measure the incomes of the agrarian self-employed who constitute the bulk of our sample (Deaton 1997).

[4] This specification was previously developed and used in an examination of rural poverty in Tanzania (World Bank 1996).

household,[5] a dummy variable if the head of the household was "self-employed in agriculture," a dummy variable for female-headed households, and an index of nonland, nonagricultural, physical assets.[6] There are two village-level variables besides social capital. The first is the median distance of dwellings in the cluster to a market for crops, included as a proxy for the market integration of the village.[7] In addition, a set of dummy variables for six agroclimatic regions of Tanzania is also included to control partially for the economic and agroclimatic diversity of the country.

However, while investigating the impact of the associational life of one set of individuals on the incomes of another may show that the effect is truly *social* and not merely that richer individuals tend to have denser networks of social contacts, it does not answer the question of causation. It could be that greater "social capital" or associational life may simply be a normal consumption good so that richer households consume more; that is, perhaps associational life is not "capital" but "consumption," consumed more by households with greater income or leisure.[8] If richer individuals lived together, one would tend to find that richer villages were associated with higher village social capital. In the United States, for example, the average income of neighborhoods would be associated with higher ownership of luxury cars, but this does not imply that if poorer neighborhoods had an abundance of Mercedes cars it would make them richer. We answer this objection about the direction of influence between social capital and income in three ways. First, we use instrumental variables estimation to show that the *village's* social capital associated with greater degrees of trust matters for incomes. The SCPS survey posed questions about individuals' "trust" in various groups. We posit that certain of these "trust" variables, particularly an individual's trust in strangers and in various government officials, are

---

[5] The average of both male and female adults is used for simplicity, although it is worth noting that when the genders are included separately the average education of adult females in the household had a much larger estimated impact on incomes than male schooling.

[6] The HRDS has a list of assets which were given the following weights to create an index: bicycles 16, radios or cameras 8, watches 4.

[7] In the above-mentioned World Bank study of rural poverty, distance to market was interacted with an index of road quality and produced a strong income effect. In our case we were not able to replicate the road quality index with our HRDS sample and so used the simpler, but less appealing, measure of distance alone.

[8] This argument is weakened by the fact that the social capital index is only partly a measure of associational *activity*, as it more reflects the nature of groups of which individuals are members—which is at least plausibly less related to income than is the magnitude of activity. To use Putnam's illustration, it may well be that richer individuals bowl more, but it is less clear why they should bowl more in groups when they do bowl (Putnam 1995).

valid instruments—in that they are not affected directly by household income and they do not affect income directly—but that greater levels of trust do lead to higher village social capital.[9] However, we acknowledge that econometric methods can never be fully persuasive in debates about causality and, after presenting the instrumental variables estimates, we also present some evidence on some theoretically plausible causal mechanisms whereby social capital affects outcomes.

Columns 1 and 2 of table 2 show the results of regressing the incomes of households from the HRDS on the village's social capital index we constructed from the SCPS (controlling for the other household and cluster variables calculated from the HRDS) using instrumental variables estimation techniques. The estimated impact is large and statistically significant in both the household and cluster-averaged regressions— that is, the social capital of the households interviewed in the SCPS has an impact on the incomes of *other* households in their village (surveyed two years previously) as well as on their *own* incomes. This finding is clear evidence that a significant fraction of benefits of associational life on economic outcomes is that it creates a "capital" that is (locally) "social"—in other words, one whose benefits are not entirely private.

The estimates suggest that increase in village social capital increases the income of all households in the village by approximately 20 percent. In more concrete terms, if half the village are members of one group (with average characteristics) this village would have a social capital index that is higher by one standard deviation than a village in which group membership was zero.[10] While increasing average membership by one-half group per household (or changing group characteristics to a similar degree) is a substantial shift in social behavior, the estimates suggest that this would increase expected incomes by an impressively large amount. These impacts are large relative to other well-known determinants of income, such as schooling or physical assets. A one standard deviation increase in education, which is an additional three years of schooling per adult, would increase incomes by only 3–5 percent. Similarly, increasing nonfarm physical assets by one standard deviation is associated with only a 19–22 percent increase in expenditures.

---

[9]    A recent investigation using cross-national data from the World Values Survey does find a strong bivariate correlation between expressed degrees of trust and membership in associations (La Porta, Lopez-de-Silanes, Shleifer, and Vishny 1997).

[10]    Since the index is multiplicative between group membership, since the characteristics of groups matter, and since the index is normalized twice, it requires some working back to find out that, evaluated at the average group characteristics, increasing group membership by .5 would increase the social capital index by one standard deviation.

TABLE 2: HOUSEHOLD EXPENDITURES PER PERSON AND SOCIAL CAPITAL, COMPARING THE VILLAGE AND HOUSEHOLD LEVEL AND USING HRDS DATA FOR INCOMES

| Column | 1 | 2 | 3 |
|---|---|---|---|
| Source of data on expenditures | Human Resource and | | |
| Level of aggregation of | Development Survey | | |
| nonsocial capital variables | Household | | Cluster[c] |
| Type of estimation[a] | IV[e] (a) | IV (b) | IV |
| Village social capital | .193 | .227 | .208 |
| | 2.31 | 1.71 | 2.56 |
| Household size | −.080 | −.079 | .019 |
| | 10.5 | 10.3 | 1.04 |
| Average adult schooling[b] | .021 | .021 | −.057 |
| | 2.87 | 2.79 | 1.42 |
| Female head of household | −.009 | −.010 | .345 |
| (1=yes) | .150 | .173 | 1.19 |
| Asset ownership (ln)[b] | .143 | .143 | .245 |
| | 5.26 | 5.20 | 3.88 |
| Self-employed in agriculture | −.068 | −.069 | −.325 |
| (1=yes) | 1.69 | 1.68 | 1.19 |
| Distance to nearest market | −.0087 | −.0087 | −.004 |
| (clstr)[b] | 2.21 | 2.21 | 1.05 |
| Agroclimatic zone dummies[d] | — | — | — |
| Regression statistics | | | |
| Number of observations | 1505 | 1505 | 84 |
| Adjusted R-squared | — | — | — |
| First stage incremental R[b] | .116 | .061 | .092 |
| Instrument test (p-level) | .783 | .786 | .618 |

—. Not available.
a. The t-statistics are based on Huber corrected standard errors that are heteroskedasticity consistent and account for stratified sampling.
b. If any of these variables was missing, then a value was imputed for that household and a missing dummy variable was set equal to one.
c. Cluster-level social capital index excludes household's own response.
d. Included in the regressions but not reported are dummy variables for each of six agroclimatic zones and the three missing value dummy variables.
e. The instrument sets are *a* and *b*; *a* includes trust in strangers, tribesman, cell leader, village chairman (government), district officials, and central government—while instrument set *b* excludes strangers.
*Source:* Narayan and Pritchett (1999).

## Social capital and causal mechanisms

Our understanding of this result is enhanced by comprehending the proximate mechanisms through which social capital affects incomes in rural Tanzania. The previous literature has suggested five plausible channels of influence: (a) more effective public services, (b) better cooperative action, (c) more rapid diffusion of information, (d) better functioning markets, and (e) informal insurance. Direct evidence on any of these channels is difficult to come by, but the combination of the HRDS and SCPS data do allow some exploration of the connection between social capital and various effects.

Tanzania since independence has been controlled by the same party, which—although government is organized along provincial and district lines—has exercised centralized control over nearly all government and party activities. While there has been large emphasis on "cooperative" and "village" level organizations these were not autonomous, locally controlled organizations, but a monopoly of the party.[11] Any effect of social capital on the effectiveness of publicly provided services must work indirectly, perhaps through greater cooperation of villagers in monitoring the performance of government, rather than directly through the formal political apparatus.

The HRDS has data on the quality of two public services, schools and health clinics, as subjectively assessed by the respondents, and a series of questions about the level of parental and community involvement in the schools, which allow us to construct an index of parental participation.[12] The HRDS also asked individuals about their attendance at "meetings where issues important to the community, such as health and education, could be discussed." Table 3 shows that the social capital index as measured in the SCPS survey is associated with higher reported levels of parental participation in schools and attendance at community meetings in the HRDS data (which surveyed different individuals from those used to measure social capital). Moreover, higher social capital was associated with higher levels of school quality. These findings trace out a possible chain of causation from greater social capital to more parental and community involvement in schools, and ultimately to better quality schools. There is, however, no link at all between health facility quality and social capital. This is perhaps not surprising as the major

---

[11] In particular during the 1970s the government pursued a policy of forced "villagization," which was neither particularly well received by those affected, nor successful.

[12] The questions asked about the closest government primary school were: "Are parents asked to participate in decisions affecting the school [NAME]?" Does the school have an active parents/teacher committee?" "Does the school [NAME] have open days for parents to visit?" "Does the school report grades?"

factors for health clinics were drug availability and qualified doctors (see Appendix)—factors that are largely beyond village control.[13]

Another possible channel for the impact of social capital is the management of resources that are treated as common property within the village (or perhaps among a few villages) such as improved water supplies, local irrigation capabilities, and local roads. Unfortunately on this question we have very little data, but in the SCPS households were asked whether they participated in joint activities aimed at building or maintaining roads. Villages with more social capital are more likely to have had community road building activities (table 3). This does suggest another possible link through village cooperative activity.

Much more important as a proximate determinant of incomes than public services is that households in villages with larger social capital are a lot more likely to have used fertilizer, agrochemical inputs, or improved seeds (table 4). A standard deviation increase in village social capital increases the probability of using agrochemicals by 42 percent (6.7 percentage points above a mean of 16), of using fertilizer by 38 percent (5 percentage points), and of using improved seeds by 17 percent (2 percentage points). We also find that in villages with higher social capi-

TABLE 3: CORRELATION OF SOCIAL CAPITAL WITH INDICATORS OF PARENTAL PARTICIPATION IN SCHOOLS, SCHOOL QUALITY, AND HEALTH FACILITY QUALITY

|  |  | Bivariate rank correlations | |
| --- | --- | --- | --- |
|  | *Survey* | *Social capital index* | *Group functioning subcomponent* |
| Median parental | HRDS | .243 | .202 |
| participation in schools |  | (.025) | (.065) |
| Attendance at community | HRDS | .296 | .117 |
| meetings |  | (.006) | (.291) |
| School quality | HRDS | .176 | .238 |
|  |  | (.108) | (.029) |
| Health facility quality | HRDS | .132 | −.039 |
|  |  | (.228) | (.724) |
| Participation in joint efforts | SCPS | .147 | .272 |
| at road repairs |  | (.182) | (.012) |

*Note:* p-levels in parenthesis.

*Source:* Author.

---

[13] While we do confirm an association between social capital, community involvement and better public services, we should point out that strictly speaking this does not go far in "explaining" the income effect of social capital as a proximate determinant—as we have no evidence on the magnitude of the link from better schools to higher incomes. And moreover, in the data above, the link with income and the quantity of schooling is quite weak in table 3.

tal a larger fraction of households report using credit for agricultural improvements. Since only 9 percent of households report using credit, the one standard deviation of social capital has the effect of increasing credit use by almost a third (2.7 percentage points). As with the income effects, these results are surprisingly strong. The positive association of the adoption of improved practices and credit use with social capital holds true whether one controls for the individual's self-reported land quality or the extent of the individual's contact with an extension agent.

These results on the adoption of improved practices are consistent with at least three of the stories about the effect of social capital: innovation diffusion, overcoming market failures caused by imperfect information, and informal insurance. There are arguments for and against each of these explanations of the differences in agricultural practices.

TABLE 4: HOUSEHOLD PROBABILITY OF ADOPTING IMPROVED AGRICULTURAL PRACTICES (DF/DX CALCULATED FROM PROBIT ESTIMATES)[a, b]

|  | Used agrochemicals | Used fertilizer | Used improved seeds | Used credit for agricultural improvements |
|---|---|---|---|---|
| Village social capital | .057 | .075 | .015 | .027 |
|  | (2.35) | (2.45) | (.737) | (1.66) |
| Household size | .012 | −.006 | .004 | −.0019 |
|  | (3.25) | (1.43) | (1.03) | (.742) |
| Average household adult education | .019 | .0078 | .010 | .0044 |
|  | (5.00) | (1.56) | (2.30) | (1.21) |
| Female head | −.102 | −.112 | −.114 | .0035 |
|  | (2.89) | (3.46) | (3.51) | (.143) |
| Assets | .049 | .110 | .058 | .0069 |
|  | (2.45) | (6.28) | (2.63) | (.606) |
| Self employed in agriculture | .046 | −.035 | −.037 | .027 |
|  | (1.49) | (.958) | (1.06) | (1.03) |
| Median distance to market | −.013 | .005 | −.005 | −.0052 |
|  | (2.34) | (.855) | (1.16) | (1.51) |
| Observed probability | .217 | .197 | .169 | .093 |
| Predicted probability at means | .155 | .129 | .125 | .078 |
| Number of observations | 772 | 734 | 765 | 842 |
| Pseudo R-squared[c] | .204 | .254 | .147 | .071 |

a. The t-statistics reported are the Huber corrected for the probit regression coefficients, not the t-statistics of the reported marginal effects.
b. Included in the regression but not reported were dummy variables for agroclimatic zones, and for missing values of the assets, schooling, and distance to market variables
c. Since the model is non-linear, the R-squared is not applicable, but this is a measure of goodness of fit for Probit models.
*Source:* Narayan and Pritchett (1999).

## Social capital: the elephant

While we have presented our evidence on social capital, fitting this into the existing empirical literature and drawing out policy implications is problematic. Social capital, while perhaps not all things to all people, is many things to many people: it is the proverbial elephant felt by the five blind men. In order to fit empirical results into an overall pattern, a overarching framework is needed that answers two questions:

■ What is social capital?

■ How does social capital, thus defined, affect social, political, or economic outcomes?

What would such a framework look like? We will begin with an abstract definition of a "society" as consisting of N distinct nodes (which may be households, if intrahousehold relations are ignored, or individuals). Between any two nodes $i$ and $j$ there is a directional (that is, not necessarily symmetric) connection, which could be called the intensity of a given social relationship between $i$ and $j$. This social relationship can be anything from a disposition or attitude (for example, a feeling of mutual trust, a "willingness to postpone reciprocation in the fulfillment of obligations"), to a culturally defined and construed kin, ethnic, or social group identification (for example, cousins, tribe, or clan), or to a joint, voluntarily adopted social tie (for example, a friend, or a member of same voluntary club). In this abstraction of a society a general definition of "social capital" is some aggregation of the relationships between the nodes.

To make this definition of social capital specific and empirically implementable requires three interrelated choices. The first involves the level at which social capital is to be measured. One can talk about the degree of social capital of an individual or household (that is, the magnitude and value of the relationships to other nodes "owned" by a given individual), of a socially defined group, or of a geographically or politically defined society (that is, the value of all the nodes in a given village, city, province, or nation).

Second, to measure social capital one must specify which particular dimensions of social experience "count" as a social relationship. Some authors choose to focus on attitudes and dispositions toward individuals or socially defined actors (for example, trust in government officials) or groups (for example, attitudes toward ethnic groups). Others focus on associational activities (such as bowling in groups, or attending church). Still others focus on socially defined relationships such as kin and clan.

Third, a definition must have a rule for how to combine and "weight" each of these relationships. The rule for assigning weights will not be simple, as the weight assigned may be highly nonlinear and the weight given to a relationship between $i$ and $j$ may depend in a complex way on other relationships. Suppose a society has two groups, A and B, that are relatively densely linked within the groups but with no linkages between each other; and suppose two individuals $i$ and $j$ are going to establish a new social relationship. How much this relationship between $i$ and $j$ adds to aggregate social capital depends on whether both are members of A (or both members of B), in which case it may add very little, or whether they are members of different groups, in which case the existence of a relationship between $i$ and $j$ may receive a large weight in "social capital."

Much of the current debate about the many definitions of social capital stems from the fact that the different literatures on social capital work through these questions with specific hypotheses and theories determining the choices. That is, the implementation of definitions of social capital, the level of analysis, social relationships examined and weights used, are topic-driven and functional. Researchers typically begin from a particular outcome under consideration (for example, local cooperation, national public policy choices, incidence of individual high school dropping out) and work back to a functional definition by asking which social phenomena are likely to influence the outcome. In this case different researchers will naturally come to very different views on the appropriate level of analysis, which social relationships count, and by how much, in defining social capital.

For instance, one could begin with the question of under what conditions the collective action problems inherent in the use of common pool resources are solved successfully. Certainly social characteristics of the groups facing such problems, such as the sentiments of group affiliation and trust, will be important in determining outcomes. In this case one could call those social characteristics that lead to beneficial outcomes in this particular problem "social capital." Alternatively, one could begin with the question of why certain socially defined ethnic groups dominate certain markets, such as the domination of credit markets by minority Asian groups in Africa. Again, certainly the social characteristics of the groups determine those outcomes and the aspects of these groups that lead to superior outcomes *for these groups* could be labeled as their social capital.

But the problem of reaching a consensus definition of social capital is even trickier, for two reasons. First, the same relationships that constitute social capital for these groups may well have value by serving to exclude others and hence would not be the same factors that would contribute to social capital in the case of some other type of collective action, even in the same social setting. That is, successful maintenance of irrigation channels may depend on social cohesion among potential users. However, if these potential users of irrigation are not the same group that is important for another collective action problem, such as soil erosion, the cohesion that is conducive to maintenance may or may not serve to facilitate cooperation on soil erosion.

The problems are worse still, as consideration of "social capital" by economists leads to a double meaning in the use of the word "social"—in that it classifies both a type of capital (social as opposed to "physical" or "human" capital) and a level of action (social as opposed to "private"). So in investigating social capital the direct and indirect benefits may differ at different levels of analysis and some social relationships will have positive weight as an individual's or group's social capital but negative weights on a society's social capital. Let us, for instance, take the example of a social group that is formed with the express object of suppressing another social group, such as the Ku Klux Klan. Then we might want to count each additional member as having additional "social capital" relative to his or her private individual (and group) objectives. In other words, the individual (and group) has a certain kind of relationship with other individuals—which is classified as social, and which has value to them in relation to their objectives; and hence it is capital. But since the purpose of the use of these individuals' social capital is to oppress other individuals then this certainly should be counted as negative "social capital" for all other groups. Greater membership in some social organizations could lead to *less* society-wide social capital, as the capital relative to the members' private objectives has negative effects on others and hence has a negative social impact.

In addition, these functional definitions run the risk of becoming circular and tautological. That is, if one defines social capital as "those elements of the social structure that contribute to better social outcomes," then obviously it has been assumed rather than shown that social structures do matter for outcomes. The proliferation of topic-oriented functional definitions of social capital will never lead to a consensus. With functional definitions social capital is what social capital does and what social capital *does* depends on whether the topic is schools, irrigation canals, credit markets, or local politics. This means that the same data could show that what is social capital with respect to collective action is not social capital with respect to capital markets or with respect to cooperation on public goods. But this lack of consensus does not have to be either a criticism of the existing literature or a barrier to the productivity of future research—as long as the choices inherent in the different definitions of social capital are made explicit within their theoretical context and the possibly functional roots of the definitions made clear.

### *Three streams, one river?*

There are three streams of thought, each of which is related to—and has adopted or been adopted by—the notion of "social capital." The first is country-level politics, the second is the efficacy of the public sector, the third is the resolution of market failures. Within each of these there are contributions that have been made prior to the resurgence of the notion of "social capital."

*Country-level politics, policies, and growth.* Easterly and Levine (1996) have shown that a measure of "ethnic heterogeneity" is empirically associated with the adoption of bad economic policies, which they attribute to the importance of distributional conflict among groups. Alesina, Baqir, and Easterly (1997) show that greater ethnic fragmentation in U.S. cities leads to lower spending on productive public goods (for example, education, roads, sewers) and is negatively related to the share of local spending on welfare. While not able to measure efficacy directly, the results also suggest higher public employment with greater fragmentation, possibly the results of higher patronage.

Others have examined the connection between society-wide indicators and investment and growth rates. Knack and Keefer (1997) for instance, examine the relationship between trust, norms of civic cooperation, associational activity, and aggregate economic growth and investment rates.

At the country level explaining economic performance by such "cultural" characteristics such as the "Protestant work ethic" or "Confucianism" has a long and checkered history, since it easily veers to self-congratulation (or flagellation) of one's own culture or a particularly ugly condescension toward other cultures as incompatible with development. Recent entries in the country-level explanation include Harrison (1992) on culture and Fukuyama's (1995) examination of trust—and the various attitudes toward different "civilizational" cultures and economic modernization are nicely summarized in Huntington (1996).

*Public sector efficacy.* The fascinating analysis of the variations in *public sector efficacy* (Putnam, Leonardi, and Nanetti 1993) of the newly created regional governments in Italy suggests that regions of Italy in which people had greater degrees of horizontal connections had more efficacious governments. He documents a close connection between the numbers of voluntary associations and the efficacy of the regional government. Putnam finds that the more likely a region's citizens are to join football clubs and choral societies the faster the regional government is in reimbursing health care claims. One way of understanding this result is that monitoring the performance of the government is facilitated by greater social capital, either directly (because the government agents themselves are more embedded in the social network), or perhaps indirectly (because the monitoring of the public provision of services is a public good)—and this is true even if the publicly provided service is itself a private good, as long as quality cannot be individually differentiated.

In addition, the institutional "capacity" either of specific government agencies or of governments in general created by the social relationships among the staff may be considered an important part of encouraging performance—and hence of social capital. Tendler's (1997) analysis of the improvement of health in Brazil shows that the interrelationship between motivated cadres of government agents and the beneficiaries they intend to reach is an important dimension to public sector efficacy.

Wade (1988) documents wide variations in the extent of cooperation within villages in southern India, which he attributes to a significant degree to differences in the benefits from cooperation, and to differences in the physical characteristics of the irrigation network serving the villages. Social capital may facilitate greater cooperation in the provision of services outside of governmental channels, which benefit all, or select, members of the community.

*Resolution of market failures.* This is obviously an economist-centric intellectual organizing device, but it does lead one to see certain lines of research in light of their commonalities.

*Common pool resources.* Ostrom's (1990) work suggests that the ability of local groups to cooperate plays a large role in avoiding the negative consequences of the excessive exploitation or undermaintenance of assets that would result from purely individualistic behavior under open access. She points out that the infamous "tragedy of the commons" based on purely individualistic behavior is only one possible outcome, and that cooperative action can be a stable outcome. Role of group or community *cooperative* action in solving problems with local "common property" elements is potentially important. Ajuha (1996) shows that in Cote d'Ivoire the degree of land degradation is worse in more ethnically heterogeneous villages, suggesting that a difference in the effectiveness of community controls and cooperation depends on social factors.

A second market failure exists in the *diffusion of innovations*, which might be facilitated by greater linkages among individuals. In his review of empirical work on the diffusion of innovations Rogers (1983) reports studies that suggest that "social participation," "interconnectedness with the social system," "exposure to interpersonal communication channels," and "belonging to highly interconnected systems" are each positively associated with the early adoption of innovations. Recent research on the adoption of Green Revolution innovations suggest that village-level spillovers played a role in individuals' adoption decisions, but it does not examine the role that social capital may have played in mediating the village-level effects (Besley and Case 1994, Foster and Rosenzweig 1995).

Third, *imperfect information* leads to large transactions costs and market failures in a wide range of markets. Social links among parties to economic transactions may increase their ability to participate in economic transactions that involve some uncertainty about compliance, such as credit. There are two possible mechanisms at work. Social capital could lead to a better flow of information between creditors and borrowers and hence may involve less adverse selection and moral hazard in the market for credit. Social capital also potentially expands the range of enforcement mechanisms for defaulting on obligations in environments in which recourse to the legal system is costly or impossible.

Fourth, *markets for insurance*, particularly for income insurance, are plagued, often to the point of nonexistence, by the problems of adverse selection and moral hazard. Social relationships may contribute to *informal insurance*, which allows households to pursue higher returns but involves more risky activities and production techniques. If this is so then a social safety net that mitigates the consequences of adverse outcomes would lead farmers to undertake activities involving higher returns but also higher risk (Morduch 1995). Increased social capital could lead to greater risk-sharing among villagers and act as an informal safety net.

### Implications for government and donor actions

Often the most perplexing question facing development practitioners is not *what*, but *how*. How does one create the right institutional mechanisms whereby societies can provide themselves with the basic public services in a socially and politically sustainable and cost-effective manner? An early blush of naive optimism among Western aid agencies and newly liberated governments may have once suggested that a simple transplanting of the public sector bureaucracies combined with a massive expansion in supply was the answer. However, the failure of the model of central government provision of basic services to thousands of scattered communities in many sectors (from water to irrigation, schooling, health, and credit) has led to both widespread disillusionment with the possibilities of the traditional modes of government, and experimentation in institutional options for reaching the poor. These experiments, all coming from different directions seem to be discovering (and rediscovering) basic themes: community development, participation, the importance of local organizational capacity, and orientation of providers to demand. All of these in one way or another emphasize the role of social capital in creating effective public action.

#### Community-driven development

One of the most important applications of social capital is in the delivery of sustainable basic services to the poor, and local infrastructure and natural resource management.

The last two decades have seen a resurgence of interest in **community-driven** development, with community groups in charge and the focus shifting to local initiative, self help, local organizational capacity, and demand orientation. Community-driven development is defined as a process in which community groups initiate, organize, and take action to further common interests or achieve common goals. Communities are not homogenous entities, but marked by great power and interest differences—hence the focus on groups and households rather than assuming that the interests of community *leaders* or elite are the same as all the other **social** groupings in a community.

Across the world, there are more failures than *successes* in this area of *large-scale* **induced** *community development.* Analysis of the global experience across sectors highlights three features that are essential for successful community-driven development within a national policy framework that supports the adaptation of these principles to the nature of the good, as well as the local physical and social context (Ostrom and Gardner 1993; Pathan, Arul, and Poffenberger 1993; Esman and Uphoff 1984; Subramanian, Jagannathan, and Meinzen-Dick 1997). The three features of community-driven development are participation, local organizational capacity or local-level social capital, and demand orientation (Narayan 1997). Social Funds are project types that attempt to structure funds to respond to community demand, and thus have great potential as instruments for community building using infrastructure and service provision as a means for strengthening local social capital at the community level.

## Participation

Like social capital, "participation" is a many splendored word which means different things to different people. In the context of community-driven development, participation refers to community group authority and control over decisions and resource allocation including financial resources. Information dissemination and consultation are essential preconditions for effective participation. Participatory processes through which community groups are enabled to make informed decisions lead to strengthening social capital or local organizational capacity and further problem solving beyond the lifetime of particular projects and programs.

Participatory processes that emphasize local involvement in decision-making are quite different from seeing community groups as merely the suppliers of free labor, collectors of local materials, and caretakers of operation and maintenance after contractors have finished building infrastructure, water points, markets, clinics, schools, and so on. The evidence of contribution of client involvement in decision-making to sustainability is strong (Esman and Uphoff 1984; Khan 1992; Freedheim 1993; Hodgkin and Kusumahadi 1993; Narayan 1995b; Isham, Narayan, and Pritchett 1994; NIACONSULT 1994; Ostrom, Lam, and Lee 1994).

The lag is in the transfer of this research and practitioners' knowledge to the design of government- or international agency–financed programs. A recent review of World Bank–financed Social Investment Funds showed that community participation in planning was high but that it dropped off during implementation (Narayan and Ebbe 1997). Only half the projects appraised local participation while reviewing subproposals for funding; 34

percent had mechanisms in place to assess whether the interests of the poor and other excluded groups were reflected in subproposals; and 10 percent gave community groups hiring, firing, supervisory, contracting, and procurement authority. The latter innovations are now rapidly spreading to other projects based on evidence that giving community groups control actually helps rather than hinder project implementation.

### Local organizational capacity

Local organizational capacity is the ability of people—in their desire to achieve agreed-upon goals—to work together, trust one another, and organize to solve problems, mobilize resources, resolve conflicts, and network with others (Narayan 1997). When people cooperate and work together they can overcome problems related to risk, information, and skills. Two elements appear to be critical in the initial stages of local organization building. First, groups have to develop rules for self-governance; and second, the groups must be embedded in the existing social organization. Since the poor rarely have strong organizations to make their voices heard, projects that aim to reach the poor must invest in strengthening the capacity of local groups to take action.

Unfortunately, most donor-financed projects and government-managed programs rarely make local organizational capacity a central objective or indicator of success, without which capacity building—which in the initial stages takes more time and requires a different type of technical skills—gets sacrificed as pressure builds to produce infrastructure or disburse the money.

Projects that aim to invest in local-level social capital have to carefully craft institutional rules and technology choices, and invest in social intermediation to ensure that processes and incentives support capacity-building of local groups and networks. In the recent review of Social Funds, only 17 percent of projects[14] invested in community development training, although this is currently changing. In most community-based projects across sectors, since social intermediation strategies have not been given the same attention as technical design, it is impossible to obtain cost estimates on social intermediation—as they are often buried in administrative costs and overheads. The greatest advance has been made in the water sector—in terms of both irrigation and drinking water—in which engineering and technology choice issues and the community capacity issue are being packaged together (Meinzen-Dick, Reidinger, and Manzardo 1995).

Social intermediation to build knowledge, skills, and organizational capacity can be achieved through mass media information dissemination strategies and through interpersonal face-to-face contact with field workers. One

---

[14] The term was first used by Lynn Bennett, World Bank.

of the most remarkable emerging trends is that when community groups are given the choice of intermediaries, their first choice is often not nongovernmental organizations (NGOs), which are widely perceived to be representatives of the poor. In several Social Funds or social fund–type projects in Malawi, Zambia, Bangladesh, and Ethiopia, communities are choosing intermediaries from within village groups or retrained government workers whose incentive has shifted to serve community groups over NGO intermediaries external to the community (Narayan and Ebbe 1997).

*Demand orientation*

The design of projects and programs that enable participation of community groups in decision-making and investment in local organizational capacity requires a shift in agency rules to support demand orientation. What does a demand-oriented agency or program look like?

Demand orientation is evidenced when projects offer community groups a range of options from which to choose (for example, options in goods and services, technology, or service levels); provide impartial information, especially about costs and benefits to assist clients in making informed choices; and require evidence of commitment or interest before construction or release of funds. During implementation demand orientation is maintained by giving community groups control and authority over decision-making with accountability measures in place. The key features of demand orientation are highlighted in table 5.

The analysis of Social Funds is revealing. The combination of several features determines whether a project is demand-oriented and maintains demand orientation throughout the implementation process. Overall, 40 percent of Social Fund projects were rated as having between three to six mechanisms for ensuring demand orientation. The six features were community initiation of subproject, upfront community contributions, contributions during implementation, creation of project committees, creation of operation, and maintenance committees.

Other important features that reflect the underlying incentives are inclusion in statement of objectives, in monitoring and evaluation criteria, degree of choice, investment in outreach workers, and information dissemination strategies.

The most obvious way of ensuring demand orientation is putting in place mechanisms for self-selection into the project. All Social Funds require groups to submit proposals. In the current portfolio of Social Funds, in 58 percent of projects the initiative comes clearly from the community group with or without support from NGO intermediaries. To respond to the challenge of ensuring that the initiation process is not dominated by the perception of needs by the intermediaries, Social Funds are increasingly giving community groups choices of technical assistance for proposal development.

TABLE 5: KEY FEATURES OF DEMAND ORIENTATION AT COMMUNITY AND AGENCY LEVELS

| Community level—households, groups | Agency level |
|---|---|
| 1. *Groups/community identify priorities.*<br>• Poor, vulnerable, women identify their priorities.<br>• Groups/community reach consensus on priorities. | 1. *Agency conducts or facilitates demand assessment, including:*<br>• Willingness to pay studies.<br>• Beneficiary assessments.<br>• Social assessment to identify key stakeholders and their interests and power. |
| 2. *Groups/community initiate action, including:*<br>• Contact with agency.<br>• Preparation of proposal and plans.<br>• Self-selection into project. | 2. *Agency informs and educates clients through:*<br>• Information campaigns about nature of project rules, funds.<br>• Clear eligibility criteria contingent on demand.<br>• Outreach mechanisms, field presence, and clear rules of engagement. |
| 3. *Groups/community choose among options.*<br>• Groups/community have information on costs and benefits of a range of options.<br>• Groups/community have authority and control over choice of service providers and funds for proposal development. | 3. *Agency offers options and choices.*<br>• Field workers offer impartial information on cost implications of options (technology, infrastructure, program content, loans).<br>• Community is offered choice of service providers, including assistance for proposal development, if needed. |
| 4. *Groups/community make contributions.*<br>• Upfront cash contributions.<br>• Upfront contributions—materials, land.<br>• Percentage contributions toward capital costs.<br>• Percentage contributions toward recurrent costs. | 4. *Agency outlines cost-sharing arrangements, specifying:*<br>• Clear rules for community contributions, linked to service level and conditions for project approval.<br>• Funding mechanisms that reach communities quickly. |

- Clear resource and land titles (clarify ownership issues).

5. *Groups/community complete self-organization prior to funds' release.*
   - Organize project group or committee prior to release of project funds.
   - Agree on rules: membership, roles, costs, benefits.
   - Create operation and maintenance fund, collect money.
   - Create and train operation and maintenance committees.

6. *Groups/community exercise control and authority during implementation.*
   - Manage funds.
   - Manage technical assistance.
   - Hire and fire workers.
   - Use transparent rules and systems for accountability.
   - Manage operation and maintenance.

- Mobilization of resources to fulfill commitment on recurrent costs agreed upon with communities.

5. *Agency supports capacity building for community organizational capacity.*
   - Provides training funds.
   - Provides choice of facilitators to support capacity building.
   - Provides support through staff attitudes and skills.

6. *Project rules and incentives support demand orientation and community control throughout process.*
   - Project objectives focus on supporting community self-help, demand, local control, and capacity building.
   - Achievement of these objectives is reflected in indicator of success.
   - Staff skills, incentives, and rewards support community control and capacity building.
   - Clear, agreed-upon rules and sanctions of disengagement are in place.

*Source:* Narayan and Ebbe (1997).

Two other trends are worth noting. First, Social Funds are opening up their menu of options offered to community groups rather than preallocating by sector. For example, the Argentina, Zambia, and Angola Social Funds set aside the bulk of their funds—between 75 percent to 88 percent of project funds—for unspecified subprojects. Second, Social Funds are beginning to invest in community and trust building. The Jamaican Social Fund includes investment in youth clubs, conflict mediation, and counseling to respond to the needs of communities afflicted by crime and violence. Other projects in West Bank and Gaza and in land management in India are spending money for activities designed to build upfront trust between community groups and government and nongovernment intermediaries, which, because of negative experiences in the past have become distrustful of official interventions.

Social Funds, like other community development programs, are putting in place a series of hurdles that community groups have to overcome as a means of ensuring genuine interest and commitment in the absence of full payment for services. This includes requiring community groups to raise money to cover some percent of capital costs and operation and maintenance costs, and the completion of organizational tasks such as consulting with all community members, clearing land titles, and creating working committees to undertake the project.

The collective experience in community development in developing countries and the industrialized world demonstrates that community action can be induced by crafting institutional design—which factors in local social and political realities—to bring about dramatic changes in trust, productivity, and quality of service provision much faster than is implied by Robert Putnam's seminal study of Italy which traces back present-day differences to different starting points two centuries ago.

## Conclusion

The debate on what social capital is, what it is not, and what it does has just started and will continue for many years. When we combine our Tanzania study results with the vast experience in inducing community-driven approaches on a large scale by governments, donors, and civil society, what is clear is that this application of social capital—facilitating collective action by community groups—will remain one of the most important in poverty reduction strategies. The challenge for national governments and policymakers across sectors is to formulate policies and the framework of rules that allow for infinite variations in the form, speed, and duration of collective action that is instrumental in generating and managing local resources; and to provide the resources that create incentives for private sector and civil society intermediaries to support participatory decisionmaking and organizational capacity—especially among the poor.

# Appendix

TABLE A1: SCHOOL AND HEALTH FACILITY QUALITY INDICATORS

| Schools | | | Health facility | | |
|---|---|---|---|---|---|
| *Characteristic* | *Mean weight* | *Mean ranking* | *Characteristic* | *Mean weight* | *Mean ranking* |
| Well-qualified teachers who teach children well | .252 | 3.18 | Drugs always available when you visit | .261 | 2.29 |
| Excellent headmaster who manages the school well | .188 | 3.41 | Well-qualified, trustworthy doctors and nurses | .228 | 3.12 |
| Enough supplies so each child has a desk and workbooks | .245 | 2.46 | Close to your homes, in the village or ward | .165 | 2.91 |
| Clean building with toilets and playground | .163 | 2.75 | Clean, with toilet, safe water, covered waiting area | .155 | 2.93 |
| Emphasizes academics, requiring no self-reliance work | .149 | 3.15 | Public services: sanitation, immunization, control of pests | .189 | 2.98 |

*Source:* HRDS survey.

# Bibliography

The word *processed* describes informally reproduced works that may not be commonly available through libraries.

Ajuha, Vinod. 1996. "Land Degradation, Agricultural Productivity and Common Property: Evidence from Cote d'Ivoire." Processed. University of Maryland, Baltimore.

Alesina, Alberto, Reza Baqir, and William Easterly. 1997. "Public Goods and Ethnic Divisions." Processed.

Besley, Timothy, and Anne Case. 1994. "Diffusion as a Learning Process: Evidence from HYV Cotton." Discussion Paper No. 174: 1–19. Princeton University Woodrow Wilson School of Public and International Affairs Research Program in Development Studies.

Binswanger, Hans P., Shahidur R. Khandker, and Mark Rosenzweig. 1993. "How Infrastructure and Financial Institutions Affect Agricultural Output and Investment in India." *Journal of Development Economics* 41: 337–66.

Borjas, George J. 1994. "Ethnicity, Neighborhoods, and Human Capital Externalities." *American Economic Review* 85(3): 365–90.

Case, Anne, and Lawrence Katz. 1991. "The Company You Keep: The Effects of Family and Neighborhood on Disadvantaged Youths." NBER Working Paper No. 3705 (May). National Bureau of Economic Research, Cambridge, Mass.

Coleman, James Samuel. 1990. *Foundations of Social Theory.* Cambridge, Mass.: Harvard University Press.

Deaton, Angus. 1997. *The Analysis of Household Surveys: A Microeconometric Approach to Development Policy.* Baltimore: Johns Hopkins University Press.

Easterly, William, and Ross Levine. 1996. "Africa's Growth Tragedy: Policies and Ethnic Divisions." Processed. World Bank, Washington, D.C.

Esman, M. J., and N. Uphoff. 1984. *Local Organizations: Intermediaries in Rural Development.* Ithaca, New York: Cornell University Press.

Foster, Andrew, and Mark R. Rosenzweig. 1995. "Learning by Doing and Learning from Others: Human Capital and Technical Change in Agriculture." *Journal of Political Economy* 103: 1176–1209.

Freedheim, Sara Beth. 1993. "Why Fewer Bells Toll in Ceara: Success of a Community Health Worker Program in Ceara, Brazil." Masters thesis. Massachusetts Institute of Technology, Department of Urban Studies and Planning, Cambridge, Mass.

Fukuyama, Francis. 1995. *Trust: the Social Virtues and the Creation of Prosperity.* New York: Free Press.

Greif, Avner. 1993. "Contract Enforceability and Economic Institutions in Early Trade: The Maghribi Traders' Coalition." *American Economic Review* 83: 525–48.

Harrison, Lawrence E. 1992. *Who Prospers?: How Cultural Values Shape Economic and Political Success.* New York: Basic Books.

Hodgkin, J., and M. Kusumahadi. 1993. *A Study of the Sustainability of CARE-Assisted Water Supply and Sanitation Projects, 1979–1991.* Burlington, Vermont: Associates in Rural Development.

Huntington, Samuel P. 1996. *The Clash of Civilizations and the Remaking of World Order.* New York: Simon and Schuster.

Isham, Jonathan, Deepa Narayan, and Lant Pritchett. 1994. "Does Participation Improve Performance: Establishing Causality with Subjective Data." *World Bank Economic Review* 9(2): 175–200.

Khan, A. H. 1992. *Orangi Pilot Project Programs.* Karachi, Pakistan: Orangi Pilot Project, Research and Training Institute.

Knack, Stephen, and Philip Keefer. 1997. "Does Social Capital Have an Economic Payoff? A Cross-Country Investigation." *Quarterly Journal of Economics* 112 (November): 1251–88.

La Porta, Rafael, Florencio Lopez-de-Silanes, Andrei Shleifer, and Robert Vishny. 1997. "Trust in Large Organizations." Processed.

Meinzen-Dick, Ruth, Richard Reidinger, and Andrew Manzardo. 1995. "Participation in Irrigation." Environment Department papers, No. 3, Participation series. World Bank, Washington, D.C.

Morduch, Jonathan. 1995. "Income Smoothing and Consumption Smoothing." *Journal of Economic Perspectives* 9(3): 103–14.

Narayan, Deepa. 1995a. "The Contribution of People's Participation in 121 Rural Water Projects." ESD Occasional Paper Series No. 1. World Bank, Washington, D.C.

———. 1995b. "Designing Community Based Development." Environment Department Papers, Participation Series No. 7. World Bank, Washington, D.C.

———. 1997. "Voices of the Poor: Poverty and Social Capital in Tanzania." Environmentally Sustainable Development Studies and Monographs series, No. 20. World Bank, Washington, D.C.

Narayan, Deepa, and Katrinka Ebbe. 1997. "Design of Social Funds—Participation, Demand Orientation, and Local Organizational Capacity." World Bank Discussion Paper No. 379. World Bank, Washington, D.C.

Narayan, Deepa, and Lant Pritchett. 1997. "Cents and Sociability." World Bank Policy Research Working Paper No. 1796. World Bank, Washington, D.C.

Narayan, Deepa, and Lant Pritchett. 1999. "Cents and Sociability: Household Income and Social Capital in Rural Tanzania." *Economic Development and Cultural Change* 47(4): 871–989.

NIACONSULT. 1994. *Farmers' Participation in National Irrigation Systems in the Philippines: Lessons Learned.* Washington, D.C.: World Bank.

Olson, Mancur. 1996. "Distinguished Lecture on Economics in Government: Big Bills Left on the Sidewalk: Why Some Nations are Rich, and Others Poor." *Journal of Economic Perspectives* 10(2): 1–24.

Ostrom, Elinor. 1990. *Governing the Commons: the Evolution of Institutions for Collective Action.* Cambridge (UK): Cambridge University Press.

Ostrom, Elinor, and R. Gardner. 1993. "Coping with Asymmetries in the Commons: Self-Governing Irrigation Systems Can Work." *Journal of Economic Perspectives* 7(4): 93–112.

Ostrom, Elinor, W. F. Lam, and M. Lee. 1994. "The Performance of Self-Governing Irrigation Systems in Nepal." *Human Systems Management* 13(3): 197–207.

Pathan, R. S., N. J. Arul, and M. Poffenberger. 1993. "Forest Protection Committees in Gujarat: Joint Management Initiatives." Reference Paper 8, prepared for Sustainable Forest Management Conference. Ford Foundation, New Delhi.

Platteau, Jean-Philippe. "Behind the Market Stage Where Real Societies Exist (Part I and II)." Processed.

Putnam, Robert D. 1995. "Bowling Alone: America's Declining Social Capital." *Journal of Democracy* 6(1): 65–87.

Putnam, Robert D., Robert Leonardi, and Raffaella Nanetti. 1993. *Making Democracy Work: Civic Traditions in Modern Italy*. Princeton, New Jersey: Princeton University Press.

Rogers, Everett. 1983. *Diffusion of Innovations*. New York: The Free Press.

Subramanian, Ashok, N. Vijay Jagannathan, and Ruth Meinzen-Dick. 1997. "User Organizations for Sustainable Water Services." World Bank Technical Paper No. 354. World Bank, Washington, D.C.

Tendler, Judith. 1997. *Good Government in the Tropics*. Baltimore: Johns Hopkins University Press.

Wade, Robert. 1988. *Village Republics*. Cambridge (UK): Cambridge University Press.

World Bank. 1993. *Tanzania Social Sector Review*. Washington, D.C.: World Bank.

World Bank. 1995. *World Development Report 1995: Workers in an Integrating World*. New York: Oxford University Press.

World Bank. 1996. "Tanzania—The Challenge of Reforms: Growth, Incomes and Welfare." Vol. 1, Main Report. Country Operations Division, Eastern Africa Department, Africa Region. World Bank, Washington, D.C.

# Social capital, the state, and development outcomes

Ajay Chhibber[1]
*World Bank*

*Social capital constitutes the informal rules and norms that along with the formal rules establish the institutional framework determining economic outcomes. The state plays a key role in establishing the formal rules; and through its own behavior it also affects the informal rules that constitute social capital. This paper tries to quantify through qualitative surveys how important the institutional environment is for economic outcomes—and the impact of informal rules on the institutional environment.*

Fifty years ago, World War II had ended, many developing countries had just emerged from colonialism, and the future seemed full of promise. The difficulties of economic development were not yet haunting us. Economic development and with it an improvement in people's lives seemed easily attainable through ideas, technical expertise, and resources. In some cases it did work out well. But in others it did not. And despite five decades of remarkable human progress we still see enormous disparity in the quality of life of people around the world; some even argue that the disparities have increased.

While the question over differences in living standards across countries has remained the same, the answers to it have changed over the years. For a long time the availability of resources—land, minerals— was considered an essential prerequisite for development. Large portions of Africa, Asia, and Latin America were colonized to acquire these resources, and countries went to war to fight over them. Gradually, think-

---
[1] I am especially grateful to Gregory Kisunko for much of the empirical work in this paper. The paper draws on the work of my colleagues, Commander, Davoodi, and Lee (1996) and that of Brunetti, Kisunko, and Weder (1996) and other background work prepared for the forthcoming *World Development Report*. I am also grateful to Brian Levy for comments on the paper.

ing shifted and physical capital—machines, equipment—came to be identified as the key prerequisite for development, and "industrialized" became synonymous with "developed." But about the middle of this century it was recognized that these explanations were too simplistic. Embodied in machines and equipment was physical capital as well as technology—knowledge and ideas. And there was no straightforward explanation of why technology developed better and faster in some parts of the world. As a result a large gap remained in our understanding of development (Solow 1994).

Since then other factors—such as human capital—have commanded a lot of attention in explaining both differences in income and in the ability of poorer countries to catch up with the richer ones. Human capital leads to new knowledge and ideas, and it increases the speed with which these are absorbed, disseminated, and used in a country (Becker, Murphy, and Tamura 1990).

Since the 1980s attention began to focus on policies that hinder the accumulation of human and physical capital. The focus was on why countries accumulated human and physical capital at different rates. More recently, the emphasis has shifted further toward the quality of a country's institutions (North 1990, 1993). These shifts in thinking reflect a search for deeper sources of differences in development outcomes. New and more complex questions have emerged. What institutional arrangements best allow markets to flourish? What is the role of the state both as a direct agent (mostly in the provision of services) and as a shaper of the institutional context in which markets function? How do policies and institutions interact in the development process?

Institutions affect human behavior. Organizations (firms, nongovernmental organizations, companies, central banks) produce goods and services that are used by society. The rules that determine a society's institutions can be formal or informal. Even when formal rules are similar, informal rules or *social capital* can in some situations explain a significant part of the reason why some societies progress faster than others. Putnam, Leonardi, and Nanetti (1993) explain significant differences between the standard of living in various segments of Italian society through differences in informal rules or social capital across these communities.

The state produces goods and services in singular or joint production but at the same time it produces the formal rules that constitute the institutional environment (figure 1). These formal rules, along with the informal ones—or social capital—make up the institutional environment. The state is therefore a unique organization because it must establish the formal rules (institutions) through a social and political process. It must also play by these rules as an organization (Stiglitz 1989).

In what way can state action influence performance? First, it establishes the formal rules by which economic agents—households, firms,

FIGURE 1: STATE, INSTITUTIONS, AND ECONOMIC OUTCOMES

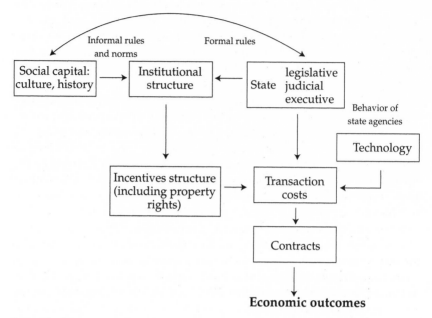

*Source:* Author.

and labor—must play the game. But the state and its agencies must also abide and play by these rules. The state cannot be above the law.

History also teaches us that the state can do enormous harm.

This can be done by, first, establishing inadequate rules for the creation of wealth. The former Soviet Union and India pre-1990 provide examples of these types of states.

Second, the state can do damage not by the impact it has on the institutional environment, but by the manner in which its organizations apply them. It can apply a heavy tax on private wealth through misaligned prices such as overvalued exchange rates, or through agricultural marketing boards that tax agriculture. It can also impart huge transactions costs on the process of setting up a new business or restructuring an old business—and it may require the payment of bribes.

Third, the state can impose an even heavier cost on society through the uncertainty its actions can create. If it often changes the rules or does not clarify the rules by which the state itself will behave, then uncertainty rises and business and common citizens must adopt costly strategies to try to protect themselves against such behavior; going underground, hiding wealth, and capital flight are some of the stratagems used.

Fourth, the state can destroy social capital through inappropriate formal rules—the informal rules that bind society together (Coleman 1990).

Colonial formal systems superimposed inappropriately destroyed many informal rules of functioning across colonized societies. Many aid-sponsored technical assistance projects intended to reform legal and civil services and other formal rules have also inadvertently had the same effect. But Putnam (1993) and Evans (1997) argue for the more positive "synergy" between the formal rules of the state and the informal rules that constitute social capital (figure 1).

In this paper we report on the impact of this "synergy"—or its lack thereof—on the overall quality of the institutional structure and its impact on private sector investment, growth, and economic outcomes. We report three results that have been developed for the *World Development Report 1997* to try and make a strong empirical case for refocusing on the quality of a country's institutions and the capability of the state to bring institutions into the mainstream of our thinking on development outcomes.

The first result uses a panel data set for 30 years for 94 countries—developed and developing—prepared for the *World Development Report 1997* to show that policies, quality of institutions, and government size all matter for economic growth and other quality-of-life indicators, such as infant mortality (see Commander, Davoodi, and Lee 1996). The variable used in this particular set is based on ICRG (International Country Risk Guide) and BERI (Bureaucratic Efficiency Ratings Index) and is similar to that used by Knack and Keefer (1995). These results are reported in the next section of the paper.

The measurement of the quality of institutions is taken a step further in the subsequent section. Here we report on a survey of over 3,700 local firms done for the *World Development Report 1997* in 69 countries. We show that the quality-of-institutions variable that emerges from this survey affects both growth and investment (see Brunetti, Kisunko, and Weder 1996).

This is followed by a section in which we turn to how the quality of institutions affects not just the business environment, but also the overall environment for effective development. We take the results from the survey on the quality of institutions and show that they explain the rate of return to development projects financed by the World Bank.

In the last section of the paper we offer some brief concluding comments, and discuss a framework for improving the effectiveness of the state, and its impact on the institutional environment.

### Economic growth and quality of institutions[2]

The state plays a highly central role in fostering economic growth:

■ By providing a macroeconomic and microeconomic incentive environment that is conducive to efficient economic activity;

---

[2] This section is based on the results reported in Commander, Davoodi, and Lee (1996).

- By providing the institutional infrastructure that provides property rights, peace, law and order, and rules that encourage efficient long-term investment; and

- By providing basic education, health care, and infrastructure required for economic activity.

But it must constantly try to provide these collective goods at the lowest cost to society. If not, it taxes society too heavily. These tradeoffs between the desire to get the state to provide these collective goods and the costs of providing them must be constantly weighed. We turn to this tradeoff between what the state does and how well it does it in this section by reporting on the impact of policies, size (government consumption), and the quality of its institutions (using BERI and ICRG data).

Taking all these factors into account, figure 2 shows their impact on income growth over the last three decades across 94 developed and developing countries. In countries with weak institutions and poor policies, per capita income grew only at about 0.4 percent per year (figure 2). In contrast, in countries with strong institutions and good policies, per capita income grew at an average of 3 percent per year. Over a 30-year period, these differences in income growth would make a huge difference to the quality of people's lives. A country with an average per capita income of $300 in 1965, with distorted policies and weak institutional capability would over 30 years only reach an income level of about $338 at 1965 prices. By contrast, a country with strong institutional capability and good policies would more than double its average income to $728 at 1965 prices. In fact many countries in East Asia have done even better than that.

Good policies by themselves also produce beneficial outcomes but these benefits are magnified in a country where the institutional quality is also much higher, where the policies and programs are implemented better, and where there is greater certainty in the minds of citizens and investors on government's actions. Good policies alone, such as those now being pursued by many countries in Latin America and Africa, would increase growth of per capita income by around 1.4 percent per year and would mean that a country starting with an average per capita income of $300 in 1965 would see it rise to about $450 after 30 years. But if institutions are strong, the impact of good policies would be stronger. Message: reforms should focus both on improvements in policies and on institutional strengthening.

## Institutional quality: the local investors' view[3]

The surest way to get an idea about the private sector's perception of the institutional environment is to ask private entrepreneurs directly.

---

[3]    This section relies on Brunetti, Kisunko, and Weder (1996).

FIGURE 2: INSTITUTIONAL QUALITY IMPROVES ECONOMIC GROWTH
(INSTITUTIONAL QUALITY, POLICY DISTORTION, AND GROWTH IN 94 COUNTRIES, 1964–93)

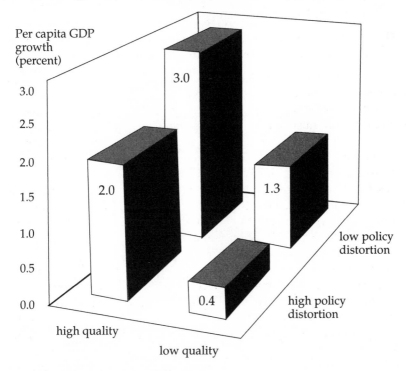

*Note:* Controlling for income, and education.
*Source:* Commander, Davoodi, and Lee (1996).

So, in preparation for the *World Development Report 1997* from which these results are drawn, a large-scale private sector survey collected responses from over 3,700 firms in 69 countries. The survey sought to capture the institutional environment made up of formal rules and informal arrangements that entrepreneurs can face.

Sometimes the source of uncertainty is in the stability of the formal rules to which firms are subject. Two key indicators are:

■ *Predictability of rule-making,* or the extent to which entrepreneurs have to cope with unexpected changes in rules and policies: whether they expect their government to stick to announced major policies, whether they are usually informed about important changes in rules, and whether they can voice concerns when planned changes affect their business.

■ *Perception of political stability:* Whether changes in government (constitutional and unconstitutional) are usually accompanied by far-reaching policy surprises that could have serious effects on the private sector.

At other times, uncertainty relates to the extent to which entrepreneurs can rely on these rules being enforced and, more broadly, on their property rights being protected. The enforcement of these rules is heavily dependent on their compatibility with the informal rules and the strength of social capital more broadly defined. Relevant indicators here include:

- *Crime against persons and property*: Whether entrepreneurs feel confident that the authorities would protect them and their property from criminal actions, and whether theft and crime represent serious problems for business operations.

- *Reliability of judicial enforcement*: Whether the judiciary enforces rules arbitrarily, and whether such unpredictability presents a problem for doing business.

- *Freedom from corruption*: Whether it is common for private entrepreneurs to have to pay some irregular additional payments to get things done.

Firms ranked each indicator on a scale ranging from one (extreme problem) to six (no problem), and the answers were averaged to give an overall indicator of how reliable private entrepreneurs perceived in each region the institutional framework to be (figure 3). The answers were also averaged for each of the individual components of the institutional quality (IQ) indicator by regions (figure 4). Bearing in mind the usual caveats about regional averages, consider these regional patterns:

- As a region, the Commonwealth of Independent States (CIS, the countries of the former Soviet Union excluding the Baltics) has the worst overall IQ rating. Entrepreneurs particularly fear crime and theft, but they also have little faith in the judiciary or in the predictability of the rule-making process, and they complain about corruption and disruptive political instability.

- On most indicators average ratings are similar for Central and Eastern Europe (including the Baltics and Turkey) and Africa. Entrepreneurs in both regions are troubled by basic problems of probity—corruption, unpredictability of the judiciary, and crime and theft—though not to the same extent as their counterparts in the CIS. They are similarly concerned about the unpredictability of rule-making. African entrepreneurs, however, are much more concerned about political instability, and many entrepreneurs appear to lack even the most basic guarantees of property security and personal safety.

■ Latin America's entrepreneurs found problems of probity—crime and theft, judicial unpredictability, and corruption—to be somewhat greater than did entrepreneurs in Africa and Central and Eastern Europe.

■ In South Asia corruption is a serious problem for the conduct of business, as well as security of property. In the Middle East and North Africa a weak judicial system and political instability are considered serious problems.

FIGURE 3: INSTITUTIONAL QUALITY (IQ) IS HIGHEST IN THE OECD AND LOWEST IN THE CIS

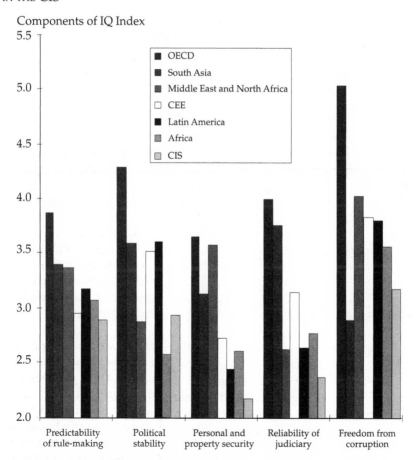

Components of IQ Index

*Source:* Brunetti, Kisunko, and Weder (1997).

FIGURE 4: THE SUBCOMPONENTS VARY ACROSS REGIONS

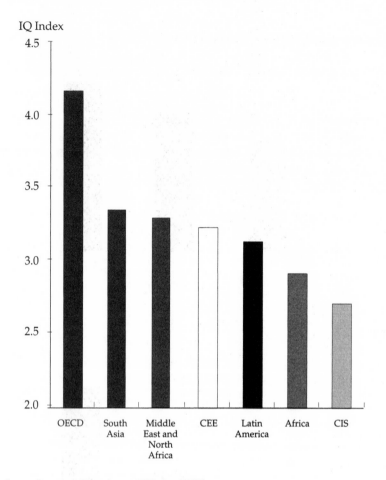

*Source:* Brunetti, Kisunko, and Weder (1997).

More revealing than these regional variations in IQ indicators are the relations between countries' IQ ratings and their growth and investment performance. Even controlling for other variables, there is a strong positive association between IQ and investment (figure 5), a finding that is consistent with expectations. Investments usually require some upfront commitment of resources that can be lost if the business environment turns unfavorable. These sunk costs make entrepreneurs wary of investing in environments with high uncertainty—they prefer to adopt a wait-and-see strategy. Higher IQ affects economic growth as well (figure 5) both through its impact on investment and on the return to that investment.

FIGURE 5: INSTITUTIONAL QUALITY (IQ) AND ECONOMIC PERFORMANCE GO HAND IN HAND

Gross investment, 1984–93 (percent of GDP)

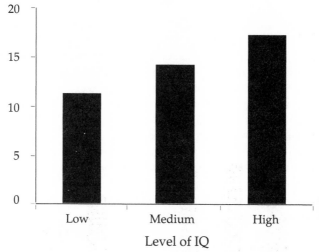

Level of IQ

GDP growth, 1984–93 (percent)

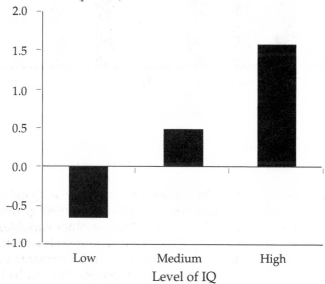

Level of IQ

*Note:* Controlling for income, policies, and education.
*Source:* Brunetti, Kisunko, and Weder (1997).

### Institutional quality and project rates of return

We turn here to how the quality of institutions affects not only the business environment but also the environment for implementation of development projects more generally. The same factors—crime, theft, corruption, and uncertainty—from the policy regime and judiciary affect the outcome for all development projects. One reason why this happens is that these factors are part and parcel of any contractual environment and human behavior. If corruption affects the private sector it is likely to be equally prevalent in determining the outcome of development projects.

A second reason is that many public projects are implemented by private contractors who are subject to the same behavioral problems implicit in an environment of weak institutions. The contractor gets a project, pays off corrupt officials, and gets more projects even if they are not effectively implemented. Pilferage, theft, and the problems of enforcement are even more prevalent in many public projects than in the private sector. Many projects are delayed because of cost overruns brought on by poor coordination.

Figure 6 shows the impact of the institutional quality variable (IQ) on project rates of return taken from 293 projects in 28 countries. A shift from a weak IQ environment to a strong IQ environment makes on average a difference of around 8 percentage points in the economic rate of return of World Bank–funded projects.

These results control for economic policies and other project and country variables and show how strongly institutions matter in determining project outcomes.

### Refocusing on state capability and institutional quality

This brief review of international evidence on the relationship between the institutional quality and income, growth, and several indicators of well-being has emphasized the importance of refocusing attention on the ingredients of institutional quality, both the formal rules and their synergy with informal norms and rules—in other words, the social capital. As the survey of entrepreneurs shows, the predictability and consistency of the institutional environment also matter a great deal in delivering economic outcomes. In many developing countries, weak and arbitrary governments can intensify the climate of uncertainty that comes from weak and underdeveloped markets. In many parts of the world an institutional vacuum now threatens economic and social development.

The key to predictable and consistent implementation is a good fit between the state's institutional capabilities and its actions. In well-developed states, administrative capabilities are normally strong, and institutionalized checks and balances restrain arbitrary action, even as they provide government organizations with the flexibility to pursue

FIGURE 6: ECONOMIC RATES OF RETURN AND QUALITY OF INSTITUTIONS

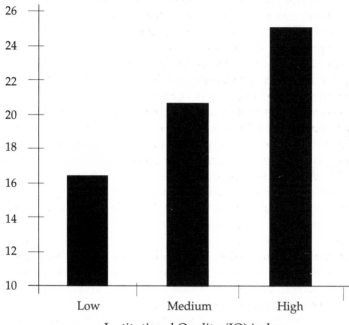

Rate of return on projects
(percent, calculated at evaluation)

Institutional Quality (IQ) index

*Source:* Author.

their public mandates. By contrast, states with weaker institutions need to give special attention to signaling credibility to firms and citizens that they will refrain from arbitrary actions.

Three central incentive mechanisms can be used in different settings and with different emphasis to improve the state's capability and its ability to provide a better institutional framework.

■ *Rules and professionalism.* Simple merit-based systems that reward rule-based behavior, that use merit to improve bureaucracy. A state that plays by the rules and the rule of law will have more credibility when it tries to get others do the same.

■ *Competitive pressure.* This can come from a variety of sources: from outside the state, such as through the scrutiny of economic policies provided by financial markets, or from the inside, through contracts. These pressures lead to more effective and responsive government.

■  *Listening and partnership.* Governments must listen to be an effective partner—to business councils, consumer groups, and any
number of other groupings. Institutional working arrangements
with community groups drawing on social capital may also be
needed. Listening and partnership help achieve more open and
accountable government.

The state's actions are therefore central to the quality of a country's
institutions. Citizens, households and firms try to improve their outcomes by investing in economic activity within a given set of institutions. But they also try to change institutions through a political process
to alter the behavior of the state. Voting out government, social protest,
capital flight, and migration are responses to dissatisfaction with the
state. This dissatisfaction, with the state and the institutional environment, can result in political and social instability, destroy social capital,
and affect the maintenance of an environment that is suitable for the
creation of wealth.

## Bibliography

The word *processed* describes informally reproduced works that may not
be commonly available through libraries.

Alston, Lee. 1996. "Empirical Work in Institutional Economics: an Overview." In Lee J. Alston, Thráinn Eggertsson, and Douglass C. North,
eds., *Empirical Studies in Institutional Change.* Cambridge (UK) and
New York: Cambridge University Press.

Alston, Lee, Thráinn Eggertsson, and Douglass C. North, eds. 1996.
*Empirical Studies in Institutional Change.* Cambridge (UK) and New
York: Cambridge University Press.

Becker, Gary S., Kevin M. Murphy, and Robert Tamura. 1990. "Human
Capital, Fertility, and Economic Growth." *Journal of Political Economy,*
Part 2, 98(5): 12–37.

Brunetti, Aymo, Gregory Kisunko, and Beatrice Weder. 1997. "Economic
Growth with 'Incredible' Rules: Evidence from a Worldwide Private Sector Survey." Background paper for *World Development Report 1997.* Processed.

Coleman, James S. 1990. *Foundations of Social Theory.* Cambridge, Mass.:
Harvard University Press.

Commander, Simon, Hamid Davoodi, and Une J. Lee. 1996. "The Causes and Consequences of Government for Growth and Well-Being." Background paper for *World Development Report 1997*. Processed.

Evans, Peter. 1997. "Government Action, Social Capital and Development: Creating Synergy across the Public-Private Divide." Processed. World Bank, Washington, D.C.

Knack, Stephen, and Philip Keefer. 1995. "Institutions and Economic Performance: Cross-Country Tests Using Alternative Institutional Measures." *Economics and Politics* 7(3): 207–27.

North, Douglass C. 1990. *Institutions, Institutional Change and Economic Performance*. Cambridge (UK) and New York: Cambridge University Press.

———. 1993. Paper prepared for the Nobel Prize Lecture in Economic Science, Stockholm.

Olson, Mancur, Jr. 1996. "Distinguished Lecture on Economics in Government. Big Bills Left on the Sidewalk: Why Some Nations are Rich, and Others Poor." *Journal of Economic Perspectives* 10(2): 3–24.

Putnam, Robert D. 1993. "The Prosperous Community." *American Prospect* 13 (Spring): 35–42.

Putnam, Robert D., R. Leonardi, and R. Nanetti. 1993. Making Democracy Work: Civic Traditions in Modern Italy. Princeton: Princeton University Press.

Romer, Paul M. 1994. "The Origins of Endogenous Growth." *Journal of Economic Perspectives* 8(1): 3–22.

Shleifer, Andre. 1996. "Government in Transition." Discussion Paper No. 1783, Harvard Institution of Economic Research, Cambridge, Mass.

Solow, Robert. 1956. "A Contribution to the Theory of Economic Growth." *Quarterly Journal of Economics* 70 (February): 65–94.

———. 1994. "Perspectives on Growth Theory." *Journal of Economic Perspectives* 8(1): 45–54.

Stiglitz, Joseph. 1989. "On the Economic Role of the State." In Joseph E. Stiglitz and Arnold Heertje, eds., *The Economic Role of the State*. Oxford: Basil Blackwell.

# Trust in large organizations

Rafael La Porta, Florencio Lopez-de-Silanes, Andrei Shleifer, and Robert W. Vishny*

Several recent studies, including those in Diego Gambetta (1988), as well as studies by James Coleman (1990), Robert Putnam (1993), and Francis Fukuyama (1995), argue that trust or social capital determines the performance of a society's institutions. These studies view trust or social capital as a propensity of people in a society to cooperate to produce socially efficient outcomes and to avoid inefficient noncooperative traps such as that in the prisoner's dilemma. Putnam (1993), for example, examines social capital as a determinant of the performance of local governments across Italian regions. He demonstrates that the Italian regions in which the public actively participates in civic activities (viewed as manifestations of a high tendency to cooperate) are also the regions in which local governments exhibit higher objective measures of performance, such as the delivery of public goods. Fukuyama (1995) argues further that high trust among citizens accounts for the superior performance of all institutions in a society, including firms.

In this paper, we provide an overview of the existing theory of trust, develop some of its implications, and test them on a cross section of countries. We find a striking confirmation of the theory in the data. We also ask: what are the forces that encourage the formation of trust? According to Putnam (1993), hierarchical religion discourages "horizontal" ties between people and hence the formation of

* La Porta, Lopez-de-Silanes, and Shleifer: Department of Economics, Harvard University, Cambridge, MA; Vishny: Graduate School of Business, University of Chicago, Chicago, IL. We are grateful to Olivier Blanchard, Edward Glaeser, Henry Hansmann, Larry Katz, and Richard Thaler for helpful comments and to Andrew Prihodko and Magdalena Lopez-Morton for research assistance.

trust. Indeed, we find a strong negative association between trust and the dominance of a strong hierarchical religion in a country, most notably Catholicism.

## I. Argument

Economists have developed two views of trust as a tendency to cooperate. One view, rooted in repeated game theory, holds that trust is a prior that an opponent is cooperative rather than fully rational (e.g., plays only tit-for-tat in a repeated prisoner's dilemma). A higher prior in a repeated prisoner's dilemma leads to a greater likelihood and duration of cooperation (David Kreps and others 1982). Another view, rooted in economic experiments, holds that people cooperate even in one-shot encounters, such as the dictator game or the ultimatum game (Colin Camerer and Richard Thaler 1995). These experiments suggest that people expect certain fair or cooperative behavior of their opponents even when they do not expect to see them again. Both of these views suggest that higher trust between people in a population should be associated with greater cooperation.

These views of trust share an important implication, namely, that trust should be more essential for ensuring cooperation between strangers, or people who encounter each other infrequently, than for supporting cooperation among people who interact frequently and repeatedly. In the latter situations, such as families or partnerships, reputations and ample opportunities for future punishment would support cooperation even with low levels of trust. This implies that trust is most needed to support cooperation in large organizations, where members interact with each other only infrequently because they are only rarely involved in joint production. Take, for example, administrative interactions between members of different departments in a university, or interagency task forces in the government. Here cooperation is less sustainable without trust because interactions are too few to allow reputations to develop.

One such large organization is the government, where bureaucrats must cooperate with a large number of other bureaucrats whom they encounter only infrequently, as well as with private citizens they may never see again, to produce "public goods." Significant trust is then needed to ensure cooperation. Local governments in Italy might perform better in high-trust regions because trust enables individual bureaucrats to cooperate better with each other and with private citizens, making government more effective.

Civic groups or associations, where participation is largely voluntary and success depends on many people cooperating, may also rely on trust for their success. Putnam (1993) actually *measures* social capital by participation in civic groups and associations, even though participation must itself be a consequence of some underlying beliefs about the behavior of other people in the society.

Finally, corporations are also large organizations that would benefit from trust among their employees. Fukuyama (1995) stresses the need for cooperation between strangers for the success of large firms, and the dependence of such cooperation on trust. He contrasts large public firms in high-trust countries to smaller family firms that prevail in low-trust societies.

## II. Evidence

We test the hypotheses developed above on a cross section of countries. We are interested in the effect of trust on the performance of large organizations, measured here by government effectiveness, participation in civic organizations, size of the largest firms relative to GNP, and the performance of a society more generally. Our measure of trust comes from the World Values Survey, which in the early 1980's and again in the early 1990's surveyed 1,000 randomly selected people in each of 40 countries. One of the questions was: "Generally speaking, would you say that most people can be trusted or that you can't be too careful in dealing with people?" The percentage of people answering yes is our measure of trust within a country (see also Stephen Knack and Philip Keefer 1996). The correlation across countries between trust in the 1980's and in the 1990's is 0.91, so we use the later, more complete, data. The highest-trust countries are in Scandinavia, where almost two-thirds of the respondents believe that strangers can be trusted; many of the lowest-trust countries are in Latin America.

Here we briefly summarize our variables; Table 1 provides details. For government effectiveness we use (subjective) estimates from investor surveys of the efficiency of the judicial system, corruption, bureaucratic quality, and tax compliance (a proxy for effectiveness of the tax authorities). For civic participation we use the extent of participation in civic activities and in professional associations. To measure the relative success of large firms, we use total sales of the largest 20 publicly traded firms (by sales) in a country relative to its GNP. Some of our measures of social success proxy for the effectiveness of government only; others reflect the success of other institutions in the society as well. We look at education (high-school graduates relative to the relevant population and educational adequacy as estimated by a business group), health (logarithm of infant mortality rate), infrastructure (an estimate of its quality by one business group and an estimate of its adequacy by another), and two general measures of social success: per capita GDP growth between 1970 and 1993 and (the logarithm of) inflation over the same period. Our goal is to establish the robustness of the results through the use of multiple variables and data sources; we have looked at many other variables as well, with similar results.

Table 2 presents the regressions of our measures of performance of large organizations on trust, controlling for the log of 1994 per capita GNP. In most regressions, we have fewer than 40 observations because we do not have dependent variables for socialist countries. Controlling for per capita GNP reduces the effect of trust, since trust is higher in richer countries. This may cause the effect of trust to be underestimated if trust is an input in the production of wealth. In other (unreported) specifications, we also control for inequality without much effect. We interpret the coefficients using a one-standard-deviation change in trust, about 15 percentage points.

TABLE 1: DESCRIPTION OF THE VARIABLES USED IN TABLES 2 AND 3

| Variable | Definition |
| --- | --- |
| Trust in people | Percentage of respondents who answered that most people can be trusted when asked: "Generally speaking, would you say that most people can be trusted or that you can't be too careful in dealing with people?" Source: *World Values Survey 1990–93 (WVS)*. |
| Efficiency of the judiciary | Assessment or the "efficiency and integrity of the legal environment as it affects business, particularly foreign firms." Average between 1980 and 1983. Scale from 0 to 10, with lower scores indicating lower efficiency levels. Source: *Business International Corporation* (1984). |
| Corruption | Low ratings if "high government officials are likely to demand special payments and illegal payments are generally expected throughout lower levels of government in the form of bribes connected with import and export licenses, exchange controls, tax assessment, policy protection, or loans." Scale from 0 to 10. Average of the months of April and October of the monthly index between 1982 and 1995. Source: *International Country Risk Guide (ICRG)*. |
| Bureaucratic quality | High scores indicate "autonomy from political pressure" and "strength and expertise to govern without drastic changes in policy or interruptions in government services." Scale from 0 to 10, with higher scores for greater efficiency. Average of the months of April and October of the monthly index between 1982 and 1995. Source: ICRG. |
| Tax compliance | Assessment of the level of tax compliance. Scale from 0 to 6, where higher scores indicate higher compliance. Source: *The Global Competitiveness Report 1996 (GCR)*. |

*(continues on next page.)*

TABLE 1.  (*continued*)

| Variable | Definition |
| --- | --- |
| Civic participation | Percentage of civic activities in which an average individual participates. The activities included are: (i) social-welfare services for elderly and deprived, (ii) education, art, and cultural activities, (iii) local community affairs, (iv) conservation, environment, ecology, (v) work with youth, (vi) sports or recreation, and (vii) voluntary associations for health. Source: WVS. |
| Participation in professional associations | Percentage of respondents who answered positively when asked if they belonged to professional associations. Source: WVS. |
| Sales' top 20/GNP | The ratio of sales generated by the top 20 publicly traded firms to GNP for 1994. Firms within a country are ranked by sales. Source: *WorldScope Global 1996* data base. |
| Infrastructure quality | Assessment of the "facilities for and case of communication between headquarters and the operation, and within the country," as well as the quality of the transportation. Average data for the years 1972–1995. Scale from 0 to 10 with higher scores for superior quality. Source: *BERI's Operations Risk Index.* |
| Adequacy of infrastructure | Average or five scores measuring the extent to which a country's infrastructure meets business needs in each of the following areas: (i) roads, (ii) air transport, (iii) ports, (iv) telecommunications, and (v) power supply. Scale from 0 to 6, where higher scores are for a superior infrastructure. Source: GCR. |
| Log infant mortality | Logarithm of the number of deaths of infants under one year of age per one thousand live births for 1993 or the most recent year available. Source: *Health-For-All Global Indicators Database.* |
| Completed high school | Percentage or the 1985 mile population aged 25 and over that has completed high school. Source: Robert Barro and Jong-Wha Lee (1994). |
| Adequacy of educational system | Assessment of the extent to which the educational system meets the needs of a competitive economy. Score from 0 to 6, where higher scores are for a superior educational system. Source: GCR. |
| Log inflation | Logarithm of the geometric average annual growth rate of the implicit price deflator for the time period 1970–1993. Source: *World Development Report 1995* (WDR95). |

| Variable | Definition |
|---|---|
| GDP growth | Average annual growth in per capita GDP for the period 1970–1993. Source: WDR95. |
| Log GNP per capita | Logarithm of the GNP per capita expressed in dollars of 1994 unless otherwise noted. Source: *World Development Report 1996.* |
| Trust in family | Rating based on respondents' answers to how much they trust their families. Scale from 0 to 4. The highest (lowest) rating is awarded when respondents manifest that they trust (distrust) their families. Source: WVS. |
| Hierarchical religion | Percentage of the population of each country that are Roman Catholic, Eastern Orthodox, or Muslim. Sources: *Worldmark Encyclopedia of the Nations 1995, Statistical Abstract of the World 1994.* |
| Ethnolinguistic fractionalization | Probability that two randomly selected persons from a given country will not belong to the same ethnolinguistic group in 1960. Source: *World Handbook of Political and Social Indicators.* |

The effects of trust on performance are both statistically significant and quantitatively large. Holding per capita GNP constant, a standard-deviation increase in trust raises judicial efficiency by 0.7, the anticorruption score by 0.3, bureaucratic quality by 0.3, and tax compliance by 0.3 of a standard deviation. Putnam's (1993) results for Italy appear to be confirmed worldwide. Furthermore, a standard-deviation increase in trust raises participation in civic activities by 0.7 and participation in professional associations by one standard deviation. The effect of trust on large firms' share of the economy is also large: a one-standard-deviation increase in trust raises that share by 7 percentage points, or half of a standard deviation. These results support Fukuyama's (1995) argument that trust facilitates all large-scale activities, not just those of the government.

Indeed, Fukuyama goes further and argues that, for firms in particular, trust replaces another mechanism of cooperation—the family. He believes that family strength is detrimental to the growth of firms. We can actually test this hypothesis since the World Values Survey asks respondents if they trust their families. When we run the relative share of the top 20 firms on both a measure of trust in strangers and a measure of trust in family, the coefficient on trust in people is 0.654 ($t = 4.1$), and the coefficient on trust in family is –0.563 ($t = -3.1$). Consistent with Fukuyama's argument, strong family ties are bad for the development of large firms.

TABLE 2: TRUST IN PEOPLE AND PERFORMANCE

| Dependent variable | Independent variables | | | Adjusted $R^2$ [N] |
|---|---|---|---|---|
| | Log GNP per capita | Trust in people | Intercept | |
| *Government Efficiency* | | | | |
| Efficiency of the judiciary | 0.2959 | 8.2093** | 2.2769 | 0.6343 |
| | (0.2213) | (1.3652) | (1.7766) | [27] |
| Corruption | 0.9214** | 4.8068** | −2.3608** | 0.7316 |
| | (0.1022) | (0.7509) | (0.9050) | [33] |
| Bureaucratic quality | 1.1596** | 3.9797** | −4.0842* | 0.6806 |
| | (0.1927) | (1.3544) | (1.6763) | [33] |
| Tax compliance | 0.3595** | 1.7330** | −0.9124 | 0.3540 |
| | (0.0913) | (0.5840) | (0.7873) | [32] |
| *Participation* | | | | |
| Civic participation | 0.0127** | 0.1224** | −0.0921** | 0.4614 |
| | (0.0038) | (0.0329) | (0.0308) | [33] |
| Participation in | −0.0072 | 0.3056** | 0.0330 | 0.5492 |
| professional associations | (0.0099) | (0.0669) | (0.0730) | [33] |
| *Large Organizations* | | | | |
| Sales' top 20/GNP | 0.0103 | 0.4927** | −0.0374 | 0.2433 |
| | (0.0325) | (0.1657) | (0.2798) | [26] |
| *Social Efficiency* | | | | |
| Infrastructure quality | 1.0269** | 2.3261** | −3.7162** | 0.6783 |
| | (0.1413) | (0.7970) | (1.2331) | [33] |
| Adequacy of infrastructure | 0.5943** | 1.2511** | −1.6559** | 0.7222 |
| | (0.0604) | (0.4200) | (0.5837) | [32] |
| Log infant mortality rate | −0.4598** | −1.0283* | 6.9682** | 0.7141 |
| | (0.0484) | (0.5176) | (0.4495) | [40] |
| Completed high school | 1.2884** | 10.9714** | −7.4405* | 0.3474 |
| | (0.4416) | (3.4633) | (3.5336) | [29] |
| Adequacy of education | 0.2200** | 1.2334* | 0.8525 | 0.2107 |
| system | (0.0858) | (0.6771) | (0.7736) | [32] |
| Log inflation | 0.0371 | −3.4128** | 3.1306** | 0.2059 |
| | (0.0787) | (1.1502) | (0.6494) | [37] |
| GDP growth | −0.2738† | 2.0266† | 3.5847** | 0.0072 |
| | (0.1548) | (1.2152) | (1.3625) | [39] |

*Notes:* Ordinary least-square regressions of the cross section of 40 countries. There are 14 dependent variables classified in four different groups including (i) Government Efficiency, (ii) Participation, (iii) Large Organizations, and (iv) Social Efficiency Coefficients are shown, and Halbert White (1980) corrected standard errors are given in parentheses underneath. The number of observations is given in brackets.
† Statistically significant at the 10-percent level.
* Statistically significant at the 5-percent level.
** Statistically significant at the 1-percent level.

The last panel of Table 2 presents the results for social outcomes. Trust has a relatively small but significant effect on infrastructure quality and adequacy, a significant effect on infant mortality, and a larger effect on the measures of educational achievement. A one-standard-deviation increase in trust raises the percentage of high-school graduates in the population by one-half of a standard deviation, and school adequacy by one-third of a standard deviation. Trust is also associated with lower inflation and weakly associated with a higher per capita GNP growth (about 0.3 percent per annum per standard deviation increase in trust). This result for growth was also obtained by Knack and Keefer (1996). In sum, trust enhances economic performance across countries.

## III. Where does trust come from?

Trust may not be truly exogenous; it may increase with good past performance of a society's institutions. According to Putnam (1993), trust is a habit formed during a centuries-long history of "horizontal networks of association" between people, covering both commercial and civic activities. Putnam argues that the independent city-states of Northern Italy encouraged the formation of such horizontal networks, in contrast to the more authoritarian political regimes of the South. Can we measure something even more basic than trust?

Putnam (1993) argues that the Catholic Church, by imposing a hierarchical structure on the society, often in symbiosis with the state, has discouraged the formation of trust: "Vertical bonds of authority are more characteristic of the Italian Church than horizontal bonds of fellowship" (p. 107). His argument can be applied more generally to any dominant, hierarchical, organized religion in a country and hence can be tested empirically across countries.

Specifically, for every country, we consider the percentage of the population belonging to a hierarchical religion, defined as Catholic, Eastern Orthodox, or Muslim. The mean of this variable in the sample is 55 percent, and its correlation with trust is a remarkable –0.61 (see Figure 1). This correlation (and all of the following results) is driven mostly by the correlation of –0.47 between percentage Catholic and trust, although predominantly Moslem and Eastern Orthodox countries have very low trust as well. In Table 3, we use this hierarchical-religion variable as an independent variable to explain organizational performance. Holding per capita income constant, countries with more dominant hierarchical religions have less efficient judiciaries, greater corruption, lower-quality bureaucracies, higher rates of tax evasion, lower rates of participation in civic activities and professional associations, a lower level of importance of large firms in the economy, inferior infrastructures, and higher inflation. The results for infant mortality, educational achievement, and growth are less clear-cut. Still, the evidence that hierarchical religions are bad for the performance of large organizations is strong. We have also run two-stage specifications, in which hierarchical religion is used as an instrument for trust. The results are similar to those in Table 2 in both magnitude and statistical significance.

This evidence suggests that hierarchical religion and distrust may both reflect some underlying basic "factor" in a society that is detrimental to the performance of large organizations. This factor may reflect dysfunctional institutions in a society, but if so, this is largely a long-term disfunctionality associated in part with a hierarchical religion (and not just with recent events). Interestingly, this factor does not reflect the ethnic heterogeneity in a society, which might be viewed as a source of distrust: the correlation between trust and a standard measure of ethnolinguistic heterogeneity is only –0.12, and the inclusion of that measure in the regressions in Table 2 does not change the importance of trust.

FIGURE 1: TRUST IN PEOPLE PLOTTED AGAINST THE PERCENTAGE OF THE POPULATION BELONGING TO A HIERARCHICAL RELIGION

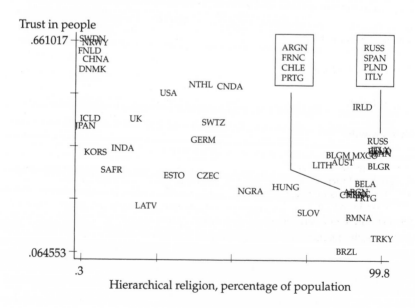

TABLE 3: RELIGION AND PERFORMANCE

| Dependent variable | Independent variables | | | Adjusted $R^2$ [N] |
|---|---|---|---|---|
| | Log GNP per capita | Hierarchical Religion | Intercept | |
| *Government Efficiency* | | | | |
| Efficiency of the judiciary | 0.7420** | −0.0233** | 2.4936 | 0.5245 |
| | (0.2357) | (0.0067) | (2.4613) | [27] |
| Corruption | 1.0740** | −0.0148** | −1.1331 | 0.7025 |
| | (0.1171) | (0.0051) | (1.2028) | [33] |
| Bureaucratic quality | 1.2376** | −0.0214** | −2.1445 | 0.7583 |
| | (0.1493) | (0.0054) | (1.5465) | [33] |
| Tax compliance | 0.3985** | −0.0088** | −0.1415 | 0.4335 |
| | (0.0767) | (0.0029) | (0.6727) | [32] |
| *Participation* | | | | |
| Civic participation | 0.0164** | −0.0003** | −0.0589* | 0.4106 |
| | (0.0035) | (0.0001) | (0.0274) | [33] |
| Participation in | 0.0002 | −0.0010** | 0.1393 | 0.5256 |
| professional associations | (0.0105) | (0.0002) | (0.1104) | [33] |
| *Large Organizations* | | | | |
| Sales' top 20/GNP | 0.0370 | −0.0020** | 0.0077 | 0.3387 |
| | (0.0263) | (0.0006) | (0.2668) | [26] |
| *Social Efficiency* | | | | |
| Infrastructure quality | 1.0725** | −0.0172** | −2.3035* | 0.7835 |
| | (0.0955) | (0.0039) | (0.8967) | [33] |
| Adequacy of infrastructure | 0.6252** | −0.0057* | −1.1572* | 0.7480 |
| | (0.0550) | (0.0021) | (0.5270) | [32] |
| Log infant mortality rate | −0.5044** | 0.0016* | 6.9040** | 0.6919 |
| | (0.0473) | (0.0018) | (0.4794) | [40] |
| Completed high school | 1.7590** | −0.0409** | −5.4915 | 0.3814 |
| | (0.4573) | (0.0142) | (4.3376) | [29] |
| Adequacy of education system | 0.2680** | −0.0016 | 0.9735 | 0.1597 |
| | (0.0820) | (0.0028) | (0.7854) | [32] |
| Log inflation | −0.0915 | 0.0087* | 2.5343** | 0.0991 |
| | (0.0784) | (0.0035) | (0.7381) | [37] |
| GDP growth | −0.1944 | −0.0030 | 3.8230* | −0.0206 |
| | (0.1622) | (0.0069) | (1.6884) | [39] |

Notes: There are 14 dependent variables classified in four different groups including (i) Government Efficiency, (ii) Participation, (iii) Large Organizations, and (iv) Social. We report coefficients for heteroscedasticity-corrected OLS (White 1980). Standard errors are shown in parentheses. The number of observations is given in brackets.
* Statistically significant at the 5 percent level.
** Statistically significant at the 1 percent level.

## IV. Conclusion

Trust promotes cooperation, especially in large organizations. Data on government performance, participation in civic and professional societies, importance of large firms, and overall performance of different societies support this hypothesis. Furthermore, trust is lower in countries with dominant hierarchical religions, which may have deterred the formation of "horizontal networks of cooperation" among people. Despite economists' skepticism (see Robert Solow 1995), theories of trust hold up remarkably well when tested on a cross section of countries.

## References

The word *processed* describes informally reproduced works that may not be commonly available through libraries.

Barro, Robert, and Jong-Wha Lee. 1994. Unpublished data set for a panel of 138 countries, Harvard University.

*BERI's Operations Risk Index.* Business environmental risk intelligence indicators obtained by the Center for Institutional Reform and the Informal Sector (IRIS), University of Maryland, various years.

Business International Corporation. 1984. *Introduction to the Country Assessment Service.* New York: Business International Corporation.

Camerer, Colin, and Richard H. Thaler. 1995. "Anomalies: Ultimatums, Dictators, and Manners." *Journal of Economic Perspectives* 9(2): 209–20.

Coleman, James. *Foundations of Social Theory.* 1990. Cambridge, Mass.: Harvard University.

Fukuyama, Francis. 1995. *Trust.* New York: Free Press.

Gambetta, Diego, ed. 1988. *Trust: Making and Breaking Cooperative Relations.* Cambridge (UK): Blackwell.

*Global Competitiveness Report 1996.* 1996. Geneva, Switzerland: World Economic Forum.

*Health-For-All Global Indicators Database.* 1996. Geneva, Switzerland: World Health Organization.

*International Country Risk Guide.* East Syracuse, New York: Political Risk Services, Institutional Reform and Informational Sector, various years.

Knack, Stephen, and Philip Keefer. 1996. "Does Social Capital Have an Economic Payoff? A Cross-Country Investigation." Processed, University of Maryland.

Kreps, David, Paul Milgrom, John Roberts, and Robert Wilson. 1982. "Rational Cooperation in the Finitely Repeated Prisoner's Dilemma." *Journal of Economic Theory* 27(2): 245–52.

Putnam, Robert. 1993. *Making Democracy Work: Civic Traditions in Modern Italy.* Princeton, New Jersey: Princeton University Press.

Solow, Robert. 1995. "But Verify" (Review of Fukuyama). *New Republic,* 11 September 1995, p. 36.

*Statistical Abstract of the World 1994.* 1994. New York: Gale Research.

White, Halbert. 1980. "A Heteroskedasticity-Consistent Covariance Matrix Estimator and a Direct Test for Heteroskedasticity." *Econometrica* 48(4): 817–38.

*World Development Report 1995.* 1995. New York: Oxford University Press.

*World Development Report 1996.* 1996. New York: Oxford University Press.

*World Handbook of Political and Social Indicators III, 1948–1982 (ICPSR 7761).* 1983. Ann Arbor, Mich.: Inter-University Consortium for Political and Social Research.

*World Values Survey, 1981–1984 and 1990-1993 (ICPSR 6160).* 1994. Ann Arbor, Mich.: Inter-University Consortium for Political and Social Research.

*Worldmark Encyclopedia of the Nations 1995,* 8th ed. 1996. Detroit, Mich.: Gale Research, 1996.

*WorldScope Global 1996.* 1996. Bridgeport, Conn.: WorldScope Disclosure Partners.

# Overview

# Economic progress and the idea of social capital

Partha Dasgupta
*University of Cambridge*

*This essay came about at Ismail Serageldin's behest. He felt that it would be a worthwhile exercise if I were to try to connect the ideas developed in Dasgupta (1993) with those in Putnam with Leonardi and Nanetti; hereafter referred to as Putnam (1993), to see whether the concept of social capital has potency for an understanding of the kinds of institution that are most likely to protect and promote human well-being in poor countries. This essay is about that. If the understanding I reached in my earlier work and also reach here is somewhat different from Putnam's, it may well be because I have been studying certain aspects of rural life in Sub-Saharan Africa and the Indian subcontinent, while Putnam has been investigating the functioning of civil society in contemporary Italy (more recently, the United States; Putnam 1995). The point is not so much that the context matters; rather, it is that widening the set of contexts exposes the complexity of the idea of social capital and its efficacy.*[1]

*A recurrent item on the agenda of social and political scientists has been to seek the most tolerable location for the boundary that separates the private and the public spheres of life, and to identify those agency roles, rights, expectations, and responsibilities that would define each sphere. It is not uncommon to view cultural differences in terms of the way different societies have "solved" this most critical of problems. But not all solutions have been effective in protecting and promoting human well-being. While an accumulation of social capital is necessary if the private and public spheres, no matter how they are conceived, are to flourish, it can also get in their way. The character of social capital matters greatly. In this essay I explore these complexities.*

*Mary Douglas, Ira Katznelson, Dale Jorgenson, Paul Seabright, Ismail Serageldin, Giancarlo Spagnolo, and Gavin Wright commented on an earlier*

---

[1] Having heard Professor Putnam's exceptional Marshall Lectures at the University of Cambridge in May 1999, I believe his views are closer to mine now than they were as expressed in his earlier writings. I will nevertheless take his published writings to be my point of departure in this essay.

*draft of the paper. Over the years I have benefited greatly from discussions with them, and with Luca Anderlini, Kenneth Arrow, Kaushik Basu, Carol Dasgupta, Paul David, Stefan Dercon, Stanley Engerman, Diego Gambetta, David Good, Jack Goody, Avner Greif, Robert Hinde, Sarwat Hussain, David Landes, Simon Levin, Karl-Göran Mäler, Eric Maskin, Elinor Ostrom, Thomas Pantham, Alaknanda Patel, Kate Plaisted, Robert Putnam, Robert Solow, Joseph Stiglitz, and Simon Szreter. To them all I am most grateful.*

*A number of the ideas presented here were developed in my Kenneth Arrow Lectures, Stanford University (April 1997); the Tagore Lectures, M.S. University, Baroda (December 1997); the Yrjö Reenpää Lecture, Finnish Cultural Foundation, Helsinki (September 1998); and the Gaston Eyskens Lectures, the Catholic University in Leuven (December 1998). Research support from the World Bank's Vice Presidency for Environmentally Sustainable Development and from the Beijer International Institute of Ecological Economics, Stockholm, is gratefully acknowledged.*

## Introduction

The idea of social capital sits awkwardly in contemporary economic thinking. Even though it has a powerful, intuitive appeal, it has proven hard to track as an economic good. Among other things, it is fiendishly difficult to measure. This is not because of a recognized paucity of data, but because we do not quite know what we should be measuring. The components of social capital are many, varied and, in many instances, intangible—as they consist of different types of relationships and engagements.

One can argue that it is misleading to use the term "capital" to refer to whatever that thing is we are trying to identify, because capital is usually identified with tangible, durable, and alienable objects, such as buildings and machines, whose accumulation can be estimated and whose worth can be assessed.[2] There is much to agree with in this observation. From another perspective, however, in regard to both heterogeneity and intangibility, social capital would seem to resemble knowledge and skills. Thus, one can also argue that since economists have not shied away from regarding knowledge and skills as forms of capital, we should not shy away in this case either. This said, there is a temptation to use "social capital" as a peg on which to hang all those "informal" engagements we like, care for, and approve of. For example, it is not uncommon today to hear the view that if a society harbors widespread opportunistic behavior, such as free-riding, rent-seeking, and bribery

---

[2] See Solow (1995, 1999) and Arrow (1999).

and corruption, it is because citizens have not invested sufficiently in the accumulation of social capital. But if the concept is to serve any purpose, this particular temptation should be resisted. Even though the term is probably here to stay because of its heuristic appeal, one conclusion I draw from the analysis that follows is that we should avoid regarding social capital on a par with physical, human, knowledge, and environmental capital. I will also argue that rather than interpreting cooperative engagements in terms of the social capital they are thought to embody, we would be better employed continuing to study *institutions* (economists call them "resource allocation mechanisms"), understand their character, and identify measures that could improve them and their mix. Aggregate concepts can help us focus on matters of importance, but they can also prove to be a distraction.

Thus, in the field of economic development there is now a large and valuable literature on what are called "informal institutions." As part of this body of work's aim has been to identify these institutions' rationale, a good deal of the literature in fact concentrates on their virtues. But in focusing on the benefits such institutions offer, one can be distracted from asking whether their continued existence could prevent more productive social arrangements (for example, in the shape of formal markets) from becoming established. One can even ask whether they were ever as good as they are frequently made out to have been. The temptation to regard observed practices as socially optimal is no doubt strong, especially when their rationale has been detected; but it should be resisted.[3]

Social capital has been identified with those "features of social organization, such as trust, norms, and networks that can improve the efficiency of society by facilitating coordinated actions" (Putnam 1993, p. 167). As a characterization this appears beguiling, but it suffers from a weakness: it encourages us to amalgamate incommensurable objects, namely (and in that order), beliefs, behavioral rules and such forms of capital assets as interpersonal networks—without offering a hint as to how they are to be amalgamated. One of my intentions here is to show that they cannot be amalgamated. Since this would imply that we must study them separately if we are to understand what they are about and how they are connected, the bulk of this essay is an attempt to do just that.

Some authors have focused on trust.[4] Others have studied those components of social organization (for example, horizontal networks, such

---

[3] Platteau (1994a, 1994b, 1996) provide thoughtful readings that reflect both genres. See Ogilvie (1995) for a chilling portrait of life constrained by communitarian rules in the Black Forests of Wurttemberg in the early Modern period, and persisting until the nineteenth century.
[4] Arrow (1972, 1974), Luhmann (1979), Dasgupta (1988), Gambetta (1988), Good (1988), Fukuyama (1995), Knack and Keefer (1997), La Porta and others (1997), Seabright (1997), and Hollis (1998), among others.

as rotating savings and credit associations, commercial guilds, credit cooperatives, civic associations, and the better types of marriages) that make social capital a productive asset.[5] Still others have considered a broader sense of the notion, by including extended kinship, lobbying organizations, and such hierarchical relationships as those associated with patronage (for example the Hindu *jajmani* system and the Sicilian Mafia) and street gangs, so that dense networks do not inevitably result in overall economic betterment, at least not in the long run.[6] Case studies of the management systems of local common-property resources in poor countries have offered further insights into the character of resource allocation mechanisms (in particular, self-management systems) that enable mutually beneficial courses of action to be undertaken by interested parties.[7] In all these accounts the engagements that rely on social capital occur somewhere between the individual and the State: they are conducted within "informal institutions." When applied to horizontal networks, social capital is therefore identified with the workings of civil society.[8]

Of central importance in all this is the notion of *trust*. But how should trust be defined? Is trust a public good, as is frequently claimed? Moreover, if created, how is trust maintained? What are we to make of the suggestion that trust is a "moral good," in that, unlike economic commodities, it grows with use and decays with disuse (Hirschman 1984)? Furthermore, is trust at the interpersonal level a substitute for the courts and the rule of law, or is it a complement? More generally, what are the links between macrolevel institutions, such as the legislative, judicial and executive branches of government, and microlevel institutions such as personal networks, which would appear to embody social capital?

---

[5]    See, for example, Geertz (1962), Netting (1981, 1997), Besley, Coate, and Loury (1993), Greif (1993, 1994, 1997a, 1997b), Putnam (1993, 1995), Seabright (1993, 1997), Banerjee, Besley, and Guinnane (1994), Besley and Coate (1995), Helliwell (1996), Helliwell and Putnam (1995), Narayan and Pritchett (1997), Serageldin (1996), and Serageldin and Grootaert (1997). See the section on "values, emotions, and credibility" below.

[6]    Olson (1982), Coleman (1990), Dasgupta (1993, 1995), Gambetta (1993), Putnam (1993), Glaeser, Sacerdote, and Scheinkman (1996), Fukuyama (1997), Hayami and Platteau (1997), Ogilvie (1997), Eshel, Samuelson, and Shaked (1998), and Rae (1999), among others.

[7]    The literature is both illuminating and extensive. See, for example, McKean (1986, 1992), Cordell and McKean (1986), Howe (1986), McCay and Acheson (1987), Wade (1988), Chopra, Kadekodi, and Murty (1990), Feeny and others (1990), Ostrom (1990, 1992, 1996), Bromley and Feeny (1992), Ostrom and Gardner (1993), Ascher (1995), White and Runge (1995), Baland and Platteau (1996, 1997), Lam (1998), and Seki and Platteau (1998). See the section on "markets and networks" below.

[8]    Zamagni (1999) provides a brief, but fine history of the development of the idea of civil society in post-Renaissance Europe.

Do these institutions reinforce one another, or does each type tend to displace the other?

How do markets relate to social capital? Is there anything in the intuition that the process of modernization and economic development (for example, the growth of markets) comes in tandem with a shrinkage of social capital as a "factor" of production; and the closely related question, do long-established social networks act as a deterrent to the modernization process? What does one mean by the terms "culture of trust" and "culture of distrust"? Moreover, is culture related to social capital—and if so, in what way?

Is social capital a public good, such as shared knowledge, or is it more like a private good, such as human skills? Or to put the matter technically, should an economy's social capital be regarded as a shift factor in its aggregate production function, or should we view it as a private input in production, much like the human capital that appears routinely in macroeconomic growth models (as in, for example, Barro and Sala-i-Martin 1995; Romer 1996)? Or is social capital merely another name for good institutions? Then again, is social capital a pure capital good, or is it, like many kinds of knowledge, simultaneously something that offers direct enjoyment? Should we try to construct an index of aggregate social capital, and if the answer is "yes," how should we go about it? Moreover, it has been argued by Putnam (1993) that, in situations with political openness, networks of civic associations help keep government accountable, thereby making government agents perform better than they otherwise would. If he is right, an indirect way to infer the productivity of such forms of social capital would be to inquire whether economies in which citizens enjoy greater civil liberties tend also to perform better in terms of economic indicators, such as national income per head, life expectancy at birth, and domestic rates of return on foreign aid. And finally, the biggest of all questions: what do we know about the character of those institutions in which citizens have the best chance of pursuing lives that are well-lived?

### Trust[9]

Trust is central to all these questions. That it is a key ingredient in transactions is not controversial.[10] And yet, until recently economists rarely

---

[9]  This section is taken from Dasgupta (1988).

[10]  Consider Arrow (1972, p. 357), who writes: "Virtually every commercial transaction has within itself an element of trust, certainly any transaction conducted over a period of time. It can be plausibly argued that much of the economic backwardness in the world can be explained by the lack of mutual confidence." Or Coleman (1990, p. 304): "Social capital ... is embodied in the *relations* among persons. ... a group whose members manifest trustworthiness and place extensive trust in one another will be able to accomplish much more than a comparable group lacking that trustworthiness and trust."

discussed the notion. It was treated rather like background environment, present whenever called upon, a sort of ever-ready lubricant permitting voluntary participation in production and exchange to take place. In the standard model of the market economy, for example, it is taken for granted that households meet their budget constraints: they do not spend in excess of their wealth. Moreover, they always deliver the goods and services they said they would. But the model is silent on the reasons agents are honest. We are not told whether they are persons of honor, conditioned by their upbringing always to meet the obligations they have chosen to undertake, or whether there is a background agency (the State) that enforces contracts, credibly threatening to mete out punishment if obligations are not fulfilled—a punishment sufficiently stiff to deter consumers from ever failing to fulfill them. The same assumptions are made about producers.

In a similar vein, until recently models of government in welfare economic theory have assumed that agents of the State (for example, members of the legislature, the civil service, the police, and the judiciary) are trustworthy. For example, in their influential textbooks on public economics, Atkinson and Stiglitz (1980) and Myles (1995) are careful to model the possibility that State agencies (for example, tax authorities) cannot trust citizens to disclose private information of relevance to the proper functioning of these agencies—unless, that is, citizens have the right incentives. But the authors assume that citizens can always, and at no resource cost, trust agents of the State to act efficiently and honestly. In other words, while the State in relation to its citizens is assumed to face an agency problem, the citizens compared with their State are assumed not to.[11]

While there are a number of senses in which the word "trust" is used in colloquial language, it acquires an important role in the efficacy of various resource allocation mechanisms when it is placed squarely within agency relationships. With this in mind, I will be using the word "trust" in the context of an individual forming expectations about actions of others that have a bearing on this individual's choice of action, when that action must be chosen before he or she can observe the actions of those others. Trust is important because its presence or absence can have a bearing on what we choose to do, and in many cases what we can do.

The clause concerning the inability to observe others' actions at the time one chooses one's own action is central. But it should be noted that this inability need not be caused by one's choice of action temporally preceding those of others. For example, it could be that what I ought now to do depends on whether you have done what you said you would

---

[11]  Recent work in mathematical political economy has gone far to remove this asymmetry. For book-length treatments of the literature, see Laffont and Tirole (1993), Dixit (1996), and Laffont (1999).

do, in circumstances in which I cannot now, or possibly ever, verify whether you have actually done it.

This account of trust places significance on other people's unobservable *actions* for the choice of one's own course of action. But there is another class of cases in which trust, in this same sense, comes into play. This is when others *know* something about themselves or the world, which the person in question does not, and when what that person ought to do depends on the extent of his or her ignorance of these matters. For example, an agreement between myself and such other people may call upon them to disclose their information. But can I trust them to be truthful? In other words, can I trust them to send me the correct messages, those they would send me if they were truly trustworthy?[12]

The former class of cases concerns unobservable actions, whereas the latter addresses problems of hidden information. As the two involve similar analytical considerations, I propose to conflate them.[13]

Luhmann (1988) reserves the term "confidence" (or a lack of it) in referring to our expectations of the *ability* of social institutions (for example, markets or State agencies) to function adequately. It is clear enough, though, that his usage can be extended to cover our expectations of the ability of experts to do their job well (for example, confidence in our physicians to diagnose our ailments correctly). In contrast, trust (or a lack of it) rears its head when we have cause to be concerned about someone's underlying disposition, motivation, and incentives. For example, we would lack confidence in the ability of the local police to protect our homes from theft if there were not enough of them to make the rounds. By the same token, we would have no trust in that same police force to do what should be expected of them if we knew their members to be corrupt. Thus too for the civil service and the law.

A number of points follow immediately:

(1) If there were no suitable punishment for breaking agreements or contracts, people would not have the appropriate incentives to fulfill them. If this were generally recognized, people would not want to enter into transactions with one another. Thus, what could in principle have been mutually beneficial relationships would not be initiated.

(2) The threat of punishment for errant behavior must be credible, or else the threat would be no threat. If people are to trust one another generally, they must have both confidence in the enforcement agency to do what is expected of it and trust in the agents to carry out their responsibilities.

---

[12] Formally, of course, they do not have to be truthful for me to be able to rely on them. As long as I can interpret their messages correctly, I can trust them. Thus the ancient Cretan was as informative as the knowledgeable saint.

[13] The terms *moral hazard* and *adverse selection* are used for a not too dissimilar classification (Hart and Holmstrom 1987). Space considerations prohibit me from going into these distinctions.

(3) The enforcement agency may be society "at large," not the State. Social ostracism, and the sense of shame society can invoke in one, are examples of such punishment. A special case of the latter is one in which the enforcement agency is the injured party to the transaction: the injured party can, for example, punish the errant party by ceasing to transact with him.

(4) You do not trust a person (or an agency) to do something merely because he says he will do it. You trust him only because, knowing what you know of his disposition, his available options and the consequences of his various possible actions, his knowledge base, ability, and so forth, you expect that he will choose to do it. In short, his promise must be credible. That is why we like to distinguish between "trusting someone" and "trusting someone blindly," and think the latter to be ill-advised.

(5) This follows from the previous point: when you decide whether to enter into an agreement with someone, you need to look at the world from *her* perspective as it is likely to be when it comes to her having to fulfill her part of the agreement. This is why game theorists instruct us to calculate backward, against time, and not forward, with time.[14]

(6) Trust and confidence among persons and agencies are interconnected. If your trust (even confidence) in the enforcement agency falters, you will not trust people to fulfill their terms of an agreement and thus will not enter into that agreement. By the same token, as democrats have long noted, you should not trust the enforcement agency (for example, government) to do on balance what is desired of it if you do not trust that it will be thrown out of power, through the ballot box or armed rebellion, if it does not do on balance what is desired of it.[15] It is this interconnectedness that makes trust such a fragile commodity. If it erodes in any part of the mosaic, it can bring an awful lot down with it. This is one reason why the medical and legal professions had, and in many cases still have, not only stern codes of conduct instilled into their members, but also powerful guild rules for members if they are to belong. It has been argued that there was a need for these professions to break the intricate link alluded to above, so that vital transactions concerning health and protection could be entered into even if enforcement costs were to rise owing to an erosion of trust elsewhere in the economy, through rapidly changing social mores, or whatever other possible reason (Arrow 1963).

---

[14] There are logical problems with backward induction as a reasoning device in social interactions (Binmore 1997). Moreover, there are now good empirical grounds for thinking that we do not apply it in all circumstances (Ostrom 1998, offers a fine account of the evidence). In the section on "exploitative relationships" I will try to summarize what evolutionary psychology has to say on this.

[15] Przeworski (1991) presents a mathematical model of the idea.

(7) An immediate corollary of this is that the production of trust is riddled with external economies. This means that there is likely to be an underinvestment in the production of trust. But this does not make trust a public good; rather, it involves what economists call "network externalities" (she trusts you, now you trust me, so she now trusts me, and so forth; Farrell and Saloner 1985; Katz and Shapiro 1985).

(8) Trust is based on reputation, and reputation is acquired on the basis of observed behavior over time. Reputation is an asset, so people invest in it, in that they forego immediate gains for the purpose of enjoying benefits later. But it is not only people who can acquire a reputation, good or bad; institutions and groups can also acquire it and maintain it. It is not easy to model the link between personal, group, and institutional reputation. However, the link needs to be studied if we are to understand the idea of social capital.

(9) How far people can trust one another depends in part on the extent to which actions are observable. So the efficiency of an institution depends, among other things, on the ease with which chosen actions can be monitored by interested parties. The ability to impose effective sanctions depends on the extent to which breaches of agreement are observable. Peer monitoring, for instance, could be a way of reducing opportunistic behavior within an organization such as a firm. As monitoring is not free of cost, the peer would need to have adequate incentives to do the peering.[16] The firm also needs to be kept in line. For example, a public agency would be needed to monitor its effluent discharge so as to discourage it from breaking environmental standards. But the public agency also needs to be kept in check. So it could be that a free and competitive press is necessary for this purpose. In each case there is call for an institutional solution to the problem of creating trust, and the problems are connected.

(10) Even though there is no natural system of units in which trust, or a reputation for being trustworthy, can be measured, it does not matter in principle, because in any given context you can measure their worth by the extent to which mutual benefits can be realized.[17] Admittedly,

---

[16] Stiglitz (1990) has explored the role of joint liability among individual borrowers of funds. Because liability is joint, borrowers have an incentive to monitor one another's choices. Stiglitz' immediate purpose in the article was to find an explanation for the phenomenal success of the famous Grameen Bank in Bangladesh in recovering loans. Negative features of group-lending schemes (for example, adding to the risks borne by individual borrowers) have been studied by Besley and Coate (1995) and Madajewicz (1997). Credit cooperatives, which borrow from a source (a bank, for example) and distribute the fund among members as loans, constitute another institutional form with a built-in incentive structure for peer monitoring (Banerjee, Besley, and Guinnane 1994).

[17] But in practice the measurement problems may be insurmountable. See the section on "culture" below.

this would only be a measure of their instrumental value, but perhaps one should not expect more. In this sense also, trust and a reputation for trustworthiness are rather like knowledge; they are valuable both intrinsically and instrumentally.

These observations will appear rather obvious. But I have found it useful to keep them in mind. They are necessary ingredients of any reasonable account of social capital. Repeatedly we will find use for them in the analysis that follows.

### Cooperative ventures

Consider a group of people who have identified a mutually advantageous course of actions. We imagine that they have reached agreement on the allocation of rights and obligations. The agreement could be on the sharing of benefits and burdens associated with the management of a common-property resource (for example, an irrigation system, a grazing field, a coastal fishery); or it could be on the provision of a public good (for example, the construction of a drainage channel in a watershed) or on some general collective action (for example, civic engagement, lobbying); or a transaction in which purchase and delivery of the commodity cannot be synchronized (for example, credit and insurance); or exchanges that amount to reciprocity ("I help you, now that you are in need, with the understanding that you will help me when I am in need"); and so on. In figure 1, which depicts a two-person case, the net benefit (payoff) enjoyed by person 1 is measured along the horizontal axis, while that of person 2 is measured along the vertical axis. The curve BC denotes the set of efficient allocations. Regarding the agreement point, I assume for the moment that it lies to the northeast of A. Two possible points are shown in figure 1: D (which lies on the efficient frontier, BC) and $D^1$ (which lies below BC).

Three questions arise: (a) How have the members of the group come to know one another? (b) As there probably were many other courses of action also available, why did they settle on this particular one? (c) How can the parties feel secure that the agreement will be kept?

The questions are related. The connection between (a) and (c) is obvious. But even (b) and (c) are related: what is agreed upon is unlikely to have been independent of the reasons the parties had for thinking that the agreement would be honored. Here I am mostly concerned with (a) and (c). The reason for neglecting (b) is that the theory of bargaining is even now rudimentary. It does not offer much guidance on how the benefits and burdens of cooperation would be shared. We should note as well that "benefits" and "burdens" can only be measured in terms of the state of affairs that would prevail in an absence of cooperation. So we have to be clear what that state is. In figure 1 it has been denoted by A, but the figure does not tell us how A is to be interpreted.

FIGURE 1: COOPERATIVE VENTURES: A TWO-PERSON CASE

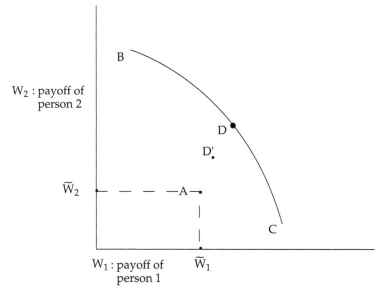

*Source:* Author.

It could be that the group comprises people who are only loosely linked. If so, A could denote payoffs the parties would obtain if they continued to be engaged in whatever they currently were doing, for instance, in employment elsewhere. In this case A would denote the status quo. Another possibility would be that the group is engaged in what amounts to a Prisoners' Dilemma game. In that case A would denote payoffs that would result if people were to choose their dominant strategies.[18] In more general circumstances A could simply be a noncooperative equilibrium of the underlying social situation.

The problem remains that interpreting A does not tell us why D should have been chosen. There is of course a temptation to appeal to that old war-horse of cooperative game theory, the Nash bargaining solution,

---

[18] Here is the two-person Prisoners' Dilemma game (the N-person case is a direct generalization). Let U ("unrestrained" behavior) and R ("restrained" behavior) be two possible alternatives open to each person. Write by (U, R) the choice of U by individual 1 and R by individual 2, and so on for the remaining three combinations. Imagine that 1 prefers (U, R) to (R, R), (R, R) to (U, U), and (U, U) to (R, U); and that 2 prefers (R, U) to (R, R), (R, R) to (U, U), and (U, U) to (U, R). Clearly U is the dominant strategy for each party: each would most prefer to choose U irrespective of what the other were to choose. So (U, U) is the unique noncooperative equilibrium pair of choices. But both prefer (R, R) to (U, U). Hence the dilemma.

and to identify D as that solution.[19] But excepting for one (Chopra, Kadekodi, and Murty 1990), I do not know of any study that has used it to interpret sharing arrangements in poor countries. The Nash bargaining solution (like other cooperative solution concepts) is independent of the context in which negotiation is assumed to take place. Nash (Border and Segal 1997) regarded this as a virtue and was explicit on the point. But this feature of the solution makes it all the more likely that it does not often find application.[20]

It is frequently not even possible to judge whether the agreement point is efficient (for example, whether in figure 1 D lies on BC, or whether it lies to the left of it, at a point such as $D^1$). For this reason, social scientists tend to study cooperative allocations qualitatively. Asymmetries in distributions are traced to differences in the parties' circumstances, while symmetries are traced to their similarities. For example, in her work on collectively managed irrigation systems in Nepal, Ostrom (1990, 1996) has accounted for differences in rights and responsibilities among users (who gets how much water and when, who is responsible for which maintenance task of the canal system, and so forth) in terms of such facts as that some farmers are head-enders while others are tail-enders. Head-enders have a built-in advantage, in that they can prevent tail-enders from receiving water. Without cooperation their fortunes would differ greatly. So cooperative arrangements display asymmetries. In fact a general finding from studies on the management of common property systems is that entitlements to products of the commons are and were almost always based on private holdings. They thus reflect inequalities in private wealth (McKean 1992).

Gaspard and others (1997) have studied a central drainage channel in the Ethiopian highlands. They found that those households having more to gain from the collective endeavor (for example, the ones owning more land, or owning land centrally located in the basin) contributed more labor to its construction. This is another example of a built-in asymmetry, giving rise to an asymmetric outcome. However, Baland and

---

[19] In the figure, $W_1$ and $W_2$ denote the payoffs of persons 1 and 2, respectively. $\tilde{W}_1$ and $\tilde{W}_2$ are their reservation values. The Nash bargaining solution is that point on BC at which the function $(W_1-\tilde{W}_1)(W_2-\tilde{W}_2)$ is maximized. For accounts of the Nash bargaining solution, see Fudenberg and Tirole (1991).

[20] Over the past several millenia a wide variety of *contextual* solutions have been proposed for the problem of dividing an "object" among claimants.

If the number of parties were more than two, matters would be especially problematic: every bilateral negotiation would now have to be sensitive to the remaining parties. In addition to the Nash bargaining solution, there are other solution concepts in cooperative game theory, such as the core, the nucleolus, and the Shapley value. I have not seen any of them being used in applied studies on the local commons.

Platteau (1996) have collated examples in which communities practice systems of rotation among users of heterogeneous common-property resources, such as inland and coastal fisheries, grazing land, and sources of firewood and fodder. Rotation enables community members to have equal access to the resource over the long run, a sensible allocation rule for similarly placed actors.

### If they are made, why are agreements kept?

Assuming then that an agreement has been reached, how can the parties be sanguine that it will be kept? Broadly speaking, there would appear to be three types of situation in which parties to an agreement could expect everyone to keep to their side of the bargain: (1) there is an external enforcer, (2) people are honorable, and (3) recourse is taken to mutual enforcement.[21]

In practice the three situations would be expected to shade into one another. Moreover, it can often prove difficult empirically to distinguish between them. For example, someone employed by the parties to act as a referee, or coordinator, or information transmitter can easily appear to an outsider to be in overall authority. Nevertheless, for the sake of clarity, I am going to treat the three as being distinct.

*External enforcement*

It could be that the agreement is translated into an explicit contract and enforced by an established structure of power and authority; which is to say that the agreement is enforced by a "third" party. This may be the State, as in the case of contracts in the large numbers of markets operating throughout the world. But it need not be the State. In rural communities, for example, the structure of power and authority are in some cases vested in tribal elders (as in nomadic tribes in Sub-Saharan Africa), in others in dominant landowners, feudal lords, chieftains, and priests.

On occasion there are attempts to make rural communities minirepublics in certain spheres of life. Village Panchayats in India try to assume that form. The idea is to elect offices, the officials being en-

---

[21] Of course, none may work in a particular context, in which case people will find themselves in a hole they cannot easily get out of, and what could have been mutually beneficial agreements will not take place. The behavior reported in the Mezzogiorno by Banfield (1958) is an illustration of this possibility. Ostrom (1990, 1996) and Baland and Platteau (1996) cite a number of cases in which cooperative arrangements have not been entered into, or have broken down. We will return to such matters later in the essay. Sen (1977) calls failure to cooperate the consequence of people being "rational fools."

trusted with the power to settle disputes, enforce contracts (be they explicit or only tacit), communicate with higher levels of State authority,
and so forth. Wade's account of local enforcement of the allocation of
benefits and burdens in rural South India describes such a mechanism
in detail (Wade 1988). Forty-one villages were studied, and it was found
that downstream villages (those facing a particularly acute scarcity of
water) had an elaborate set of rules, enforced by fines, for regulating the
use of water from irrigation canals. Most villages had similar arrangements for the use of grazing land. Wade reports that elected village councils (Panchayats) appoint agents who allocate water among different
farmers' fields, protect crops from grazing animals, collect levies, and
impose fines.[22]

The question why such a structure of authority may exist and be accepted by people is a higher-order one, akin to the question why people
accept the authority of the State. The answer is that general acceptance
itself is self-enforcing behavior: when a sufficiently large number of others accept the structure of authority, each has an incentive to accept it,
the personal cost of noncompliance (for example, a stiff jail sentence)
being too high. General acceptance is an equilibrium. Contrariwise, when
sufficiently large numbers do not accept it (for example, during tensions leading to riots or civil wars), individual incentives to accept it
weaken, and the system can unravel rapidly to an equilibrium characterized by nonacceptance. General acceptance of the structure of authority is held together by its own bootstraps, so to speak (Dasgupta 1993).
This yields the corollary that even if a government backed by the apparatus of the State were viewed by most citizens to be unworthy, it would
remain in power if each citizen were to suppose that most others would
continue to accept its authority.[23]

For a third-party to enforce agreements it has to be possible to verify
publicly whether the terms of a contract have been fulfilled. But this can
prove costly (as is confirmed by the enormous costs, relative to incomes,
that litigation involves even in modern industrial societies); in some cases
it can prove impossible. Because of this and possibly other reasons, societies rely also on other mechanisms to facilitate cooperation. We discuss them next.

### Prosocial disposition

People would trust one another to keep agreements if they were sanguine that most others had a disposition to be trustworthy. Such dispo-

---

[22]  Baland and Platteau (1996, p. 217) write about "water masters" in fishing
groups in the Niger River delta who regulated the use of the local fisheries.
[23]  Models of multiple equilibria of social systems abound. They will be a recurrent theme here. I provide examples below.

sition is to a greater or lesser extent formed through communal living, role modeling, education, and receiving rewards and punishments. The process begins at the earliest stages of our lives.[24] The development of personal morality is related to this, but the two are not the same. Note too that we not only internalize moral norms, such as that of paying our dues, helping others at some cost to ourselves, and returning a favor; we also practice such norms as those prescribing that we punish people who have hurt us intentionally; and even such metanorms as shunning people who break agreements, on occasion frowning on those who socialize with people who have broken agreements; and so forth. By internalizing such norms, a person enables the springs of her actions to include them. She therefore feels shame or guilt in violating the norm, and this prevents her from doing so, or at the very least it puts a break on her, unless other considerations are found by her to be overriding. In short, her upbringing ensures that she has a disposition to obey the norm, be it moral or social. When she does violate it, neither guilt nor shame would typically be absent, but frequently the act will have been rationalized by her. Summarizing a number of studies conducted in the West, Rotter (1980) reported that on average people who are more willing to trust others are themselves more trustworthy, in that they are less likely to lie, cheat, or steal. They are also less likely to be unhappy or maladjusted, and are more liked by friends and colleagues.

Often enough the disposition to be honest would be toward members of some particular group (for example, one's clan, neighbors, or ethnic group), not others. This amounts to group loyalty. One may have been raised to be suspicious of people from other groups, one may have even been encouraged to dupe such others if and when the occasion arose. Society as a whole wastes resources when the disposition for honesty is restricted to particular groups. A general disposition to abide by agreements, to be truthful, to be able to trust one another, and to act with justice is an essential lubricant of societies. Theoretical considerations imply that the larger is the population over which this disposition is cast by all, the better is the collective outcome. Landes (1998) offers powerful historical evidence of this. Later we will formulate a model that builds on the idea that communities in which civic virtues prevail save on transaction costs. There lies the instrumental worth of civic virtues, and explains why mechanisms for the growth of social capital consist in part of establishing pathways by which these virtues could be made to flourish.

---

[24] Rest (1983), Shantz (1983), Eisenberg and Mussen (1989), Hinde and Groebel (1991), and Coles (1997) contain accounts of what is currently known of the development processes through which people from their infancy acquire prosocial dispositions—for example, by learning to distinguish accidental effects from intentional effects of others' actions.

In the world as we know it, the disposition to be trustworthy at both the personal and impersonal spheres is present in varying degrees. When we refrain from breaking the law, it is not always because of a fear of being caught. However, if for instance, relative to the gravity of the misdemeanor the pecuniary benefits from malfeasance were high, some transgression could be expected to occur. Punishment assumes its role as a deterrence because of the latter fact.

### Mutual enforcement

However, in cases in which people encounter one another repeatedly in similar situations, agreements could be honored even if people are not disposed to be honest, and even if an external authority is not available to enforce agreements. This mechanism, in which people are engaged in long-term relationships, is an ingredient in theories of social capital.[25]

Let us assume then that figure 1 represents opportunities faced by the various parties in each of an indefinite number of periods. We call the social engagements that are possible in each period the "stage game." Opportunities over time can then be derived from repetitions of this stage game.

Consider now a group of farsighted people who know one another, who prepare to interact indefinitely with one another under repeated plays of the stage game, and who understand the details of the agreement.[26] By a farsighted person I mean someone who applies a low rate to discount future costs and benefits of alternative courses of action. This means that the parties in question are not independently mobile (although they could be collectively mobile, as in the case of nomadic societies); otherwise the chance of future encounters with one another would be low, and people would discount heavily the future benefits of cooperation.

The basic idea is this: if people are farsighted, a credible threat by others that they would impose sufficiently stiff sanctions on anyone who broke the agreement would deter everyone from breaking it. The problem is to arrange matters so that the threats in question are credible. This can pose a problem because the character of the agreement can matter, which means that the kind of sanctions that are intended for use to punish transgressors can matter. In the following two sections we study how the basic argument and some of its many generalizations work.

---

[25] The theoretical chapter in Putnam (1993), Chapter 6, makes the connection, but does not develop the formal structure of the mechanism. I give the details below, both for completeness and because I will need the account subsequently. The classic articles on the subject are Friedman (1971), Rubinstein (1979), Fudenberg and Maskin (1986), and Kandori (1992a).

[26] I am not assuming that the parties are bound to meet forever. Rather, I am assuming that no matter how far a date into the future one cares to name, there is some chance that the parties in question will be on hand to be able to cooperate.

## Norms and reputations

The discussion will benefit by means of examples.

*Social norms*

Consider a group of herdsmen enjoying exclusive rights to a grazing field. We may imagine that being similarly placed, they are engaged in a symmetric many-person Prisoners' Dilemma game on a period-by-period basis.[27] The herdsmen recognize that if they were interested only in the current outcome, each person's most preferred course of action would be to introduce too many animals into the commons. But if all were to do so, profits would be lower than they would have been if they had all exercised restraint. In figure 1, which denotes the two-person case, A denotes profits in each period if the parties were to behave in an unrestrained manner and D their profits if they were to exercise restraint. The herdsmen have agreed to cooperate and practice restraint, but they all recognize that each would be tempted to break the agreement unilaterally unless some suitable sanctions on opportunistic behavior were put in place.

Imagine that each herdsman's actions are observable by the others, though not necessarily verifiable by an outside party. I assume also that everyone has a perfect memory. This means that people can build a reputation for honest behavior.[28] Now, one might think that a social norm, requiring people to keep their word, has a role to play. But it merely begs the question: we would want to know why the norm is accepted by all, that is, what incentives people have for not violating it. By a "norm" I mean a behavioral strategy (in other words, rules such as, "Do this if that happens," or "Do that if he does this"). By a "social norm" I mean a behavioral strategy that is subscribed to by all. But the strategy would have to be self-enforcing if it were to be subscribed to by all. So for a norm to be a social one it would have to be in the interest of each party to act in accordance with it if all others were to act in accordance with it—in short, it would have to be an equilibrium strategy. We want to see how norms can be so fashioned as to be social norms.

---

[27]  This is the famous example in Hardin (1968). Dasgupta and Heal (1979, chapter 3) contains a formal economic model that yields such dilemmas.

[28]  Each of these qualifications can be relaxed somewhat (Fudenberg and Tirole 1991). Hardin's (1968) statement on the fate of common-property resources, that they erode because people "free-ride" on others, was telling for such globally mobile resources as the atmosphere and the open seas, because individual actions are very hard to observe. In the text I am referring to geographically localized commons, or the local commons for short.

Ostrom's account of the management of irrigation water in Nepalese villages contains details of how arrangements have been so designed that any one person's actions can be observed by at least one other person (Ostrom 1990, 1992).

In a pioneering article, Friedman (1971) studied a "grim" norm. For our herdsmen it would go as follows: begin by exercising restraint and continue to act in a restrained way as long as all others have exercised restraint, but switch forever to the unrestrained behavior in the period following the first time someone has broken the agreement by behaving in an unrestrained manner. The norm is grim because it is unforgiving of a single failure to comply with the agreement. The threat of sanctions is credible because sanctions amount to a permanent switch to the unique equilibrium action in the stage game (namely, unrestrained behavior). However, the norm is a social norm only for "farsighted" herdsmen. If herdsmen were not farsighted, the norm would not have potency. Future sanctions would not be viewed as being costly, so people would behave opportunistically from the start. This is exactly what intuition suggests.

Even among farsighted herdsmen cooperation is not the only possible outcome. For example, behaving in an unrestrained manner in each period is also an equilibrium strategy; so permanent noncooperation is also an equilibrium outcome. And so on—repeated games have many equilibria.[29] I am at this point discussing how cooperation can be sustained, not how it might have been reached by a community. To understand the latter would require of us to study the community's history, pure analysis would not get us far.

The grim norm is special. In settings more general than repeated plays of the Prisoners' Dilemma game, sanctions need to be more subtly designed if they are to be credible. I turn to these matters, first by studying social environments that are not repeated games, then by exploring repeated settings in which the social interactions embodied in the stage game are more complex than the Prisoners' Dilemma.

*Group reputation*

Interactions that may recur over the indefinite future are farfetched: people are known to have finite lives. But dynasties are a different matter. Parents care about their children's standard of living, children in turn could be relied on to care about their children's standard of living, and so on down the generations. One can now extend the previous argument by enabling an entire dynasty of herdsmen to acquire a reputation for being trustworthy. If each generation of herdsmen care sufficiently about their children's standard of living, period-by-period cooperation could be sustained if they were to act in a restrained manner so long as no one ever reneged on the original agreement—and if, in the event that anyone did, they were to move permanently to unrestrained

---

[29] The precise statement regarding this is called the Folk Theorem. See Fudenberg and Tirole (1991).

behavior the period following the first defection by someone. This would amount to a use of the grim norm in an intergenerational setting.

Thus, reputation can be a capital asset even for dynasties. In many situations sanctions can be so designed as to be targeted at the descendents of transgressors (recall, for example, that in traditional societies it was not uncommon for fathers' debts to be inherited by their sons). Interestingly, the threat of *intra*dynastic sanctions can be a means by which exchanges across generations take place. In a wide-ranging essay on social norms, Elster (1989, p. 113) has argued that this is not possible: "Intergenerational reciprocity is … found between parents and children. Assuming that parents cannot disinherit their children, the latter have no incentive to take care of their parents in old age…. Yet, most societies have a norm that you should help your parents; in return for what they did for you when you were at a similarly helpless stage." Elster used this and other considerations to argue that norms must be internalized if they are to work.

But the argument is not quite correct. To see why, call someone deserving if and only if he has looked after a deserving parent. Consider a norm stating that those who had not taken care of deserving parents in their old age would not be deserving of being cared for by their children when they themselves became old. Now imagine that the intergenerational game begins with the young of the dynasty choosing to look after the old. One could then always tell who is deserving and who is not. So, if the young were sufficiently farsighted to care that they themselves will need looking after later in life, they would as a matter of self-interest look after their parents.[30]

Kreps (1990) has carried the argument farther by showing how reputation can be bought and sold. He has even identified circumstances in which reputation serves a purpose *only* if there is a market for it. Suppose that in every period, $t$, a different pair of individuals, $M_t$ and $N_t$, face an opportunity for cooperation. For concreteness, suppose the two can undertake a production venture, in which $M_t$ has first to supply labor, to be followed by $N_t$ requiring to market the produce and paying $M_t$ an agreed-upon portion of the proceeds. We take it that the venture can be concluded within period $t$.

The problem for $M_t$ is that she cannot trust $N_t$, because $N_t$ has every incentive to abuse trust by absconding with the proceeds. But we may imagine that $N_t$ has a life to lead after $t$, and that he needs resources in order to survive. So Kreps supposes that there is a firm called N-Associates. At the beginning of $t$ the firm has a member $N_{t-1}$, who has just concluded a successful venture with $M_{t-1}$. As it happens, N-Associates has a reputation for never abusing trust, because the firm has never abused trust. So now imag-

---

[30] Kandori (1992b) contains a definitive treatment of the way finitely lived overlapping groups can sustain cooperation by a reliance on social norms. The pioneering work on this is Hammond (1975).

ine that $M_t$ is willing to trust $N_t$ if $N_t$ is a member of N-Associates, but not otherwise. In fact, imagine that all the Ms choose to trust members of N-Associates so long as no previous member of the firm has ever abused the trust of some previous M. This means that $N_t$ would be willing to buy a position in the firm at some price, implying that a position in the firm will have a market value. Meanwhile, as he needs resources for life after t–1, $N_{t-1}$ would be willing to sell his position in the firm to $N_t$ if the price were right. For there to be cooperation in each period, the price of a position in the firm at the beginning of each $t$ must be sufficiently low to make it worthwhile for $N_t$ to purchase it, and sufficiently high for $N_{t-1}$ to be willing to sell it.[31]

### Exploitative relationships

Figure 1 depicts a social setting in which parties have agreed on a mutually advantageous course of actions. Since much of the literature on social capital has focused on this sort of case, it not infrequently offers a picture of free and comfortable citizens getting together on a lucrative venture. There is a distinct scent of seventeenth-century Dutch burghers in the analysis.

But there are long-term relationships amounting to one class of people exploiting another. They are not uncommon in poor countries. What to an outsider could appear to be a mutually advantageous course of actions among a group may in fact be a state of affairs in which some members find themselves worse off than they would have been had the group not been engaged in the relationship. That there can be exploitation in long-term relationships is not to be doubted. Beteille (1983), for example, has reminded us that in Indian villages access to local common-property resources is often restricted to the privileged (for example, caste Hindus), who are also among the bigger landowners. The outcasts (euphemistically called members of "schedule castes") are often among the poorest of the poor.

Consider a village community, where to exit would for some (for example the landless) be to invite destitution. Those more fortunately placed (for example, landowners and priests) are then in a position to exercise considerable bargaining power over them. For expositional ease I return to the case of repeated interactions. To make the idea of exploitation precise, define each party's "min-max value" in the stage game to be the lowest payoff others can push the person to by suitable choice of their strategies, provided the person foresees this and chooses his best response to it. A person's min-max value is sometimes referred to also as her "reservation value," because any arrangement upon which the group seeks to agree should be expected to yield each person a payoff at least as high as her min-max value. Note though that someone's min-max value could well be much

---

[31]   It could be that if $N_{t-1}$ cannot sell it at a high enough price, it is worthwhile for him to continue to retain his position in the firm and work less productively in it.

lower than her payoff in any noncooperative equilibrium of the stage game. This is a fact of considerable theoretical and practical importance.[32]

Imagine that the agreed-upon course of actions yields members of some subgroup payoffs that are lower than what they would be in any noncooperative equilibrium of the stage game. It would not be unreasonable to call that subgroup the exploited. There are of course others in the group who expect to thrive under the arrangement: they are the exploiters. In figure 2 various payoffs under the stage game are depicted for a case involving two people. I am going to assume that the stage game has a unique equilibrium, denoted by A. B is a feasible allocation of benefits and burdens at which both parties are better off than at A. C is a feasible allocation at which both parties have higher payoffs than their respective min-max values. However, at C person 1 is worse off than she would be at A, and person 2 is better off than he would be at B. The question that arises is whether C can be sustained as the outcome of an agreement under a long-term relationship.

FIGURE 2: EXPLOITATIVE RELATIONSHIPS: A TWO-PERSON CASE

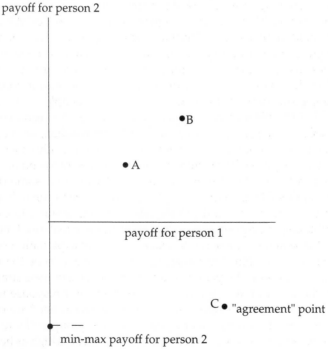

*Source:* Author.

---

[32] Recall that in the Prisoners' Dilemma game payoffs when everyone plays their dominant strategies are min-max values. The stage game now being discussed in the text is not a Prisoners' Dilemma game.

The question is not trivial. The problem is to devise credible sanctions, so that the "agreement" sticks. To see the point in concrete terms, consider that in the Indian subcontinent landless workers need consumption loans during the lean season and in emergencies (marriage, birth, illness, and death in the family), while landlords need additional labor during the busy season and in emergencies (for example, storms and floods). Lacking collateral, the landless laborer has no access to the formal credit market. A landlord in turn would rather avoid the vagaries of the casual labor market in times of need. But if the worker were to pledge his labor whenever the landlord were to call upon it, the pledge itself could be a collateral. So landlords and workers are able to enter into long-term relationships in which credit and labor supply are interlinked in the stage game.[33] Note though that while the landlord can do without the worker (he can in principle employ workers from neighboring villages), the worker is at the mercy of the landlord. The worker's min-max value would then be expected to be extremely low. But if others were to press a worker down to his min-max value, say, by having nothing to do with him, one of the landlords would have to search for workers in distant villages, and this could prove very costly. How can sanctions be made credible in such situations?

We take it that the agreement assigns various privileges and duties to landlords and workers on a period-by-period basis. A system of norms that suggests itself is to make it even more costly for someone not to impose sanctions when called upon to do so than it is to impose them. Here is how this can be achieved in the form of a norm that is embedded in a hierarchy of metanorms. I will begin by presenting an argument that works when neither landlords nor workers discount future costs and benefits. I will then discuss the case in which they do discount the future, albeit at a low rate.

Call a person a "conformist" if and only if she cooperates with all who are conformists. This sounds circular, but, as in the case of the "deserving parents" of the previous subsection (on "group reputations"), it is not, because we now suppose that the norm requires all parties to begin the process of repeated interactions by keeping to their agreement. By recursion it is possible for any party in any period to determine who is a conformist and who is not. If someone's actions in any period made him a nonconformist, the norm would enjoin each of the other parties to impose a sanction on him by pushing him to his min-max value for a sufficiently large number of periods. Putting it more elaborately, the norm requires not only that sanctions be imposed on those in violation of an agreement; but also that sanctions be imposed on those who fail to im-

---

[33] See Braverman and Stiglitz (1982) and Braverman and Gausch (1984) for theoretical explorations. Bardhan (1984) and Rudra (1984) contain accounts of interlinked rural markets from a sample of West Bengal villages.

pose sanctions on those in violation of the agreement; on those who fail to impose sanctions on those who fail to impose sanctions on those in violation of the agreement; … and so on, indefinitely. This indefinite chain of metanorms makes the threat of sanctions against deviant behavior credible, because, if all others were to conform to the norm, it would not be worth anyone's while to violate the norm. In short, abiding by the agreement would be self-enforcing.[34]

Even though I am neglecting details here, there is a problem with the above argument that cannot be ignored. It occurs if people discount future costs and benefits, even if ever so slightly. The problem is that the argument does not work if someone's payoff when helping to force someone else to their min-max value is less than that someone's own min-max value. In this case the norm needs to be supplemented by something to make the threat of sanctions on nonconformists credible. Toward this end Fudenberg and Maskin (1986) constructed an ingenious supplement. They showed that under suitable conditions people can be induced to impose sanctions when they are required to if they are *rewarded* for a period after they comply (see also Abreu 1988). There is clear empirical resonance in this. We are rewarded by society for following its strictures, not necessarily by having gifts showered on us, but mostly by being shown approval. And it often works, because social approval matters to us.

These arguments show how long-term relationships among farsighted people can be sustained. The qualification "farsighted" means that people expect to interact with one another repeatedly. This is a good assumption to make if one wants to understand exchanges in traditional societies. Long-term relationships are prevalent there. In this section I have stressed that such relationships are not necessarily equitable (they may even be exploitative) or inevitable. Repeated games contain many equilibria, including those involving no cooperation. While the theory of games has proved invaluable in explaining how certain allocation rules can be sustained, we need to study history to understand why and how at any particular place the prevailing allocation rule, not others, got selected. This is why the applied literature on both cooperative and noncooperative behavior consists largely of case studies. Later in the essay I will describe a few.

### Emotive behavior

It would seem unlikely that people are such effortless calculators and information storers that they are able to act on the basis of an ever-growing chain of metanorms similar to those constructed in the ac-

---

[34] Notice though that, as cooperation is self-enforcing, there would be no deviance along the path of cooperation; so, no sanctions would be observed. The metanorms pertain to behavior *off* the path of cooperation.

count of relationships in which sanctions are extremely costly to those who are required to impose them. Norms often do involve imposing sanctions on someone breaking an agreement (not much forgiveness there!), and on someone who does not impose a sanction on someone breaking an agreement.[35] This said, I know of no empirical study that reports on a people who would impose sanctions on those who do not impose sanctions on those who do not impose sanctions on those who do not impose sanctions... and so on. The grim norm is known to prevail in reciprocal relationships (Czako and Sik 1988), but the impression I have gained from the literature is that it is in force mostly in those environments in which the parties have access to formal markets as an alternative. In rural communities in poor countries matters are different, since formal markets are often far away. In a number of accounts I have read (for example, Ostrom 1992), sanctions are graduated; the first misdemeanor is met by a small punishment, subsequent ones by a stiffer punishment, persistent ones by a punishment that is stiffer still, and so forth. How does one reconcile these findings with theoretical reasoning?

In cases in which formal markets and reciprocal relationships coexist (see upcoming sections on "the local commons in poor countries: successes and failures" and "macroevidence: scale versus change"), the grim norm could be expected to prevail, as it involves permanent sanctions— which is a needed device for preventing people from engaging in opportunistic behavior when good, short-term opportunities appear elsewhere from time to time. But if there were no alternatives to nonmarket relationships, and the community were something of an enclave, communitarian arrangements would be of high value to all. It should not be surprising then that any single instance of misbehavior would be interpreted as an error on the part of the miscreant, or as "testing the water" (to check whether others were watching). This would explain why graduated sanctions are often observed.

But I have heard of no evidence of an infinite chain of metanorms; so the question is whether human motivation is such that they are in fact not required. Now, it is not difficult to imagine people being moved to sacrifice personal resources to benefit those who have shown kindness and to sacrifice personal resources to punish those who have been unkind. We may call such emotions as those that prompt one to make these gestures emotions of "reciprocity" (Rabin 1993).[36] Other than introspec-

---

[35] For example, rural tradition in parts of India involves several layers of norms. Not only is it considered "unclean" if one has behaved in certain ways, but to have contact with someone who is unclean can also make one unclean.

[36] It needs stressing that "reciprocity," as the term is being used here, is *not* the same as behavior in accordance with the tit-for-tat strategy popularized by Axelrod (1984). In our usage no mention has been made, for example, about how long the punishment is inflicted on those who have hurt us.

tion, what evidence is there that people are thus motivated? In a famous experiment on bargaining (Güth, Schmittberger, and Schwarz 1982), a sum of money was made available for allocation among a pair of individuals, one of whom was chosen as the proposer of how the money would be divided, the other the responder. The proposer was asked to suggest a division and the responder was instructed to say whether he would accept the offer. It was stipulated that if the responder accepted the offer the money would be divided in accordance with the proposal; but if it was rejected neither party would receive anything. Given the one-shot nature of the game, it has been christened the Ultimatum Game.

If each of the parties cared only about the amount *she* received (this is frequently regarded as the way a rational person would necessarily care!), the Ultimatum Game would have a simple solution: the proposer would offer at most a tiny amount to the responder and the responder would accept. But this is not how participants played the game. Generally speaking, divisions about 60:40 were offered by the proposer and, commonly, offers of less than 25 percent to the responder were rejected because they were regarded as unfair. The literature on the Ultimatum Game is now huge (see Roth 1995, for an excellent review). A natural interpretation of the finding that generous divisions are offered by proposers is that proposers know responders would reject unfair divisions, even though it would mean having to forego a pecuniary benefit.

In a set of ingeniously designed one-shot experimental games in which profit-maximizing firms offered labor contracts to potential workers, Fehr, Gächter, and Kirchsteiger (1997) found that both types of subjects had a disposition to practice reciprocity. In one set of experiments workers frequently responded to generous offers by not shirking (an instance of "gift exchange"); while in another, firms at some cost to themselves rewarded workers subsequently if they had worked hard, but punished them if they had shirked. The experiments were so designed that both firms and workers benefited from having a disposition to reciprocate.

In another set of experiments, again involving one-shot games, Fehr, Kirchsteiger, and Riedl (1998) found that if buyers of a commodity offer high enough prices, sellers at some cost to themselves set product quality above levels enforceable by buyers. Buyers, in anticipation of this form of gift exchange, offer higher prices than they would have offered if they had not expected firms to be so motivated. The experiments were designed so as to enable both sets of parties to benefit from having the disposition to reciprocate. The findings provide an explanation for the fact that people frequently, and rationally, infer product quality by its price.[37]

---

[37] Ostrom, Gardner, and Walker (1994) contains reports on a number of experimental games on the sharing of common-property resources in which subjects displayed reciprocity. Ledyard (1995) provides a review of experimental games on the voluntary provision of public goods. Subjects were found frequently not to play opportunistically.

People in any given context would appear to have a sense of fairness that matters to them. It is not "irrational" to reject a demeaning offer even when there are pecuniary gains to be enjoyed from accepting it. Of course, if the total amount of money were large relative to one's income, an offer of even 5 percent in the Ultimatum Game might be acceptable to most. There is here the familiar clash of values and desires we all experience. Similarly, a person may choose to cease cooperating with someone who has cheated him. Put in colloquial terms, the person's ego could be involved, he could even be angry at being cheated.[38]

Why? Why are bygones not invariably treated as bygones? One ready answer (there are others) is that emotions sometimes get in the way. If one were to ask why we experience such emotions, it would be suggested that minds capable of particular types of feeling emerged under selection pressure. But a number of evolutionary psychologists have gone farther. They have explored the thesis that the mind consists of a set of adaptations designed to solve the long-standing problems humans encountered as hunter-gatherers, such as that of enabling them to face threats and to engage in social exchange (Barkow, Cosmides, and Tooby 1992). They argue that the human mind has a built-in capacity to learn norms of reciprocity and those general social rules that enhance the returns from cooperative behavior. They hypothesize that in order to behave adaptively humans needed among other things a map of the persons, relationships, motives, interactions, emotions, and intentions that make up the social world. On the basis of the results of a body of psychological experiments, Cosmides and Tooby (1992) have concluded that we do not have a general-purpose ability to detect violations of conditional rules ("if $p$ then $q$"), but rather, that human reasoning has been designed to detect violations of conditional rules when they can be interpreted as cheating on a social contract.[39] Cosmides and Tooby have also argued that algorithms governing reasoning about social contracts

---

[38]   Our innate need to seek retribution for injuries we have suffered has been the basis of some of the finest literature over the ages. But scholars of revenge tragedy have noted a great deal more than merely the human desire to seek retribution; among other things they have noted our need also for subtle forms of demonstration: "The root of revenge," writes Kerrigan (1996, pp. 85–86), "is *deik-*, 'indication.' A revenger who (like Hamlet) kills with a goblet and unbaited, venomed rapier, is exacting punishment precisely by making his violence indicate a message." See also Williams (1993) for a discourse on the way shame and the felt necessity of taking tragic actions appear in the epics of the ancient Greeks. It would be argued by evolutionary psychologists that the need we feel for such demonstration itself has had a long-term instrumental role. See below in the text.

[39]   Our general inability to detect violations of rules of the propositional calculus reveals itself in the reasoning fallacies that subjects in numerous experiments have been observed to make. We are prone too to making the Concorde fallacy, namely, our inclination not to regard sunk costs as costs that have been sunk (Arkes 1996).

operate even in unfamiliar situations, that the definitions of cheating that are embodied are not independent of one's perspective (that is, the context matters), and that the algorithms are just as good at computing the cost-benefit representation of a social contract from the perspective of one party as from that of another.[40]

But if people were intrinsically disposed toward imposing sanctions on those who have cheated us, as opposed to being merely strategically so directed, and if this disposition was commonly known, cooperation could be sustained among farsighted people even without having to take recourse to an elaborate structure of metanorms discussed earlier. If it were commonly known that people are so disposed, the threat of sanctions would be credible. If those who had been betrayed became angry, they would *want* to punish betrayers; they would not need a strategic reason for doing so. Communities could then rely in part on people's disposition to act in accordance with a common sense of fairness and justice, and in part on incentives.

### Networks, sanctions, and long-term relationships: examples

The theory of repeated games has been put to use in a wide variety of contexts. Greif (1993), for example, has used it to explain the emergence of a number of institutions that facilitated the growth of trade in medieval Europe. He has shown how the Maghribi traders during the eleventh century in Fustat and across the Mediterranean acted as a collective to impose sanctions on those of their agents who violated their commercial codes. Elsewhere, Greif, Milgrom, and Weingast (1994) have offered an account of the rise of merchant guilds in late medieval Europe. Guilds afforded protection to members against unjustified seizure of their property by city-states. Guilds decided if and when trade embargoes against such states were justified.[41] In a related work, Milgrom, North, and Weingast (1990) point to the role of merchant courts at the Champagne fairs. The courts helped members to impose sanctions on those who had transgressed on agreements.

Enforcement mechanisms based on group reputation has been studied by Greif (1997a). He has argued that the establishment of community responsibility systems in Italy during the twelfth and thirteenth

[40] Given how particular their claims are, it should not be surprising that the Cosmides-Tooby theory is not uncontroversial. For a critique of the way Cosmides and Tooby have interpreted their findings, see Davies, Fetzer and Foster (1995). Their critique, however, was not designed to argue that the theory is necessarily wrong. An alternative theory of human-reasoning schemas is offered by Cheng and Holyoak (1985).
[41] Guilds, in short, are not viewed in these accounts as rent-seeking institutions. This view should be contrasted with the one in Ogilvie's account of producers' guilds in the duchy of Wurttemberg in the early Modern period (Ogilvie 1997).

centuries enabled credit, insurance, and futures markets to be established. Under a community responsibility system transgressions by a party are met by a group (to which the injured belongs) imposing sanctions on another group (to which the transgressor belongs). So it is not an individual who acquires a reputation for honesty, rather, it is his community that acquires it. While there are obvious disadvantages in such systems, there can be one distinct advantage: by creating an incentive for peer monitoring, the system is efficient when transport costs are high and the legal system weak. Greif suggests that the emergence of these markets in turn enabled long-distance trade to develop after a long period of economic decline.

Local common property resources have provided the venue for a number of investigations into communal management systems. In his work on the local commons in the Swiss Alps, Netting (1981) reported that elected village councils marked equivalent shares of standing timber for community members, who in turn drew lots for the shares. Sanctions were imposed on those who took more than their entitlements of firewood. Moreover, in the summer cattle owners were entitled to graze only as many beasts on the communal alp as they were able to feed from their private supply of hay during the preceding winter. This way the total number of animals was kept roughly in line with the fodder potential of the village meadows. Netting traced the origins of such communal schemes in the Alps to the fifteenth century.

But if academics were asked to point to a self-governing and self-regulating institution, they would inevitably think of academia. The institution is driven by norms. They cover such matters as the disclosure of research findings, public acknowledgement of priority, secrecy over work in progress, training of students, refereeing submissions, and peer review. During the academic year I find myself engaged in little else outside norm-driven behavior. The rights, privileges, and obligations are frequently only implicit in academia, but they are fiercely guarded.

Why is academia so norm-driven? One reason has to do with the fact that the output of research is nonrivalrous (one's use of a piece of knowledge does not reduce the amount available for use by others). Moreover, the sort of research the institution seeks to encourage is especially risky and is geared toward the production of the kind of knowledge of use as an input to further research. These features, taken together, explain why academic research is supported by public subsidy and why the institution encourages the practice of "open science," but they do not explain many other aspects of the institution's character. Two other features of research activity help explain some of them.

First, the production of knowledge is subject to serious moral hazard (it is not possible for others to decipher how hard a scientist is working at his task). Secondly, much of the output of research is understandable only by fellow researchers. So a scientist's quality can only be judged by her peers, meaning that both individual and group reputations need to be cultivated. But building a reputation involves both cooperation and competition among scientists, a hallmark of academic life. So a reliance on social norms within academia is an institutional response to the problems societies face in screening what is and what is not productive research, identifying who is and who is not a good researcher, and creating an incentive for scientists to disclose their findings.[42]

To take an example, consider that both individual and group reputation are involved in the ubiquitous practice of "tenure" in academia. How? Since a department's reputation for research enhances members' personal status (inevitably, academia has also encouraged the cult of status), it is in the interest of each that their department employs the best. Department members are generally also more expert than others in the university to screen potential recruits for ability. They may also be best placed to judge their own department's needs (for example, balance of research interests). Security of tenure offers academics the incentive to perform both tasks well. Their own jobs not being under threat, they can afford to select the very best from among those who have applied for posts.[43]

Even as competitive a field of activity as research and development in the modern private sector involves cooperation among rivals. Ruthlessly competitive behavior, such as maintaining total secrecy (worse still, misleading rivals), in regard to one's research findings is known to be wasteful all round. Powell (1990) has shown how scientists in rival firms even in the biotechnology industry share certain kinds of information among themselves, while maintaining secrecy over other matters (see also Powell and Brantley 1992). The balance between disclosure and secrecy is a delicate one, but in any given state of play a common understanding would seem to prevail on the kinds of information members of a network of scientists are expected to disclose if asked, and the kinds one is expected not even to seek from others. In any such environment noncooperation would be costly to the individual scientist. If he refused to share information, or was discovered to have misled others by giving false information about his own findings, he would be denied access to information others share. There is evidence that sharing private findings is not clandestine practice among scientists. People in management are not only aware of it, they positively

---

[42] This line of reasoning has been developed in Dasgupta and David (1987, 1994). David (1998) contains a historical account of the rise of open science in late Renaissance Europe. Stephan (1996) contains a fine account of the economics of science.

[43] See Carmichael (1988). Complementarity between teaching and research activities enables tenure to be a viable practice (Arrow 1962).

encourage their scientists to join the prevailing network. Scientists who are well-connected in this sense are particularly valued. In a market economy at least a part of the benefits of building networks is captured in one's salary.

But to speak of "social norms" and "reciprocity," it is poor countries in the contemporary world that should come to mind first. Among the Kofyar farmers in Nigeria, for example, agricultural land is privatized, but free-range grazing is permitted once the crops have been harvested (Stone, Netting, and Stone 1990). The agricultural labor market is next to nonexistent. The Kofyars have in its stead instituted communal work on individual farms. Although some of this is organized in clubs of 8–10 individuals, there are also community-wide work parties. A household not providing the required quota of labor without good excuse is fined (as it happens, in jars of beer!). If fines are not paid, errant households are punished. Punishment assumes the form of a denial of communal labor; it also involves social ostracism.[44]

In a study of the Kuna tribe in Panama, Howe (1986) described an intricate set of sanctions that are imposed on those who violate norms of behavior designed to protect a common source of fresh water. In a study of sea tenure in northern Brazil, Cordell, and McKean (1986) uncovered a system of codes that have served to protect the fishery. Violations of the codes are met with a range of sanctions that include both shunning and the sabotaging of fishing equipment.

Udry (1994) has offered an illuminating account of reciprocity as practiced among villagers in northern Nigeria in their attempt to smoothen consumption by borrowing and lending. A sample of 400 households in four villages were surveyed. It was found that nearly all credit transactions were either between relatives or between households in the same village. No written contracts were involved, and the agreements did not specify the date of repayment or the amount repaid. Social codes were implicitly followed. Interestingly, the amount repaid was found to depend not only on the amount borrowed, but also on the economic circumstance of the borrower *and* the lender at the time of repayment. This, as Udry (1990) noted in an earlier report, makes credit transactions resemble insurance. It can be shown that if judiciously chosen, mixed credit-insurance schemes provide incentives to those who borrow not to renege on their obligations. This in turn provides incentives to those who are in a position to do so, to lend (Thomas and Worrall 1996). Of course, in village life norms of behavior can be enforced also by such means as the threat of social ostracism, and Udry reports that this too is wielded if

---

[44]  "The price of community is common, institutionalized labour; the withdrawal of community for one of its mutually vulnerable members is social death." (Netting 1997, p. 29).

necessary. It would appear to be inessential, though: less than 10 percent of the loans reported in Udry's study were in default.

Long-term relationships are more likely to persist if they are dense rather than thin, because if a group were to link the various transactions its members might wish to engage in, it would raise individual stakes, so to speak, by making the personal cost of opportunistic behavior in any single relationship that much greater. In India, for example, long-term relation among landlords, laborers, priests, and artisans are dense. Informal markets are often linked.[45]

Civic cooperation does not appear in a vacuum. Of particular relevance today is the potential role of the government and nongovernment organizations in helping to build local institutions through which community members could get to realize the advantages of collective action. Such help involves, among other things, devising clearly defined rules concerning the allocation of burdens and benefits. In their study of migration, property rights and environmental-resource use in a sample of six villages in Northwest India, Chopra and Gulati (1998) found that the effect of a conscious attempt to build local institutions has been powerful. Distress migration out of a village was lower where nongovernment organizations had been at work than in a village where there had been little attempt to create institutions for managing water and pasture land on a communal basis. Significantly, they found that the probability of participation in communal pasture land was higher among villagers who were participating in communal water management schemes than among villagers who were not.

Cooperation enables members to learn about one another's traits—for example, that they are trustworthy. So it is frequently remarked that successful cooperation begets further cooperation. In a study of milk-producers' cooperatives in South Indian villages, Seabright (1997) found that prior history of cooperative institutions in the community is a positive predictor of a cooperative's success.[46] He reports too that cooperation among producers was more successful in those villages in which members had previously organized communal religious festivals, as opposed to villages in which festivals had been segmented by caste.

Seabright's findings parallel those of Putnam (1993) on the comparative economic performance of the 20 provinces of Italy since 1970.

---

[45] In his review of the work in experimental psychology on cooperative behavior, Good (1988) draws this as a central conclusion of the research. See also Granovetter (1985) for an inquiry into the embeddedness of social relationships. The theory of linked games articulates this, on which Spagnolo (1999) is the key reference.
[46] The cooperatives in question require small farmers to sell milk at less than open market prices in return for such collective benefits as finance and infrastructure. For an earlier report on the findings see Seabright (1993).

Putnam found that civic traditions, even as measured in such seemingly flippant indexes as memberships in choral groups and soccer clubs, are a better predictor of economic performance than are past levels of economic development. Modernity, in Putnam's sample, would appear not to be an enemy of civility, quite the contrary. Putnam was also able to trace the roots of civic community far back, to the earliest years of medieval Italy. These two sets of findings offer evidence that trust begets trust.

Putnam (1993, p. 173) writes: "Networks of civic engagement, like the neighborhood associations, choral societies, cooperatives, sports clubs, mass-based parties, and the like ... represent intense horizontal interaction. Networks of civic engagement are an essential form of social capital: the denser such networks in a community, the more likely that its citizens will be able to cooperate for mutual benefit." Our analysis offers an explanation of why it would be so. But the analysis has also revealed a dark side to social capital, missing from much of the literature, that long-term relationships can involve vast inequities. Moreover, the analysis has given hints that even benign long-term relationships within what Putnam calls "horizontal networks" can prove to be an obstacle to economic betterment. They can prevent people from pursuing their own projects and purposes. Later we will confirm this.

### The local commons in poor countries: successes and failures

Communitarian systems of management have protected local resources in many places from the tragedy of the commons. Understandably, this fact has influenced writings on social capital (Feeny et al. 1990; Bromley and others 1992). So it pays to study the successes and failures of such systems. A great many studies are about management practices in poor countries, and so I will concentrate on them.

In poor countries the local commons include grazing lands, threshing grounds, swidden fallows, inland and coastal fisheries, rivers, woodlands, forests, village tanks, and ponds. Are they extensive? As a proportion of total assets, their presence ranges widely across ecological zones. In India the local commons are most prominent in arid regions, mountain regions, and unirrigated areas, they are least prominent in humid regions and river valleys (Agarwal and Narain 1989). There is an economic rationale for this, based on the human desire to reduce risks. An almost immediate empirical corollary is that income inequalities are less in cases in which common-property resources are more prominent. Aggregate income is a different matter, though, and it is the arid and mountain regions and unirrigated areas that are the poorest in this regard. This needs to be borne in mind when public policy is devised. As would be expected, dependence on common-property resources even within dry regions declines with increasing wealth across households.[47]

Jodha (1986, 1995) studied evidence from over 80 villages in 21 dry districts in India to conclude that, among poor families, the proportion of income based directly on the commons is for the most part in the range of 15–25 percent. Moreover, as sources of income, they often complement private-property, which are in the main labor, milch and draft animals, agricultural land, and tools. Common-property resources also provide the rural poor with partial protection in times of unusual economic stress. For landless people they may be the only nonhuman asset at their disposal. A number of resources (such as firewood and water, berries and nuts, medicinal herbs, resin and gum) are the responsibility of women and children.

In a study of 29 villages in Southeastern Zimbabwe, Cavendish (1998, 1999) arrived at even larger estimates: the proportion of income based directly on the commons is 35 percent, the figure for the poorest quintile being 40 percent. A similar picture emerges from Hecht, Anderson, and May (1988), who offered qualitative descriptions of the importance of babassu products among the landless in Maranho, Brazil. The products offer support to the poorest of the poor, most especially the women among them. They are an important source of cash income in the period between agricultural-crop harvests.[48]

Are the local commons managed? In many cases they are, or have been. They are frequently not open-access resources, but are open only to those having historical rights, through kinship ties, community membership, and so forth. Communitarian management of the commons makes connection with social capital viewed as a complex of interpersonal networks. It hints at the basis upon which cooperation has traditionally been built. A large empirical literature has confirmed that resource users in many cases cooperate, on occasion through not undemocratic means.[49]

We noted earlier that the distribution of benefits and burdens in a long-term relationship would be expected to depend on how the users would have fared if they had not reached an agreement (as in figure 1). In cases in which users are symmetrically placed, distributions would

---

[47] In his work on South Indian villages, Seabright (1997) has shown that producers' cooperatives, unconnected with the management of local commons, are also more prevalent in the drier districts.

[48] For a similar picture in the West African forest zone, see Falconer (1990).

[49] Ostrom (1990, chapter 3) and Baland and Platteau (1996, chapter 10) contain much evidence. The former ranges over a number of long-enduring common-property resources in Nepal, the youngest of which has been found to be 100 years old, the oldest more than 1,000 years old. The latter contains accounts of not only successful management practices, but also of some in which a commons remained unmanaged.

be expected to be symmetric—a subtle matter to devise if the resource is heterogeneous. Rotation of access to the best site is an example of how this can be achieved. It is practiced in coastal fisheries, fuel reserves in forest land, and fodder sites in the grasslands. Rotation enables users to get a fair shake.

But if there are substantial differences among community members in the ownership of private property, entitlements to the products of the commons would be expected to reflect those inequalities.[50] For example, among Kofyar farmers in Nigeria obligatory labor on both communal projects and individual farms is drawn equally from all member households, but this benefits large cultivators disproportionately. It is also all too possible that the relationships are exploitative (as in figure 2). We noted earlier, for example, that in India, access to the commons is often restricted to the privileged (for example, caste Hindus), who are also among the bigger landowners. In many parts of the poor world women are systematically excluded from such networks of relationships as those involving credit, insurance, and savings. Rampant inequities exist too in patron-client relationships.

Site-specific information about the local ecology is held by those who work on the commons. Local participatory democracy offers a mechanism by which relevant local knowledge can inform the design of public policy.[51] As women are often the ones to work on the commons, they are an important repository of knowledge. But they are frequently the ones who are shut out of the local political arena. The State apparatus can be helpful here, by enabling women to participate in the democratic process, and by ensuring that local decisions are made in an open way. It would help prevent local economic powers from maintaining control. Good management of the commons requires more than mere local participation; it needs enlightened government (third-party) engagement as well.

It is worth distinguishing, once again, between verifiability and observability of actions, and between reaching a collective agreement and ensuring that the agreement is kept. The State may be able to guide the workings of local democracy even when it cannot enforce agreements. It would be able to do so if the costs of monitoring participatory democracy at work were low and the costs of verifying that agreements have been broken were high. This tension, the simultaneous need for increased decentralization in rural decision-making and for government involvement in ensuring that the seats of local decisions are not usurped by the powerful, poses a central dilemma in the political economy of rural development. It is a dilemma because of the conflicting nature of

---

[50]  McKean (1992) and Ostrom and Gardner (1993) have stressed this point.
[51]  On this see Esman and Uphoff (1984), Wignaraja (1990), Ghai and Vivian (1992), and Ostrom (1992, 1996).

underlying incentives: the practice of democratic decision-making at the village level may expose government to a greater pressure to be accountable. But the guardian is itself subject to a problem of incentives. This is a situation in which a free, competitive media (namely, the press, radio, and television) have an instrumental role to play.[52]

The local commons matter greatly to the poorest of the rural poor, who happen, generally speaking, to be the landless. When the commons erode, such people are often at risk of economic disenfranchisement even if the aggregate economy enjoys growth. In recent years this has been documented extensively for the poorest regions of the Indian subcontinent (C.S.E. 1982, 1985; B. Agarwal 1986). This heightened vulnerability of the poorest, which is often more real than perceived, is the cause of some of the greatest tragedies in contemporary societies.

Why should the local commons have eroded in those cases in which they previously had been managed in a sustained manner? A recent intellectual tradition attempts to provide an explanation: the reason the poor degrade their local resource base is that their poverty forces them to discount future incomes at unusually high rates (Bardhan 1996, p. 62). Unless the poor were so impoverished as to be facing starvation, this argument alone does not amount to much. Poverty, in any case, is not a recent phenomenon. If the thesis were correct, many of the local commons that have survived would have disappeared long ago. On the basis of responses from rural households in Indonesia, Zambia, and Ethiopia to questionnaires on preferences for current over future consumption, Holden, Shiferaw, and Wik (1998) infer in their interesting paper that the respondents discounted their future consumption rates greatly, sometimes even as high as 100 percent per year.

This is one empirical study on the question; there are not many others. In any case, such high rates are difficult to interpret. If the natural growth rate of local environmental resources were as high as even 10 percent per year, there would be a 90 percent gap between rates of return on foregone consumption and consumption rates of discount. But such a large gap would be expected to result in extremely high rates of resource degradation, far higher than the rates reported in the studies with which I am familiar (for example, Cleaver and Schreiber 1994). One possible way in which the figures can be reconciled is that extracting resources requires labor. Even so, a gap of 90 percent between natural

---

[52] These matters are discussed more fully in Dasgupta (1993, chapter 17, 1996). See also Bardhan and Mookherjee (1998) for a mathematical formalization of a similar tension. They consider a case in which the central government wants to invest in a local project. To permit the locals to make decisions relating to the investment is desirable because many matters of importance are known only locally. But there is a weakness with decentralization, in that local bosses can usurp the local decision-making process.

growth rates and consumption discount rates would imply serious labor scarcity (for example, high disutility of labor). This does not seem to ring true for Sub-Saharan Africa and Indonesia.

Poverty can be a cause of high discounting if the poor face binding credit constraints (Deaton 1991; Dasgupta 1993). Since credit constraints are symptomatic of institutional failure, I consider a different explanation for the erosion of the local commons: low private rates of return from the resource base owing to the failure of institutions.[53]

There are many ways in which institutional failure manifests itself. Civil wars (more generally, uncertain property rights) are a prime example, of course. It does not serve much purpose investing in a resource base if there is a high chance of it being usurped or destroyed by others. In a subsequent section on "creating networks" we will study a mechanism that weakens even the disposition to cooperate as the resource base becomes more valuable in the wake of economic development. Moreover, cooperation can also break down (or not be initiated) if migration accompanies the development process. As opportunities outside the village improve, those with lesser ties (for example, young men) are more likely to take advantage of them and make a break with those customary obligations that are enshrined in prevailing social norms. Those with greater attachments would perceive this, and so infer that the expected benefits from complying with agreements is now lower. Either way, norms of reciprocity could be expected to break down, making certain groups of people (for example, women and the elderly) worse off. Earlier I noted this possibility in the context of formal models of long-term relationships. This is a case in which improved institutional performance elsewhere (for example, growth of markets in the economy at large) has an adverse effect on the functioning of a local, nonmarket institution (Dasgupta and Mäler 1991; Dasgupta 1993).

Rapid population growth can itself be a trigger if institutional practices are unable to adapt to changing economic circumstances. In Cote d'Ivoire, for example, growth in rural population has in recent years been accompanied by increased deforestation and reduced fallows. Biomass production has declined, as has agricultural productivity. Lopez (1998) estimates that income at the village level has declined by some 15 percent.

The local commons also erode because of unreflective public policies. Sadly, there are also direct causes, such as predatory governments and thieving aristocracies. For example, Binswanger (1991) has shown that in Brazil the exemption from taxation of virtually all agricultural income and the enactment of laws that see logging as proof of land occupancy have provided strong incentives for the rich to acquire and convert forest land. Binswanger argues that the subsidy the government

---

[53] This thesis has been explored more fully in Dasgupta and Mäler (1991) and Dasgupta (1993, 1996, 1997).

has provided to the private sector to engage in deforestation has been so large that a reduction in the activity is in Brazil's interests, and not merely in the interest of the rest of the world.[54]

Corrupt practice by rulers is commonplace. For example, when Chambers (1988) studied institutions governing canal irrigation in South Asia, he discovered that political leaders there had routinely auctioned jobs to irrigation engineers. Many of these jobs are posts of short tenure. But as they offer a scope for earning illegal income (for example, from contractors and farmers), they are much in demand. And Colchester (1995) has recounted that political representatives of forest-dwellers in Sarawak, Malaysia, have routinely given logging licenses to members of the state legislature. Primary forests in Sarawak are expected to be depleted within the next few years.

Even well-meaning economic aid can prove harmful. In a report on communal irrigation systems in Nepal, Ostrom (1996) observed that originally the canals had consisted of temporary, stone-trees-and-mud headworks, constructed and managed by the farmers themselves. Canal systems that had been improved by the construction of permanent headworks were found frequently to be in worse repair and to be delivering less water to tail-enders than previously. Ostrom also reported that water allocation was more equitable in traditional farm-management systems than in modern systems managed by external agencies, such as government and foreign donors. She has estimated from her sample that agricultural productivity is higher in traditional systems.

Ostrom has an explanation for this. She argues that unless it is accompanied by countermeasures, the construction of permanent headworks alters the relative bargaining positions of the head- and tail-enders. Head-enders now do not need the labor of tail-enders to maintain the canal system. So the new sharing scheme involves even less water for tail-enders. Head-enders gain from the permanent structures, but tail-enders lose disproportionately.[55]

Resource allocation rules practiced at the local level are not infrequently overturned by central fiat. A number of States in the Sahel imposed rules that in effect destroyed communal management practices in the forests. Villages ceased to have authority to enforce sanctions on those who violated locally instituted rules of use. State authority turned the local commons into free-access resources.[56]

---

[54] In a wider discussion of the conversion of forests into ranches in the Amazon basin, Schneider (1995) has shown that the construction of roads through the forests has been a potent force. Roads have made forest resources economically more valuable.

[55] For other examples in which projects designed to benefit the recipients of aid have been destructive, see Coward (1985), Chambers (1988) and Ascher and Healy (1990).

[56] See Thomson, Feeny, and Oakerson (1986) and Baland and Platteau (1996).

All this is to say that resource allocation mechanisms that do not take advantage of dispersed information, that are insensitive to hidden (and often not-so-hidden) economic and ecological interactions, that do not take the long view, and that do not give a sufficiently large weight to the claims of the poorest within rural populations, are not to be commended. The examples tell us something about the way communitarian solutions to resource allocation problems break down and are displaced by other allocation mechanisms, some of which are worse. But this does not mean that communitarian management systems are inevitably efficient, or that they themselves may not delay the appearance of more efficient resource allocation mechanisms. We will study these matters subsequently.

### Dispositions, beliefs, and economic performance: the trust game

So far I have elaborated on the role social norms play in enabling trans-actions to take place. Some involve long-term relationships. But people are known to transact with one another without recourse to social norms. The most prominent examples are formal markets, which rely greatly on the enforcement of contracts by the State. To be sure, even market exchanges are often based in part on reputation, something firms work hard to acquire. Firms with a good reputation enjoy a competitive edge. As resource allocation mechanisms, institutions are blends; they rarely assume a pure form.

Perhaps the most delicate mechanism on which agreements can be based relies on people trusting one another to fulfill their obligations simply because people have a disposition to be honest. It is a delicate mechanism because it relies not only on people having prosocial dispositions, but also on their beliefs about the extent to which such dispositions are prevalent. The way in which the two are related and the way in which they in turn influence behavior is not at all simple, so our grasp of this mechanism is hopelessly inadequate. Nevertheless, we need to explore what little we do know if we are to understand the role of social capital in economic development. This section and the following six are devoted to this matter. The analysis I can offer is very tentative.

Consider the following example:[57]

There is a large group of individuals, who in every period meet in random pairs to engage in a transaction. Each party at each encounter can choose one of two courses of action: X (transact honestly) and Y (cheat a bit). To have an interesting problem, I suppose that each party chooses in ignorance of the other's choice. Imagine now that each person would rather choose X if the individual she encounters were to choose X (not only does one feel shame in not being honest when dealing with honest behavior, the overall transaction is also less productive

---

[57]  Taken from Dasgupta (1988).

if one has cheated), but would rather choose Y if the individual she encounters were to choose Y (it is unpleasant being a sucker). Assume next that each party prefers the situation in which both choose X to both of them choosing Y (each would rather experience bilateral honesty than bilateral cheating, not only because honesty is nice, but also because the transaction is more profitable).

Imagine that, even though they are indistinguishable, there are two types of individuals in the population: type 1 and type 2. The possibility that a type-1 person will have an honest disposition is greater than that for a type-2 person. In table 1 the payoffs of a type-1 person are presented. She is assumed to choose a row (the party with whom she is transacting is assumed to choose a column). In table 2 the payoffs of a type-2 person are presented, and he is assumed to choose a row (the party with whom he is transacting is assumed to choose a column). The payoff matrices are the same, but for the northwest cell. The difference captures the idea that someone of type 1 has a greater disposition to be honest than someone of type 2. Finally, we take it that people choose on the basis of their expected payoffs. I will call this the "trust game."

<table>
<tr><td colspan="3">TABLE 1: PAYOFFS OF TYPE-1 PERSON</td></tr>
<tr><td></td><td>X</td><td>Y</td></tr>
<tr><td>X</td><td>30</td><td>5</td></tr>
<tr><td>Y</td><td>5</td><td>10</td></tr>
</table>

*Source:* Dasgupta (1988).

<table>
<tr><td colspan="3">TABLE 2: PAYOFFS OF TYPE-2 PERSON</td></tr>
<tr><td></td><td>X</td><td>Y</td></tr>
<tr><td>X</td><td>20</td><td>5</td></tr>
<tr><td>Y</td><td>5</td><td>10</td></tr>
</table>

*Source:* Dasgupta (1988).

Here I want to avoid the use of social norms as a coordinating device. So I will assume that the population is so large that when two people meet at random they meet for the first time. Imagine too that no one's record of past actions is known to anyone else. In these circumstances what should one do when randomly meeting a person? Clearly, his best course of action depends on what he thinks the other person will do. But what thought should one rationally entertain?

Consider first someone of type 1. Her best choice would be X if she were to regard the chance that the other person would choose X to be in excess of $1/6$, but her best choice would be Y if this chance was less than $1/6$.[58] Now consider someone of type 2. His best choice would be X if he were to regard the chance that the other person would choose X to be in excess of $1/4$, but his best choice would be Y

---

[58] To confirm this, let the chance be $p$. Then for someone of type 1 to be indifferent between X and Y, $p$ must satisfy the condition $30p + 5(1–p) = 5p + 10(1–p)$, which yields $p = 1/6$.

if this chance was less than $1/4$.[59] Let the proportion of type-1 persons in the population be P. This is taken to be common knowledge. Let us now study equilibrium behavior.

Notice that if each person expects all others to choose X, everyone would choose X, whereas if each person expects all others to choose Y, everyone would choose Y. In short, the outcomes in which everyone chooses X and those in which everyone chooses Y are both social equilibria. The role of expectations is crucial: if everyone were to believe that everyone else would act honestly, then everyone would act honestly, whereas if everyone were to expect everyone else to cheat a bit, everyone would cheat a bit. Notice though that everyone would enjoy a higher payoff in the honest equilibrium than in the cheating equilibrium.[60]

What of disequilibrium beliefs? Consider a simple (and possibly naive!) learning rule, according to which people in each period believe the behavior they are likely to encounter to be the previous period's economy-wide average behavior (assuming such macrodata were publicly known) and then choose to behave on the basis of such expectations. This kind of behavioral adjustment is known as "best-response dynamics." It is simple to confirm that under this dynamics both equilibria are locally, asymptotically stable, in that a slight departure from either set of equilibrium-beliefs brings beliefs back to equilibrium. So if people were cynical about one another ("I cannot really trust the person I encounter to deal honestly with me"), everyone would be worse off than if people were to trust one another sufficiently. Moreover, if the X-equilibrium were to prevail, an observer would conclude that the society in question had developed a culture of honesty. Contrariwise, if the Y-equilibrium were to prevail, the observer would conclude that this otherwise same society had sunk into a culture of dishonesty.[61]

The population mix P has not entered the analysis so far. It has an interesting role to play if it lies between $1/6$ and $1/4$. Consider any figure in this range. It is easy to confirm that, in addition to the two equilibria we have already identified, there is a third, in which each person of type 1 chooses X and each of type 2, Y. It is common knowledge in this equilibrium that type-1 people behave honestly and type-2 people cheat. But since at no encounter does either party know with whom they are dealing, behavior according to type sustains itself. One can check

---

[59]  $1/6$ being less than $1/4$, a person of type 1 needs less persuasion to choose X.

[60]  There is in fact a third equilibrium. It involves mixed strategies, one for each type. However, it is of no interest to us because it is unstable (see the section on "conformism and contagion" below).

[61]  Variations of this model have been studied in a number of recent papers in which the underlying game is referred to as a "coordination game." See Foster and P. Young (1990), Ellison (1993), Kandori, Mailath, and Rob (1993), H. P. Young (1993), Matsui and Matsuyama (1995) and Burdzy, Frankel, and Pauzner (1997). In the section on "culture" below, I will provide an account of these works.

that this equilibrium too is locally, asymptotically stable under the best-response dynamics. Note as well that if this mixed-equilibrium were to prevail, an observer would conclude that the society in question consists of two interacting "cultural types," each behaving in its own manner. Imagine then that the observer asks a random sample of people if they trust others to behave honestly in their dealings. If the respondents were to answer on the basis of their previous period's experience only, a proportion P of the sample would say that they trusted others (those who had encountered honesty), while the remaining proportion (1–P) would say that they did not.

The example on its own cannot, of course, tell us which equilibrium would prevail in the long run. For this we need more information, for example, an initial set of expectations. We have in any event considered a very special system of belief formation, in which each period's experience is expected to be the previous period's average experience. One would expect the dynamics of beliefs to be more complex.[62]

It is instructive to calculate the economy's average payoff in each of the equilibria we have just studied, assuming that payoffs are interpersonally comparable. In the X-equilibrium, in which all behave honestly, average payoff can be shown to be $(10P + 20)$, whereas in the Y-equilibrium, in which everyone cheats, average payoff is 10. If P lies in the interval $(1/6, 1/4)$, of interest is the mixed equilibrium, in which type-1 persons choose X and type-2 persons choose Y. The economy's average payoff is $(30P^2 - 10P + 10)$. This increases with P in the interval $(1/6, 1/4)$, which means that the greater is the proportion of honest people in the population, the greater is the economy's average level of payoff.

La Porta and others (1997) have constructed a measure of trust in societies from the World Values Survey, which in the early 1980s and again in the early 1990s surveyed 1,000 randomly selected individuals in each of 40 countries and asked them, among other questions, if generally speaking they would say that most people could be trusted or that they could not be too careful in dealing with people. The measure of trust adopted by La Porta and his colleagues was the percentage of people who replied that most people could indeed be trusted (correlation across countries between trust in the 1980s and in the 1990s was found to be a high 0.91).[63] The authors found that, controlling for gross domestic product (GDP) per head, trust is positively correlated with judicial efficiency, tax compliance, bureaucratic quality, civic participation, the relative success of large firms, the infant survival rate, educational achievement, and growth in GDP per head—and negatively cor-

---

[62] Fudenberg and Levine (1998) is an account of what is currently understood on the dynamics of learning rules.
[63] The highest "trust" countries in the sample, which consists predominantly of European countries, are in Scandinavia, many of the lowest are in Latin America.

related with government corruption. In a more detailed regression analysis Knack and Keefer (1997) have reported a similar finding from the World Values Survey data. They have found that, controlling for income per head in 1980, primary- and secondary-school enrollment rates in 1960, and the price of investment goods in 1980, growth in GDP per head during the period 1980–1992 was higher in countries in the sample in which people trusted one another more.[64]

No one should claim that these cross-country findings reflect comparisons of the mixed equilibrium with different values of P in the model we have just studied, but it is a case in which theory and empirics are not pointing in different directions. In the social sciences this should not be taken lightly. Of particular interest is an additional finding in Knack and Keefer (1997), that the "impact" of trust on growth of GDP per head during 1980–1992 was higher in countries that were poorer at the start of the period. This is consistent with one of the hypotheses I have been exploring in this essay, that interpersonal trust can be a substituted for confidence in the ability of formal markets to function adequately.

But leaving aside all the recognized problems associated with cross-country statistics and multivariate analysis, there are problems of interpretation in the findings that cannot be swept aside. The World Values Survey does not identify the reasons why the degree of trust in each of the sample countries is what it is. Nor do La Porta and his colleagues, for example, reflect much on what the data they have collated may be trying to tell us. They regard their index of trust to be an independent variable in what is a string of multivariate analyses. Moreover, they take government corruption to be the *dependent* variable in one of their regression equations. This is puzzling. For suppose we were to step outside the extreme confines of the trust game as the laboratory in which to interpret their findings. Then it could be that the rule of law is more reliably applied in countries where trust among citizens is greater, and is the reason why it is greater. As the trust game demonstrates, trust in a society is not ex-

---

[64] Writing by $g(y)$ the percentage rate of change in GDP per head over the period 1980–1992, and by $x_1$, $x_2$, $x_3$, $x_4$, and $x_5$ for GDP per head in 1960, primary-school enrollment in 1960, secondary-school enrollment in 1960, the price of investment goods in 1980, and the index of trust, respectively, the equation Knack and Keefer (1997) estimated by using the ordinary-least-square technique was:

$$g(y) = a + b_1x_1 + b_2x_2 + b_3x_3 + b_4x_4 + b_5x_5 + å$$

where å is an independent random variable reflecting measurement errors, and $a$ and $b_i$ (i = 1,2,3,4,5) are constants. That one would expect estimates of $b_2$ and $b_3$ to be positive and $b_4$ to be negative is obvious enough. However, theories of economic growth suggest that other things being the same, poorer countries would be expected to grow faster. That is why $x_1$ is included in the regression equation, and also why one expects the estimate of $b_1$ to be negative. Each of these expectations was confirmed in the data. The point of the Knack-Keefer exercise was, of course, to show that the estimate for $b_5$ is positive and significant.

ogenously given even if people's dispositions are. Nor can trust be created from vacuum. It may be that people trust one another because they are aware of the benefits long-term relationships enable all to enjoy (we studied this in the previous five sections), but it could also be because of good governance on the part of the State (for example, lack of corruption in enforcing the law of contracts). In the latter case the background institution responsible for trust would have little to do with social capital as generally understood.

It can be argued of course that the accumulation of social capital is a prerequisite for good governance, a point stressed by Putnam (1993) in his now classic work on Italy. But when one tries to pin down the notion of social capital, as Putnam did by measuring associational activities, such as membership in choral societies and football clubs, one risks running into problems in other data sets, some of which have revealed that civic associations can be another name for lobbyists and rent-seekers and, therefore, not so good for governance and economic performance (Olson 1982; Knack and Keefer 1997). At this point I am trying to give as much scope as possible to the notion that social capital is an engine of economic development. So I am interpreting empirical findings in terms of the ingredients of social capital. But it is as well to appreciate that the interpretations could be otherwise. Later we will explore them.

## Conformism and contagion

The trust game has shown that an economy can harbor equilibrium allocations in which different types of people behave in the same way (the X- or Y-equilibrium), as well as those in which they behave differently (the mixed equilibrium). The moral is banal: we should distinguish values from disposition, disposition from preferences, preferences from beliefs, and beliefs from actions. So a general question arises: when people conform in their behavior, why do they?

### Why conform?

Earlier we studied a number of environments in which people discover a personal need to go along with the rest. Norms of conduct (be they personal or social) provided the basis on which influence was seen to work. But there is another class of processes leading to conformity. These operate when people accept information from others as evidence of what the world is like. This influence can arise in a particularly subtle form when people are not able to learn directly what others know, but try to infer it by observing their behavior (Banerjee 1992; Bikhchandani, Hirshleifer, and Welch 1992, 1998). As they are frequently confounding, it is not a trivial matter to keep the two sets of reasons for conformity apart in experimental studies. But analytically they are distinct.

It has proven hard to obtain formal evidence of conformity, so there is not much of it. The famous experiments of Sherif and Asch, in which subjects were set to perform visual discrimination tasks (for example, the task of comparing lengths without the aid of a measuring rod), showed not only that people are more influenced by others' opinions when the facts in question are more uncertain, but also that people may conform simply to avoid censure, ridicule, and social disapproval (Hogg and Vaughan 1995, chapter 6). Smith and Bond (1993) reviewed a number of such studies. They classified the findings in a way that implies that conformity is lower in the "individualistic" cultures thought to embody North American and North and West European societies than in the "collectivist" (or "communitarian") cultures widely taken to represent societies in Africa, Asia, Oceania, and South America. This may appear intuitively plausible to many. To me, however, it hints at how difficult it is to separate various types of conformism, how problematic it is to talk of conformism unless the domain of behavior over which conformism is thought to prevail has been specified. The point is that a society could be individualistic in some respects even while it is deeply conformist in others.[65]

People conform in their purchase of such goods as the telephone, the fax machine, and the personal computer because there are interpersonal complementarities in their use-value (my use for a telephone increases as the number of others who rely on telephones increases, and so on; Farrell and Saloner 1985; Katz and Shapiro 1985). Other patterns of conformism could be attributable to shared disposition. Thus, for example, surveys in a number of countries where an "individualistic" culture is thought to prevail have revealed that substantial growth in per capita income has not translated into any significant increase in reported happiness (Easterlin 1974; Scitovsky 1976; Oswald 1997). A natural conclusion to draw from this is that in these cultures personal happiness depends on one's income or expenditure relative to the mean income or expenditure of some reference group (for example, per capita national income; Easterlin 1974). But if this were true, and if people acted in such ways as to increase their personal happiness, one of two broad types of outcome would arise. To see why and how, imagine that people are similar both in endowments and motivations. Then if it is relatively easy for everyone to earn more income (because of, for instance, increases in labor productivity owing to technological change), the individual urge to beat the Joneses would result in a race in which everyone strives to earn more than the average. So long as the rate of technological progress remains high, the race continues. Some would be ahead for a while, only to be overtaken by others, who in turn would be overtaken by yet oth-

---

[65] Goody (1996, 1998) offers wide-ranging evidence of this in the context of Europe and Eurosia.

ers, and so forth. This is the hallmark of a "rat race" and is one possibility. Another occurs when it proves really hard for people to earn more because productivity growth is low, perhaps nil. In this case the economy equilibrates quickly at a distribution of income in which everyone earns something that is close to the low, average income of their reference group.

To formalize these ideas, consider a situation in which an individual's most-preferred level of personal income is an increasing function of the economy's per capita income (y). This is depicted in figure 3 by the curve ABCDEF.[66] We are to imagine that in each period each individual gets to learn of the previous period's average income level in the economy (something that may be possible in the presence of mass communication) and proceeds to earn his most-preferred level of income, which is to say that the economy in disequilibrium adjusts in accordance with "best-response dynamics." In figure 3 there are two stable equilibrium income levels, $\tilde{y}_1$ and $\tilde{y}_3$—one low, the other high. $\tilde{y}_2$ is an unstable equilibrium lying between $\tilde{y}_1$ and $\tilde{y}_3$. If, for whatever reason, initial income per head were slightly greater than $\tilde{y}_2$, the economy would experience a period of growth as it moved toward $\tilde{y}_3$. If, however, initial income per head were less than $\tilde{y}_2$, the economy would travel to $\tilde{y}_1$ and settle there.

It may be asked why technological change is rapid in one society and negligible in the other. A visiting social scientist might remark that since the spirit of enterprise and progress prevails in the society galloping toward $\tilde{y}_3$, but does not in the one resting at $\tilde{y}_1$, there must be differences of motivation in the two societies, perhaps even in their national character. But, as the two economies are not intrinsically different, the remark would mislead: the economies differ in their behavior because entrepreneurs in one expect demand for their products to grow, and discover that their expectations are self-fulfilling; whereas in the other they expect demand to stagnate, and discover that their expectations are self-fulfilling. Differences in behavior occur because the opportunities in the two communities differ, current differences having been brought about by earlier experiences, perhaps even caused by accidental differences in experience. To be sure, the society comprising "enter-

---

[66] The way I have phrased the matter may seem odd: why should a person's most-preferred income level be finite? The answer is that there is a cost to earning more (for example, additional sweat). The model being described is in a reduced form; it implicitly takes such costs into account when estimating the most-preferred income level. To illustrate, imagine that people are identical. Let $v(y_i, y)$ denote individual $i$'s scalar index of happiness (net of the cost of earning income), where $y_i$ is $i$'s personal income and $y$ is per capita income. Easterlin's hypothesis in a generalized form is that $\partial v/\partial y_i > 0$ and $\partial v/\partial y < 0$. In the text I am making an additional assumption: $\partial^2 v/\partial y \partial y_i > 0$. It implies that $i$'s most preferred income level is an increasing function of per capita income (figure 3). In a discussion of people's desire for durable consumption goods, Duesenberry (1949) christened this the "demonstration effect."

FIGURE 3: INFLUENCES ON CONFORMITY

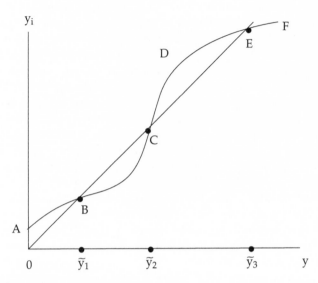

*Source:* Author.

prising people" will eventually settle down at $\tilde{y}_3$ (if nothing else, ecological constraints would be expected to bring long-run growth to a halt).
Despite this, living standards in the two societies would be vastly different, even if reported happiness were discovered to be pretty much
the same.[67]

Assuming that personal happiness counts socially, both economies would be regarded as suffering from collective inefficiency: the
benefit to someone from an increase in their income or expenditure would
exceed the benefit to society as a whole. The resource waste at $\tilde{y}_3$ would
be especially discernable, but in both places people would gain if a suitable income or expenditure tax were introduced.[68]

*Local conformity and the prospects of contagion*

Proximity matters. Face-to-face encounters are different from letters,
telephone conversations, and communication over the Internet. To observe a person's behavior at close quarters is not the same as hearing or

---

[67] Aghion and Howitt (1998) contains models of endogenous technological
change with multiple equilibria. Keynes' reading of short-run involuntary unemployment (Keynes 1936), that it can be caused by depressed expectations, is
also similar to the argument in the text. Cooper and John (1988) have formalized
the idea. In the text, we are concerned with long-term phenomena.
[68] Frank (1997) elaborates on this point.

reading about it. Studies in applied psychology have shown that empathy in many spheres is strongest when the interchange is face to face. This applies regarding influence as well, be it benign or malign (Rutter 1984; Sally 1995; Frey and Bohnet 1996; Good 1996). So, in many spheres of activity, especially those involving spatially localized interactions, the desire to conform with others would amount to regarding such others as being those in one's neighborhood. But localities overlap. The question is whether conformity spreads relentlessly or remains geographically contained. While in the latter case society would become segmented into distinct neighborhoods, each with its own behavior pattern, in the former case a single pattern of behavior would take over the whole of society. Models of "contagion" capture these issues. Those in which behavior is contained offer the beginnings of an explanation of why poverty, education, and crime display high variance across space, in many cases across neighborhoods within cities.[69] Those in which behavior spreads provide an account of how certain fads and fashions can become an epidemic, while other patterns of behavior die or are stillborn under selection pressure.[70]

Kandori, Mailath, and Rob (1993) have studied best-response dynamics in an extreme version of the trust game: they assume that there is only one type of person in the economy (for example, type 1). They then add the qualification that in each period each person fails to choose his best response with a small probability—because people like to experiment, perhaps, or because they are capable of making a mistake. This proved to be an ingenious modeling device in their study, because the economy was found to converge to the honest equilibrium (the X-equilibrium) no matter what the starting distribution of behavior happened to be. Honest behavior spreads and the Y-equilibrium gets eliminated under selection pressure. Even a vanishingly small probability of making a mistake ensures that honest behavior will become entrenched.[71]

Ellison (1993) explored an alternative dynamics for the same model. He took it that in each period individuals know the previous period's average behavior of only a finite number of their neighbors, not that of the entire economy. This could be because each person interacts only

---

[69] See, for example, Bernheim (1994), Anderlini and Ianni (1996), Glaeser, Sacerdote and Scheinkman (1996), and Eshel, Samuelson, and Shaked (1998).

[70] See, for example, Schelling (1978), Banerjee (1992), Bikhchandani, Hirshleifer, and Welch (1992, 1998), Kandori, Mailath, and Rob (1993), H. P. Young (1993), Ellison (1993), and Bernheim (1994). The study of cellular automata has spawned a parallel literature on contagion (Holland 1995). For an excellent commentary on contagion models, see Brock and Durlauf (1999).

[71] H. P. Young (1993) independently obtained the same convergence result, but in his paper individuals were assumed to choose their current actions on the basis of their own past choices, rather than on the choices of others in the previous period.

with his neighbors. Ellison also found that the economy converges to the honest equilibrium. But surprisingly, the speed of convergence was found to be orders of magnitude *higher*. Contagion spreads much faster if imitative behavior is founded on local rather than global influence. The intuition behind the result is that as interactions are local, honest behavior is able to gain a foothold somewhere; and since neighborhoods overlap, the behavior is able to spread. I do not know whether the result generalizes in any interesting direction.

One would think that people conform to the prevailing norm especially when it comes to reproductive behavior. It has often been remarked in the context of Sub-Saharan Africa that procreation is not only a private matter, it is also a social obligation, influenced by both family experiences and cultural presumptions (Goody 1976; Fortes 1978). So it is tempting to seek evidence of imitative behavior in reproduction. The working hypothesis I have adopted in this essay is that if a norm prevails, it should be interpreted as equilibrium behavior. Conformism in reproductive behavior would arise if, for example, each individual's most desired family size were an increasing function of the average family size in the community (Dasgupta 1993, chapter 12).

To see this, let us return to figure 3 and reinterpret $y$ to mean the average fertility rate of a community. The curve ABCDEF would now denote the fertility rate a typical household seeks to attain in response to the prevailing fertility rate in the community. Depending on its initial value, the fertility rate would adjust to one of two values, $\bar{y}_1$ and $\bar{y}_3$— one low, the other high. Even though the two communities are not intrinsically different, they would appear very different, one being significantly more pronatalist than the other. Moreover, as externalities are inherent in imitative behavior, both communities would have cause to seek remedies. Reproductive externalities are a reason why societies can in principle get locked into serious population problems.

Demographers have made only a few attempts to discover evidence of imitative behavior—that is, behavior guided in part by an "attention to others." The two exceptions with which I am familiar are Easterlin, Pollak, and Wachter (1980) and Watkins (1990). The former studied intergenerational influence in a sample of families in the United States and reported a positive link between the number of children with whom someone had been raised and the number of children they themselves had.

In her study of demographic change in Western Europe over the period 1870–1960, Watkins (1990) showed that variations in fertility and nuptiality within each country has declined. She found that in 1870, before the large-scale declines in marital fertility had begun in most areas of Western Europe, demographic behavior varied greatly within countries. Provinces (for example, counties and cantons) within a country differed considerably, even while variations within provinces was low. There were thus spatial clumps within each country, suggesting the importance of local communities. In 1960 variations within each country were less than what they were in 1870. Watkins explains this in terms of increases in the geographical reach national governments have enjoyed over the 90 years in question.

There is one recent finding that could also be pointing to imitative behavior. Starting in 1977, 70 "treatment" villages were serviced by a massive program of birth control in Matlab Thana, Bangladesh, while 79 "control" villages were offered no such special service. The contraceptive prevalence in the treatment villages increased from 7 to 33 percent within 18 months, and then more gradually to a level of 45 percent by 1985. The prevalence also increased in the control villages, but only to 16 percent in 1985. Fertility rates in both sets of villages declined, but at different speeds, and by 1980 the difference in fertility rates had reached a figure of 1.5, even though there had been no difference to begin with (Hill 1992). If we were to assume that even though influence travels, geographical proximity matters, we could explain why the control villages followed those "under treatment," but did not follow them all the way. The contagion did not spread completely.

## Culture

In his famous work on the influence of culture on economic development, Weber (1930) took a community's culture to be its shared values and dispositions. Studies as widely cast as Weber's cannot easily be summarized, but the causal mechanism Weber himself would seem to have favored in his work on the Protestant ethic and the spirit of capitalism leads from religion, through political culture, to institutions, and so to economic performance.

Using culture to explain economics has not been popular among social scientists in the postwar period.[72] But there has been a recent revival. Schama (1987) has drawn a portrait of civic culture among the Dutch burghers of the late sixteenth century to explain the remarkable economic prosperity the Dutch enjoyed during the following hundred years or so. For Schama, the burgher was a citizen first and *homo economicus* second. His thesis is that the obligations of civic life conditioned the opportunities of prosperity, so that if any one obsession linked together the burghers' several concerns with family, the fortunes of state, the power of their empire and the condition of their poor, their standing in history and the uncertainties of geography; it was the moral ambiguity of good fortune. Schama's account of Dutch prosperity turns on the way the nation's burghers coped with that ambiguity.

---

[72] For a spirited critique of Weber on grounds that his inferences are biased because he truncated time-series data, see Geddes (1990).

Since Weber the most ambitious appeal to culture to understand differences in economic performance has been Landes (1998), who asks why it is that since the middle of the sixteenth century countries in northern Europe managed to race ahead of several others elsewhere that had been seemingly better placed at the time. Technological progress and its rapid diffusion among populations was the key to that success. But the progress itself needs explaining. The one Landes offers is distinctive, because it gives importance to the evolution (or a lack of it) of different types of attitudes and beliefs in various regions of the world. Landes argues that these differences gave rise to institutional differences, which help explain why some countries became winners, while others enjoyed a brief period of success before losing to the winners, while yet others merely suffered from atrophy.

Schama and Landes offer historical narratives, drawing what could be called "suggestive inferences."[73] They are in the grand tradition. An alternative strand of inquiry makes use, when available, of statistical evidence. The two strands complement each other. We noted earlier that Putnam (1993), La Porta and others (1997), and Knack and Keefer (1997) have used cross-section data to study possible links between civic culture and economic growth. Granato, Inglehart, and Leblang (1996a) have also used the World Values Survey, but to construct an index of a different notion of culture, reflecting the personal motivation to achieve. The authors have made use of answers to one of the questions asked in the survey, which was to identify from a list of qualities the one the respondent regarded most important. The list consisted of thrift, saving money and things, determination, obedience, and religious faith. Granato, Inglehart, and Leblang took the index of the motivation to achieve to be the sum of the percentage in each country emphasizing the first two goals, minus the percentage emphasizing the last two goals. They found that, controlling for gross domestic product per head and the level of primary education in 1960, differences in economic growth in the period 1960–1989 in a sample of 25 countries are positively and significantly correlated with their index of personal motivation.[74]

The finding should not be given a causal interpretation, nor do the authors suggest that it should. Earlier we noted that even disposition can be a determined rather than determining factor.[75] When it is the former, an observed link between culture and economic development

---

[73]  I owe this term to Stanley Engerman.

[74]  The idea of using culture in the sense of shared values for explaining differences in economic performance grates on many (see Jackman and Miller 1996a). For a spirited commentary on Granato, Inglehart, and Leblang (1996a), see Jackman and Miller (1996b). But see the reply by Granato, Inglehart, and Leblang (1996b).

[75]  This viewpoint contrasts with ones that see culture as determining (see, for example, Triandis 1991).

should be interpreted at best as an equilibrium relationship between two endogenous variables, nothing more.

But disposition is not the only way to view culture, the latter can also be regarded as patterns of behavior differentiating groups. For example, much has been written on differences between Japanese firms and firms in western industrial countries (see, for example, Aoki and Dore 1994). In the former, there would appear to be more emphasis on sharing information, whereas in the latter information is more decentralized. Studies have shown that firms do not necessarily adopt what might be thought to be the most efficient mode of organization for the *industry* to which they belong; rather, they adopt modes that reflect the organizational practices of the country of origin. To explain this Aoki (1996) has stressed that skill is involved in operating efficiently within any given mode. To the extent labor does not move across national boundaries, these skills would be specific to the information processing habits among the country's population. The firm is an organization in which production units are managed and coordinated. This being the case, differences in practice may so evolve as to be a source of comparative advantage for different countries. Cultural diversity among firms should then be expected. It may even be desirable.[76]

But practices are grounded on beliefs. Anthropologists have taught us to interpret cultural differences in terms of differences in the beliefs people hold about the way the world works (for example, the role of ancestors and of spirits and gods in shaping our lives). The point of view I want to explore now is somewhat different. I want to use "culture" to denote differences in the beliefs people hold about one another. Earlier we noted that in repeated relationships, shared beliefs about the actions that various parties would choose if matters were otherwise (a counterfactual) can act as a focal point, leading people to choose one set of actions rather than another, and thereby sustain one set of institutions and technology rather than another.

Greif (1994, 1997b) has applied this idea to differences in patterns of trade in the medieval Mediteranean. He interprets differences in agency relations that appeared to have prevailed between Maghribi traders of the eleventh century on the one hand and Genoese traders of the twelfth century on the other in terms of differences in expectations: Maghribi merchants expected their colleagues to impose sanctions on agents who cheated any member of their network, whereas Genoese merchants did not entertain such expectations. Greif argues that this can even account for differences in the investible surplus of the two regions, leading to differences in their subsequent economic fortunes. Recently Hayami (1997, 1998) has argued that Japan's postwar economic success was in

---

[76] Hayami (1997) offers a similar view. For a contrasting account of the history of differences between Japanese and U.S. firms, see Moriguchi (1997).

part attributable to the possibilities arising from a system of trust among investors and banks, a system grounded on a shame culture. Each thesis is based on the beliefs people are thought to hold about others' reaction to their actions.

Beliefs can play an even more complex role than the one discussed here so far. Economists have shown how cultural stereotypes can persist even when there are no intrinsic differences among groups.[77] Imagine, for example, that to be qualified to do a demanding (but personally rewarding) job requires investment, and that investment costs differ among people, dependent as the costs are on a person's intrinsic ability. Imagine too that a person's intrinsic ability has been drawn from the same genetic urn: there are no group differences, only individual differences. Assume now that innate ability cannot be observed by employers, to an extent that even if one has made the investment and is thus qualified for the demanding job, employers are unable to judge this beforehand with unerring accuracy. If, however, employers harbor negative stereotypes against a particular group's ability, they are likely to use a stiffer criterion for assigning workers of that group to the difficult, but personally more rewarding job. Among workers belonging to that group, this practice would lower the expected return on the investment that makes them suitable for the more rewarding job. This means that smaller numbers of them would make the investment. This in turn means that there would be fewer of them suitable for the rewarding job, which in its turn could confirm the cultural stereotype and justify the use of the stiffer criterion by employers. In other words, it is possible for people's beliefs about group differences to be confirmed by the consequences of the actions that members of those groups take in response to the practice people follow in response to those beliefs. This is once again an instance of one equilibrium outcome out of possibly many, for if employers did not hold negative cultural stereotypes against any group, there would not be such a differentiated outcome among groups. Discrimination occurs and persists because of a self-fulfilling system of prejudicial beliefs.

Such findings as these have been deployed by Lindbeck (1995a, 1995b, 1997) and Lindbeck, Nyberg, and Weibull (1999) in modeling the attitude of citizens toward work on the one hand, and toward the volume of taxes and the character of public transfers on the other. The authors assume that a person's desire to live off the state increases with the proportion of those who live off the state—there is little stigma attached when the proportion is large, but a good deal when it is small. Citizens vote on levels of taxes and transfers, and choose in the light of the prevailing situation whether to work. This model (along with others like it)

---

[77] The key contributions are Arrow (1973), Akerlof (1976), Starrett (1976) and Coate and Loury (1993). The example in the text is taken from the Coate-Loury paper.

is attractive because it treats such matters as the degree of civic cooperation as something to be explained; these issues are not taken to be explanatory variables. A significant feature of the model is that, like the trust game, it readily admits multiple equilibria, each characterized by a particular degree of civic cooperation. Therefore rates of cooperation, high or low, can be held together by their own bootstraps. This means that societies that are identical in their innate characteristics could have different rates of compliance.

The accounts here have not treated culture as an explanatory variable. Provided the analysis is designed to address the long run, the idea is to try to explain cultural differences in terms of differences in primitives, such as our material needs, the large-scale ecological landscape, the shared knowledge base, pure historical accidents, even self-fulfilling beliefs. Cultural differences would be correlated with differences in economic performance, they would not be the cause of them.

But different types of variables should be expected to change at different speeds—some slowly, others fast. It could be that certain types of (cultural) beliefs are slow to adapt. Since slow variables are for all intents and purposes fixed in the short run, it would not be unreasonable to regard them as parameters for short-run analyses. This is the approximation social scientists make when they offer cultural explanations for economic performance—for example, the success of Japan in the postwar era (Hayami 1997, 1998).

For the long run matters are different. Individual motivation and beliefs are influenced by values and the practice of norms, and they in turn are influenced by the products of society, such as institutions, artifacts, and technologies.[78] Furthermore, any process that ties individual motivations and beliefs to values and norms and thereby to the choices made, and back again, would be expected to be path-dependent. There is little evidence though that trade and imitation may not lead to convergence in those spheres of culture that have a sizeable effect on economic performance. This is one of the messages we gathered from models of contagion. It is also possible that the *effect* of any particular aspect of a people's culture changes over time even when the culture itself is not changing. Like many factors of production, the various components of culture are in different degrees complementary to other factors. So it is possible for a particular component to lie dormant for decades, even centuries, only to become a potent force when circumstances are "right." By the same token, this same component could become ineffective, even dysfunctional, when circumstances change again. This is why there is no logical flaw in such claims as that Japan's remarkable economic success in the postwar period has been attributable in part to some aspects of the nation's culture, even though those same aspects did not have

---

[78] See especially Douglas (1982) and Wildavsky (1987, 1994).

potency in earlier centuries and may in the future prove even to be dys-functional.

In an important and interesting article, Sethi and Somanathan (1996) have explored a model that illustrates a number of these ideas in a simple way. They imagine a collective undertaking (for example, managing a common-property resource) that recurs indefinitely. The engagement is among a large group of people, each of whom behaves either opportunistically or cooperatively, as in a many-person version of the Prisoners' Dilemma game. But in contrast to the Prisoners' Dilemma, or the trust game we studied earlier, Sethi and Somanathan assume that in every period each person can be identified by a behavioral rule. Three types of people are considered: (a) those who behave opportunistically, (b) those who cooperate (in other words, who are prosocial) and forgive opportunists, and (c) those who cooperate, but punish opportunists. To be punished means a loss in personal well-being—the greater the number of people punishing one, the greater the loss—but it is assumed as well that to punish someone involves resource costs (for example, time) for the person inflicting the punishment.

Although in each period a person is of a particular type, the mix of types in the population can change because of, for instance, imitation. The authors assume that in each period the percentage rate of change in the proportion of people of any given type is itself proportional to the difference between the current well-being of a person of that type and the average well-being of the entire population. So if a type is currently doing better than the population average, its proportion in the population will increase; if it is doing worse, its proportion will decline; and if it is doing exactly as well, its proportion will remain the same. Such dynamics could be the result of learning behavior, in a world in which learning does not take place all at once among everyone, but occurs at different threshold levels across the population. The assumption is that successful behavior is emulated increasingly. The aim is to study long-run civic behavior.[79]

Sethi and Somanathan show that a society consisting solely of opportunists is always a locally, asymptotically stable equilibrium, which is to say that if there is a sufficiently large proportion of opportunists in the population today, there will be an even greater proportion of opportunists tomorrow. Society would continue to deteriorate until it became totally dysfunctional, with everyone behaving opportunistically. So opportunistic behavior can be contagious. This is the bad news. The good news is that, if the private cost in being punished is sufficiently high,

---

[79]  In evolutionary biology such adjustment mechanisms are called "replicator dynamics." Maynard Smith (1982) is a pioneering statement on evolutionary stability. Weibull (1995) contains an extensive account. Note the difference between replicator dynamics and the best-response dynamics we studied earlier.

there is a stable class of equilibria consisting of mixtures of the two types of civic-minded people.[80] The interesting finding is that each equilibrium mixture contains a sizeable proportion of prosocial, but stern, people. We are to understand that if the proportion of opportunists is small, but positive today, and there is a sizeable proportion of prosocial, but stern, people, the extent of cooperation tomorrow will be even greater, and the day-after-tomorrow greater still. Provided cooperative behavior is widespread to begin with, and provided there are sufficiently large numbers of stern people, civic behavior is contagious.

In an equilibrium consisting solely of civic-minded people, those who are stern do not have to mete out punishment (there are no opportunists *to* punish!). So stern people do exactly as well as those who are forgiving. That is why they survive. Their presence is required, though; otherwise if even a small band of opportunists were to appear, they would take over. The model shows that cooperation would not survive if there were no sanctions on opportunists. It also shows that the presence of people who are civic-minded, but stern, enable those who are civic-minded, but forgiving, to survive. Those who forgive may be loveable, but there is a definite sense that they free-ride. To forgive is commendable, but the trait can clash with the need for incentives.

A number of further observations can be made. Integration with outside markets would reduce the personal cost of being punished (one can now leave one's village for work elsewhere and not care about social sanctions in the village); it could also make opportunistic behavior more profitable (because, for example, of an increase in the market value of the common-property resource). Thus, a community could tilt from a culture of cooperation to one of opportunism if it became more integrated with the outside world. Exogenous shocks that previously did not have a lasting effect owing to the stability of cooperative behavior could now shift the community to a regime in which cooperation unraveled.[81] So the very process of economic development can bring in its wake a loss of resilience in a community's capacity to cooperate and thrive. The breakdown can occur rapidly, causing suffering to specific groups (such as women and children and the elderly) if there are no accompanying countermeasures to soften the blow, such as improved third-party enforcement of agreements, social security, alterations in property rights (for example, asset transfers), and so forth.

We have in turn looked upon culture as common behavior, shared beliefs, and common values and dispositions. In each case I have been

---

[80] Formally, these equilibria (there is a continuum of them) is Liapunov-stable: if the system in equilibrium is perturbed a tiny bit, it remains within a small neighborhood of the equilibrium.

[81] Technically speaking, the basin of attraction of the noncooperative equilibrium can expand in response to market integration.

concerned with the study of equilibrium outcomes. This has helped to identify a number of mechanisms by which a traditional culture can erode when it comes into contact with modernizing forces such as, for example, formal markets. We are studying ways in which people are able to cooperate. The transition from one system of cooperation to another is never easy. As there are some who get hurt when traditional forms of cooperation get eroded, it is important to know who they typically might be. This is not to romanticize about traditional systems; it is only to point to an obvious truth that protective measures need to be put into place during changing circumstances.

### Creating social networks

In all this I have taken it that people get to interact with one another without having to search for trading partners. But as search requires resources, we need to study pathways by which networks themselves get formed.

One may think of social networks as systems of communication channels, protecting and promoting personal relationships. This is a wide notion. It covers as tightly-knit a network as a nuclear family and one as extensive as a voluntary organization. We are born into certain networks and we enter new ones over the course of a lifetime. So networks are themselves connected to one another. Network connections can also be expressed in terms of channels, although a decision to establish channels that link networks could be a collective one.

An elementary channel connects a pair of individuals directly. But one can establish indirect links. A builds an elementary channel connecting her to B, C builds an elementary channel connecting him to B, and so forth. A is then connected to C, albeit once removed. Indeed C's motive for establishing an elementary channel with B could be because of his desire to be linked to A. And so on.

To establish a channel involves costs (for example, time), as it does to maintain it. In some contexts they would be called by the suitably vague term, "transaction" costs (Coase 1960). The desire to join a network on someone's part could be because of a shared value.[82] Networks also play a role in enabling coalitions to form and act, a matter central to Putnam's (1993) view of civic engagement. Generally speaking, the decision to invest in a channel could come about because it would contribute directly to one's well-being (for example, investing in friendship), it could be because it makes economic sense (for example, joining a guild), or it could be because of both (for example, entering a marriage). On occa-

---

[82]  Fukuyama (1997, lecture 2) takes this to be the defining characteristic: "A network is a group of individual agents that share *informal* norms or values beyond those necessary for market transactions."

sion the time involved is not a cost at all, as the act of trying to create a channel can itself be pleasurable. One imagines that many of the benefits and costs of joining a network and continuing one's membership are unanticipated. The immediate motivation could be direct pleasure (for example, enjoyment in relating to someone or being a member of a congenial group); its economic benefits an unanticipated side effect. But the direction could go the other way (for example, joining a firm and subsequently making friends among colleagues). Regardless of the motivation, expenditure in a channel involves a resource allocation problem, with all its attendant difficulties.

The clause "personal relationships" in the notion of networks is central. It involves trust without recourse to third-party engagement.[83] There is also the suggestion we noted earlier, that the practice of civic cooperation leads to a heightened disposition to cooperate. It amounts to forming personal taste by sampling experiences. But if social engagement fosters trust and cooperation, there would be synergy between civic engagement and a disposition to be so engaged. The synergy would be tempered by the fact that the private cost of additional engagements (for example, time) would rise with increasing engagements.[84]

As elsewhere in resource allocation theory, it helps to think first of networks in equilibrium and to then study their dynamics. We may take it that each person has available to him a set of channels from which he can choose. Some would have been inherited (the decision problem concerning these would be whether to maintain them and, if so, at what level of activity), others he would have to create. Imagine that for any configuration of channels that others select, there is an optimal set of channels for each individual. An equilibrium network of channels is then a feasible network that is optimal for each party's choice of channels, given that others establish their respective channels in the network in question. Equilibrium networks can be expected to contain strategically placed individuals. They are the fortunate people, having inherited or made the most valuable connections, in a literal sense. There would be others with connections of not much economic worth, even if their emotional worth were high.[85]

Installing channels is a way to create trust. Plausibly, someone's knowledge of someone else's character declines with the number of elementary channels separating them, as in the example of perhaps

---

[83] Compare Putnam (1993, p. 171): "Social trust in complex modern settings can arise from two related sources—norms of reciprocity and networks of civic engagement."

[84] Putnam (1993, pp. 86–91) discusses this influence. He even suggests (p. 90) that "taking part in a choral society or a bird-watching club can teach self-discipline and an appreciation for the joys of successful collaboration."

[85] Boorman (1975) and Bala and Goyal (1997) are formal studies of equilibrium networks.

knowing very little personally about a friend of a friend of a friend, knowing rather more about a friend of a friend, and knowing even more about a friend.[86] This creates the necessary tension between the benefits and costs of establishing elementary channels. But one can be misled by this chain-postulate into thinking that weak ties are not valuable. In fact they can be extremely valuable. In a famous report based on interviews with professional and technical workers in a town outside Cambridge, Massachusetts, Granovetter (1973, 1974) revealed that more than half had found their jobs through a personal connection. Surprisingly, the majority of personal connections were not close friends, they were mere acquaintances.

On reflection, the latter finding should have been expected. The reason weak ties are especially useful in job search is that they cover a greater range of links than strong ties do. Weak ties connect one to a wide *variety* of people, and thereby to a wider information base.[87] However, among rural populations in poor countries there are few weak ties, ties are mostly intense. This narrows possibilities. But it creates an avenue for migration. An enterprising member of the community moves to the city. He is followed by others in a chain-like fashion, as information is sent home of job prospects. Migrant workers may even recommend to their bosses village relations, employing whom would reduce a moral hazard problem for employers. This would explain the still largely anecdotal evidence that city mills often employ disproportionate numbers of workers from the same village. The emotional costs of adaptation to new surroundings would also be lower for later migrants, with the implication that migration in response to new opportunities in the city should be expected to be slow to begin with but would pick up strength as costs decline (Carrington, Detragiache, and Vishwanath 1996). Formal evidence of chain migration, though sparse, does exist. Caldwell (1969) has confirmed its occurrence in Sub-Saharan Africa and B. Banerjee (1983) has provided evidence from an Indian sample.

Wintrobe (1995) postulates that parents invest in channels and pass them on to their children in return for security in old age. This probably has had force in poor countries, where capital markets are largely unavailable to rural households. But there is a lot more in our desire to transfer capital assets to the young. One type of capital we give our offspring in abundance is what falls broadly under the term "cultural values." Why do we do this? It can be argued that we imbue our chil-

---

[86]    Compare this account with Putnam (1993, pp. 168–69): "Mutual trust is lent. Social networks allow trust to become transitive and spread: I trust you, because I trust her and she assures me that she trusts you."

[87]    For an elegant exposition of this fact, in the form of a profile of an acquaintance of the writer, see Gladwell (1999). Mortensen and Vishwanath (1994) provide a theory of how even salaries depend on whom one knows.

dren with values we cherish not merely because we think it is good for *them*, but also because we desire to see our values survive. Our descendents do something supremely important for us: they add a certain value to our lives our mortality would otherwise deprive them of. Procreation itself is a means of making one's values durable. So there are reasons other than intergenerational exchange why we invest in channels and pass them on to our children.[88]

Wintrobe (1995) also asks the interesting question why networks frequently operate along ethnic lines and why they are multipurpose and dense, unlike specialized "professional" networks. In answer he observes that exit from and entry into ethnic networks are impossible, and that the threat of sanctions by the group prevents children from reneging on the implicit contract to work within it. We have seen how the theory of linked games among overlapping generations gives substance to this mechanism.

But there are probably additional forces at work. It should not be surprising that the channels people bequeath to their children in traditional societies frequently amount to ethnic networks (who else is there with whom one can form connections?). But while it is true that exit from one's ethnicity is literally impossible, children do have a choice of not using the ethnic channels they may have inherited. So Wintrobe's thesis needs to be extended if we are to explain why those particular networks are so active; their mere denseness would probably not suffice. The way to do it is to observe first that investment in channels is irreversible: one cannot costlessly redirect channels once they have been established. Moreover, if trust begets trust, the cost of maintaining a channel would decline with repeated use (witness that we take our closest friends and relatives often for granted). So using a channel gives rise to an externality over time (much as in "learning by doing" in the field of technology use).[89] The benefits of creating new channels are therefore low if one has inherited a rich network of relationships. This is another way of saying that the cost of not using inherited channels is high. Out-

---

[88] Alexander Herzen's remark, that human development is a kind of chronological unfairness, since those who live later profit from the labor of their predecessors without paying the same price, and Kant's view, that it is disconcerting that earlier generations should carry their burdens only for the sake of the later ones, and that only the last should have the good fortune to dwell in the completed building, or in other words, the thought that we can do something for posterity but it can do nothing for us (see Rawls 1972, p. 291), is a reflection of an extreme form of alienation: alienation from one's own life. These matters are discussed in greater detail in Dasgupta (1994).

[89] Solow (1997) contains a discussion of the dynamics of a macroeconomy when technological change involves learning-by-doing. For a study of the evolving structure of an industry in which firms experience learning-by-doing, see Dasgupta and Stiglitz (1988).

side opportunities have to be especially good before one severs inherited links. It explains why we maintain so many of the channels we have inherited from our family and kinship, and why norms of conduct pass down the generations. We are, so to speak, locked in from birth.[90]

The establishment and maintenance of channels create externalities not only across time, but also among contemporaries. If the externalities are positive, as in the case of making friends (or becoming literate and numerate as a prelude to enjoying advanced communication links), there would typically be an undersupply. Diamond (1982) famously showed this in the context of people seeking those others with whom they would be able to exchange goods they had produced. Since one may run into people who have not got appropriate goods to exchange, search is costly. When someone with goods searches more intensively, she benefits because she is more likely to find someone with whom to trade. But she also benefits those others who possess goods that are appropriate for exchanges with her because they are more likely to run into her. Simulations suggest that such externalities can have powerful effects. Diamond's purpose in constructing the model was to show how an economy could find itself in a depression if transactions involved search. People would produce little if they thought they had to wait a long while before being able to sell (maintaining inventories is costly). It could even be a self-fulfilling thought. If so, equilibrium production and search would both be less than efficient.[91]

There can also be negative externalities in the creation of channels, such as those between members of hostile groups. One would expect an oversupply of them.[92] But be they positive or negative, externalities give rise to collective inefficiency. Positive externalities point to an argument for public subsidy, and negative ones produce one for investment in such institutions as those whose presence would detract from them ("taxing" them would be another possibility). Local authorities frequently apply this argument when establishing youth centers, social clubs, and the like.

---

[90]  Such a lock-in effect is not unique to social capital, of course. In a well-known study in economic history, David (1976) argued that the reason the mechanical reaper took time to be introduced in England was the character of the country's rural landscape in the mid-nineteenth century. David noted that individual fields in some parts were separated by hedgerows; in others the terrain was interspersed with irrigation trenches and water-cuts. These were installed physical capital. They had served, and were continuing to serve, a purpose, but they did make the use of the mechanical reaper overly expensive at the level of the individual farmer.

[91]  Formally, Diamond's model is identical to our trust game with only one type of person in the population, not two.

[92]  In his analysis of the Sicilian Mafia, Gambetta (1993) studies the character of such negative externalities.

There are types of influence that are able to travel great distances, for example, via television, newspaper, and the Internet. They would be expected to push society toward greater homogeneity of individual projects and purposes. Of course, local influences can have this effect too, as in simple models of contagion (see especially Ellison 1993). We remarked on this earlier. Whether contagions spread or are geographically contained appears to be sensitive to model specification. The models are nevertheless united in one thing: they all tell us that channels of communication create twin pressures, one leading to clusters of attitudes and behavior, the other to homogeneity. These pressures work on different, crisscrossing spheres of our lives. Both in turn interact with markets.

Network formation is an extremely difficult subject. One expects that people often have only a hazy notion of what constitutes a productive channel. Moreover, the dynamics of even the simplest constructs are nonlinear. So it is not evident whether the system self-organizes into an equilibrium structure or not, or what the structure looks like if it does organize by itself. Explorations in cellular automata have proved to be so inconclusive as to leave one bemused. The literature on the economics of search (for jobs, for bargains, for exchanges generally), by contrast, has identified tractable models (for example, Diamond 1982), as has the literature on simple contagion models mentioned earlier. They affirm that social environments that harbor equilibria can possess multiple equilibria and that the equilibria are not necessarily efficient or just.[93] The trust game would appear to be canonical. We have seen repeatedly that it can be interpreted in many ways.

Locally interacting systems are of obvious interest for an understanding of many of the social networks we observe. They capture the fact that elementary channels are not public goods. The creation of a channel by someone gives rise to externalities, but they are local externalities. Likewise, the creation of trust gives rise to externalities, but they too are local externalities. Moreover, the externalities are not anonymous, they are personalized. Names matter. In this sense also they differ from public goods.

Burt (1992) and Burt, Hogarth, and Michaud (1998) have found among business firms in the United States that controlling for age, education and experience, employees enjoying strategic positions in social networks are more highly compensated than those who are not. Their findings confirm that at least some of the returns from investment in network creation are captured by the investor. The findings also imply that memberships in networks are a component of what economists call "human capital." The point is that if firms pay employees on the basis of what

---

[93] Bala and Goyal (1997) have constructed an ingenious example of a network equilibrium that is both unique and collectively efficient. As would be expected, the model has many special features.

they contribute to profitability, they would look not only at the conventional human capital employees bring with them (for example, education, experience, personality), but also the personal contacts they possess. In their important work on human capital formation in the United States, Jorgenson and Fraumeni (1989, 1992a, 1992b) estimated that the country's stock of human capital is more than ten times as large as its stock of marketable physical capital. They also found that investment in human capital is more than five times as great as investment in marketable physical capital. The Jorgenson-Fraumeni estimates of human capital include in them the privately captured reward for the accumulation of network capital. It would be informative to untangle network capital from the rest of human capital. This could reveal the extent to which returns from network investment are captured by the investor. But measurement problems abound. They may be insurmountable precisely because of the pervasive externalities. We will return to these matters in the two sections following the next one.

### Markets and networks

Earlier I offered a classification of the various pathways by which agreements can be kept. Attention was drawn to third-party enforcement and to mechanisms relying on personal reputation. We noted that impersonal markets are able to function extensively only if agreements can be enforced by a third party. We noted too that a necessary condition for this to be possible is that states of affairs that matter be verifiable. The apparatus of government is relevant here. Impersonal markets (markets for short) can function well only if contracts can be written in detail and the law is impartial and effectively administered. I am thinking of contracts bearing on such matters as the quality of goods and services, delivery date, and hours worked. If the State is weak, or oppressive, or merely corrupt, social networks assume importance in ensuring that agreements are kept. Dense networks help give weight to informal agreements. Inevitably, transactions have to be personalized in such cases.[94]

Social networks are the embodiment of "social capital." A defining feature of networks is that they are personal (members of networks must have names, personalities, and attributes). Social networks are exclusive, not inclusive, otherwise they would not be social networks. The terms of trade within a network are different from those prevailing across a group of networks. An outsider's word is not as good as an insider's word. Names matter. To be sure, the distinction between personalized and impersonal exchanges is not sharp, and even in a sophisticated

---

[94]    See Gambetta (1993) on this in his discussion of Sicilian society and Rose (1995) on Russian society.

market (for example, modern banking), reputation matters (for example, credit rating of the borrower). But the distinction is real.

Dense networks can be suffocating for members, but networks in general need not be suffocating. Earlier we noted how networks can be an invaluable source of information, enabling markets to function well. We noted also that networks can be a means by which markets get established (for example, long distance trade in earlier times). In many cases they are necessary if markets are to function at all. Rauch (1996a, 1996b) for example, has applied the theory of search to study the character of international trade in differentiated products. There are specialized commodities, such as footwear, that are traded internationally but not in organized markets—they do not have reference prices listed for them, either. Why? Rauch observes that there are so many fine differences in the characteristics of footwear that a price observed at one location offers little information about the commodity's worth at any other location. So, traders search for buyers and sellers to find a good match. In this search proximity is helpful, as is common language; and this implies that an important effect of immigration on trade would be through the establishment of business contacts (Gould 1994). Evidence from the Organisation for Economic Co-operation and Development (OECD) countries is consistent with these observations.[95]

All societies rely on a mix of impersonal markets and communitarian institutions. The mix shifts through changing circumstances, as people find ways of circumventing difficulties in realizing mutually beneficial transactions. In poor countries both insurance and credit markets are underdeveloped. Udry (1994) reports that as recently as the late 1980s more than 90 percent of the value of all loans in Nigeria were obtained from what in the development literature is called the "informal sector," which includes not only informal moneylenders, but also networks of family and kin.

The transmission and retrieval of knowledge affords another illustration of the changing mix, albeit an extreme one. In preliterate societies an important role of social capital was the transmission of knowledge (for example, a society's history). The elderly were particularly valued as repositories of wisdom (Goody 1986). Today, both transmission and retrieval are in large measure a private act, not a collective endeavor.[96]

In an oft-quoted passage, Arrow (1974, p. 33) expressed the view that organizations are a means of achieving the benefits of collective action

---

[95] For a more general investigation into the role of personal contacts in the geographic distribution of trade, see Egan and Mody (1992).

[96] Manguel (1997) interprets the evolution of reading in these terms. Johann Gutenberg's printing of the Bible by movable type is justifiably regarded as an event of the greatest importance (Landes 1998, pp. 51–52).

in situations in which the price system fails. This formulation, if interpreted literally, gets the historical chronology backward, but it has an important converse: certain types of organization can prevent markets (and thereby an effective price system) from coming into existence. Earlier we noted that when markets displace communitarian institutions in the production of goods and services, there are people who suffer unless countermeasures are undertaken. I am talking now of the other side of the coin: communitarian institutions can prevent markets from functioning well; in extreme cases they can prevent the emergence of markets. When they do, communitarian institutions are a hindrance, not an engine of economic development. They may have served a purpose once, but they are now dysfunctional.

The key point is that the links between markets and communitarian institutions are shot through with externalities. Transactions in one institution have effects that spill over to another without being accounted for. Kranton (1996) studies this. She begins by observing that to be engaged in market transactions can involve search. As we noted earlier, search gives rise to externalities: if a person increases her search, others benefit, in that their search costs decline. So, if people are largely involved in communitarian institutions (for example, if they transact on the basis of norms of reciprocity), private incentives to enter markets are low owing to high search costs. But it could be that the market has the potential to offer a greater range of goods and services and is, in fact, the superior institution of production and exchange. Kranton shows that if, for whatever reason, there are insufficient numbers of people entering markets, communitarian institutions could not only survive, but keep the more efficient institution from coming into being. This would be a collective loss.

Externalities introduce a wedge between private and social costs, and between private and social benefits. Repeatedly in this essay we have seen how equilibrium behavior can yield inefficient outcomes in the presence of externalities. That individuals are able to explain their actions as being in their own best interest does not imply that the institution in which they operate is defendable. They themselves may find the institution undefendable if they were to recognize its underlying mechanism for translating choices into consequences. So too with dysfunctional norms of behavior. Such practices as female circumcision are frequently packaged as "cultural values" for the benefit of outsiders, a sure way to forestall critical inquiry into them. These simple truths are easy to overlook, but have wide ramifications for the way we should perceive our own institutions and those of other places and other times.

Consider, for example, that the parental costs of procreation are low when the cost of rearing children is shared among the kinship. In Sub-Saharan Africa, fosterage within the kinship is commonplace: children are not raised solely by their parents, the responsibility is more diffuse within the kinship group (E. Goody 1982; Caldwell 1991; Bledsoe 1994). Fosterage in the African context is not adoption. It is not intended to, and in fact it does not break ties between parents and children. The institution would seem to afford a form of mutual insurance protection. There is some evidence that, as savings opportunities are few in the low-productivity agricultural regions of Sub-Saharan Africa, fosterage also enables households to smoothen their consumption across time.[97] In parts of West Africa, up to half the children have been found to be living with their kin at any given time. Nephews and nieces have the same rights of accommodation and support as do biological offspring. There is a sense in which children are seen as common responsibility.

All this sounds good. Unfortunately, the arrangement creates a free-rider problem if the parents' share of the benefits from having children exceeds their share of the costs (Dasgupta 1993, 1995). From the point of view of the parents, taken as a collective, too many children would be produced in these circumstances. Related to this is a phenomenon noted by Guyer (1994) in a Yoruba area of Nigeria. In the face of deteriorating economic circumstances, some women have been bearing children by different men so as to create immediate lateral links with them. Polyandrous motherhood enables women to have access to more than one resource network.

If we view the networks that enable these social practices to exist as risk-sharing arrangements and consumption-smoothening devices, they are to the good. But they are not *all* to the good, because their presence lowers the benefits to people of transacting in insurance and capital markets when such markets appear on the scene. The benefit would be even lower if the emotional costs of moving from one system to another were included (economists would call this a "stock effect"). Admittedly, like capital markets, insurance markets suffer from many imperfections. Of central importance is the imperfection that arises from the moral hazard to which commercial firms are subject: it is difficult for firms to monitor the extent to which the insured have taken precautions against accidents. But one great advantage of insurance markets is that they are able to pool more risk than communitarian insurance schemes are able to. In this sense at least, they are superior to fosterage and polyandrous motherhood. However, mutual insurance among members of a community (for example, household, kinship, village) can be expected to be less fraught with problems of moral hazard. If it *is* less fraught, people would have an incentive to take out insurance in both institutions. But to the extent people take part in communitarian insurance arrangements, markets are "crowded out." This is an externality, and markets would be excessively crowded out if even communitarian institutions suffer

---

[97] This latter motivation has been explored by Serra (1996).

from some moral hazard (Arnott and Stiglitz 1991). In any event, there is a collective loss unless judicious government policies are put in place. One concludes that past accumulation of certain kinds of social capital can act as a drag on economic development, by preventing more efficient institutions from spreading.

The point then is this. Social networks can be a help or a hindrance, it all depends on the uses to which networks are put. It also depends on the state of technology. Networks can offer powerful aid to the good functioning of markets when they are used for transmitting information, both among network members and between members and non-members. In such cases networks and markets are complementary in their roles.[98] However, networks can be destructively competitive with markets if they are involved in the production and exchange of "marketable" goods through communitarian arrangements, such as those operating on the basis of norms of reciprocity.

The growth of impersonal markets would seem to be necessary for long-run improvements in the standard of living. Both theory and empirics testify to this (Adelman and Morris 1967; Dasgupta 1993; Landes 1998). The reason has been familiar since Adam Smith: transactions limited to a group are likely to be less productive than those that can involve the entire population. Standardization of products enables unit costs of production to decline with the volume of output. Standardization is, of course, also intimately connected with the growth of markets. In addition, it is possible to show theoretically that the more dissimilar are transactors, the greater are the potential gains from transaction. To the extent associations are a dense network of engagements, they are like economic enclaves. But if associations act as enclaves, they retard economic development. For example, social impediments to the mobility of labor imply that "talents" are not able to find their ideal locations. This can act as a drag on technological progress (Galor and Tsiddon 1997). More generally, resources that should ideally flow across enclaves do not do so—which creates inefficiency.

### Macroevidence: scale versus change

So far I have adopted a microeconomic perspective. How does the analysis translate into the macroeconomy?

In a review of Fukuyama (1995), Solow (1995) observed that if social capital is to be treated on a par with other types of capital, it had better show up in the statistics of growth accounting. To illustrate, consider the simplest formulation of economy-wide production possibilities. Let K and L, respectively, denote an economy's stock of physical capital and

---

[98] Even here, the role of networks can be expected to diminish as it becomes easier and easier to transmit and access information in the marketplace.

labor-hours employed, and suppose that production possibilities of aggregate output, Y, are given by the functional relation,

$$Y = AF(K,L), \text{ where } A > 0. \tag{1}$$

We will suppose that F satisfies properties that would enable textbook resource allocation theory to run smoothly.[99]

In equation (1) A is the scale factor of the production function. Economists refer to it as the "total factor productivity" of the economy and regard it as a combined index of institutional capabilities and publicly shared knowledge. However, for reasons I will suggest below, economists have not tried to develop independent ways of measuring total factor productivity. Instead, as Solow (1995) remarks, a standard exercise in the economics of development has been to decompose the observed *change* in output of an economy into its sources: How much can be attributed to the change in labor-force participation, changes in population size, net accumulation of physical capital, and so on. If some part of observed change in output cannot be credited to any measured factor of production, economists call it the "residual." We now use equation (1) to obtain growth accounts.

To do this, differentiate both sides of the equation with respect to time to obtain:

$$d(\ln Y)/dt = [AKF_K/Y]d(\ln K)/dt + [ALF_L/Y]d(\ln L)/dt + d(\ln A)/dt. \tag{2}$$ [100]

Equation (2) is useful because it decomposes the change in gross national product (the left-hand side) into three components: (a) the contribution of the change in the stock of physical capital (the first term on the right-hand side), (b) the contribution of the change in the quantity of labor-hours in production (the second term), and (c) the contribution of the change in total factor productivity (the third term) or, in other words, the residual.[101] Solow (1995) remarked that if social capital has bite as a concept, it would show up in international time series as a residual.

In fact it does not. The contribution of the residual to the phenomenal economic growth of East Asian countries in recent years has been negligible; the first two terms on the right-hand side of equation (2) explain

---

[99] These properties are such that F is constant-returns-to-scale in K and L, that it is an increasing function of K and L, and that it increases at diminishing rates. I am ignoring environmental capital because there are no systematic international time series of it. I have also suppressed time subscripts from Y, A, K, and L.
[100] "lnY" denotes the logarithm of Y, and so forth. $F_K$ is the partial derivative of F with respect to K, and so on.
[101] Change here refers to the percentage rate of change.

almost all the growth that has been enjoyed there since the 1960s.[102] And yet East Asian societies are widely viewed as being rich in precisely the kinds of social capital that would have helped foster economic growth. How is this to be explained?

The question occurs in less aggregated data as well. We noted earlier that in his analysis of statistics from the 20 administrative regions of Italy, Putnam (1993) found civic tradition to be a strong predictor of contemporary economic indicators. He showed that indexes of civic engagement in the early years of this century were highly correlated with employment, income, and infant survival in the early 1970s. He also found that regional differences in civic engagement can be traced back several centuries and that, controlling for civic traditions, indexes of industrialization and public health have no impact on current civic engagement. As he put it, the causal link appears to be from civics to economics, not the other way around.[103]

The same question appears, albeit indirectly, in even less aggregated data. Narayan and Pritchett (1997) have analyzed statistics on household expenditure and social engagements in a sample of over 50 villages in Tanzania, to discover that indexes of village-level social capital (namely, memberships in village-level associations) were strongly associated with mean household expenditure. They have also provided statistical reasons for arguing that more social capital results in higher household expenditure rather than the other way around.

The residual does not appear in any of these cross-section studies. I will now argue that it is not necessary for it to do so.

Consider two communities, labeled $i = 1, 2$. To make the analytical points I want to make here in a sharp way, we will suppose that in both communities there is a single, all-purpose, nondeteriorating commodity that can be either consumed or set aside for saving. Let us continue to imagine that there is only one kind of labor.[104] Finally, suppose that both communities are autarkic and operate with the same body of technical knowledge concerning the ways labor and physical capital can be combined to produce output. This means that any difference in the total factor productivity of the two economies would be attributable entirely to differences in their institutional capabilities. For the moment let us call the latter "social capital."

---

[102] The key papers on this are Kim and Lau (1992) and A. Young (1993). Rodrik (1997) contains a good commentary.

[103] See also Helliwell and Putnam (1995). But see Knack and Keefer (1997), who have found no association between memberships in formal groups and trust and improved economic performance in their sample of countries.

[104] The reason I am postulating an all-purpose commodity and a single kind of labor at this point is that I want to avoid aggregation problems. See below for elaboration.

Let the stock of physical capital and labor in $i$ be $K_i$ and $L_i$. We use the notation in equation (1) to denote aggregate output, $Y_i$, by the functional relation,

$$Y_i = A_iF(K_i, L_i), \text{ where } A_i \text{ (> 0)}; \quad i = 1, 2. \tag{3}$$

There are any number of microeconomic accounts that could be provided for this formulation. For example, the social structure underlying the trust game (tables 1 and 2) could give rise to the aggregate production function in equation (3). So could the more general model involving quasivoluntary compliance account for it. Now if civic cooperation were to increase in community $i$ (for example, if there is a shift from a low compliance to a high compliance equilibrium owing to changes in population-wide expectations), it would translate into a higher value of $A_i$. But this would mean that the same quantities of physical capital and labor-hours would combine to produce more output, because greater trust and trustworthiness would make possible a more efficient allocation of resources in production.

By the same token, if civic cooperation were greater among people in community 1 than in community 2, we would have $A_1 > A_2$. If they possessed identical amounts of physical capital and identical quantities of labor, community 1's output would be larger than community 2's output. An observer would discover a positive association between a community's "social capital" (in other words, total factor productivity) and its mean household income. This is one way to interpret the finding reported in Narayan and Pritchett (1997).

Consider now a different thought experiment. Imagine that in the year 1900 the two communities had been identical in all respects but for their social capital, of which community 1 had more (that is, $A_1 >$ $A_2$ in 1900). Imagine next that since 1900 total factor productivity has remained constant in both communities. Suppose that people in both places have followed a simple saving rule: a constant fraction, s (> 0), of aggregate output has been invested each year in accumulating physical capital. In order to make the comparison easy, suppose finally that the communities have remained identical in their demographic features. It is then a simple matter to confirm that in 1970 community 1 would be richer than community 2 in terms of consumption, output, and physical wealth. Note though that the residual in the time series of growth accounts in both communities would be nil ($dA_i/dt = 0$, for $i = 1, 2$).

We can reinforce the story. The presumption that the two communities have saved at the same rate is unsatisfactory. To see why, it will be noticed from equation (3) that in 1900 the marginal product of physical capital would have been higher in community 1. This would suggest that the private rate of return on investment in physical capital was higher in community 1 in that year.[105] But this would have provided people in community 1 a reason for investing a greater fraction of their incomes than those in community 2, thereby spurring 1's growth rate even more. By 1970 the economic disparity between the two communities would have been greater. I conclude that an absence of a residual in growth accounts does not mean that social capital has not had an influence on the macroeconomy.

As the communities are both autarkic, there is no flow of physical capital from the one to the other. This is an economic distortion for the combined communities: the rates of return on investment in physical capital in the two places remain unequal. The source of the distortion is the enclave nature of the communities, occasioned in our example by an absence of markets linking them. There would be gains to be enjoyed if physical capital could flow from community 2 to community 1.

Autarky is an extreme assumption, but it is not a misleading assumption. What the model points to is that to the extent social capital is exclusive, it inhibits the flow of resources—in this case a movement of physical capital from one place to the other. Put the other way, if markets do not function well, capital does not flow from community 2 to community 1 to the extent it ideally should. Social networks within each community block the growth of markets, so their presence inhibits economic development. That is the moral to be drawn.

### Measuring social capital

Is it reasonable to model the externalities generated by social networks as total factor productivity, or should social capital be regarded on a par with physical, environmental, and human capital as factors of production? In either case, how should it be measured?

Earlier, we noted that if the market for labor and skills works reasonably well, wages and salaries would in part consist of the profits employees make for their employers by virtue of the "contacts" they possess (Burt 1992). Therefore, to the extent the social worth of such contacts is reflected in wages and salaries, social capital is a part of measurable human capital, which means that it can be thought of as a privately owned factor of production.[106] But we also noted that social networks involve externalities, which

---

[105] If markets in each community were perfectly competitive, the private rate of return on investment in physical capital would equal the marginal product of physical capital. Since we are discussing the importance of social capital in production, I am, of course, assuming that markets are vastly imperfect in each community. What I am assuming, though, is that they are similarly imperfect, in the sense that differences in the marginal products of physical capital in the two communities translate into differences in their private rates of returns on investment in physical capital. This is a weak assumption to make.

[106] However, unlike physical capital, human capital is nontransferable; it is person-specific.

typically would not be reflected in wages and salaries. So then, how is one to measure the externalities?

We have already considered one possibility, in regarding social capital to be embodied in total factor productivity. Two others suggest themselves. First, we could entertain the eminently sensible suggestion that labor involves not only time (and effort), but also skill, or in other words, it involves human capital. We could then imagine that aggregate output (Y) is a function of labor-hours (L) and a composite index of capital that includes both physical and human capital (K and H, respectively). Let the composite index of capital be BM(K, H), where B is a scale factor and M is an increasing function of K and H. Then, in place of equation (1), we would have:

$$Y = AF(BM(K, H), L), \text{ where } A, B > 0. \tag{4}$$

In this formulation, B captures social-network externalities.

Lau (1996) reports on a series of studies that have specified the aggregate production function to be of the form $Y_t = F(B_t K_t^a H_t^{(1-a)}, L_t)$, where $0 < a < 1$. In its form this is a special case of equation (4). The studies have uncovered that, since the end of the Second World War, the contribution of $B_t$ to growth in $Y_t$ in today's newly industrialized countries has been negligible.

However, following the studies he was reporting, Lau interpreted B to be the economy's knowledge base, not social network externalities. A stagnant B in that interpretation would mean an absence of technological change, which the studies attempted to show has been the case in East Asia since the end of the Second World War. Here we are considering the idea that B could as well represent social-network externalities. Let us see how it would work.

Consider once again two autarkic communities (i = 1, 2). Suppose B is constant in both places and $B_1 > B_2$. Then it must be that $H_1 > H_2$, since, by definition, a worker's human capital includes the social networks to which she belongs. If L and K were the same in the two communities in some base year, $Y_1$ would have exceeded $Y_2$ in that year. If L were to remain constant in both places and the savings rates in the two were the same, accumulation of physical capital would be greater in community 1, which in turn means that the standard of living would be higher. All this would be true even though time series would show that the "residual" ($[dB_t/dt]/B_t$) in both communities was zero. Interestingly, in the base year the marginal product of physical capital in community 1 would have been *lower* than in community 2, which means that ideally, physical capital ought to have moved from 1 to 2, and it would have moved had there been perfect capital markets.[107]

---

[107] This follows from the assumption that F satisfies diminishing marginal factor products with increasing factor inputs.

A second alternative for modeling social networks would be to construct a composite index of labor, which includes not only labor-hours, L, but also the capital embodied in labor (in other words, human capital, H). Thus, let the composite index be CN(L, H), where C is a scale factor and N is an increasing function of L and H. Then, in place of equation (1), we would have

$$Y = AF(K, CN(L, H)), \text{ where } A, C > 0. \tag{5}$$

This formulation has different implications from the previous one, but it is similar to the first, which saw social capital as being embodied in total factor productivity, A. Consider once again two autarkic communities, 1 and 2. Suppose C is constant in both places and $C_1 > C_2$. Then it must be that $H_1 > H_2$, since, by definition, a worker's human capital includes the social networks to which he belongs. If L and K were the same in the two communities in some base year, $Y_1$ would have exceeded $Y_2$ in that year. If L were to remain constant in both places and the savings rates in the two were the same, accumulation of physical capital would be greater in community 1, which in turn means that the standard of living would be higher. All this, even though time series would show that the "residual" ($[dC_t/dt]/C_t$) in both communities was zero. In contrast to the previous model, though, in the base year the marginal product of physical capital in community 1 would have been *higher* than in community 2—which means that, ideally, physical capital ought to have moved from 2 to 1, and it would have moved had there been perfect capital markets. I conclude that embodying social capital in total factor productivity and in the scale factor C in equation (5) have similar implications, but that they both differ from the implications of embodying it in the scale factor, B, in equation (4). I know of no data set that would enable one to determine which of the three macroeconomic formulations of social networks is most compelling.

Putnam (1993, p. 174) observes a critical difference between horizontal and vertical networks:

"A vertical network, no matter how dense and no matter how important to its participants, cannot sustain social trust and cooperation. Vertical flows of information are often less reliable than horizontal flows, in part because the subordinate husbands information as a hedge against exploitation. More important, sanctions that support norms of reciprocity against the threat of opportunism are less likely to be imposed upwards and less likely to be acceded to, if imposed. Only a bold or foolhardy subordinate lacking ties of solidarity with peers, would seek to punish a superior."

There is a third reason:

Imagine a network of people engaged in long-term economic relationships, one in which relationships are maintained by the practice of social norms (for example, norms of reciprocity). Suppose new economic opportunities arise outside the enclave, for instance, because markets have developed. Horizontal networks are more likely to consist of members who are similarly placed. If one of the parties discovers better economic opportunities outside the enclave, it is likely that others too will discover better economic opportunities there. Both parties would then wish to renegotiate their relationship.

Vertical (or hierarchical) networks are different. Even if the subordinate (for example, the landless laborer) finds a better economic opportunity in the emerging markets, it is possible that the superior (that is, the landlord-creditor) does not; in which case the former would wish to renegotiate, but the latter would not. It is no doubt tempting to invoke the Coase argument (Coase 1960), that the subordinate would be able to compensate the superior and thus break the traditional arrangement. But this would require the subordinate to be able to capitalize his future earnings, something typically not possible for people who are subordinates in rural economies in poor countries. A promise to pay by installments is not an appealing avenue open to a subordinate, either. He would have to provide a collateral. As this could mean that his family would be left behind, the worker could understandably find it too costly to move.

The distinction between horizontal and vertical networks, and between benign and malign networks, and an absence of prices that would reflect the worth of networks makes estimation of social capital especially hard. Putnam (1993, 1995) circumvented the problems in an ingenious manner, counting membership sizes of groups in civil society, such as sports clubs, bowling leagues, choral societies, parent-teacher associations, literary societies, and political clubs. But he did not try to aggregate them into a single measure. In his empirical work he regressed each against other indexes, such as government accountability and economic growth. Narayan and Pritchett (1997) and Fukuyama (1997) have both enlarged the domain of networks for consideration and have sought to aggregate them. They have suggested measuring a community's social capital as the weighted sum of the sizes of its various social networks. Fukuyama (1997) takes a network's weight to be an aggregate of its various characteristics—for example, the network's internal cohesion and the way it relates to outsiders. A network can therefore have a negative weight (for example, for street gangs), in which case it would contribute negatively to a community's stock of social capital. All this has heuristic value, but there are problems.

When economic statisticians aggregate various kinds of capital equipment in a market economy into a measure of physical capital, they need prices to use as weights. To be sure, markets are most frequently imperfect and are often missing. Nevertheless, market prices offer a benchmark for estimating ideal prices (they are called "shadow," or "accounting" prices). A route that is not dissimilar can be followed for estimating the value of human capital (see, for example, Jorgenson and Fraumeni 1989) and for certain types of environmental capital, such as soil, forests, and fisheries (for example, Repetto and others 1989).

Social capital is in a different category from these because it has its greatest impact on the economy precisely in those areas of transaction in which markets are missing. The examples we have studied in this article were in part designed to bring this out. The examples have also shown why estimating the accounting prices that would be needed to build an aggregate measure of social capital could pose insurmountable difficulties. These difficulties are a deep fact, not an incidental one, and are a reason why it is premature to regard social capital in the same way as we do physical capital and the measurable forms of environmental capital.

This is not a pessimistic conclusion. Before we try to measure anything, we ought to ask why we wish to measure it. I do not believe we lose anything of significance in not being able to arrive at an estimate of social capital in a country, a region, a city, or wherever. The concept of social capital is useful insofar as it draws our attention to those particular institutions serving economic life that might otherwise go unnoted. Once attention is drawn to them, we need to try to understand them and find ways of improving them or building around them. But this is the very stuff of economics. Not having an estimate of social capital is not an impediment to such exercises.

### Democracy, civil liberties, and economic development

The government is an institution. Social networks enable citizens to acquire information about the workings of government apparatus, to form coalitions against government malfeasance and, more generally, to exercise their rights. Civic engagement, if appropriately channeled, can make government more accountable. Putnam (1993) offered this as one explanation for his finding that those Italian provinces where citizens have been more involved in civic engagement enjoy a better living standard.

The World Bank (1997) has recently described work with a similar motivation. On the basis of responses to an international questionnaire, it was found that the strength of public institutions is quantitatively a significant determinant of economic development as measured by such diverse indexes as infant survival, income growth, and rates of return on investment.[108] Government policy is a determinant too; what this new finding shows is that the quality of public institutions matters as well. Predictability in the making of rules, political

---

[108] Chhibber (1997) contains a summary of the findings.

stability, an absence of multilayered corruption and crime, and reliability in the judiciary reflect the capability of public institutions. The models developed in this essay tell us how we may account for these findings.

The agency view of government offers a particular interpretation of the findings. The thought is that political democracy and civil liberties together are a means by which government can be made accountable.[109] But the view used to be questioned often for poor countries, for it is not uncommon to hear the argument that citizens of poor countries cannot afford such luxuries as civil and political rights, that they are inimical to economic development. The question is, are they?

Dasgupta (1990) and Dasgupta and Weale (1992) explored possible links between political and civil liberties and *changes* in the standard of living. The study was restricted to poor countries. Since indexes of political and civil rights have no cardinal significance, only ordinal information was used. No attempt was made to search for causality in the relationships that emerged.

The sample consisted of countries where, in 1970, real national income per head was less than $1,500 at 1980 international dollars. There were 51 such countries with populations in excess of 1 million (Summers and Heston 1988). The period under observation was the decade of the 1970s. It was found that:

(a) Political and civil rights were positively and significantly correlated with real national income per head *and its growth*, with improvements in infant survival rates, and with increases in life expectancy at birth.

(b) Real national income per head and its growth were positively and significantly correlated, and they in turn were positively and significantly correlated with improvements in life expectancy at birth and infant survival rates.

(c) Improvements in life expectancy at birth and infant survival rates were, not surprisingly, highly correlated.

(d) Political and civil rights were not the same; but they were strongly correlated in the sample.

(e) Increases in the adult literacy rate were not related systematically to incomes per head, to their growth, or to infant survival rates. They were positively and significantly correlated with improvements in life expectancy at birth. But they were negatively and significantly correlated with political and civil liberties.

These observations suggest that literacy stands somewhat apart from other "goods." It does not appear to be driven with the three other mea-

---

[109] The literature is huge. Dahl (1989) contains a good summary. In Dasgupta (1993, chapters 5 and 17) I have gone into these issues in more detail.

sures of the living standard. Furthermore, regimes that had bad records in political and civil rights were associated with good performances in this field. I still have no explanation for this.

A criticism of cross-country statistical inquiries into the links between civil and political liberties, on the one hand, and improvements in the standard of living, on the other, has been that they have often arrived at contradictory results. But it is as well to check the methodologies deployed in such studies before worrying whether their answers tally. Numerical indexes of civil and political liberties have no cardinal significance, they make only ordinal sense. However, the majority of published studies have run linear regressions between indexes of freedom and measures of the living standard. That the findings in such studies are not consonant with those that make use only of ordinal information is no reason to think that the latter are uninformative.

Do our findings tally with those others that are based on ordinal measures? Barro (1996) is one of the few studies to have taken the ordinal nature of political and civil rights indexes seriously.[110] His sample contains 100 countries, and he finds that middle-level democracy (as measured by the same indexes of political civil liberties as the ones in Dasgupta 1990) is more favorable for growth in living standards than low levels. As the sample of countries studied in Dasgupta (1990) and Dasgupta and Weale (1992) contains at best middle-level democracies (and at worst, the worst there is in the field of human rights), Barro's finding is consonant with the earlier findings.[111]

Of course, the correlations observed in the data do not imply causation. Nor should one expect to find causality. Each of the indexes would be "endogenous" in any general political theory. For example, it is most probable that democracy is correlated with some omitted feature (such as the character of the constitution, the extent to which the rule of law is exercised or rights to property are secure, citizens' engagement in associational life, or the state's reliability in providing public services) that enhances growth in national income per head, or life expectancy at birth.[112] This essay has been

---

[110] But only in the second half of the article. The first half was devoted to running linear regressions.

[111] Isham, Kaufmann, and Pritchett (1997) have studied cross-national data on the performance of government investment projects financed by the World Bank. They have found a strong empirical link between civil liberties and the performance of government projects. Even after controlling for other determinants of performance, countries with the strongest civil liberties have projects with an economic rate of return that is 22 percent higher than countries with the weakest civil liberties.

[112] Weingast (1997) views "constitutions" as coordinating devices. In fact they are precommitment devices, a different matter entirely. But they are "devices," no more. A nation may have a sound constitution, but if it is violated, naught comes of it.

in large part an attempt to provide the links that make the required connection. We should also bear in mind that indexes of political and civil liberties can change dramatically in a nation, following a coup d'état, a rebellion, an election, or a similar event; and with a six-year average index, we must be careful in interpreting the statistical results.[113] Subject to these obvious cautions, what the evidence seems to be telling us is that, statistically speaking, of the 51 poor countries on observation, those whose citizens enjoyed greater political and civil liberties also experienced larger improvements in life expectancy at birth, real income per head, and infant survival rates. The argument that political and civil rights are luxuries poor countries cannot afford is belied by the data. This seems to me to be eminently worth knowing.

In an earlier work, I suggested that a recognition among citizens of the distinction between the private and the public realms, of the fact that the two realms have distinct claims on us, may well be central to economic development.[114] While it can be argued that differences between the "republican school of civic humanists" and their "liberal" counterparts have been overdrawn in recent writings among political scientists, the emphasis the latter group placed on the need for keeping our attitudes, aims, and passions in the two realms separate was entirely appropriate. Good citizenship involves our being able to change ourselves constantly, as we move back and forth between the two realms each day of our lives.

## References

The word *processed* describes informally reproduced works that may not be commonly available through libraries.

Abreu, Dilip. 1988. "On the Theory of Infinitely Repeated Games with Discounting." *Econometrica* 56: 383–96.

Adelman, Irma, and Cynthia Taft Morris. 1967. *Society, Politics and Economic Development: A Quantitative Approach.* Baltimore: Johns Hopkins University Press.

Agarwal, Anil, and Sunita Narain. 1989. *Towards Green Villages: A Strategy for Environmentally Sound and Participatory Rural Development.* New Delhi: Centre for Science and Development.

Agarwal, B. 1986. *Cold Hearths and Barren Slopes: The Woodfuel Crisis in the Third World.* New Delhi: Allied Publishers.

---

[113] As a matter of fact, though, changes in political and civil liberties indexes over the period 1973–79 were slight for most countries in the sample.
[114] Dasgupta (1993). Public and private realms are not to be identified with the public and private sectors.

Aghion, Philippe, and Peter Howitt. 1998. *Endogenous Growth Theory*. Cambridge, Mass.: MIT Press.

Akerlof, G. 1976. "The Economics of Caste and of Rat Races and Other Woeful Tales." *Quarterly Journal of Economics* 90: 599–617.

Anderlini, L., and A. Ianni. 1996. "Path Dependence and Learning from Neighbors." *Games and Economic Behaviour* 13: 141–77.

Aoki, Masahiko. 1996. "An Evolutionary Parable of the Gains from International Organizational Diversity." In R. Landau, T. Taylor, and G. Wright, eds., *The Mosaic of Economic Growth*. Stanford, Calif.: Stanford University Press.

Aoki, Masahiko, and Ronald P. Dore, eds. 1994. *The Japanese Firm: The Sources of Competitive Strength*. Oxford: Oxford University Press.

Arkes, H. R. 1996. "The Psychology of Waste." *Journal of Behavioural Decision-Making* 9: 213–27.

Arnott, Richard, and Joseph E. Stiglitz 1991. "Moral Hazard and Nonmarket Institutions: Dysfunctional Crowding Out or Peer Review?" *American Economic Review* 81: 179–90.

Arrow, Kenneth J. 1962. "Economic Welfare and the Allocation of Resources for Inventions." In R. Nelson, ed., *The Rate and Direction of Inventive Activity*. Princeton: Princeton University Press.

———. 1963. "Uncertainty and the Economics of Medical Care." *American Economic Review* 53: 941–73.

———. 1972. "Gifts and Exchanges." *Philosophy and Public Affairs* 1: 343–62.

———. 1973. "The Theory of Discrimination." In O. Ashenfelter and A. Rees, eds., *Discrimination in Labor Markets*. Princeton, New Jersey: Princeton University Press.

———. 1974. *The Limits of Organization*. New York: W. W. Norton.

———. 2000. "Observations on Social Capital." In Partha Dasgupta and Ismail Serageldin, eds. *Social Capital: A Multifaceted Perspective*. Washington, D.C.: World Bank.

Ascher, William. 1995. *Communities and Sustainable Forestry in Developing Countries*. San Francisco: ICS Press for International Center for Self-Governance.

Ascher, William, and Robert G. Healy. 1990. *Natural Resource Policymaking in Developing Countries: Environment, Economic Growth, and Income Distribution.* Durham, North Carolina: Duke University Press.

Atkinson, Anthony Barnes, and Joseph E. Stiglitz. 1980. *Lectures in Public Economics.* New York: McGraw Hill.

Axelrod, Robert M. 1984. *The Evolution of Cooperation.* New York: Basic Books.

Bala, V., and S. Goyal. 1997. "Self-Organization in Communication Networks." Processed, Department of Economics, McGill University, Montreal, Canada.

Baland, Jean-Marie, and Jean-Philippe Platteau. 1996. *Halting Degradation of Natural Resources: Is There a Role for Rural Communities?* Oxford: Clarendon Press.

Baland, Jean-Marie, and Jean-Philippe Platteau. 1997. "Division of the Commons." Cahiers de la Faculte des Sciences Economiques, Sociales et de Gestion N° 200, Facultes Universitaires Notre-Dame de la Paix, Namur, France.

Banerjee, Abhijit V. 1992. "A Simple Model of Herd Behaviour." *Quarterly Journal of Economics* 107 (August): 797–818.

Banerjee, Abhijit V., Timothy Besley, and Timothy W. Guinnane. 1994. "Thy Neighbor's Keeper: The Design of a Credit Cooperative with Theory and a Test." *Quarterly Journal of Economics* 109 (May): 491–515.

Banerjee, B. 1983. "Social Networks in the Migration Process: Empirical Evidence on Chain Migration in India." *Journal of Developing Areas* 17: 185–96.

Banfield, Edward C. 1958. *The Moral Basis of a Backward Society.* Chicago: Free Press.

Bardhan, Pranab K. 1984. *Land, Labor, and Rural Poverty: Essays in Development Economics.* New York: Columbia University Press.

———. 1996. "Research on Poverty and Development Twenty Years after *Redistribution with Growth.*" *Proceedings of the Annual World Bank Conference on Development Economics, 1995.* Supplement to the *World Bank Economic Review* and the *World Bank Research Observer,* pp. 59–72.

Bardhan, Pranab K., and D. Mookherjee 1998. "Expenditure Decentralization and the Delivery of Public Services in Developing Countries." Working Paper No. C98-104. Center for International and Development Economics Research, University of California, Berkeley.

Barkow, J. H., L. Cosmides, and J. Tooby, eds. 1992. *The Adapted Mind: Evolutionary Psychology and the Generation of Culture.* New York: Oxford University Press.

Barro, R. J. 1996. "Democracy and Growth." *Journal of Economic Growth* 1: 1–27.

Barro, R. J., and X. Sala-i-Martin. 1995. *Economic Growth.* New York: McGraw Hill.

Bernheim, B. Douglas. 1994. "A Theory of Conformity." *Journal of Political Economy* 102 (October): 841–77.

Besley, Timothy, and S. Coate. 1995. "Group Lending, Repayment Incentives and Social Collateral." *Journal of Development Economics* 46: 1–18.

Besley, Timothy, S. Coate, and G. Loury. 1993. "The Economics of Rotating Savings and Credit Associations." *American Economic Review* 83: 792–810.

Beteille, Andre, ed. 1983. *Equality and Inequality: Theory and Practice.* Delhi: Oxford University Press.

Bikhchandani, Sushil, David Hirshleifer, and Ivo Welch. 1992. "A Theory of Fads, Fashion, Custom, and Cultural Change as Informational Cascades." *Journal of Political Economy* 100: 992–1026.

Bikhchandani, Sushil, David Hirshleifer, and Ivo Welch. 1998. "Learning from the Behaviour of Others: Conformity, Fads, and Informational Cascades." *Journal of Economic Perspectives* 12: 151–70.

Binmore, Ken. 1997. "Rationality and Backward Induction." *Journal of Economic Methodology* 4: 23–41.

Binswanger, Hans. 1991. "Brazilian Policies that Encourage Deforestation in the Amazon." *World Development* 19: 821–29.

Bledsoe, C. 1994. " 'Children Are Like Young Bamboo Trees': Potentiality and Reproduction in Sub-Saharan Africa." In K. Lindahl-Kiessling and H. Landberg, eds., *Population, Economic Development, and the Environment: The Making of Our Common Future.* Oxford: Oxford University Press.

Boorman, S. 1975. "A Combinatorial Optimization Model for Transmission of Job Information through Contact Network." *Bell Journal of Economics* (Spring): 216–49.

Border, Kim C., and Uzi Segal. 1997. "Preferences over Solutions to the Bargaining Problem." *Econometrica* 65(1): 1–18.

Braverman, A., and J. L. Gausch. 1984. "Capital Requirements, Screening, and Interlinked Sharecropping and Credit Contracts." *Journal of Development Economics* 14: 359–74.

Braverman, A., and J. E. Stiglitz. 1982. "Sharecropping and the Interlinking of Agrarian Markets." *American Economic Review* 72: 695–715.

Brock, W. A., and S. N. Durlauf. 1999. "Interactions-Based Models." Social Systems Research Institute, University of Wisconsin, Madison. Forthcoming, in J. J. Heckman and E. Leamer, eds., *Handbook of Econometrics, 5.* Amsterdam: North Holland.

Bromley, Daniel W., David Feeny, eds. 1992. *Making the Commons Work: Theory, Practice and Policy.* San Francisco: ICS Press.

Burdzy, K., D. M. Frankel, and A. Pauzner. 1997. "Fast Equilibrium Selection by Rational Players Living in a Changing World." Working Paper No. 7–97, Foeder Institute for Economic Research, Tel-Aviv University.

Burt, R. S. 1992. *Structural Holes: The Social Structure of Competition.* Cambridge, Mass.: Cambridge University Press.

Burt, R. S., R. M. Hogarth, and C. Michaud. 1998. "The Social Capital of French and American Managers." Processed, Graduate School of Business, University of Chicago.

Caldwell, J. C. 1969. *African Rural-Urban Migration.* Canberra: Australian National University.

———. 1991. "The Soft Underbelly of Development: Demographic Transition in Conditions of Limited Economic Change." In *Proceedings of the Annual Bank Conference on Development Economics 1990.* Supplement to the *World Bank Economic Review* and the *World Bank Research Observer,* pp. 207–54.

Carmichael, H. L. 1988. "Incentives in Academics: Why Is There Tenure?" *Journal of Political Economy* 96: 453–472.

Carrington, W. J., E. Detragiache, and T. Vishwanath. 1996. "Migration and Endogenous Moving Costs." *American Economic Review* 86: 909–30.

Cavendish, W. 1998. "The Complexity of the Commons: Environmental Resource Demands in Rural Zimbabwe." Processed, Centre for the Study of African Economies, University of Oxford.

Cavendish, W. 1999. "Poverty, Inequality and Environmental Resources: Quantitative Analysis of Rural Households." Processed, TH Huxley School, Imperial College of Science, Technology and Medicine, London.

Chambers, Robert. 1988. *Managing Canal Irrigation: Practical Analysis from South Asia.* Cambridge (UK): Cambridge University Press.

Cheng, P. W., and K. J. Holyoak. 1985. "Pragmatic Reasoning Schemas." *Cognitive Psychology* 17: 391–416.

Chhibber, Ajay. 1997. "Institutions, Policies and Development Outcomes." Processed, World Bank, Washington, D.C.

Chopra, K. R., and S. C. Gulati. 1998. "Environmental Degradation, Property Rights and Population Movements: Hypotheses and Evidence from Rajasthan (India)." *Environment and Development Economics* 3: 35–57.

Chopra, K. R., G. K. Kadekodi, and M. N. Murty. 1990. *Participatory Development: People and Common Property Resources.* New Delhi: Sage.

Cleaver, K. M., and G. A. Schreiber. 1994. *Reversing the Spiral: The Population, Agriculture, and Environment Nexus in Sub-Saharan Africa.* Washington, D.C.: World Bank.

Coase, R. H. 1960. "The Problem of Social Cost." *Journal of Law and Economics* 3: 1–44.

Coate, Stephen, and G. C. Loury. 1993. "Will Affirmative-Action Policies Eliminate Negative Stereotypes?" *American Economic Review* 83: 1220–40.

Colchester, M. 1995. "Sustaining the Forests: The Community-Based Approach in South and South-East Asia." *Development and Change* 25: 69–100.

Coleman, James S. 1990. *Foundations of Social Theory*. Cambridge, Mass.: Harvard University Press.

Coles, Robert. 1997. *The Moral Intelligence of Children*. New York: Random House.

Cooper, Russell, and Andrew John. 1988. "Coordinating Coordination Failures in Keynesian Models." *Quarterly Journal of Economics* 103 (August): 441–63.

Cordell, J., and M. McKean. 1986. "Sea Tenure in Bahia, Brazil." In National Research Council, *Proceedings of the Conference on Common Property Resource Management*. Washington, D.C.: National Academy Press.

Cosmides, L., and J. Tooby. 1992. "Cognitive Adaptations for Social Exchange." In J. H. Barkow, L. Cosmides, and J. Tooby, eds., *The Adapted Mind: Evolutionary Psychology and the Generation of Culture*. Oxford: Oxford University Press.

Coward, E. W. 1985. "Technical and Social Change in Currently Irrigated Regions: Rules, Roles and Rehabilitation." In M. M. Cernea, ed., *Putting People First: Sociological Variables in Rural Development*. Oxford: Oxford University Press.

C.S.E. (Centre for Science and Environment). 1982, 1985. *The State of India's Environment*. New Delhi: Centre for Science and Environment.

Czako, Á., and E. Sik. 1988. "Manager's Reciprocal Transactions." *Connections* 11: 23–32.

Dahl, Robert Alan. 1989. *Democracy and Its Critics*. New Haven, Conn.: Yale University Press.

Dasgupta, Partha. 1988. "Trust as a Commodity." In Diego Gambetta, ed., *Trust: Making and Breaking Cooperative Relations*. Oxford: Basil Blackwell.

———. 1990. "Well-Being and the Extent of Its Realization in Poor Countries." *Economic Journal* 100 (Supplement): 1–32.

———. 1993. *An Inquiry into Well-Being and Destitution.* Oxford: Clarendon Press.

———. 1994. "Savings and Fertility: Ethical Issues." *Philosophy & Public Affairs* (Spring): 99–127.

———. 1995. "The Population Problem: Theory and Evidence." *Journal of Economic Literature* 33: 1879–1902.

———. 1996. "The Economics of the Environment." *Environment and Development Economics* 1: 387–428.

———. 1997. *Environmental and Resource Economics in the World of the Poor.* Washington, D.C.: Resources for the Future.

Dasgupta, Partha, and G. M. Heal. 1979. *Economic Theory and Exhaustible Resources.* Cambridge (UK): Cambridge University Press.

Dasgupta, Partha, and P. A. David. 1987. "Information Disclosure and the Economics of Science and Technology." In G. Feiwel, ed., *Arrow and the Ascent of Modern Economic Theory.* New York: New York University Press.

Dasgupta, Partha, and P. A. David. 1994. "Toward a New Economics of Science." *Research Policy* 23: 487–521.

Dasgupta, Partha, and K.-G. Mäler. 1991. "The Environment and Emerging Development Issues." *Proceedings of the World Bank Annual Conference on Development Economics 1990.* Supplement to the *World Bank Economic Review* and the *World Bank Research Observer,* pp. 101–32.

Dasgupta, Partha, and J. E. Stiglitz. 1988. "Learning by Doing, Market Structure and Industrial and Trade Policies." *Oxford Economic Papers* 40: 246–68.

Dasgupta, Partha, and Martin Weale. 1992. "On Measuring the Quality of Life." *World Development* 20(1): 119.

David, P. A. 1976. "The Landscape and the Machine: Technical Interrelatedness, Land Tenure, and the Mechanization of the Corn Harvest in Victorian Britain." In *Technical Choice, Innovation and Economic Growth: Essays on American and British Experience in the Nineteenth Century.* Cambridge (UK): Cambridge University Press.

———. 1998. "Common Agency Contracting and the Emergence of 'Open Science' Institutions." *American Economic Review* 88 (Papers & Proceedings): 15–21.

Davies, F. H., J. H. Fetzer, and T. R. Foster. 1995. "Logical Reasoning and Domain Specificity: A Critique of the Social Exchange Theory of Reasoning." *Biology and Philosophy* 10: 1–37.

Deaton, A. 1991. "Saving and Liquidity Constraints." *Econometrica* 59: 1221–48.

Diamond, P. 1982. "Aggregate Demand Management in Search Equilibrium." *Journal of Political Economy* 90: 881–94.

Dixit, Avinash K. 1996. *The Making of Economic Policy: A Transaction-Cost Politics Perspective*. Cambridge, Mass.: MIT Press.

Douglas, M. 1982. "Cultural Bias." In M. Douglas, ed., *In the Active Voice*. London: Routledge & Kegan Paul.

Duesenbery, J. S. 1949. *Income, Savings and the Theory of Consumer Behavior*. Cambridge, Mass.: Harvard University Press.

Easterlin, R. 1974. "Does Economic Growth Improve the Human Lot? Some Empirical Evidence." In P. A. David and M. Reder, eds., *Nations and Households in Economic Growth: Essays in Honor of Moses Abramowitz*. New York: Academic Press.

Easterlin, R., R. Pollak, and M. Wachter. 1980. "Toward a More General Model of Fertility Determination: Endogenous Preferences and Natural Fertility." In R. Easterlin, ed., *Population and Economic Change in Developing Countries*. Chicago: University of Chicago Press.

Egan, M. L., and A. Mody. 1992. "Buyer-Seller Links in Export Development." *World Development* 20: 321–34.

Eisenberg, Nancy, and Paul Henry Mussen. 1989. *The Roots of Prosocial Behaviour in Children*. Cambridge (UK): Cambridge University Press.

Ellison, Glenn. 1993. "Learning, Local Interaction, and Coordination." *Econometrica* 61: 1047–72.

Elster, Jon. 1989. *The Cement of Society: A Study of Social Order*. Cambridge (UK): Cambridge University Press.

Eshel, Ilan, Larry Samuelson, and Avner Shaked. 1998. "Altruists, Egoists, and Hooligans in a Local Interaction Model." *American Economic Review* 88: 157–79.

Esman, M. J., and N. T. Uphoff. 1984. *Local Organizations: Intermediaries in Rural Development.* Ithaca, New York: Cornell University Press.

Falconer, Julia. 1990. *The Major Significance of "Minor" Forest Products.* Rome: Food and Agricultural Organization.

Farrell, Joseph, and Garth Saloner. 1985. "Standardization, Compatibility, and Innovation." *Rand Journal of Economics* 16: 70–83.

Feeny, David, et al. 1990. "The Tragedy of the Commons: Twenty-Two Years Later." *Human Ecology* 18: 1–19.

Fehr, Ernst, Simon Gächter, and George Kirchsteiger. 1997. "Reciprocity as a Contract Enforcement Device: Experimental Evidence." *Econometrica* 65 (July): 833–60.

Fehr, Ernst, G. Kirchsteiger, and A. Riedl. 1998. "Gift Exchange and Reciprocity in Competitive Experimental Situations." *European Economic Review* 42: 1–34.

Fortes, M. 1978. "Parenthood, Marriage and Fertility in West Africa." *Journal of Development Studies* 14 (Special Issue on Population and Development): 121–49.

Foster, Dean, and Peyton Young. 1990. "Stochastic Evolutionary Game Dynamics." *Theoretical Population Biology* 38: 219–32.

Frank, R. H. 1997. "The Frame of Reference as a Public Good." *Economic Journal* 107: 1832–47.

Frey, B. S., and I. Bohnet. 1996. "Cooperation, Communication and Communitarianism: An Experimental Approach." *Journal of Political Philosophy* 4: 322–36.

Friedman, J. 1971. "A Noncooperative Equilibrium for Supergames." *Review of Economic Studies* 38: 1–12.

Fudenberg, Drew, and David K. Levine. 1998. *The Theory of Learning in Games.* Cambridge, Mass.: MIT Press.

Fudenberg, Drew, and E. Maskin. 1986. "The Folk Theorem in Repeated Games with Discounting or with Incomplete Information." *Econometrica* 54: 533–56.

Fudenberg, Drew, and Jean Tirole. 1991. *Game Theory.* Cambridge, Mass.: MIT Press.

Fukuyama, Francis. 1995. *Trust: The Social Virtues and the Creation of Prosperity.* New York: The Free Press.

———. 1997. *Social Capital.* Tanner Lectures, Brasenose College, Oxford; Processed, Institute of Public Policy, George Mason University, Fairfax, Virginia.

Galor, Oded, and Daniel Tsiddon. 1997. "Technological Progress, Mobility, and Economic Growth." *American Economic Review* 87 (June): 363–82.

Gambetta, Diego. 1988. "Can We Trust Trust?" In D. Gambetta, ed., *Trust: Making and Breaking Cooperative Relations.* Oxford: Basil Blackwell.

———. 1993. *The Mafia: A Ruinous Rationality.* Cambridge, Mass.: Harvard University Press.

Gaspard, Francoise, M. Jabbar, C. Melard, and J.-P. Platteau. 1997. "Participation in the Construction of a Local Public Good: A Case Study of Watershed Management in the Ethiopian Highlands." Cahiers de la Faculte des Sciences Economiques, Sociales et de Gestion N° 181, Facultes Universitaires Notre-Dame de la Paix, Namur, France.

Geddes, B. 1990. "How the Cases You Choose Affect the Answers You Get: Selection Bias in Comparative Politics." *Political Analysis* 2: 131–50.

Geertz, C. 1962. "The Rotating Credit Association: A 'Middle Rung' in Development." *Economic Development and Cultural Change* 10: 241–63.

Ghai, Dharam P., and Jessica M. Vivian, eds. 1992. *Grassroots Environmental Action: People's Participation in Sustainable Development.* London: Routledge.

Gladwell, Malcolm. 1999. "Six Degrees of Lois Weisberg: The Secret Power of the Woman Who Knows Everybody." *New Yorker,* January 11, pp. 52–63.

Glaeser, Edward L., B. Sacerdote, and J. A. Scheinkman. 1996. "Crime and Social Interactions." *Quarterly Journal of Economics* 111: 507–48.

Good, D. 1988. "Individuals, Interpersonal Relations, and Trust." In D. Gambetta, *Trust: Making and Breaking Cooperative Relations.* Oxford: Basil Blackwell.

———. 1996. "Patience and Control: The Importance of Maintaining the Link between Producers and Users." In B. Gorayska and J. L. Mey, eds., *Cognitive Technology: In Search of a Humane Interface.* Amsterdam: Elsevier Science.

Goody, Esther N. 1982. *Parenthood and Social Reproduction: Fostering and Occupational Roles in West Africa.* Cambridge (UK): Cambridge University Press.

Goody, Jack. 1976. *Production and Reproduction.* Cambridge (UK): Cambridge University Press.

———. 1986. *The Logic of Writing and the Organization of Society.* Cambridge (UK): Cambridge University Press.

———. 1996. *The East in the West.* Cambridge (UK): Cambridge University Press.

———. 1998. *Food and Love: A Cultural History of East and West.* London: Verso.

Gould, David M. 1994. "Immigrant Links to the Home Country: Empirical Implications for US Bilateral Trade Flows." *Review of Economics and Statistics* 76 (May): 302–16.

Granato, Jim, Ronald Inglehart, and David Leblang. 1996a. "The Effect of Cultural Values on Economic Development: Theory, Hypotheses, and Some Empirical Tests." *American Journal of Political Science* 40: 607–31.

Granato, Jim, Ronald Inglehart, and David Leblang. 1996b. "Cultural Values, Stable Democracy, and Economic Development: A Reply." *American Journal of Political Science* 40: 680–96.

Granovetter, M. S. 1973. "The Strength of Weak Ties." *American Journal of Sociology* 78: 1360–80.

———. 1974. *Getting a Job: A Study of Contacts and Careers.* Chicago: University of Chicago Press.

———. 1985. "Economic Action and Social Structure: The Problem of Embeddedness." *American Journal of Sociology* 90: 481–510.

Greif, Avner. 1993. "Contract Enforceability and Economic Institutions in Early Trade: The Maghribi Traders' Coalition." *American Economic Review* 83: 525–48.

———. 1994. "Cultural Beliefs and the Organization of Society: A Historical and Theoretical Reflection on Collectivist and Individualist Societies." *Journal of Political Economy* 102: 912–50.

———. 1997a. "On the Social Foundations and Historical Development of Institutions that Facilitate Impersonal Exchange: From the Community Responsibility to Individual Legal Responsibility in Pre-Modern Europe." Processed, Department of Economics, Stanford University.

———. 1997b. "Cultural Beliefs as a Common Resource in an Integrating World: An Example from the Theory and History of Collectivist and Individualist Societies." In P. Dasgupta, K.-G. Mäler, and A. Vercelli, eds., *The Economics of Transnational Commons*. Oxford: Clarendon Press.

Greif, Avner, P. Milgrom, and B. Weingast. 1994. "Coordination, Commitment, and Enforcement: The Case of the Merchant Guild." *Journal of Political Economy* 102: 745–76.

Güth, Wilfried, R. Schmittberger, and B. Schwarz. 1982. "An Experimental Analysis of Ultimatum Bargaining." *Journal of Economic Behaviour and Organization* 3: 367–88.

Guyer, J. L. 1994. "Lineal Identities and Lateral Networks: The Logic of Polyandrous Motherhood." In C. Bledsoe and G. Pison, eds., *Nuptiality in Sub-Saharan Africa: Contemporary Anthropological and Demographic Perspectives*. Oxford: Clarendon Press.

Hammond, P. J. 1975. "Charity: Altruism or Cooperative Egoism?" In E. Phelps, ed., *Altruism, Morality and Economic Theory*. New York: Russell Sage Foundation.

Hardin, G. 1968. "The Tragedy of the Commons." *Science* 162: 1243–48.

Hart, O., and B. Holmstrom. 1987. "The Theory of Contracts." In T. Bewley, ed., *Advances in Economic Theory*. Cambridge (UK): Cambridge University Press.

Hayami, Yujiro. 1997. *Development Economics: From the Poverty to the Wealth of Nations*. Oxford: Clarendon Press.

———. 1998. "Toward an East Asian Model of Economic Development." In Y. Hayami and M. Aoki, eds., *The Institutional Foundations of East Asian Economic Development*. London: Macmillan.

Hayami, Yujiro, and Jean-Philippe Platteau. 1997. "Resource Endowments and Agricultural Developments: Africa vs. Asia." Facultes Universitaires Notre-Dame de la Paix, Namur, France. Faculte des Sciences Economiques et Sociales. Cahiers: Series Recherche (Belgium), No. 192 (June): 1–54.

Hecht, S. B., A. B. Anderson, and P. May. 1988. " Subsidy from Nature: Shifting Cultivation, Successional Palm Forests, and Rural Development." *Human Organization* 47 (Spring): 25–35.

Helliwell, John F. 1996. "Economic Growth and Social Capital in Asia." NBER Working Paper 5695, National Bureau of Economic Research, Cambridge, Mass.

Helliwell, John F., and Robert D. Putnam. 1995. "Economic Growth and Social Capital in Italy." *Eastern Economic Journal* 21: 295–307.

Hill, K. 1992. "Fertility and Mortality Trends in the Developing World," *Ambio* 21: 79–83.

Hinde, Robert A., and Jo Groebel, eds. 1991. *Cooperation and Prosocial Behaviour*. Cambridge (UK): Cambridge University Press.

Hirschman, Albert O. 1984. "Against Parsimony: Three Easy Ways of Complicating Some Categories of Economic Discourse." *American Economic Review* 74 (Papers & Proceedings): 88–96.

Hogg, M. A., and G. M. Vaughan. 1995. *Social Psychology: An Introduction*. London: Prentice Hall/Harvester Wheatsheaf.

Holden, S. T., B. Shiferaw, and M. Wik. 1998. "Poverty, Market Imperfections and Time Preference: Of Relevance for Environmental Policy?" *Environment and Development Economics* 3: 105–30.

Holland, J. H. 1995. *Hidden Order: How Adaptation Builds Complexity*. Reading, Mass.: Addison-Wesley.

Hollis, Martin. 1998. *Trust within Reason.* Cambridge (UK): Cambridge University Press.

Howe, James. 1986. *The Kuna Gathering: Contemporary Village Politics in Panama.* Austin, Tex.: University of Texas Press.

Isham, Jonathan, Daniel Kaufmann, and Lant H. Pritchett. 1997. "Civil Liberties, Democracy, and the Performance of Government Projects." *World Bank Economic Review* 11(2): 219–42.

Jackman, R. W., and R. A. Miller. 1996a. "A Renaissance of Political Culture?" *American Journal of Political Science* 40: 632–59.

Jackman, R. W., and R. A. Miller. 1996b. "The Poverty of Political Culture." *American Journal of Political Science* 40: 697–716.

Jodha, N. S. 1986. "Common Property Resources and the Rural Poor." *Economic and Political Weekly* 21: 1169–81.

———. 1995. "Common Property Resources and the Environmental Context: Role of Biophysical versus Social Stress." *Economic and Political Weekly* 30: 3278–83.

Jorgenson, D. W., and B. M. Fraumeni. 1989. "The Accumulation of Human and Non-Human Capital, 1948–1984." In R. E. Lipsey and H. S. Tice, eds., *The Measurement of Income, Saving and Wealth.* Chicago: University of Chicago Press.

Jorgenson, D. W., and B. M. Fraumeni. 1992a. "The Output of the Education Sector." In Z. Griliches, ed., *Output Measurement in the Services Sector.* Chicago: University of Chicago Press.

Jorgenson, D. W., and B. M. Fraumeni. 1992b. "Investment in Education and US Economic Growth." *Scandinavian Journal of Economics* 94: 51–70.

Kandori, Michihiro. 1992a. "Social Norms and Community Enforcement." *Review of Economic Studies* 59 (January): 63–80.

———. 1992b. "Repeated Games Played by Overlapping Generations of Players." *Review of Economic Studies* 59 (January): 81–92.

Kandori, Michihiro, G. J. Mailath, and R. Rob. 1993. "Learning, Mutation and Long Run Equilibria in Games." *Econometrica* 61: 29–56.

Katz, M. L., and C. Shapiro. 1985. "Network Externalities, Competition, and Compatibility." *American Economic Review* 75: 424–40.

Kerrigan, John. 1996. *Revenge Tragedy: Aeschylus to Armageddon*. Oxford: Clarendon Press.

Keynes, J. M. 1936. *The General Theory of Employment, Interest and Money*. London: MacMillan.

Kim, J.-I., and L. J. Lau. 1992. "The Sources of Economic Growth of the Newly Industrialized Countries on the Pacific Rim." Processed, Department of Economics, Stanford University.

Knack, Stephen, and Philip Keefer. 1997. "Does Social Capital Have an Economic Payoff: A Cross Country Investigation." *Quarterly Journal of Economics* 112 (November): 1251–88.

Kranton, R. E. 1996. "Reciprocal Exchange: A Self-Sustaining System." *American Economic Review* 86: 830–51.

Kreps. David M. 1990. "Corporate Culture and Economic Theory." In J. E. Alt and K. A. Shepsle, eds., *Perspectives on Positive Political Economy*. New York: Cambridge University Press.

Laffont, J.-J. 1999. *Incentives and Political Economy*. Oxford: Clarendon Press.

Laffont, J.-J., and J. Tirole. 1993. *A Theory of Incentives in Procurement and Regulation*. Cambridge, Mass.: MIT Press.

Lam, W. F. 1998. *Governing Irrigation Systems in Nepal: Institutions, Infrastructure, and Collective Action*. Oakland, Calif.: ICS Press for International Center for Self-Governance.

Landes, David S. 1998. *The Wealth and Poverty of Nations: Why Some Are So Rich and Some So Poor*. London: Little, Brown and Company.

La Porta, Rafael, Florencio Lopez-de-Silanes, Andrei Schleifer, and Robert W. Vishny. 1997. "Trust in Large Organizations." *American Economic Review* 87 (Papers & Proceedings): 333–38.

Lau, L. J. 1996. "The Sources of Long-Term Economic Growth: Observations from the Experience of Developed and Developing Countries." In R. Landau, T. Taylor, and G. Wright, eds., *The Mosaic of Economic Growth*. Stanford, Calif.: Stanford University Press.

Ledyard, J. O. 1995. "Public Goods: A Survey of Experimental Research." In J. H. Kagel and A. E. Roth, eds., *The Handbook of Experimental Economics*. Princeton, New Jersey: Princeton University Press.

Lindbeck, Assar. 1995a. "Welfare State Disincentives with Endogenous Habits and Norms." *Scandinavian Journal of Economics* 97: 477–94.

————. 1995b. "Hazardous Welfare-State Dynamics." *American Economic Review* 85 (Papers & Proceedings): 9–15.

————. 1997. "Incentives and Social Norms in Household Behavior." *American Economic Review* 87 (Papers & Proceedings): 370–77.

Lindbeck, Assar, S. Nyberg, and J. W. Weibull. 1999. "Social Norms and Economic Incentives in the Welfare State." *Quarterly Journal of Economics* 114: 1–36.

Lopez, R. 1998. "The Tragedy of the Commons in Cote d'Ivoire Agriculture: Empirical Evidence and Implications for Evaluating Trade Policies." *World Bank Economic Review* 12: 105–32.

Luhmann, Niklas. 1979. *Trust and Power*. Chichester, UK, and New York: John Wiley.

————. 1988. "Familiarity, Confidence, Trust: Problems and Alternatives." In D. Gambetta, ed., *Trust: Making and Breaking Cooperative Relations*. Oxford: Basil Blackwell.

Madajewicz, M. 1997. "Capital for the Poor: the Role of Monitoring." Processed, Department of Economics, Harvard University.

Manguel, Alberto. 1997. *A History of Reading*. London: Flamingo.

Matsui, Akihiko, and Kiminori Matsuyama. 1995. "An Approach to Equilibrium Selection." *Journal of Economic Theory* 65(2): 415–34.

Maynard Smith, J. 1982. *Evolution and the Theory of Games*. Cambridge (UK): Cambridge University Press.

McCay, B. J., and J. M. Acheson, eds. 1987. *The Question of the Commons: The Culture and Ecology of Communal Resources*. Tucson, Ariz.: University of Arizona Press.

McKean, M. 1986. "Management of Traditional Common Lands (Iriaichi) in Japan." In National Research Council, *Proceedings of the Confer-*

*ence on Common Property Resource Management.* Washington, D.C.: National Academy Press.

―――. 1992. "Success on the Commons: A Comparative Examination of Institutions for Common Property Resource Management." *Journal of Theoretical Politics* 4: 256–68.

Milgrom, Paul, D. North, and B. Weingast. 1990. "The Role of Institutions in the Revival of Trade: The Law Merchant, Private Judges, and the Champagne Fairs." *Economics and Politics* 1: 1–23.

Moriguchi, C. 1997. "The Evolution of Employment Systems in the US and Japan, 1900–1960: A Comparative Historical and Institutional Analysis." Processed, Department of Economics, Stanford University.

Mortensen, D., and T. Vishwanath. 1994. "Personal Contacts and Earnings: It's Who You Know." *Labour Economics* 1: 177–201.

Myles, G. D. 1995. *Public Economics.* Cambridge (UK): Cambridge University Press.

Narayan, Deepa, and Lant Pritchett. 1997. "Cents and Sociability: Household Income and Social Capital in Rural Tanzania." Processed, World Bank, Washington, D.C.

Netting, R. McC. 1981. *Balancing on an Alp.* Cambridge (UK): Cambridge University Press.

―――. 1997. "Unequal Commoners and Uncommon Equity: Property and Community among Smallholder Farmers." *The Ecologist* 27: 28–33.

Ogilvie, Sheilagh. 1995. "Institutions and Economic Development in Early Modern Central Europe." *Transactions of the Royal Historical Society* 5, Series 6, pp. 221–50.

―――. 1997. *State Corporation and Proto-Industry: The Wurttemberg Black Forest 1580–1797.* Cambridge (UK): Cambridge University Press.

Olson, Mancur. 1982. *The Rise and Decline of Nations: Economic Growth, Stagflation and Social Rigidities.* New Haven, Conn.: Yale University Press.

Ostrom, Elinor. 1990. *Governing the Commons: The Evolution of Institutions for Collective Action.* Cambridge (UK): Cambridge University Press.

————. 1992. *Crafting Institutions for Self-Governing Irrigation Systems*. San Francisco: ISC Press for Institute for Contemporary Studies.

————. 1996. "Incentives, Rules of the Game, and Development." *Proceedings of the Annual World Bank Conference on Development Economics, 1995*. Supplement to the *World Bank Economic Review* and the *World Bank Research Observer*, pp. 207–34.

————. 1998. "A Behavioral Approach to the Rational Choice Theory of Collective Action." *American Political Science Review* 92: 1–22.

Ostrom, Elinor, and R. Gardner. 1993. "Coping with Asymmetries in the Commons: Self-Governing Irrigations Can Work." *Journal of Economic Perspectives* 7: 93–112.

Ostrom, Elinor, R. Gardner, and J. Walker. 1994. *Rules, Games & Common-Pool Resources*. Ann Arbor, Mich.: Michigan University Press.

Oswald, A. J. 1997. "Happiness and Economic Performance." *Economic Journal* 107(445): 1815–31.

Platteau, Jean-Philippe. 1994a. "Behind the Market Stage Where Real Societies Exist, Part I: The Role of Public and Private Order Institutions." *Journal of Development Studies* 30(3): 533–77.

————. 1994b. "Behind the Market Stage Where Real Societies Exist, Part II: The Role of Moral Norms." *Journal of Development Studies* 30(4): 753–817.

————. 1996. "Traditional Sharing Norms as an Obstacle to Economic Growth in Tribal Societies." Cahiers de la Faculte des Sciences Economiques, Sociales et de Gestion N° 173, Facultes Universitaires Notre-Dame de la Paix, Namur, France.

Powell, Walter W. 1990. "Neither Market nor Hierarchy: Network Forms of Organization." *Research in Organizational Behaviour* 12: 295–336.

Powell, Walter W., and P. Brantley. 1992. "Competitive Cooperation in Biotechnology: Learning Through Networks?" In Nitin Nohria and Robert G. Eccles, eds., *Networks and Organizations*. Cambridge, Mass.: Harvard Business School Press.

Przeworski, A. 1991. *Democracy and the Market*. Cambridge (UK): Cambridge University.

Putnam, Robert D. (with Robert Leonardi and Rafaella Y. Nanetti). 1993. *Making Democracy Work: Civic Traditions in Modern Italy*. Princeton, New Jersey: Princeton University Press.

Putnam, Robert D. 1995. "Bowling Alone: America's Declining Social Capital." *Journal of Democracy* 6: 65–78.

Rabin, Matthew. 1993. "Incorporating Fairness into Game Theory and Economics." *American Economic Review* 83: 1281–1302.

Rae, D. W. 1999. "Small Tyrannies of Place: The Pursuit of Democratic Liberty in 10 Tier Neighborhoods." In I. Shapiro and C. Hacker-Cordon, eds., *Democracy's Edges*. New York: Cambridge University Press.

Rauch, J. E. 1996a. "Trade and Search: Social Capital, *Sogo Shosha*, and Spillovers." Processed, Department of Economics, University of California, San Diego.

———. 1996b. "Networks versus Markets in International Trade." NBER Working Paper 5617, National Bureau of Economic Research, Cambridge, Mass.

Rawls, John. 1972. *A Theory of Justice*. Oxford: Oxford University Press.

Repetto, Robert C., W. Magrath, M. Wells, C. Beer, and F. Rossini. 1989. *Wasting Assets: Natural Resources in the National Income Accounts*. Washington, D.C.: World Resources Institute.

Rest, J. R. 1983. "Morality." In J. H. Flavell and E. M. Markman, eds., *Handbook of Child Psychology, III: Cognitive Development*. New York: John Wiley & Sons.

Rodrik, D. 1997. "The 'Paradoxes' of the Successful State." *European Economic Review* 41 (Papers & Proceedings): 411–42.

Romer, David. 1996. *Advanced Macroeconomics*. New York: McGraw Hill.

Rose, Richard. 1995. "Russia as an Hour-Glass Society: A Constitution without Citizens." *East European Constitutional Review* 4: 34–42.

Roth, A. E. 1995. "Bargaining Experiments." In J. H. Kagel and A. E. Roth, eds., *The Handbook of Experimental Economics*. Princeton, New Jersey: Princeton University Press.

Rotter, J. B. 1980. "Interpersonal Trust, Trustworthiness and Gullibility." *American Psychologist* 35: 1–7.

Rubinstein, A. 1979. "Equilibrium in Supergames with the Overtaking Criterion." *Review of Economic Studies* 21: 1–9.

Rudra, Ashok. 1984. "Local Power and Farm-Level Decision-Making." In Meghnad Desai, Susanne Hoeber Rudolph, and Ashok Rudra, eds., *Agrarian Power and Agricultural Productivity in South Asia*. Berkeley, Calif.: University of California Press.

Rutter, D. R. 1984. *Looking and Seeing: The Role of Visual Communication in Social Interaction*. Chichester, UK: Wiley.

Sally, D. 1995. "Conversation and Cooperation in Social Dilemmas: A Meta-Analysis of Experiments from 1958 to 1992." *Rationality and Society* 7: 58–92.

Schama, Simon. 1987. *The Embarrassment of Riches: An Interpretation of Dutch Culture in the Golden Age*. London: Collins.

Schelling, Thomas C. 1978. *Micromotives and Macrobehaviour*. New York: W. W. Norton.

Scitovsky, Tibor. 1976. *The Joyless Economy: An Inquiry into Human Satisfaction and Consumer Dissatisfaction*. Oxford: Oxford University Press.

Schneider, R. R. 1995. *Government and the Economy on the Amazon Frontier*. World Bank Environment Paper No. 11, World Bank, Washington, D.C.

Seabright, Paul. 1993. "Managing Local Commons: Theoretical Issues in Incentive Design." *Journal of Economic Perspectives* 7: 113–34.

———. 1997. "Is Cooperation Habit-Forming?" In P. Dasgupta and K.-G. Mäler, eds., *The Environment and Emerging Development Issues, Vol. II*. Oxford: Clarendon Press.

Seki, E., and J.-P. Platteau. 1998. "Coordination and Pooling Arrangements in Japanese Coastal Fisheries." Cahiers de la Faculte des Sciences Economiques, Sociales et de Gestion Nº 208, Facultes Universitaires Notre-Dame de la Paix, Namur, France.

Sen, Amartya. 1977. "Rational Fools: A Critique of the Behavioural Foundations of Economic Theory." *Philosophy & Public Affairs* 6: 317–44.

Serageldin, Ismail. 1996. "Sustainability as Opportunity and the Problem of Social Capital." *Brown Journal of World Affairs* 3: 187–203.

Serageldin, Ismail, and Christiaan Grootaert. 1997. "Defining Social Capital: An Integrating View." Processed, Vice Presidency for Environmentally Sustainable Development, World Bank, Washington, D.C.

Serra, R. 1996. *An Economic Analysis of Child Fostering in West Africa*. Ph.D. Dissertation, Faculty of Economics, University of Cambridge.

Sethi, Rajiv, and E. Somanathan. 1996. "The Evolution of Social Norms in Common Property Resource Use." *American Economic Review* 86: 766–88.

Shantz, C. U. 1983. "Social Cognition." In J. H. Flavell and E. M. Markman, eds., *Handbook of Child Psychology, III: Cognitive Development*. New York: John Wiley & Sons.

Smith, P. B., and M. H. Bond. 1993. *Social Psychology across Cultures: Analysis and Perspectives*. London: Harvester Wheatsheaf.

Solow, R. M. 1995. "But Verify." *The New Republic*, September 11, pp. 36–39. (Review of F. Fukuyama, *Trust: The Social Virtues and the Creation of Prosperity*. New York: The Free Press, 1995.)

———. 1997. *Learning from Learning-by-Doing*. Stanford, Calif.: Stanford University Press.

———. 2000. "Notes on Social Capital and Economic Performance."In Partha Dasgupta and Ismail Serageldin, eds. *Social Capital: A Multifaceted Perspective*. Washington, D.C.: World Bank.

Spagnolo, Giancarlo. 1999. "Social Relations and Cooperation in Organizations." *Journal of Economic Behaviour and Organization* 36: 1–26.

Starrett, D. 1976. "Social Institutions, Imperfect Information, and the Distribution of Income." *Quarterly Journal of Economics* 90: 261–84.

Stephan Paula. 1996. "The Economics of Science." *Journal of Economic Literature* 34(3): 1199–1235.

Stiglitz, Joseph E. 1990. "Peer Monitoring in Credit Markets." *World Bank Economic Review* 4: 351–66.

Stone, Glenn Davis, Robert McC. Netting, and M. Priscilla Stone. 1990. "Seasonality Labour Scheduling and Agricultural Intensification of the Nigerian Savannah." *American Anthropologist* 92(1): 7–23.

Summers, Robert, and Alan Heston. 1988. "A New Set of International Comparisons of Real Product and Prices: Estimates for 130 Countries, 1950–1985." *Review of Income and Wealth* 34: 1–25.

Thomas, J., and T. Worrall. 1996. "Informal Insurance Arrangements in Village Economies." Processed, Department of Economics, University of Warwick, UK.

Thomson, J. T., D. H. Feeny, and R. J. Oakerson. 1986. "Institutional Dynamics: The Evolution and Dissolution of Common Property Resource Management." In National Research Council, *Proceedings of a Conference on Common Property Resource Management*. Washington, D.C.: U.S. National Academy of Science Press.

Triandis, H. C. 1991. "Cross-Cultural Differences in Assertiveness/Competition vs. Group Loyalty/Cooperation." In R. A. Hinde and J. Groebel, eds., *Cooperation and Prosocial Behaviour*. Cambridge (UK): Cambridge University Press.

Udry, Christopher. 1990. "Credit Markets in Northern Nigeria: Credit as Insurance in a Rural Economy." *World Bank Economic Review* 4: 251–69.

———. 1994. "Risk and Insurance in a Rural Credit Market: An Empirical Investigation in Northern Nigeria." *Review of Economic Studies* 61(208): 495–526.

Wade, Robert. 1988. *Village Republics: Economic Conditions for Collective Action in South India*. Cambridge (UK): Cambridge University Press.

Watkins, S. C. 1990. "From Local to National Communities: The Transformation of Demographic Regions in Western Europe 1870–1960." *Population and Development Review* 1990(16): 241–72.

Weber, Max. 1930. *The Protestant Ethic and the Spirit of Capitalism*. London: George Allen & Unwin.

Weibull, J. W. 1995. *Evolutionary Game Theory*. Cambridge, Mass.: MIT Press.

Weingast, B. 1997. "Democratic Stability as a Self-Enforcing Equilibrium." In Albert Breton, G. Galeotti, P. Salmon, and R. Wintrobe, eds., *Understanding Democracy*. Cambridge: Cambridge University Press.

White, T. A., and C. F. Runge. 1995. "The Emergence and Evolution of Collective Action: Lessons from Watershed Management in Haiti." *World Development* 23: 1683–98.

Wignaraja, Ponna. 1990. *Women, Poverty and Resources*. New Delhi: Sage Publications.

Wildavsky, Aaron. 1987. "Choosing Preferences by Constructing Institutions: A Cultural Theory of Preference Formation." *American Political Science Review* 81: 3–21.

————. 1994. "How Cultural Theory Can Contribute to Understanding and Promoting Democracy, Science, and Development." In I. Serageldin and J. Taboroff, eds., *Culture and Development in Africa*. Washington, D.C.: World Bank.

Williams, Bernard Arthur Owen. 1993. *Shame and Necessity*. Berkeley, Calif.: University of California Press.

Wintrobe, Ronald. 1995. "Some Economics of Ethnic Capital Formation and Conflict." In A. Breton, G. Galeotti, P. Salmon, and R. Wintrobe, eds., *Nationalism and Rationality*. Cambridge (UK): Cambridge University Press.

World Bank. 1997. *World Development Report*. New York: Oxford University Press.

Young, A. 1993. "Lessons from the East Asian NICs: A Contrarian View." NBER Working Paper No. 4482, National Bureau of Economic Research, Cambridge, Mass.

Young, H. P. 1993. "The Evolution of Conventions." *Econometrica* 61: 57–84.

Zamagni, S. 1999. "Social Paradoxes of Growth and Civil Economy." In G. Gandolfo and F. Marzano, eds., *Economic Theory and Social Justice*. London: MacMillan.